ÆT 68.

Wendell Phillips:

THE AGITATOR.

1980

BY

CARLOS MARTYN,

Editor of "American Reformers," and author of "John Milton," "Wm. E Dodge," etc.

WITH AN

APPENDIX

CONTAINING THREE OF THE ORATOR'S MASTERPIECES, NEVER BEFORE PUBLISHED IN BOOK FORM, VIZ.:

"THE LOST ARTS."

"DANIEL O'CONNELL."

"THE SCHOLAR IN A REPUBLIC."

REVISED EDITION.

FUNK AND WAGNALLS COMPANY
NEW YORK AND LONDON

Entered, according to Act of Congress, in the year 1890, by
FUNK & WAGNALLS
In the Office of the Librarian of Congress at Washington, D. C.
[*Printed in the United States.*]

PREFACE.

WENDELL PHILLIPS was a citizen of the twentieth century sent as a sample to us of the nineteenth. There is not in biography another character more profoundly interesting and instructive. Whether judged by the length, variety, influence, or genius of his life, this man was unique. Fredrika Bremer said long ago: "The anti-slavery struggle will be the romance of American history." The Swedish novelist foretold that our future Sir Walter Scott would find in this "debatable ground" the richest materials for his "Sixty Years Hence." But where was there in the "irrepressible conflict" a more heroic figure than Mr. Phillips?

Nor was his an isolated advocacy. He identified himself as inseparably with every other reform of the age. There was no exception. He stood, "The Admirable Crichton" of progress. Would any one understand this century? Would he equip himself for usefulness? Would he catch fire from contact with one of the purest, ablest, most inspiring of men? Let him study and emulate the career of Wendell Phillips.

Biography has been defined as the story of a single soul. But the narrative becomes complex, since in its passage a single soul touches many other souls.

Hence biography expands into history. The problem is to preserve the biography in the history—to make the individual stand out in the midst of the crowd. This difficulty is intensified when the life portrayed, like the shuttle in weaving, plays into the very warp and woof of the times.

In the case of Mr. Phillips, the effort has been to give only so much of the wider view as should make his career comprehensible. In these pages everything has been subordinated to the setting forth of the man in his essential features, clean-cut and pronounced. Under this rule, a mass of interesting matter has been set resolutely aside. Many related persons have been passed over, or dismissed with a mere mention. Nothing has been admitted save what would individualize, animate, and reproduce the great reformer. This is a biography, not a history. Surely, a man should be the hero of his own life.

A vast amount of new material only just now accessible, yet essential to a just estimate of the orator, and suggestive and illustrative of his mental and personal habits, will be found within these covers, giving a near and intimate view of him. The account of his earlier and mid-career is especially full.

One great merit we may confidently claim for this volume. It abounds in copious quotations from Mr. Phillips's utterances. He is given the opportunity to state his position in his own words on every one of the great issues in which he was interested. Hence it is in some sense a handbook of his opinions.

Here are principles for the philosophical, facts for the matter-of-fact, extracts from speeches which made and vocalized history, for the admirers of eloquence, anecdotes for the lovers of *ana*, portraits for students of pictures, illustrations for teachers and speakers, tumults for those who delight in excitement—something for every one, and a good deal for all. Who loves freedom? Who desires to look into and help forward the great reforms still struggling toward accomplishment? Who is interested in the enlargement of woman's sphere, in temperance, in the question of capital and labor, in the Irish agitation, in the ethics of progress? Mr. Phillips was their consummate exponent. As well read "Hamlet," with Hamlet cut out, as hope to grasp these issues without his luminous guidance.

If at any point this narrative drops below the level of our friend Dryasdust, the charge of a lack of dignity will be cheerfully borne if it carries the reader inside of the subject. Boswell is by common consent the best of biographers. Why? Because he jots down the day's minutiæ—every occurrence from the morning bath, the chops for breakfast, the walk along Fleet Street, to the last *môt* at night. Trifles reveal character. We get at the real self most surely when the hero is off parade and in undress. Thanks to Boswell, we *know* Dr. Johnson.

The writer confesses that as he has written he has dipped his pen in his heart for ink. He has made himself not the critic, but the biographer of Mr. Phillips. The life he lived is the life described. An effort has been made to open a window into the man so that the world might look in. There is nothing to hide. The deeper the insight, the greater will be the admiration for the Agitator's talents and the reverence for his character.

To the many friends who have interested themselves in and aided his task, the author expresses again, in this formal way, his earnest thanks. Let us hope the result may compensate the effort. It will, if Wendell Phillips shall live and breathe again before our eyes and in our souls as these pages are turned.

CARLOS MARTYN.

NEW YORK CITY, March, 1890.

THERE, with one hand behind his back,
Stands Phillips, buttoned in a sack,
Our Attic orator, our Chatham ;
Old fogies, when he lightens at 'em,
Shrivel like leaves ; to him 'tis granted
Always to say the word that's wanted,
So that he seems but speaking clearer
The tip-top thought of every hearer ;
Each flash his brooding heart lets fall,
Fires what's combustible in all,
And sends the applauses bursting in
Like an exploded magazine.
His eloquence no frothy show,
The gutter's street-polluted flow,
No Mississippi's yellow flood
Whose shoalness can't be seen for mud ;
So simply clear, serenely deep,
So silent -strong its graceful sweep,
None measures its unrippling force
Who has not striven to stem its course.
—JAMES RUSSELL LOWELL.

THE greatest praise government can win is, that its citizens know their rights and dare maintain them. The best use of good laws is to teach men to trample bad laws under their feet. On these principles I am willing to stand before the community in which I was born and brought up ; where I expect to live and die ; where, if I win any reputation, I expect to earn and keep it. As a sane man, as a Christian man, and as a lover of my country, I am willing to be judged by posterity.—WENDELL PHILLIPS.

MR. PHILLIPS had all the qualities of a great orator : command of himself, warm sympathy, responsive intellect, splendid repartee, the power to flash, the power to hit close, the language of the people, a wonderful magnetism, and an earnestness that made him the unconscious hero of the cause he pleaded.—The Boston *Herald*.

CONTENTS.

BOOK I.

MORNING.

1811-1837.

	PAGE
I. GENESIS	15-24
II. ENVIRONMENT	25-33
III. SCHOOLING	34-48
IV. THE YOUNG LAWYER	49-56
V. THE MARTYR AGE	57-77
VI. THE NEW CLIENT	78-85
VII. IN FANEUIL HALL	86-102

BOOK II.

NOON.

1838-1865.

I. THE ABOLITIONISTS—MEN AND MEASURES	105-115
II. A CONUNDRUM	116-121
III. "VALE"	122-126
IV. SCENES AND EXPERIENCES IN EUROPE	127-147
V. NO. 26 ESSEX STREET	148-151
VI. THE IRISH ADDRESS	152-158
VII. A NEW BATTLE OF CONCORD	159-163
VIII. THE "COVENANT WITH DEATH"	164-173
IX. INFIDELITY IN THE 'FORTIES	174-178
X. THE AGITATOR	179-188
XI. EGERIA	189-198
XII. CONCERNING A SINGULAR EPIDEMIC	199-203
XIII. MR. CALHOUN'S IDEA OF EQUILIBRIUM	204-211

CONTENTS.

		PAGE
XIV.	INCIDENTS	212–222
XV.	THE DEVIL'S GOSPEL	223–234
XVI.	THE WOMEN, AND A MAN	235–242
XVII.	DISJECTA MEMBRA	243–250
XVIII.	GOOD WORKS	251–258
XIX.	PORTRAITS	259–266
XX.	EXCITEMENT	267–275
XXI.	GREAT EVENTS	276–288
XXII.	"IRREPRESSIBLE CONFLICT"	289–299
XXIII.	THE WINTER OF SECESSION	300–311
XXIV.	UNDER THE FLAG	312–322
XXV.	THE STRUGGLE OF TWO CIVILIZATIONS	323–337
XXVI.	SHADOW IN SUNSHINE	338–345

BOOK III.

AFTERNOON.

1866–1879.

I.	FROM BATTLE-FIELD TO FORUM	349–365
II.	IO! TRIUMPHE!	366–376
III.	"NEW OCCASIONS TEACH NEW DUTIES"	377–385
IV.	LIVING ISSUES	386–398
V.	GRANT—GREELEY—FROUDE	399–406
VI.	OLLA PODRIDA	407–417
VII.	USEFULNESS	418–430
VIII.	THE RADICAL CLUB	431–439
IX.	LYCEUM EXPERIENCES	440–447

BOOK IV.

EVENING.

1880–1884.

I.	STILL CONTENDING	451–469
II.	LENGTHENING SHADOWS	470–478
III.	SUNDOWN	479–482

		PAGE
IV.	"At Even-time it Shall be Light"	483–488
V.	The Orator	489–505
VI.	The Man	506–524
VII.	Phillipsiana	525–530

APPENDIX.

"The Lost Arts"	533–547
"Daniel O'Connell"	548–569
"The Scholar in a Republic"	570–594

Index	595–600

BOOK I.

MORNING.
1811-1837.

WENDELL PHILLIPS.

I.

GENESIS.

THE first American Phillips was an Englishman; and so was the second. Since the family began on this side of the water in a paradoxical way, it is not strange that the most illustrious member of it should have been fond of paradoxes.

The Rev. George Phillips was one of the band of conscience exiles who sailed from Great Britain for the new world, in 1630, in the "Arbella," with Winthrop and Saltonstall and Johnson; this last a landowner in three counties, after whose charming wife the chief vessel of the flotilla of ten ships was named.[1] Things were in a bad way over there, or seemed to be; although, as is apt to be the case, it was darkest just before the dawn; for within ten years Hampden

---

[1] The common orthography is Arabella, but later writers almost unanimously reject this spelling, which is founded on the often-erring authority of Mather in the "Magnalia," and of Josselyn, and accept that of John Winthrop in his Diary, of Johnson, in the "Wonder-Working Providence," and of Dudley's Epistles. These men were personally acquainted with Mr. Johnson. *Vide* Winthrop, p. 1, note.

and Pym and Vane and Cromwell revolutionized England in never-to-be-forgotten fashion. Just now, however, the situation was forlorn enough. The mother-country was parcelled out among three contending parties : The *Puritans*, who were so named because they stickled for the simplicity of the Gospel ; the *Papists*, who had swayed the sceptre under " Bloody Mary," and were destined to grasp it again a generation later under James II., and in the mean time were sleeplessly plotting ; and the *Prelatists*, Protestants by profession, Papists in practice, who were encamped at court. Charles I. now sat on the throne. He was that oddest of anomalies, a treacherous moralist. Yes, Charles was the painting of a virtue. Outwardly, he was Cato ; inwardly, he was Iago. His faction, wedded like himself to the tenets of absolutism, eagerly cried Amen to his most arbitrary acts, which they often instigated. Liberty-loving people—men and women whose Bible was the Old and New Testaments and not the Prayer-book, who worshipped God in spirit rather than in form, Christians instead of Pharisees—had a sorry time of it. Britain, emancipated from the Pope, hugged the popedom. Dissent from the State religion was heresy. The measure of a conscience was the length of a prelate's foot. Thus stood the Puritans at the date we have mentioned : popery preparing to spring upon them, while the fangs of prelacy were already buried in their throat.

Looking about for a chance to escape, these victims of persecution were attracted hither, where a colony of their fellows had been planted in 1620—the famous landers on Plymouth Rock. The newcomers disembarked to the north of the earlier settlers, at

Salem, a place so called "for the peace they had and hoped in it."[1]

George Phillips was a Puritan. He could not and would not conform to Strafford, the systematizer of tyranny in the State, and to Laud, the exponent of absolute power in the Church. A gentleman by birth, a graduate of the English Cambridge, a rector at Boxted, in Essex County, happily married and at work, he did not hesitate to tear himself up root and branch in obedience to his conscience. Come-outerism being in the blood, it should not surprise us to find the quality, an occasion having arisen, again asserting itself down the line of descent.

Soon after reaching America, Mr. Phillips lost his wife ; she, like the lady Arbella Johnson, who preceded her to the grave, dying from exposure on the voyage and hardship on land. Delicately reared and accustomed to luxurious surroundings, they were early and lovely martyrs. The widower's sorrow was too full for utterance, or he might have hymned it in those lines of Dr. Watts, so tender and pathetic :

" I was all love and she was all delight ;
   Let me run back to seasons past ;
   Ah, flowery days, when first she charmed my sight !
   But roses will not always last."

Leaving Salem, Mr. Phillips went to Watertown, now a part of Boston, where he became the first minister of the town. This pastorate he held during fourteen years, until his death, in 1644, at the age of fifty-one. He was a man of solid attainments and vigorous intellect, was associated with John Win-

---

[1] In reference to the meaning of the word Salem, *vide* Cotton Mather's " Magnalia," vol. ii., pp. 67, 68.

throp in the government of the Colony of Massachusetts, and was the earliest advocate in America of the Congregational order and discipline.[1] Thus he marches among the founders of empire—*conditores imperiorum*, to whom Lord Bacon, in his "Marshalling of the Sovereign Degrees of Honor," assigns the foremost place.

Such was Phillips the first. His eldest son, Phillips the second,[2] was born in England in 1625; crossed the sea with his parents when five years old; was among the earliest graduates of Harvard College, then recently founded;[3] entered the ministry; settled at Rowley, in Massachusetts, in 1651, where he remained until his death, in 1696, making himself known and felt as the Rev. Samuel Phillips. A twelvemonth after leaving college, he married Sarah Appleton, of Ipswich, and this couple left a large family. The second Phillips was a man of estimable character and brilliant ability—the favorite orator on anniversary occasions.[4] This characteristic, too, reappeared, later on, with added vim.

Phillips the third was named Samuel, after his father. He broke the clerical continuity and took to business, removing to Salem, where he became a goldsmith. Born in 1657, he married a granddaughter of Deputy-Governor Symonds, Mary Emerson, of Gloucester, Mass., and died in 1722, at the age of sixty-five. He was a man of unblemished reputation, had a genius for trade, and made money.

---

[1] "Phillips Genealogies," by Albert M. Phillips, p. 10.
[2] The Rev. George Phillips married a second time, and left seven children by this marriage.
[3] Opened in 1638.   [4] Gage's "History of Rowley."

He also begat children,[1] two of whom it behooves us attentively to notice. The eldest son, named Samuel after his father, jumped back into the ministry. The four chief events in his life were : his birth, in 1689 ; his graduation from Harvard College, in 1708 ; his settlement as pastor of the " Old South Church" in Andover, in 1710, and his marriage, in 1711, to Hannah White, of Haverhill, Mass., whose father was a deacon and a captain in the militia. This Phillips, of the fourth generation, continued to preach in Andover until his death, in 1771 ; was a model of industry and self-restraint, and a born leader in thought and action.[2]

He left five children, two of whom became widely useful and distinguished, viz., Samuel and John Phillips. These brothers were laymen, and settled the one in Andover, Mass., the other in Exeter, N. H. Both accumulated wealth, and they became the joint founders of the celebrated Phillips Academy, in Andover—an institution whose usefulness increases with the lapse of time. In addition to this good work, John founded the Phillips Academy, in Exeter, the twin of Andover, and also endowed a chair of theology at Dartmouth College. Living in the "times that tried men's souls," these brothers were patriots and saints—among the most eminent of all.[3] The son of the eldest, known as Judge Phillips, inherited the best qualities of both ; became lieutenant-governor of Massachusetts, and continued

---

[1] Samuel Phillips, like his grandfather, was twice married. All his children were by his first wife, save the last.
[2] "Memoir of Judge Phillips," by Rev. John L. Taylor, p. 7.
[3] *Vide* " Phillips Genealogies," pp. 15–20, *passim*.

their benefactions to the cause of learning, lavishing time, attention, money upon the Andover Academy, especially, whose constitution and course of study are the output of his brain.[1]

Having said so much regarding the elder of this fourth generation, and his immediate descendants, beguiled into it by their usefulness and eminence, we return now to the second son of Samuel Phillips, the goldsmith, whose name was John—the great-grandfather of the subject of these pages. John Phillips was born in 1701. He became a Boston merchant; married, in 1723, Mary, a daughter of Nicholas Buttolph, also of Boston; possessed marked mercantile ability, as his success shows; was a deacon in the old Brattle-street church, a justice of the peace, colonel of the Boston regiment, and many times represented the town in the General Court. He died in 1768, "and was buried with military honors."[2] This was the fourth Phillips in the direct line to Wendell. Phillips the fifth was William, only son of John and Mary Buttolph, who was born in 1737, and who married Margaret, youngest child of the Hon. Jacob Wendell,[3] a distinguished merchant of Boston, a military magnate, and one of the Governor's Council. William Phillips died early

---

[1] *Vide* "Phillips Genealogies," pp. 20-24. Judge Phillips gave many thousands of dollars in this way. Bearing in mind the difference in the purchasing power of money then and now, his gifts would be equivalent to hundreds of thousands of dollars to-day. See an interesting and valuable article on Andover in *Harper's Magazine*, vol. lv., p. 564.

[2] *Ib.*, p. 29.

[3] The Wendells were of Dutch extraction, and came to Boston from Albany, N. Y., in the early years of the eighteenth century.

—at thirty-four. His widow survived him many years.[1] It was from her that our Wendell received his name.

Their only son became famous as the Hon. John Phillips—sixth in the line from the American ancestor. He was born in 1770. Two years later his father died. His mother proved equal to the emergency. She was a woman of unusual strength of character, well educated, and a devoted Christian. On account of the advantages he would there enjoy, she sent her boy to abide under the roof-tree of his uncle, Lieutenant-Governor Phillips, at Andover, where he fitted for college at the academy of which his kinsman was such a generous patron. Entering Harvard when he was fourteen, he was graduated in 1788, and pronounced the salutatory oration. He was called to the bar shortly afterward, and leaped into an extensive and lucrative practice. In 1794 he was selected to deliver the oration on the Fourth of July, with Boston for an audience—a production familiar ever since through an extract in the schoolbooks, where it rests as a model of eloquence, and which several generations of boys have declaimed. The finger-tips of the writer tingle as they hold the pen in memory of one such occasion.

While the echoes of that speech yet resounded in the old town, Mr. Phillips married Sally Walley, whose father was a successful merchant there. This lady became one of the best of wives, one of the most devoted of mothers. Patient, watchful, considerate, self-sacrificing, she was a power for good in all the relations of home and neighborhood. She

---

[1] She died February 27th, 1823.

possessed fine natural powers of mind and heart, which she had been able carefully to cultivate. Thus she stood,

> " A perfect woman, nobly planned,
> To warn, to comfort, and command."

Aided by his own powers, admirably seconded by his wife's co-operation, John Phillips passed rapidly on and up from high to higher. In 1800, on the establishment of the Municipal Court in Boston, he was made public prosecutor, a function which, in a less official but far wider sense, his celebrated son inherited. In 1803 he was elected to the House of Representatives. In 1804 he was returned to the Senate of Massachusetts, where he remained until his death. In 1809 he became judge of the Court of Common Pleas. In 1812 he was chosen a member of the corporation of Harvard College. In 1820 he sat in the Convention for the Revision of the Constitution of the State—perhaps the most conspicuous figure in that able and dignified body. In 1821 Boston adopted a city charter. Two candidates, equally eminent, were named for the mayoralty—Harrison Gray Otis, a nephew of that James Otis whose eloquence had defied George III., and consecrated Faneuil Hall and the "Old South" Church to liberty, himself one of the most accomplished orators of that generation ; and Josiah Quincy, already decorated with honors, State and national, to which he further added, in after years, the titles of Speaker of the Massachusetts House of Representatives, Judge of the Municipal Court, and President of Harvard College. Between two such worthy competitors selection was difficult. A vote resulted in no choice, whereupon the Hon. John Phillips was pitched upon as a compromise candidate, and was immediately elected—practically without opposition. He thus became the first Mayor of Boston. His incumbency was so satisfactory that there was a universal demand for his re-election. But before the close of his term he was suddenly removed from earth by angina pectoris, an insidious disease destined more than half a century later to end the mortal career of his great son.

John Phillips was universally respected. His mind was clear and wide, his heart was warm, his hands were open and clean, his soul was anchored in deep piety. Filling as he did a great variety of offices, no one ever questioned either his integrity or his ability. He was specially gifted in speech, and this power was enhanced by a singular charm of manner. In this he was evidently the father of his son. But he is also credited by tradition with "a pliable disposition," which, just as plainly, he did not transmit to *one* of his children.

Early in the century, Mr. Phillips built for himself a spacious mansion of the colonial pattern, at the corner of Beacon and Walnut streets, which became a show place (the old engravings of Boston loved to reproduce it), and which the curious may still gaze at, though it has been somewhat altered. It was the navel of the aristocratic quarter, and stood in the "West End" of the New England London; the "Saint Germain" of the Yankee Paris. A block away, to the left, on the summit of Beacon Hill, was the Hancock house—as bold and unmistakable in the landscape as its owner's signature was in the Declaration of Independence. Next door, on the right, lived the Winthrops—the town residence of that historic family. In front stretched the forty-three acres of Boston Common. Around and about thronged the dons and doñas of the capital. Here, on November 29th, 1811, Wendell was born—the eighth in a family of nine ; a nest of brothers, with three sisters in it.[1]

---

[1] The complete list of the children of John and Sally (Walley) Phillips, with dates of birth and death, is as follows :

1. Thomas Walley, born January 16th, 1797 ; died 1859.
2. Sarah Hurd, born April 24th, 1799 ; died 1837.
3. Samuel, born 1801 ; died 1817, while a member of the Sophomore Class of Harvard College.
4. Margaret, born November 29th, 1802 ; died
5. Miriam, born ; died
6. John Charles, born November 15th, 1807 ; died 1878.
7. George William, born January 3d, 1810 ; died 1880.
8. WENDELL, born November 29th, 1811 ; died February 2d, 1884.
9. Grenville Tudor, born August 14th, 1816 ; died 1863.

Vide "Phillips Genealogies," pp. 30-35.

II.

ENVIRONMENT.

EVERY thoughtful observer of life knows that the fireside is the earliest and most influential of schools. The nursery is the child's university. When the nature is uninscribed and plastic the home writes the first and most lasting impressions. More that is elementary—a key to all the rest—is learned in the cradle and beside the mother's chair than in all after time. Here dawns upon the mind the conception of life. Here ideals are imparted. Parents decree the future. Happy the boy or girl whose heart throbs with the memory of a good and happy home! Hence in studying any human eminence the instant and critical inquiry touches this decisive point.

It was a kindly turning of Providence in Wendell Phillips's favor that he was born when and where he was. His high-chair was placed in a Puritan household. This means much. It indicates lofty thought. It stands for holy living. It implies a domestic economy regulated by gravity and decorum and virtue above the frivolities of the hour. It signifies that definite ideas of right and wrong were implanted. It shows that, in conformity with Milton's suggestion,

" To measure life learn thou betimes,"

the boy's nascent intelligence was seasonably instructed in the chief articles of human being and doing.

Then, too, that old colonial mansion was warm with plenty. John Phillips, being wealthy, was a liberal provider. Mrs. John was a model New England housewife. Consequently, their children, one after the other, opened their eyes upon delightful surroundings. Abundance laughed in the larder. Books elbowed one another on the shelves of the library. Pictures smiled down from the walls. Statuary breathed from the corners of the rooms. Thus an insensible education of the eye and ear was ever proceeding. That subtle element which we call æsthetic, at once delicate and formative, impregnated the air. Could any atmosphere be more helpful to one who should by and by become an orator?

It was further happy for young Wendell that he was one of many children. An only child is apt to be petted and spoiled. Where there are a number, each demands so much that no one can get all. Besides, it should seem to be a psychological fact that the friction of several minds from the nursery up to adult life is necessary to the best development of genius. There is scarcely an instance of an only child's achieving greatness. Even when latent, ability gasps and dies for lack of elbow-room and play. On the other hand, history is full of characters that were helped out and thrust forward by early attrition at home. Thus Napoleon was one of thirteen children; Franklin was one of seventeen; General Sherman was one of eleven; Charles Dickens was one of eight; Gladstone was one of seven. Those large American families which were universal a generation or two back—were they not so many schools of genius? Their infrequency to-day—is this not suggestive, ominous? What possibilities our fashionable mothers nowadays forego ; the possibilities of fostering genius and winning for themselves personal distinction !

John Phillips made this wise rule for his children : " Never ask another to do for you what you can do for yourself ; and never ask another to do for you what you would not do for yourself if you could." There is no end of self-reliance in this rule, and a world of sound democratic philosophy, besides. Knowing, also, the uncertainty of fortune in America —a game of blindman's-buff—and remembering, perhaps, the old Jewish saying, " He who does not teach his children a trade, brings them up to steal," he encouraged them to master whatever tools of manual labor they could handle. Accordingly, as soon as he got on his feet, Wendell began to potter about the house with hammer and chisel and saw. In later life he claimed that there was hardly an ordinary trade in vogue when he was a boy at which he had not done many a day's work.[1] Indeed, his mother said : " A good carpenter was spoiled when Wendell became a lawyer."

Moreover, he early developed another trait, more significant of his future career. Feeling the push of his clerical ancestry, he became a preacher at four or five, and placing a Bible in a chair before him, and arranging other chairs in circles about the room, he would harangue these wooden auditors (hardly more wooden than some of the human ones he afterward addressed) by the hour.[2]

---

[1] Thomas Wentworth Higginson's "Wendell Phillips," published by Lee & Shepard, Boston, 1884.
[2] Testimony of Theodore D. Weld.

"Wendell," said his father to him, one day, "don't you get tired of this?"

"No, papa," replied the speaker, "*I* don't get tired, but it's rather hard on the chairs!"

He inherited his wit from his father, who was very bright. When a member of the Convention for the Revision of the Constitution of Massachusetts, John Phillips, in debating a certain proposed change, remarked: "I hope our case may not be like that of a man whose epitaph may be read in an Italian churchyard: 'I was well; I wanted to be better; I took medicine; and here I lie!'"[1]

Wendell was of a domestic turn, sympathetic and affectionate, and open as the daylight. His love for his mother was a passion. He was also devoted to his nurse, Polly. When the birthday of this good soul came round, he gave her a needle-case, bought with his own pennies, and with it a verse which he composed, and (with a single later exception to be cited in due time) his first and only poetic flight.

The boy's nearest and dearest intimate, residing a block away, at the corner of Walnut and Chestnut streets, was J. Lothrop Motley, destined to become famous as the historian of the Netherlands. It was David and Jonathan with these two; and their friendship, beginning in the cradle, lasted to the grave. Phillips was the elder by two years; but Motley was precocious—a scholar in his childhood. Referring to this period, the orator says: "Motley could not have been eleven years old when he began writing a novel. It opened, I remember, not with 'one solitary horseman,' but with two, riding up to an inn,

---

[1] Found in the records of the Convention.

in the Valley of the Housatonic. Neither of us had ever seen the Housatonic, but it sounded grand and romantic. Two chapters were finished."[1]

Thomas Gold Appleton, the son of one of the patriarchs of New England manufactures, who had amassed a great fortune, also lived near by, and made this duo a trio. Appleton became a noted wit and *raconteur*, and joined to these gifts the charm of a graceful pen. As Phillips speaks of Motley, so Appleton tells of both : " Phillips was an old friend of mine. I remember how we used to play together long ago, and the recollection is very pleasant indeed. He was a fine, manly little fellow, and I was very proud of him as a playmate. Wendell Phillips, J. Lothrop Motley, and I frolicked in the garret of the Motley house ; and I recall that their favorite pastime used to be to strut about in any fancy costume they could find in the corners of the old attic, and shout scraps of poetry and snatches of dialogue at each other. It was a fine sight to watch them, for both were noble-looking fellows ; and even then Wendell's voice was a very pleasant one to listen to, and his gestures as graceful as could be."[2]

Mr. Appleton's account is corroborated by Oliver Wendell Holmes (a kinsman of Wendell Phillips) in his admirable "Memoir of Motley": " If one could have looked into that garret when our country was not far advanced in its second score of years, he might have found these three boys in cloaks and doublets and plumed hats, as heroes and bandits, enacting more or less impromptu melodramas."[3]

---

[1] "Memoir of Motley," by Oliver Wendell Holmes, p. 7.
[2] *Vide* Boston *Globe*, Phillips Memorial Edition, February 4th, 1884.
[3] "Memoir of Motley," p. 5.

Wendell was his mother's favorite.[1] Possessed herself of a strong character, marked by singular simplicity and keen insight, she early discerned the dormant powers of her gifted son, and never spared herself in the endeavor to put the best that was in her into him. She was profoundly religious. Her foremost purpose, therefore, was to root him in faith and hope and love. She used to take him aside and pray with and for him. Her earliest gift to him was a Bible—his inseparable companion for seventy years.[2] She taught him the catechism as he sat on her lap. And when he could hardly toddle she guided his steps, his hand in hers, to the family pew on Sunday mornings. "Wendell," she would say, "be good and do good; this is my whole desire for you. Add other things if you may—these are central."[3] Under such wholesome tuition how could the lad's moral nature do otherwise than healthily develop?

Physically, he was strong and well. Mrs. Phillips was almost as solicitous for his bodily as for his moral welfare. She taught him the laws of life and health—the gospel of hygiene—*mens sana in corpore sano*. Those habits of temperance, exercise, and purity which characterized him from first to last in a remarkable degree, were the fruitage of her in-

---

[1] His own testimony. See also the "Eulogy of Wendell Phillips," by T. D. Weld, p. 19.

[2] This he gave just before his death to his intimate friend, Mrs. E. S. Crosby, who treasures it among her jewels. In it he marked two passages, which he requested should be read at his funeral, viz., Ps. 23 and 1 Cor. 15 : 12. These were so read.

[3] Mr. Phillips repeated these words to the writer in 1868, and ten years afterward, when his attention was called to the matter, corroborated the utterance.

structions. A wise mother wisely at work fashioning the soul within, and the form, its shrine, without— what usefulness quite equals this?

Both parents were widely and variously interested in affairs beyond their door-steps. John Phillips, as we have noted, was in public life. His wife was a true helpmeet. His concerns were hers. Hence questions and issues astir out there in the streets were brought into the household, and talked over at the fireside and around the table. Persons were characterized, measures were discussed, matters of historical moment were dwelt upon, in full family conclave. In this way the children gained an intelligent acquaintance with the outside world. The hearthstone was a vantage-ground from which to survey, in seclusion, but not in exclusion, the multiform life of the commonwealth. At such times, we may be sure, no eyes and ears were wider open than Wendell's; and so he learned from the start that his neighborhood extended farther than just around the corner.

In those days the Revolutionary tradition was fresh and vigorous. This has been happily called the native air of Wendell Phillips.[1] It marked and dominated his life. Several of the chief actors in the drama were yet on the stage—Jefferson at Monticello; John Adams just at hand, in Quincy; while Elbridge Gerry sat in the Governor's chair of Massachusetts at the very moment of his birth. All about were the lofty and inspiring scenes immortalized by these and kindred heroes. Yonder, in sight from his door-sill, loomed Bunker Hill. Here was

---

[1] George William Curtis's "Eulogy of Wendell Phillips," p. 5.

the church-tower whose lantern started Paul Revere upon his ride. There was Winter Hill, whose cannon-ball struck old Brattle Street church. Across the Common was the "Old South," dedicated to God by the Puritans, and to liberty by Otis and Warren. Within five minutes' walk was Faneuil Hall, twice the cradle of freedom: the freedom of the Colonies and the freedom of the negro race in America; the birthplace and waiting theatre of this boy's own renown. And behold! the very elm under whose branches Washington first drew his sword. What an environment! What an incentive!

Moving daily among these historic associations, the boy, at once perceptive and receptive, learned to reverence the "dead but sceptred sovereigns who still rule our spirits from their urns." Having himself thrilled beneath their touch, he came to value them as "the normal school of politics." He voiced the influence of his environment, long years afterward, in speaking of revolutionary Boston:

"We had a signal prominence in those days. It was not our merit; it was an accident, perhaps. But it was a great accident in our favor that the British Parliament chose Boston as the first and prominent object of its wrath. It was on the men of Boston that Lord North visited his revenge. It was our port that was to be shut, and its commerce annihilated. It was Sam Adams and John Hancock who enjoy the everlasting reward of being the only names excepted from the royal proclamation of forgiveness.

"It was only an accident; but it was an accident which, in the stirring history of the most momentous change the world has seen, placed Boston in the van. Naturally, therefore, in our streets and neighborhood came the earliest collision between England and the Colonies. Here Sam Adams, the ablest and ripest statesman God gave to the epoch, forecast those measures which welded thirteen colonies into one thunderbolt, and launched it at George III. Here Otis magnetized every boy into a desperate rebel. Here the fit successors of Hugh Peters and Knox consecrated their pulpits to the defence of that doctrine of the freedom and sacredness of man, which the State borrowed so directly from the Christian Church. The towers of the North Church rallied the farmers to the Lexington and Concord fights; and these old walls (the 'Old South' Church) echoed the people's shout when Adams brought them word that Governor Hutchinson surrendered and withdrew the redcoats. Lingering here still are the echoes of those clashing sabres and jingling spurs that dreamed Warren could be awed to silence. Otis's blood immortalizes State Street, just below where Attucks fell (our first martyr), and just above where zealous patriots made a teapot of the harbor.

"It was a petty town of some twenty thousand inhabitants; but 'the rays of royal indignation collected upon it served only to illuminate and not to consume.' Almost every one of its houses had a legend. Every public building hid what was treasonable debate, or bore bullet-marks or bloodshed—evidence of royal displeasure. It takes a stout heart to step out of a crowd and risk the chances of support, when failure is death. The strongest, proudest, most obstinate race and kingdom on one side: a petty town the assailant; its weapons, ideas; its trust, God and the right; its old-fashioned men patiently arguing with cannon and regiments; blood the seal of the debate, and every stone, and wall, and roof, and doorway witness forever of the angry tyrant and sturdy victim.

"Boston boys had reason to be thankful for their birthright. The great memories, noble deeds, and sacred places of the old town are the poetry of history and the keenest ripeners of character."[1]

Such, then, was the home, such the instructions, and such the scenes in which were passed the earliest and most impressionable years of Wendell Phillips.

---

[1] Oration at the Old South Meeting House, for its preservation. June 14th, 1876.

III.

SCHOOLING.

To the formative influences of the home and the streets, Wendell Phillips superadded the best educational advantages. He was sent in his eleventh year to the Boston Public Latin School—prolific mother of famous sons. This landmark of ancient Boston then stood on School Street, between Washington and Tremont, upon a portion of the ground now covered by the Parker House. Mr. B. A. Gould, an ideal pedagogue, was then and long remained the head-master. The school was largely attended, and the scholars represented the blue blood and brains of young America in 1822. Motley went to Northampton to fit for college, an institution officered, in part, by the historian Bancroft;[1] so that he and Phillips did not continue their *camaraderie* during the five years from 1822 to 1827—resuming it at Harvard. But Appleton remained as the chum of Phillips. And now he met and cemented his lifelong friendship with Charles Sumner, who was his elder by nearly a year, and who was in the class a twelvemonth ahead. Sumner, as Phillips himself testifies, came from a family "long prominent in Massachusetts," a family "noted for physical as well as intel-

---

[1] See Holmes's "Memoir;" also the "Correspondence of J. Lothrop Motley," edited by George William Curtis, published by Harper & Brothers, New York, 1889.

lectual vigor."[1] The senator that was to be embodied even now the physical and intellectual traits of his ancestry ; but at the Latin School " he was a recluse and studious boy, hardly ever joining in any amusements or athletic games ; and this mood lasted through his college years."[2]

Indeed, Boston then discountenanced athletics. Schools and colleges existed for the cultivation of brain, not brawn. Now they exist for the cultivation of brawn, not brain. Probably, the truth lies in that golden mean which the classics recommend. Anyhow, Phillips was ahead of his times in this respect ; as, later, he was in other ways. For though never negligent of his books, he dearly loved athletics. He was a champion boxer and marksman, and fencer and oarsman, and horseman. Inheriting a magnificent physique, palpitating with health, he trampled prejudices under foot and would have exercise, and plenty of it.[3] His standing as a scholar was excellent,[4] as a result, no doubt, of those despised gymnastics. The curriculum[5] neces-

---

[1] Johnson's *New Universal Cyclopædia*, article " Sumner," by W. Phillips.

[2] *Ib.*   [3] Such is the united testimony of his classmates.   [4] *Ib.*

[5] Here it is as it then stood: In Greek, Valpy's " Grammar," the " Delectus Sententiarum Græcarum ;" Jacobs's " Greek Reader ;" the " Four Gospels" and two books of Homer's " Iliad ;" in Latin, Adams's " Latin Grammar," " Liber Primus," " Epiteme Historiæ Græcæ," " Vivi Romæ," " Phædri Fabulæ," " Cornelius Nepos ;" Ovid's " Metamorphoses ;" Sallust's " Catiline" and " Jugurthine War ;" Cæsar ; Virgil ; Cicero's " Select Orations ;" the " Agricola" and " Germania" of Tacitus, and the " Odes" and " Epodes" of Horace ; in the study of mythology, Tooke's " Pantheon of the Heathen Gods" served as a text-book ; in arithmetic, Lacroix was the text-book ; in reading, Lindley Murray's " English Reader." The school was so large that each class was subdivided into three divisions.

sitated diligence ; and there was head-master Gould, ferule in hand, to enforce attention and knock learning into unwilling heads.

Wendell continued in School Street those habits of declamation begun among the chairs at home and practised in Motley's garret ; but now with a larger audience. "What first led me to observe him," writes a fellow-student, "and fixed him in my memory, was his elocution ; and I soon came to look forward to declamation day with interest, mainly on his account, though many were admirable speakers. The pieces chosen were chiefly such as would excite patriotic feelings and an enthusiasm for freedom."[1] Phillips himself tells us that already he "had by heart the classic eulogies of brave old men and martyrs," and carried at the end of his silver tongue "Greek and Roman and English history."[2] Then and afterward he embraced every opportunity to hear the "masters of assemblies:" his own father, Harrison Gray Otis, Edward Everett—every greatness of the day.

In 1825 an event occurred which convulsed the continent with enthusiasm—the visit of Lafayette. When the illustrious friend of Washington landed in Boston the city was in a frenzy. Phillips shall tell us about his share in the scene in his own words, quoted from a charming address which he made in the afternoon of his career to a vast audience in the Music Hall, at the annual School Festival of Boston :[3]

"This is the first time for many years that I have participated in a school festival. I have received no invitation since 1824,

---
[1] "Life and Times of Wendell Phillips," by George L. Austin, p. 29.
[2] "Speeches and Lectures," by Wendell Phillips, p. 226.
[3] July 25th, 1865. *Vide* p. 344 of this volume.

when I was a little boy in a class in the Latin School, when we were turned out on yonder Common in a grand procession at nine o'clock in the morning. And for what? Not to hear fine music—no ; but for something better than music, that thrilled more than eloquence—a sight which should live in the memory forever, the best sight which Boston ever saw—the welcome of Lafayette on his return to this country, after an absence of a score of years. I can boast, boys and girls, more than you. I can boast that these eyes have beheld the hero of three revolutions, this hand has touched the right hand that held up Hancock and Washington. Not all this glorious celebration can equal that glad reception of the nation's benefactor by all that Boston could offer him—a sight of her children. It was a long procession ; and, unlike other processions, we started punctually at the hour published. They would not let us wander about, and did not wish us to sit down. I there received my first lesson in hero-worship. I was so tired after four hours' waiting, I could scarcely stand ; but when I saw him—that glorious old Frenchman !—I could have stood until to-day."

Amid such scenes and experiences five tranquil years of preparation were passed. The boy of ten was now the youth of fifteen—tall, lithe, and graceful as a Greek statue. Leaving the Latin School with an established reputation for every accomplishment of body and mind that suited his age, and for some more mature, he stepped up into the broader world of Harvard. This was in 1827.

Although his home was just in sight across the river Charles, it was not as easy then to get to and from Boston and Cambridge as it is now. Besides, it was thought best to give Wendell the benefit of a college *entourage*. His father was dead—had died the year after the lad was entered at the Latin School, in 1823. Thus the entire responsibility for the education and outfit in life of a large family devolved upon the mother. The sagacious manner in which she met and mastered the emergency contributed, no doubt, to give her son that respect for and appreciation of female ability which became one of his characteristic traits. But we must pity these two, separated now for the first time, though not for long. She wept on his neck, commended him to God, and cautioned him about his linen in the same breath, and told him never to forget his prayers and his Bible—and regularly to air his room! True mother and true saint; an enchanting and common combination; embodying the divine and human, and therefore not strangely mixing earth and heaven in speech and action.

When Phillips matriculated the Rev. Dr. John T. Kirkland was president. Two years later, in 1829, Josiah Quincy succeeded him, the same Quincy who had divided the suffrages of Boston with Harrison Gray Otis, when Wendell's father was elected mayor; a man both good and great, whose life God spared to a serene and honored evening of old age. The faculty and the students—all are gone! To read their names in the catalogue of 1827 is like spelling the names on the weather-stained head-stones in a graveyard. Harvard is old enough to be mellowed by time. A certain pensiveness hangs around it and mates it with European universities dating back to the Middle Ages. True, youth is on the campus, and the dormitories and the class-rooms are populous with animation and color. Just the same, yesterday shadows to-day. The old clock which has tolled away so many generations will toll away this generation.[1] The grave only waits! An historic

---
[1] See this thought developed by Professor Goldwin Smith, "Lectures on the Study of History," p. 220.

college is an isthmus separating two eternities, yet, like Suez, canalled to marry the oceans ; and it is this relation which it sustains to the past and the future which endows it with such influence over the imagination of dreamy and poetic youth.

Phillips became intimate with President Quincy — as intimate as was possible considering their difference in age and station. With the president's son, Edmund Quincy, he formed at this time an association which ran through both lives as veins run through a block of marble.

Young Quincy was several years older than Phillips ; but they got together and stayed together. Sumner was a Sophomore when Phillips entered the Freshman Class ; but in this case friendship overleaped the boundary of class, as in the case of Quincy it had of age. Now, too, Motley came to Harvard, and those Beacon-Hill relations were cemented anew. Speaking of Motley, Phillips gives interesting testimony—lets us behind the scenes :

"His quickness of apprehension was wonderful. During our first year at college, though the youngest in the class, he stood third, I think, or second in rank ; and ours was an especially able class. Yet to maintain this standing he neither cared nor needed to make any effort. Too young to feel any responsibilities, and not yet awake to ambition, he became so negligent that he was 'rusticated.' He came back sobered and worked rather more ; but with no effort for college rank thenceforward. In his room he had a small writing-table with a shallow drawer ; I have often seen it half-full of sketches, unfinished poems, soliloquies, a scene or two of a play, prose portraits of pet characters, etc. These he would read to me, though he never volunteered to do so ; and every now and then he burned the whole, and began to fill the drawer again."[1]

---

[1] "Memoir of J. Lothrop Motley," by Oliver Wendell Holmes p. 8.

It is further recorded of Motley, that one day his tutor came into his room and found the table littered up with novels instead of text-books.

"How is this?" asked the tutor.

"Well," was the answer, "you see, I am pursuing a course of historical reading. I have now reached the novels of the nineteenth century. Take them in bulk, they are tough reading!"[1]

Phillips had from the start and always retained an intense sense of the ludicrous. These and such like experiences of his crony he appreciated then and told years later with inimitable effect. Of himself, however, no such stories can be related. Though never a hermit like Sumner, neither was he a scapegrace like Motley. Between the two in age he was enough like both to win their confidence and command their respect. In college rank he stood well up toward the head.[2] But his interests were too broad and diversified for the valedictorian's crown. At Harvard, as in the Latin School, he gave a good deal of attention to athletics, and continued his boxing, fencing, boating, and horse-riding, becoming an expert in these manly accomplishments.[3] He was also an omnivorous reader, history and mechanics being his specialties.[4] His passion was horses; in later life he made a personal friend of Rarey, the horse-tamer.

When Phillips went to Cambridge the Rev. Dr. Lyman Beecher was the Jupiter of the Boston pulpit. Every Sunday, and often on week-day nights,

---

[1] "Memoir of J. Lothrop Motley," by Oliver Wendell Holmes, p. 9.
[2] The Rev. Edgar Buckingham, class-secretary of the Class of 1831.
[3] *Ib.*
[4] *Ib.*

he thundered and lightened in Hanover Street church. He shook and kindled the town. Thousands throbbed under his preaching. His special mission was to combat Unitarianism, which then sat in all the high places. One day some one said to him :

"Well, Dr. Beecher, how long do you think it will take you to destroy Unitarianism in Boston?"

"Humph!" was the gruff reply, "several years, I suppose—roots and all."

Among the many attracted to hear his discourses was young Phillips, whose immediate family was orthodox in creed. As a child he had learned his first lessons in theology with his mother's lap for an altar. Now those childish impressions were deepened and confirmed by Dr. Beecher, never afterward to change. He passed through the experience called conversion.

A personal friend asked him, not long before his death : "Mr. Phillips, did you ever consecrate yourself to God?"

"Yes," he answered, "when I was a boy fourteen years of age, in the old church at the North End, I heard Lyman Beecher preach on the theme, ' You belong to God ;' and I went home after that service, threw myself on the floor in my room, with locked doors, and prayed, ' O God, I belong to Thee ; take what is Thine own. I ask this, that whenever a thing be wrong it may have no power of temptation over me ; whenever a thing be right, it may take no courage to do it.' From that day to this it has been so. Whenever I have known a thing to be wrong, it has held no temptation. Whenever I have known a thing to be right, it has taken no courage to do it." [1]

The event here referred to occurred in 1826, a year previous to his matriculation. With this seriousness upon him, like the halo around a saint's head on the canvas of the old painters, he went to college.

Now let us stop and look at his portrait, as drawn by several of his classmates.

Referring to his religious experience, the Rev. Dr. Edgar Buckingham remarks:

"The excitement of the revival gradually passed off—that is, in a few years. But his conversion for quite a while made a deep impression on his companions, awakening their reverence (the word is not too strong) for this religious boy. I remember well his appearance of devoutness during morning and evening prayers in the chapel, which many attended only to save their credit with the authorities. Doddridge's 'Expositor' Wendell bore to college in his Freshman year (a present, I think, from his mother, a new volume), to be his help in daily thought and prayer." [2]

Another of his classmates refers to the same experience:

"Before entering college he had been the subject of religious revival. Previous to that he used to give way to violent outbursts of temper, and his schoolmates would sometimes amuse themselves by deliberately working him into a passion. But after

---

[1] Evidence of Rev. O. P. Gifford, D.D., at Eighth Annual Convention of the United Societies of Christian Endeavor. Reported in the *Golden Rule*, August 15th 1889, p. 737.

[2] Cited in Austin's "Life and Times of Wendell Phillips," p. 38.

his conversion they could never succeed in getting him out of temper."[1]

Truly, a conversion which makes a boy master of himself must be genuine! But how about other traits of the young collegian?

"To my mind," writes the Rev. Dr. Buckingham, "Phillips was the most beautiful person I ever saw—handsome, indeed, in form and features; but what I mean by his beauty was his grace of character—his kindly, generous manners, his brightness of mind, his perfect purity and whiteness of soul. His face was very fair, though it could not have been called pale; and it had a radiance from which shone forth the soul that dwelt within. He was of a wealthy family; and with manly beauty, with a most attractive face, 'a smile that was a benediction,' with manners of superior elegance, with conversation filled with the charms of literature, with biography and history, full of refined pleasantry, with never a word or thought that the purest might not know and listen to, it was no wonder that his society was courted and respected by those who had wealth at their command, and still more by those young men who came from the South. It is said that he was proud; that he was a born patrician. In a good sense of the word, he was a born patrician; in the sense of a French expression, '*noblesse oblige*,' he felt the responsibility of his birth and education—his responsibility to keep himself pure, upright, and good. I would not say that he never developed at any time anything of worldly pride also. I believe

---

[1] Cited by Theodore D. Weld, in his "Eulogy of Wendell Phillips," p. 16.

he did look down with scorn on that vulgarity, that form of professed democracy, whose virtue was to envy those better and purer than themselves, as well as loftier in position. I never knew that he scorned any one who was merely poor. But it happened, as one of the strangest of all human phenomena, that this young man who, in all his public life, had been the defender of the down-trodden and despised, was the especial pet, in his Junior and Senior years, in college, of the aristocracy in that institution. Indeed, he had the credit of being their leader; they put him up to it. The democracy of the class became excited to the highest degree—for reasons that I do not now recall, and believe I never knew (and I dare say there were none)—and it was determined to put Phillips and others of his associates down. I think he used some of his fine scorn at that time. We had then a military organization, a great pride of ours—the 'Harvard Washington Corps'—and though our uniform was black coats and white pantaloons, and the officers had gold buttons on their coats, with the usual feathers, epaulets, and sashes, yet, in my mind then, no company, however richly uniformed, made a handsomer appearance. When the time came for the election of officers by the class to which we belonged, a great struggle took place. It ended in a compromise. Phillips was not chosen captain. A young man from the South, yet not of the acknowledged aristocracy—a young man of herculean stature and proportions, one who had never taken sides in this social quarrel, and whom the whole college would have said was properly the man for the place—was chosen; and Phillips became one of the highest officers—lieutenant, I think. I never asked him what he learned about Southern pride and assumption in those days. But was it not singular that, from having been the most admired companion and most ardent champion of Southern men in his youth, he should have become in after years an opponent of Southern principles, than whom there has been none more powerful in the country?"[1]

Hear, next, what his room-mate, the Rev. John Tappen Pierce, of Illinois, has to say:

"Our acquaintance began at Harvard, in 1827, when we first met to be examined. I was then a lad of fifteen, but two weeks younger than Phillips. Though I had never seen him before I was drawn to him by irresistible attraction, and I always found him true as magnet to steel. I had engaged a roommate, otherwise we should have roomed together the first year; but, just before entering the Sophomore Class in 1828, Phillips came to my room and proposed our partnership, which I joyfully accepted; and here began our life intimacy, a sweet and enduring tie.

"I will speak first of his moral traits. He never said or did anything unbecoming to Christian character. What President Kirkland said in his 'Life of Fisher Ames' was eminently true of Phillips: 'He needed not the sting of guilt to make him virtuous.' His character shone conspicuous. He was above pretence—a sincere, conscientious, devoted friend. He had a deep love for all that was true and honorable; always detested a mean action. His Bible was always open on the centre-table. His character

---

[1] Austin's "Life and Times of Wendell Phillips," pp. 36, 38 *sq*.

was perfectly transparent; there were no subterfuges, no pretences about him. He was known by all to be just what he seemed.

"Second, his social traits: He was the favorite of the class. If any class honor was to be conferred, who so likely to have it as he? Nor would any dispute his claim. Though very modest in his self-estimate, every one willingly yielded him the palm. Upon the death of a valued classmate, Thompson, none but Phillips must pronounce the eulogy.

"Third: His standard as a scholar was among the first in a large class. This is saying not a little, when we recall the names of Motley, the historian; Simmons, the distinguished orator; Ames, United States *chargé d'affaires;* McKean, a true son of genius; the Rev. Dr. Morison, late editor of the *Unitarian Review;* Mayor Shurtleff and Dr. Shattuck, of Boston; Pickering, the Boston lawyer; Judge Durell, of New Orleans; Joseph Williams, Lieutenant-Governor of Michigan and president of a State college there.

"As an orator Phillips took the highest stand of any graduate of our day. I never knew him to fail in anything or hesitate in a recitation. In mathematics he was *facile princeps;* natural and moral philosophy, history, the ancient languages—in all pre-eminent; equally good in all branches."

The Rev. Dr. Morison, to whom Mr. Pierce refers in the above extract, testifies as follows:

"Wendell Phillips in college and Wendell Phillips six years after were entirely different men. In college he was the proud leader of the aristocracy. From what he then was no one could possibly predict what he afterward became, as the defender and personal friend of the helpless and despised. There was always the same grace and dignity of personal bearing, the same remarkable power of eloquence, whether in extempore debate or studied declamation. It was a great treat to hear him declaim as a college exercise. He was always studying remarkable passages, as an exercise in composition, and to secure the most expressive forms of language. In this he did not accept the aid of teachers. His method was his own.

"His classmates would have selected him as one born to be a power among men. No other student in those days could compare with him in that respect. He was already distinguished for his unsullied purity of character. But it was not easy to understand how this aristocratic leader of a privileged class could cast in his lot with the most despised of his race. The simple and true explanation is that a new thought had come in as the central motive of his life. His attention was drawn to the great national curse and crime of his day, and he gave himself heart and soul to the cause."[1]

While his rhetorical genius made him the easy master of the college platform, his social qualities pushed him into leadership in the numerous societies of Harvard. He was a member of the "Phi Beta Kappa," by virtue of his scholarship—that exclusive brotherhood being confined to the first sixteen in each class. He was president of the "Porcellian" and of the "Gentleman's Club"—circles which admitted only the *jeunesse dorée;* and a member of the "Hasty-Pudding Club." At this time there was nothing of the

---

[1] *Vide* Weld's "Eulogy," pp. 14, 15.

radical about him—hardly a flavor of democracy. He seemed to be the predestined leader of American conservatism, the inevitable champion of class distinctions and elegant leisure. Through these years he suggests the Cavalier, never the Puritan—Pharaoh, not Moses. He was so far from radicalism that his maiden speech at college was made against the proposed establishment of a temperance society in his class, and he killed it!

One day Phillips went into Boston to attend a Whig meeting in Faneuil Hall. It was during the Presidential campaign of 1828, when Adams was running against Jackson. As the student ascended the stairs he heard for the first time the powerful, metallic voice of Daniel Webster arguing in favor of the tariff; not very musical, he thought, as Clay's was, or Harrison Gray Otis's, but full of strength. As he entered the hall and listened he speedily detected that "his statement was argument." After this he frequently heard Webster in the courts and at political gatherings—always with admiration for his gifts. The great expounder, he found, was ponderous, almost heavy on ordinary occasions. It took a crisis to rouse him—then he was sublime.[1]

Mr. Phillips was graduated in 1831, with a class which numbered sixty-five members. What next?[2]

---

[1] "Recollections of Wendell Phillips," by F. B. Sanborn (MS.).

[2] Austin says, in his "Life and Times of Wendell Phillips," p. 34: "During his college life Mr. Phillips rarely read speeches, or even had any taste for oratory." This is an evident error, and is contradicted by the concurrent testimony of all his classmates, as witness the authorities cited.

IV.

THE YOUNG LAWYER.

The orthodox steps in the upward course of a well-born and rich young Bostonian, fifty years ago, were : First, the Public Latin School ; next Harvard College ; and then the Harvard Law School. Two of these steps Phillips had already taken ; in the autumn of 1831 he took the third, and seated himself to be instructed by Judge Story—a new Paul at the feet of a modern Gamaliel. Meantime, his college classmates were scattered everywhither—most of them dismissed into oblivion; for many graduates when they get a diploma only add a sheepskin to a sheep's-head, and provoke the spectators to cry " Bah !" Some of the Class of '33, however, drew out of the crowd of nonentities. Of those mentioned in these pages Appleton sauntered off to a life of belles-lettres enjoyment — literary gormandism. Motley sailed away to continue his studies in Berlin and Göttingen, and by and by to write himself into immortality. Sumner went, with Phillips, to the Harvard Law School, where the two continued and increased their intimacy.

Judge Story was a legal luminary of the first magnitude—the peer of Marshall. His students worshipped him. Both Phillips and Sumner shared in this feeling, and counted it as chief among their privileges that they might sit on his benches. The school was divided into three classes—the Senior, Middle, and Junior ; and the course covered three years. In those early days the attendance was comparatively small, the whole number of students being forty in 1833. This was a happy circumstance for them because they were individualized. Each received a fair share of the preceptor's personal attention, and the instruction took the form of a recitation rather than of a lecture, as now. The progress was correspondingly rapid ; while the relations of the students to the professors and to one another were close and delightful. Phillips at once took and maintained a high rank ; though he did not permit his outside interests to dwarf by disuse. The practice of athletics was rigidly adhered to, while his miscellaneous reading broadened and deepened. His one regret at this time was that his studies continued to separate him from his widowed mother, for the Law School was at Cambridge. But he knew her heart and prayers were with him, and both got consolation from frequent, if brief meetings.

He was especially fond of those aspects and principles of the law which presented it as a science, as the source and seat of human justice. The saying of Coke made a great impression on him, that " reason is the life of the law ; nay, the common law itself is nothing else but reason ;"[1] and he would have agreed with Froude, that " our human laws are, or should be, but the copies of the eternal laws, so far as we can read them."[2] But while particularly attracted toward legal philosophy, Phillips was not lacking in the grasp of details, nor reluctant to sub-

---

[1] First Institute.   [2] " Short Studies in Great Subjects," " Calvinism."

ject himself to the drudgery incidental to the mastery of forms and statutes.[1] He did not find any department of the study dry.[2] How could he, when the fire of a mind like Story's kindled it?

In a characteristic passage Mr. George William Curtis paints Wendell Phillips as his study of the law proceeded: "Doubtless the sirens sang to him, as to the noble youth of every country and time. If, musing over Coke and Blackstone, in the full consciousness of ample powers and of fortunate opportunities, he sometimes forecast the future, he saw himself succeeding Fisher Ames, and Harrison Gray Otis, and Daniel Webster, rising from the bar to the Legislature, from the Legislature to the Senate, from the Senate—who knew whither?—the idol of society, the applauded orator, the brilliant champion of the elegant repose and the cultivated conservatism of Massachusetts. The delight of social ease, the refined enjoyment of taste in letters and art, opulent leisure, professional distinction, gratified ambition—all these came and whispered to the young student. And it is the force that can tranquilly put aside such blandishments with a smile, and accept alienation, outlawry, ignominy, and apparent defeat, if need be, no less than the courage which grapples with poverty and outward hardship, and climbs over them to worldly prosperity, which is the test of the finest manhood. Only he who knows the worth of what he renounces gains the true blessing of renunciation."[3]

At this hour, however, only the anticipations were

---
[1] The remark of Judge Hopkinson, his classmate.
[2] *Ib.*, Sumner's Testimony also.
[3] "Eulogy of Wendell Phillips," pp. 6, 7.

present—the renunciation was hidden behind the impenetrable veil of futurity.

Three years, exactly, after the commencement of his legal course, Phillips found himself in the possession of his professional degree, viz., in September, 1834. With the blessing of Judge Story, who foretold for him an unprecedented career (which he had, but in a very different sense from Story's prophecy), and with the even more valued benediction of his mother, he was admitted to the bar.

Soon after this important event, he went away on a short tour, travelling as far as Philadelphia. Here, at a fashionable boarding-house, whither he had gone as the escort of a bevy of ladies, he met Trelawny, the English friend of Byron and Shelley. Trelawny was there in attendance upon Mrs. Fanny Kemble Butler, the leading actress of the day, of whom he professed to be an admirer. He had been in South Carolina, at the house of the lady's husband, Pierce Butler, and was on his way to Niagara. The Englishman, who had learned, or unlearned, his morality in the clubs of Pall Mall and with the brace of scapegrace poets with whom he had associated on the Continent, shocked the young Puritan by the open expression of atrocious sentiments respecting women—boasting of his success with them, and declaring that no woman ought to live beyond the age of twenty.[1]

Facing homeward, Phillips stopped for a few days in New York. In some way he made the acquaintance of Aaron Burr during his tarry. The slayer of Hamilton was exceedingly polite and showed him

---

[1] "Recollections of Wendell Phillips," by F. B. Sanborn (MS.).

the sights. Soon after his return Burr visited Boston. Phillips called on him at the Tremont Hotel, and offered to act the part of a *cicerone.* Among other places they went to the Athenæum, then on Pearl Street, to see the pictures and look at the library. As they walked down the hall, between the alcoves, Phillips caught sight of a bust of Hamilton, one of the ornaments of the library, which he had forgotten was there. He tried on some pretext to draw Burr in another direction; but he, too, had seen the bust and marched straight up to it. He stood facing it for a moment, then turned and said: "A remarkable man—a very remarkable man." Upon this he wheeled on both heels in military style and moved on again with great composure.[1]

Mr. Phillips's first public honor—his very earliest recognition as an orator—came from New Bedford, whose authorities, just after his graduation, invited him to deliver the Fourth of July address. The late Charles T. Congdon, an eminent journalist, paints a pen-portrait of the scene:

"When Phillips stood up in the pulpit I thought him the handsomest man I had ever seen. When he began to speak, his elocution seemed the most perfect to which I had ever listened, and I was sure that the orations of Cicero were given with smaller effect. Even then the future orator of the Abolitionists was an admirable speaker; nor did he, though scarcely past his majority, lack the grace and force of language with which the whole country has since become familiar."[2]

---

[1] "Recollections of Wendell Phillips," by F. B. Sanborn (MS.).
[2] "Recollections of a Journalist."

Desiring to prepare himself thoroughly before engaging in practice, the young lawyer went from Boston to Lowell, and entered the office of Thomas (afterward Judge) Hopkinson; his purpose being to familiarize himself with the code and with technical methods. Mr. Hopkinson had been his classmate at the Law School, but was older. He made both fame and money from the start, and welcomed the brilliant Bostonian with both hands outstretched. Fain would he have kept him in Lowell and admitted him into partnership,[1] but the pet of Judge Story had other plans. After a few months of persistent toil his object was accomplished, and he returned to Boston, not, however, before meeting and beginning an acquaintance with that singular man, Benjamin F. Butler, then an errand boy in a neighboring law office.[2]

And now at last Wendell Phillips, with all these years of diligent preparation behind him, with a mind which is a teeming storehouse of accumulated material manipulated by faculties rigorously trained, with a body which is a model of symmetry and strength, with the manners of a prince, genius in his face and honey on his lips, opens his office, hangs out his sign,[3] puts up his library, and cries, "Ready!"

How did he get on?

Here we must stop to notice and refute a singular misunderstanding. One of his biographers and one of his eulogists have given wide currency to the

---

[1] Letter of Judge Hopkinson, in possession of the writer.

[2] *Vide* the Letter of Benjamin F. Butler in Boston *Globe*, February 4th, 1884.

[3] George L. Austin, in his "Life of Wendell Phillips," p. 44.

statement that the young lawyer met with no success—that he waited in that spick-and-span office "for clients who did not come."[1] No proof is adduced of this unlikely assertion, save, in one case, the hazy recollection of an aged friend of his younger days. On the other hand, we have the probabilities of the case, which are overwhelmingly contradictory of this mistake. With his position, acknowledged ability and address, how could he fail to capture a practice? But, better still, we have the testimony of Mr. Phillips himself. "He often," writes a lady who was much in his family, and who knew him, perhaps, better than any other person save his wife, "spoke to me of his practice and the nature of it. 'Very much,' he said, 'was office work—drawing up legal papers, wills, etc.' He would sometimes say, with a smile, he did better then as a young lawyer than most young men do to-day upon entering the profession. 'Those two opening years I paid all my expenses, and few do it now.'"[2]

To the same effect speaks Mr. Sumner, who was perfectly familiar with the facts, and who declared, not long before his death, that "when Mr. Phillips became an Abolitionist he withdrew from the roll of Massachusetts lawyers the name of the greatest."[3]

Mr. A. H. Grimké, too, a learned and eloquent colored man, writes that Mr. Phillips himself informed him that his practice was extensive and successful.[4]

Nobody would be more likely to possess informa-

---

[1] George William Curtis, in his "Eulogy," p. 8.
[2] Mrs. William Sumner Crosby, quoted in the "Eulogy of W. Phillips," by Theodore D. Weld, p. 19.
[3] *Ib.*
[4] *Ib.*

tion on this point than Mr. Phillips's old friend and coworker, James Redpath, who compiled his volume of "Speeches and Lectures," and he says, in the last edition of that volume, in his biographical notice: "A large and increasing practice so occupied his time that he forgot all else. In the trial of cases at the bar he was training his eloquence, and before juries he was modulating that voice so soon to thrill humanity."[1]

We may be sure, therefore, that it was not because he was wearied from "waiting for clients who did not come," that Wendell Phillips soon took down his sign and closed his office. Future chapters will disclose the reason.

---

[1] See the volume itself.

V.

THE MARTYR AGE.

THE afternoon of October 21st, 1835, was charming, the air balmy, with a touch of tonic in it. Wendell Phillips sat beside an open window in his office on Court Street reading. Suddenly his attention was attracted by shoutings—angry, menacing, profane—accompanied by the tramp of hurrying feet along the sidewalk. The young lawyer rose and leaned over the window-sill. He saw a crowd half a block away on Washington Street. Evidently they were acting under great excitement. What was the matter? Leaving the window he put on his hat and sallied forth. Presently he was in the midst of the crowd. He found it a mob. They were confronting the Anti-Slavery office at the head of Washington Street, while four or five thousand gesticulating, vociferating men were trying to push their way up the narrow stairs and into the hall, which was up two flights.

Mr. Phillips stood and watched. Now he sees the mayor (Theodore Lyman) come on the scene. He hears him vainly *beseech* the people to disperse, instead of *commanding* them to do so. In a moment the mayor disappears; he has gone into the building. Now some thirty women, pale but composed, come down the stairs and march in procession along the street and so away amid the hoots and insults of the rabble. Among these brave ladies is one destined to become Mrs. Wendell Phillips,[1] though as yet they have not consciously met.

But look yonder! A man bare-headed, with a rope about his waist, his clothing torn and bedraggled, but with the erect head, calm face, and flashing eyes of a martyr going to the stake,[2] is dragged toward the City Hall,[3] which is just at hand. "Kill him!" "Lynch him!" "Hang the Abolitionist!" these exclamations are hurled at the composed prisoner as though they had been missiles.

"Who is that?" asks Mr. Phillips.

"That?" is the answer of a bystander. "Why, that's Garrison, the d—d Abolitionist. They are going to hang him."

The young man sees Colonel John C. Park, the commander of the Boston regiment, of which he is himself a member. Approaching him, he says: "Colonel, why doesn't the mayor call for the guns? This is outrageous!"

"Why," retorts the officer, "don't you see that the regiment is in the mob?"[4]

Profoundly astonished he observes this fact, and further notices that the mob is composed of "gentlemen of property and standing," his friends and associates on Beacon Hill![5] A mob in broadcloth! Being now shut out from further observations of the

---

[1] *Vide* "William Lloyd Garrison," by his sons, vol. ii., p. 12, note.

[2] The remark of Charles Sprague, the banker-poet, quoted in *ib.*, p. 22.

[3] *Ib.*, p. 23.

[4] *Ib.*, p. 32. See Phillips's "Speeches and Lectures," p. 213.

[5] *Ib.*, p. 33.

scene by the intervening multitude, and, indeed, supposing that the authorities would keep Mr. Garrison in the City Hall until it should be safe for him to venture to his home, Mr. Phillips walked slowly back to his office in deep thought.

On the morrow he learned that he had not seen the drama through; that Mr. Garrison had been new-clad in borrowed raiment in the mayor's room, hurried into a hack and, at the risk of his life, sent off to jail as a disturber of the peace, while the mobocrats were permitted to saunter off without any attempt at their arrest![1] He also discovered from the newspapers that the occasion of the riot had been a meeting of the "Boston Female Anti-Slavery Society." Here, too, he found that Mayor Lyman played an *opera-bouffe* part, turning the *ladies* (noble women, graced with manifold accomplishments) out-of-doors instead of the *rioters;* contributing to, not resisting, the disgrace of trampling upon the dearest right of liberty—free speech. Most surprising of all, the press of the city, with hardly an exception, extolled the mob and gloried in the shame! Himself a member of the bar, trained to feel that there was more force in the writ of a constable than in the bayonet of a soldier, supposing that he lived under the reign of law rather than mob violence, he was rudely awakened from these pleasant dreams to realize the fact that, in the country of which he was a proud citizen, an unpopular minority had no rights which the State was bound to respect, that law was not worth the parchment on which it was engrossed when it stood in the way of popular prejudice. It

---

[1] Phillips's "Speeches and Lectures," p. 216.

was his first, but by no means his last lesson in the essential weakness and limitation of republican government.

And now, at the moment when Wendell Phillips's attention was first practically drawn to the momentous issue, we pause to outline the state of the popular mind on the question of slavery.

The patriots and sages who created the United States were, almost without exception, opposed to slavery. Many of them were practical Abolitionists —Washington and Patrick Henry, for instance, freed their slaves. Nevertheless they recognized slavery as an existing institution. They believed it would eventually die; it was already dead in the North. But meantime they protected it against an uprising on the part of the slaves by the insurrectionary guarantee of the Constitution. They foisted into that fundamental document the three-fifths slave basis of representation, and thus unwittingly gave the taskmasters a powerful political motive for retaining slavery. And they agreed that the accursed slave-trade should continue in full blast for twenty years from the date of the adoption of the instrument. These were three sops to Cerberus. What did they matter? Were not the republican idea, the laws of trade, the voice of religion against the curse? The very doctrine of equality, which was the right hand of the Constitution, would—must—sooner or later, smite the system into the grave. So they reasoned. Mistaken men! "He needs a long spoon," says the proverb, "who sups with the devil." Referring to this error, Mr. Phillips said: "God gives manhood but one clew to success—equal and exact justice; that He guarantees shall be always expediency. Deviate one hair's breadth—plant only the tiniest seed of concession—you know not how 'many and tall branches of mischief shall grow therefrom.' " [1]

For a time, however, all went well. Randolph pronounced slavery "a volcano in full operation." Abolition societies sprang up everywhere. Franklin, Rush, and their compeers were glad and proud to act as their presidents. Slavery stood cap in hand and begged leave to be. Its tone was apologetic.

Presently the scene changed. In an evil hour " the devil hovered over Charleston with a handful of cotton-seed (again we quote Mr. Phillips). Dropped into sea-island soil and touched by the magic of Massachusetts brains (referring to Eli Whitney's invention of the cotton-gin, which instantly made the culture of cotton cheap and profitable), it poisoned the atmosphere. That cotton fibre was a rod of empire such as Cæsar never wielded. It fattened into obedience pulpit and rostrum, court, market-place, and college, and leashed New York and Philadelphia to its chair of State. In 1787 slave property, worth, perhaps, two hundred millions of dollars, strengthened by the sympathy of all other capital, was a mighty power. It was the Rothschild of the State. The Constitution, by its three-fifths slave basis, made slave-holders an order of nobles. This was the house of Hapsburg joining hands with the house of Rothschild. Prejudice of race was the third strand of the cable, bitter and potent as Catholic ever bore Huguenot, or Hungary ever spit on Moslem. This fearful trinity won to its side that mysterious omnipotence called *Fashion*—a power

---

[1] " Speeches and Lectures," p. 377.

which, without concerted action, without thought, law, or religion on its side, seems stronger than them all. Such was slavery. In its presence the North knelt and whispered. When slavery could not bully, it bubbled its victim."[1]

In these circumstances the early repugnance to the "peculiar institution" began to fade away. Those Abolition societies one by one disbanded. Business, quickened by the impulse which came from the gigantic traffic in cotton, stifled conscience in order to make money. Thus the great centres of trade, from New Orleans to Boston, were bribed into complicity. Society, borrowing its tone from wealth, spread its screen over human bondage. Law soon found or made precedents and sanctions, for did not a fat retainer jingle in its hands? The pulpit opened the Bible and turned back to the Book of Genesis for a scriptural warrant, in obedience to the demand of the slavery-infected pews. Ah, it was not slavery that was dying, as the fathers dreamed, it was anti-slavery! The South, which began by being apologetic, now reversed the rôle and arrogantly commanded, while the North became abject.

Serfdom in Russia was dreadful. Bondage in Brazil was wicked—it was at a good, salt-sea distance. But slavery in America was a necessity—a commercial, political, social, religious necessity, which let any one gainsay at his peril! *Here* it was entirely proper to knock men down under the hammer of the auctioneer, whip women to prostitution, and sell babies by the pound. There was money in

---

[1] "Speeches and Lectures," p. 377.

it. Traffic in human flesh ! Why, ask the minister if Abraham did not own slaves, and if Paul did not return the fugitive Onesimus ?

Such was the strangely altered condition of the public mind when, in the year 1829, suddenly uprose a young man who new-voiced the testimony of the fathers against slavery, and did it with an emphasis all his own. Who was he? His name was William Lloyd Garrison. Born in Newburyport, in Massachusetts, in 1805, his earlier years were passed as a printer's apprentice. He had a genius for ethics, and soon began to write for his master's journal, the Newburyport *Herald*, upon current, moral, and political questions, which he did acceptably. Graduating from this printing-office, his high school and college, he started a newspaper in his native town, the *Free Press*, which gasped through a few issues and then died. Mr. Garrison made his way to Boston and tried again, the *National Philanthropist* being the title of his venture. It was the first journal ever established as the champion of total abstinence. Here he met Benjamin Lundy, a middle-aged Quaker and a moral hero, who, at his own cost, was publishing in Baltimore, in slave holding Maryland, a small monthly called the *Genius of Universal Emancipation*, then the only distinctively anti-slavery periodical in America.[1] Mr. Lundy had come to Boston to solicit subscribers and to raise funds for the prosecution of his unequal war. These two men recognized in one another a kindred spirit, and Mr. Garrison's attention was now explicitly directed to the question of slavery. Soon after the young Mas-

---
[1] Johnson's *New Universal Cyclopædia*, article "Lundy."

sachusetts editor went to Bennington, in Vermont, to edit the village newspaper there (the *Journal of the Times*) in support of John Quincy Adams for the Presidency. Now he began to discuss slavery in earnest. Mr. Lundy again joined him while thus engaged and pleaded with him to unite in the publication of the Baltimore organ. This he did in 1829.[1] The partners did not agree in their views. Mr. Lundy was a gradual emancipationist, and favored the colonization of the slaves just as fast as they should be freed. Mr. Garrison, with intuitive sagacity, saw the absurdity and impossibility of this scheme in his first study of the problem, and hit at once by a stroke of genius upon the only basis on which the moral war could be waged, viz., immediate and unconditional emancipation.[2] He reasoned thus: Is slavery wrong anywhere? Then it is wrong everywhere. Is it wrong for a day? Then it is wrong for a year—wrong to the end of time. Is the wrongdoer bound to do right anywhere and at any time? Then he is bound to do right everywhere and instantly. So he hit upon his talisman and coined his war-cry.

But how, with their different views, could these two edit the same paper? Mr. Lundy proposed that each of them should sign his own contributions and feel free to publish his own doctrine. Thus the *Genius of Universal Emancipation*, like Cowper's "Orator Puff," had two "tones to its voice." One was a tone of thunder, while the other was the tone of a

---

[1] These statements are summarized from "William Lloyd Garrison," by his sons, vol. i., pp. 36-137.

[2] See Wendell Phillips's "Eulogy of Garrison," published by Lee & Shepard, Boston.

zephyr. What was the result? Mr. Lundy's teachings had no result. Even Baltimore, the centre of the domestic slave-trade, gave no heed to his mild remonstrances. It was like bombarding Gibraltar with cologne water. When Mr. Garrison spoke the city was stirred as by an earthquake. He was speedily thrown into jail. At the end of forty-nine days his fine and bill of costs (he had been tried and found guilty of libel for denouncing a certain Mr. Todd for conducting an interstate slave-trade) were paid by Arthur Tappan,[1] of New York, an eminent merchant, then a colonizationist, but known soon after as among the most active of Abolitionists; and the victim of free speech was set at liberty.

This experience taught Mr. Garrison that he had selected the wrong scene for his crusade; that a preliminary work needed to be done before slavery could be successfully assailed; that the right to *discuss* the question must be first established. Free speech was now deemed treason by the State and condemned as heresy by the Church. Where should this central truth of liberty be vindicated? Manifestly not in the midst of coffle-gangs and slave-pens, where his voice would be drowned by the rattle of shackles and the machinery of oppression in thunderous operation. Hence, dissolving his partnership with Mr. Lundy, he set out upon a prospecting tour. In giving his experience, he wrote:

"Every place that I visited gave fresh evidence of the fact that a greater revolution in public sentiment was to be effected in the free States (and particularly in New England) than at the South. I found

---

[1] "William Lloyd Garrison," by his sons, vol. i., p. 190.

contempt more bitter, opposition more active, detraction more relentless, prejudices more stubborn, and apathy more frozen than among slave-holders themselves. Of course there were individual exceptions to the contrary. This state of things afflicted, but did not dishearten me. I determined, at every hazard, to lift up the standard of emancipation in the eyes of the nation, within sight of Bunker Hill, and in the birthplace of liberty."[1]

Accordingly he returned to Boston and established the *Liberator*.[2] This was in 1831. Supposing that he would have a certain ally in the churches if he could but win them to consider the question of slavery, Mr. Garrison became an itinerant missionary and waited upon clergyman after clergyman. Being of the orthodox faith in those days, he began with the Rev. Dr Lyman Beecher.

"No," said the divine, with a shake of the head; "I have too many irons in the fire already."

"Then," was the solemn reply, "you had better take all the rest out and put this in."[3]

The truth is, that Dr. Beecher was a colonizationist. He preached immediate repentance to sinners, with a *caveat* in the case of slavery. Of all suggested remedies for slavery colonization was the most preposterous. All the shipping of the world would not have sufficed to ferry the slaves back to Africa. And had that been possible, what hope was there that the masters would consent, or if they did, that the slaves would go? The conviction is irre-

---

[1] "Garrison and his Times," by O. Johnson, pp. 41, 42.
[2] *Ib.*, p. 50. "William Lloyd Garrison," by his sons, vol. i., p. 219.
[3] "Garrison and his Times," p. 44.

sistible that many consciences, pinched by a sense of the sin of slavery, but unwilling to accept the only honest and adequate remedy, salved their aching with this fantasy. As regards Dr. Lyman Beecher, he did make vicarious atonement by the gift to Anti-Slavery, later on, of his son, Henry Ward Beecher, whose tongue became like the stone in David's sling to smite the Goliath-evil ; and of his daughter, Harriet Beecher Stowe, whose pen impaled it. The old man's loins were wiser than his head !

From Dr. Beecher, Mr. Garrison went to the Rev. Dr. William Ellery Channing, the chief of the Unitarians, with no greater success. Dr. Channing sympathized, but would not act. Then he visited Jeremiah Evarts, the famous Secretary of the "American Board of Commissioners for Foreign Missions," and an able champion of the Indians. But he considered that there was a great difference between *red* and *black*. He admired the one color and disliked the other. Besides, many of the Cherokees and Choctaws were themselves slave-holders ! [1]

Surprised but not dismayed, the editor of the *Liberator* continued his Diogenes-quest for an honest man. He flashed his lantern through the thick darkness of Boston, of Massachusetts, of New England —vainly ! Or if he met with any success, the exceptions were so few and so obscure that they only established the rule of indifference that deepened into vicious hostility. The clergy were against slavery in the abstract, but were clear that it ought not to be interfered with at the South. Abraham and Onesimus were constantly flung into the young

---

[1] " Garrison and his Times," by O. Johnson, pp. 45, 46.

Abolitionist's face. This chapter in the history of American Christianity is fitted to wring tears from the eyes of angels. It was the age of the reign of Satan in the Kingdom of God. Behold an inherent defect in the voluntary system, which puts the pulpit at the mercy of the pews, and makes it martyrdom for the minister to preach what the parish disallows.

Mr. Garrison next tried the Quakers, moved to it, perhaps, by his old relations with Mr. Lundy. They had been the immemorial friends of the oppressed, for had not the iron entered their own souls? But now they were become rich and respectable. They were the sharpest of traders, and their greed choked their consciences. Their ears were stuffed with cotton so that they could not hear the sighs of the bondmen.

There was a time, as some one has said, when one Quaker was enough to shake the country for twenty miles around; but now it required the country for twenty miles around to shake one Quaker![1] There were some bright exceptions among them, as among the other sects. John G. Whittier was one. He had already attuned his harp for freedom, and begun to sing a race into liberty and himself into immortality. Arnold Buffum, of Lynn, in Massachusetts, was another, and he became the first President of the first Anti-Slavery Society in America that was established on the principle of immediate emancipation.[2] There were others less well known.

"Well, Perez, I hope thee's done running after the Abolitionists," said a high-seat friend to one of

---

[1] "Garrison and his Times," by Oliver Johnson, p. 21.
[2] *Ib.*, p. 94.

his humbler brethren. " Verily, I have," returned Perez ; " I've caught up with and gone just a little ahead of 'em !" [1]

Meantime the *Liberator* continued to appear, and was supported as miraculously as was Elijah in the famine. How the money came or was to come God only knew. The heroic editor lived for many months on faith, and such material provender as he could procure from a neighboring bakery.[2] The office was in a garret. " Everything about it," remarks Oliver Johnson, an eye-witness of and participator in the experience, " had an aspect of slovenly decay, and Harrison Gray Otis well characterized it as ' an obscure hole—'

'Yet there the freedom of a race began.'

The dingy walls ; the small windows bespattered with printers' ink ; the press standing in one corner, the composing stands opposite ; the long editorial and mailing table, covered with newspapers ; the bed of the editor and publisher on the floor—all these make a picture never to be forgotten." [3]

The publication of the sheet which issued from these sorry quarters made a sensation. Each week its appearance was an event. Boston at the outset shook with laughter. It was a new edition of " Don Quixote." The South recognized the danger at once. This voice was like its own—resolute, commanding—the only voice its instinct made it fear. Here were conviction, indomitable will and courage never to submit nor yield.

---

[1] " Garrison and his Times," by Oliver Johnson, p. 97.
[2] *Ib.*, p. 51.   [3] *Ib.*, pp. 51, 52.

In condemning slavery as a sin; in demanding that it be repented of and forsaken immediately and unconditionally because sinful; in asserting the humanity of the negro and his consequent fitness for freedom (a fact which the whole country discredited, holding that a "nigger" was nothing but a type of cattle—an impious notion which slavery had spawned); in speaking *right out* on these points, with the directness and emphasis of Nathan when he said to the royal transgressor, "Thou art the man!" Mr. Garrison made the *Liberator* a spear of Ithuriel, whose touch transformed slave-holders into man-stealers and forced the disguised devil to disclose himself.[1]

One by one friends sought out the editor. By and by there were enough of these to permit the organization of a "New England Anti-Slavery Society." Early in 1832 the association was formed, twelve apostles signing the constitution.[2] The meeting was held in the school-room of the African Bap-

---

[1] "Him . . . they found
Squat, like a toad, close at the ear of Eve,
Assaying by his devilish art to reach
The organs of her fancy, and with them forge
Illusions as he list, phantasms and dreams;
Him thus intent, Ithuriel with his spear
Touched lightly, for no falsehood can endure
Touch of celestial temper, but returns
Of force, to its own likeness: up he starts,
Discovered and surprised."
—*Paradise Lost*, B. iv.

[2] Here are their names: William Lloyd Garrison, Oliver Johnson, Robert B. Hall, Arnold Buffum, William J. Snelling, John E. Fuller, Moses Thatcher, Joshua Coffin, Stillman B. Newcomb, Benjamin C. Bacon, Isaac Knapp, and Henry R. Stockton. *Vide* "Garrison and his Times," by O. Johnson, p. 86.

tist Church in Belknap Street, Boston, thereafter a frequent refuge of the Abolitionists in storm and tempest. As the meeting adjourned, and the twelve gentlemen stepped out into the dark night (it was snowing), Mr. Garrison remarked, impressively: "We have met this evening in this obscure schoolhouse; our numbers are few and our influence limited; but mark my prediction, Faneuil Hall shall erelong echo with the principles we have set forth. We shall shake the nation with their mighty power."[1] Surely he wore on that occasion the mantle of the old Hebrew prophet!

Toward the end of 1833 a great convention was held in Philadelphia, and the "American Anti-Slavery Society" was organized,[2] an achievement which unified the scattered forces of Abolition and challenged the attention of the nation. The example proved contagious. A number of State societies, and in some cases county and city societies, were formed soon after. The agitation became intense. Mr. Garrison could not hold forth any worldly considerations to attract adherents. His case was like that of Garibaldi, who, desiring to liberate and unify Italy, went before a crowd of young men and appealed for recruits.

"What are your inducements?" they asked.

"Poverty, hardship, battles, wounds, and—*victory!*" replied the hero. The Italians caught his enthusiasm and enlisted on the spot. In the same way did the Boston Abolitionist make headway.

The alarmed South was loud-mouthed and threat-

---

[1] "Garrison and his Times," by O. Johnson, p. 88.
[2] "William Lloyd Garrison," by his sons, vol. ii., chap. xii., *passim*.

ening. The North, as usual, cringed and asked for orders. As an indication of the spirit of the slave oligarchy read this paragraph, clipped from the Richmond *Whig:*

" Let the hell-hounds at the North beware. Let them not feel too much security in their homes, or imagine that they who throw firebrands, although from, as they think, so safe a distance, will be permitted to escape with impunity. There are thousands now animated with a spirit to brave every danger to bring those felons to justice on the soil of the Southern States, whose women and children they have dared to endanger by their hell-concocted plots. We have feared that Southern exasperation would seize some of the prime conspirators in their very beds, and drag them to meet the punishment due their offences. We fear it no longer. We hope it may be so, and our applause as one man shall follow the successful enterprise."

Here is another extract, taken from the Columbia *Telescope*, a prominent and influential journal in South Carolina :

" Let us declare, through the public journals of our country, that the question of slavery is not and shall not be open to discussion ; that the very moment any private individual attempts to lecture us upon its evils and immorality, in the same moment his tongue shall be cut out and cast upon the dunghill."

Taking their cue from such utterances as these (and these were only two solos in a diabolical chorus), Governor McDuffie, in a message to the Legislature of South Carolina, declared slavery " the corner-stone of the Republican edifice ;" asserted that the laboring class of any community, " bleached or unbleached," was a " dangerous element in the body politic ;" predicted that within twenty-five years the white laboring people of the North would be virtually reduced to slavery, and ended by demanding that the laws should be so amended everywhere as to punish any interference with or discussion of Southern institutions " with death without benefit of clergy." [1]

The Legislature of the State, responding to this message, promptly resolved, " That South Carolina, having every confidence in the justice and friendship of the non-slave-holding States, announces her confident expectation, and she earnestly requests that the governments of these States will promptly and effectually suppress all those associations within their respective limits purporting to be Abolition societies." [2]

North Carolina, Alabama, and Virginia adopted similar resolutions. And these were forwarded to the Northern Governors.[3] How did they receive such insolent demands? Precisely as the black slaves at the South received the whip. Most of them forwarded the communications to their respective legislatures with no comment at all. Two of them, however, viz., Governor W. L. Marcy, of New York, and Governor Edward Everett, of Massachusetts, outran the rest in the race of servility, echoed the demands of Governor McDuffie, of South Carolina, and recommended the legislatures of their respective States to make it a penal offence to speak or print against slavery.[4] Happily, the legislatures of New York and Massachusetts had more self-respect than their lackey-governors. The suggested legislation was attempted, but thanks to the efforts of the Abolitionists it did not carry.[5]

---

[1] *Vide* " Garrison and his Times," by O. Johnson, pp. 213, 214.
[2] *Ib.*, p. 214.   [3] *Ib.*
[4] " William Lloyd Garrison," by his sons, vol. ii., pp. 75, 76.
[5] *Ib.*, p. 76. " Garrison and his Times," by O. Johnson, pp. 214–17.

With such a domineering spirit at the South and with such servility in high places at the North, it is not surprising that the sidewalks were unsafe for Abolitionists to tread ; that public halls were denied to them for their meetings ; that their publications were excluded from the mails ; that it became increasingly difficult for them to earn a livelihood in any line of trade ; that they were marked men, under the frown of State and Church, moral pariahs, inviting abuse and regarded as fit for death.[1] To be an Abolitionist in free America was in popular estimation, fifty years ago, what it was to be a Christian in the days of Nero, or what it is to be a Nihilist in Russia now. The very word embodied contempt and rage beyond expression. Anybody, everybody, felt free to kick and cuff, to damn and hang an Abolitionist.

Theodore D. Weld,[2] who was an active participant in the scenes he describes, and who is remembered as a Demosthenes of eloquence by the few survivors of that period, paints, as only he could, the treatment which he and others like him then received :

---

[1] See T. D. Weld's " Eulogy of Wendell Phillips," pp. 21-25.

[2] Mr. Weld was born in Massachusetts in 1803. He studied at Andover, and followed Dr. Lyman Beecher to Lane Seminary, in Ohio, when that divine took charge of the institution. Here he became interested in the slavery question, abolitionized the seminary, took the field as an Anti-Slavery lecturer, and by his amazing eloquence speedily made his name and fame continental. Unhappily his excessive labors and exposures caused the loss of his voice and did what slavery could not do—silenced him. He is still living (1890), hale and hearty in a serene and honored old age, at Hyde Park, near Boston.

"Civilization presupposes a government of law. If law is abolished society sinks into barbarism. Sunk thus was this nation then in its relation to Abolitionists. Mobs had been for years everywhere in outburst against them. They were the victims of an indiscriminate ostracism. Everywhere they were doomed because they hated slavery and lived out that hate. In thousands of cases they were subjected to personal assaults, beatings, and buffetings, with nameless indignities. They were stoned, clubbed, knocked down, and pelted with missiles, often with eggs, and, when they could be gotten, spoiled ones. They were smeared with filth, stripped of clothing, tarred, feathered, ridden upon rails, their houses sacked, bonfires made in the streets of their furniture, garments, and bedding, their vehicles and harnesses were cut and broken, and their domestic animals harried, dashed with hot water, cropped, crippled, and killed. Among these outrages, besides assaults and breaches of the peace, there were sometimes burglaries, robberies, maimings, and arsons; Abolitionists were driven from their homes into the fields and the woods and their houses burned. They were dragged and thrust from the halls in which they held their meetings. They were often shot at and sometimes wounded. In one mob a number were thus wounded and one killed. For a quarter of a century our civilization was sunk to barbarism. The law, which to others was protection, to Abolitionists was sheerest mockery. Yea, more, it singled them out as its victims. Professing to protect, it gave them up to ravage and beckoned the spoilers to their prey. Of the tens of thousands who perpetrated such atrocities not one suffered the least legal penalty for those astounding violations of law !"[1]

While such was the reception of the Abolitionists here at the North and in their own homes, and when it was proposed to padlock their lips by law, slaveholders might come into the free States with a retinue of slaves as long as the triumphal procession of an old Roman emperor, and with a harem that suggested the Turkish Sultan, with none to molest them or make them afraid. And from the centre of the indecent *cortége* they denounced the Abolitionists as cut-throats. It was an outrage to attack slavery, but entirely correct to practice and defend it! Opposition was sin and defence was virtue!

Mr. Garrison, as the central figure in the accursed circle, was naturally the special target for conspirators to aim at. Already a price had been set upon his head by the State of Georgia of $5000,[2] a standing bribe to any gang of ruffians to kidnap him and deliver the Samson of Abolition into the hands of the modern Philistines. That he was not seized on some dark night, hurried to the wharf near his office, and sent on some South-bound vessel to grind in the prison-house of the oppressors or make sport in the Temple of Dagon, is a miracle—further proof of the existence and Providence of God.

Such is a crayon sketch of the public situation at the hour when the broadcloth mob fell under the eyes of Wendell Phillips in 1835—the South omnipotent and imperious, the North its errand-boy and lick-spittle; the Abolitionists few in number, unin-

---

[1] "Eulogy of Wendell Phillips," pp. 22, 23.

[2] See the legislative action of Georgia, quoted in "William Lloyd Garrison," by his sons, vol. i., pp. 247-49.

fluential in position, despised as fanatics and hated as incendiaries, banned by the slave-masters and mobbed at home, outcasts for their humanity, as the negroes were on account of their skin. America was a synonym for hell.

VI.

THE NEW CLIENT.

THE intimacy of Wendell Phillips and Charles Sumner, as we have noted, commenced at the Boston Latin School, continued at college and in the Law School, and deepened with the lapse of time. They were often together. One day (it was early in 1836) they sat conversing in Mr. Phillips's office on Court Street, when a mutual friend, a Mr. Alford, burst in upon them. He informed them of his engagement to a Miss Grew, of Greenfield, in Massachusetts. Said he :

"I am going to Greenfield with my *fiancée* to-morrow, and a cousin of hers, a Miss Ann Terry Greene, is to accompany us. Now you know that in my condition ' two's company,' etc., and I wish you would go, both of you, and take care of the other lady. She will require the two of you, for she is the aurora borealis in human form—the cleverest, loveliest girl you ever met. But I warn you that she is a rabid Abolitionist. Look out or she will talk you both into that *ism* before you suspect what she is at."

After chaffing Alford, the two friends agreed to go.

" It is only fair," remarked Mr. Sumner, " to help him out. Do as you'd be done by, eh, Wendell ? "

The next morning was furiously stormy. When

Mr. Sumner got up and looked out he muttered, " I won't go on a stage ride (no railroads then) on such a day for any woman!" and ungallantly went back to bed.

Mr. Phillips was more chivalrous—he went. While his friend devoted himself to Miss Grew he made himself the cavalier of Miss Greene, who, true to the warning he had received, talked Abolition to him to the accompaniment of the rattling stage-coach. What of that? Who cares what a charming girl talks *about*, so that she only *talks?* Besides, Mr. Phillips was already deeply interested in the question of slavery. His Anti-Slavery convictions dated back to 1831,[1] the year of his graduation. True, he held them in an inactive, theoretical fashion. But they were there, and they had been warmed into new life by the Garrison mob. The burning words of this fair enthusiast added fresh fuel to the slumbering fire. When Jean d'Arc sounds to battle where is the soldier who can refuse to buckle on his armor? All too soon did that stage-coach lumber into Greenfield!

Before they parted Mr. Phillips asked and obtained permission to continue the acquaintance. Miss Greene was a native and resident of Boston. Her admirer learned that she was an orphan and an heiress,[2] though for the heiress part of it he cared nothing, for he was himself a man of independent fortune, and one who would not have been swayed by mercenary considerations. Her home was not far from his own, with her uncle and aunt, Mr. and

---

[1] Weld's " Eulogy of Wendell Phillips," p. 20.
[2] Her father was Benjamin Greene, a wealthy trader of Boston.

Mrs. Henry G. Chapman,[1] who were warm friends and devoted adherents of Mr. Garrison.[2] The lady was beautiful, splendidly educated, a marvellous conversationalist, and possessed a rare moral nature. She had withal a singular power of insight, and after the manner of her sex, could get to the bottom of a subject by a flash of intuition, and so reach a conclusion which the male intellect might attain only by laborious reasoning. "Yes," confessed Mr. Phillips, in after years, "my wife made an out and out Abolitionist of me, and she always preceded me in the adoption of the various causes I have advocated."

No wonder the young man found the personal charms of such a woman, inspired and aglow with lofty moral purpose, irresistible! He came to see her, came again, and then kept coming. Within the year when they first met their engagement was announced.[3]

It was at the Chapman's fireside that Wendell Phillips was introduced to Mr. Garrison[4]—his final step toward Abolition. These two men, so unlike in family, training, worldly prospects, so at one in conviction, courage, devotion, were from the start attracted to each other. And thus began that wondrous alliance which was to find its consummation and benediction in the rehabilitation of American liberty.

Yet it was a strange coalition. For Mr. Garrison was a plebeian, while Mr. Phillips was an aristo-

---

[1] "Ann Phillips," a Memorial Sketch, by Mrs. Alford, p. 3.
[2] *Ib.*   [3] *Ib.*
[4] So Mr. Phillips told the writer.

crat. The one was a self-made man ; the other was the consummate product of New England culture. The first had no grace, save the highest, that of God ; the second had that highest, and added to it every other grace of mind and person that can adorn a man. The genius of the printer was the homespun genius of intense moral conviction, that treads every obstacle under foot ; the genius of the lawyer was the genius of Plato in the Academy and Burke in the Senate, with contagious morality enough thrown in to infect the continent. One of these two allies was to become the executive of the Anti-Slavery movement ; the other was to supply the eloquence that should melt the fetters from a race and transform a nation.

That meeting with Ann Terry Greene was a happy circumstance. As results of it the lady secured an ideal husband and won to a great reform its most powerful advocate. Mr. Phillips obtained a wife who became his perennial inspiration. Mr. Garrison gained his most renowned ally, and the blacks may date from it the auspicious beginning of a triumphant end.

Not long after meeting Mr. Garrison Wendell Phillips openly announced his adoption of Abolition principles and took his place among the " fanatics." The Rubicon was passed ! The boats were burned ! On June 14th, 1837, he rode out to Lynn, ten miles away, for the first time to attend an Anti-Slavery Convention.[1] It was the quarterly meeting of the Massachusetts Society. His maiden speech in the hated cause made that session forever memorable.

---

[1] " William Lloyd Garrison," by his sons, vol. ii., p. 129.

After reading a resolution which pledged the assemblage to "special consecration," he proceeded to enforce it in an address which "charmed and surprised the audience."[1] Naturally, his classic style and exquisite modulation could not fail to surprise and charm. One passage is prophetic in its aspiration, and is characteristic, too, in its generous tribute to Mr. Garrison:

"We would have ourselves the joy of seeing this work accomplished. Before our eyes are closed, we wish to see the happy day which shall proclaim liberty to the captive. If it be possible, let the shout of emancipated millions rise before his ear is dust whose voice first waked the trumpet-note which is rocking the nation from side to side. To him (need I name him?) with at least equal truth may be applied the language of Burke to Fox: 'It will be a distinction honorable to the age, that the rescue of the greatest number of the human race from the greatest tyranny that was ever exercised, has fallen to the lot of one with abilities and dispositions equal to the task; that it has fallen to the lot of one who has the enlargement to comprehend, the spirit to undertake, and the eloquence to support so great a measure of hazardous benevolence.'"[2]

With this speech Mr. Phillips began his career as a reformer. He had gained a new client. He became attorney for the people in the Court of Conscience. Like the matchless sculpture of St. Martin sharing his cloak with a beggar, so he threw over the form of shivering humanity the warm protection of his gifts and advocacy.

When it became known in Boston that the most talented of her young sons had become an Abolitionist, the town was horrified. His family, in all its branches, was torn between pity for their misguided

---
[1] "William Lloyd Garrison," by his sons, vol. ii., p. 129.
[2] *Vide Liberator*, vol. vii., p. 63.

kinsman and a bitter sense of their own disgrace. His former classmates were for a space incredulous and then aghast. Beacon Hill rent its clothes and put ashes on its head. Everybody said : "It is suicide—political, professional, and social suicide." So it was. Boston was neither as large nor as democratic then as it is now. The blue-blood feeling was marked and strong. It was as fatal to break caste in Boston fifty years ago as it would have been in India. Those old families were republicans in profession and aristocrats in practice. They prided themselves as much upon their descent as did the English nobility. And they resented as keenly any departure from conventional respectability as could the descendants of the Normans. It is at once laughable and pathetic to reflect that there was ever a time in republican and Christian America when a practical belief in the Declaration of Independence and the Sermon on the Mount was regarded as disreputable, proof that one was either a knave or a fool ! Wendell Phillips soon found that it was so. The circle in which he moved cut him dead. Old acquaintances grew strangely near-sighted when they met him on the street. Doors which before had opened to give him eager welcome were shut in his face. The class from which his professional advancement was to come withdrew their business from his hands. He saw all his bright prospects crumbling to the ground under his very eyes. He found himself an outcast in his native city—deserted and avoided as though stricken with leprosy. He was an Abolitionist. And what was that but a movable pest—corruption animate—death in life ? Any Abolitionist was despicable : he most of all, because by birth and breeding he was a gentleman. Therefore the respectability of Boston stayed only long enough to brand him as "the friend of niggers," and then turned away from him in unspeakable disgust.

In all the older towns of this country—Boston, New York, Philadelphia, Charleston, St. Louis— class distinctions were formerly rigid as the etiquette of the Court of St. James. One aristocracy always sympathizes with another. This feeling is the cement that held together the "best" families of the North and the "first" families of the South. And this explains why these families, North as well as South, abhorred the Abolitionists, who, in attacking slavery, were sapping caste itself. It was a new phase of the world-old contest between the classes and the masses. That one of their own order should go into the Abolition camp enraged the dons and doñas. It was like deserting to the enemy in time of war. Hence Wendell Phillips was looked upon as a social Benedict Arnold. The marvel is, not that *they* felt as they did, but that *he* felt as he did. The fact that he so soon and so completely emancipated himself from the narrow prejudices of such an environment, is the best proof of his moral greatness.

But did he not feel his outlawry? How could he help it? Remember his position. Think of his outlook. But it doubly endears him to posterity that he never complained, never besought, never retreated an inch, nor filed down a principle, nor softened a phrase to regain his place and conciliate esteem. He had counted the cost. He regarded his forfeited distinctions, all possible advancement within his reach, as "dust in the measure and fine dust in the balance," when weighed against the honor of standing with God and befriending those who were ready to perish. What he lost he valued ; what he gained he held as an abundant compensation. It hurt him to feel that he had disappointed those who loved him. All the more resolutely did he turn for consolation to the service of the poor and miserable and blind and naked. No such sacrifices have been made by any other American. But he had and has his exceeding great reward. All this the poet Lowell has magnificently embalmed in a descriptive sonnet which he wrote not long afterward and dedicated to Wendell Phillips :

" He stood upon the world's broad threshold : wide
   The din of battle and of slaughter rose ;
He saw God stand upon the weaker side,
   That sank in seeming loss before its foes ;
Many there were who made great haste and sold
   Unto the coming enemy their swords.
He scorned their gifts of fame, and power, and gold,
   And, underneath their soft and flowery words,
Heard the cold serpent hiss ; therefore he went
   And humbly joined him to the weaker part,
Fanatic named, and fool, yet well content
   So he could be the nearer to God's heart,
And feel its solemn pulses sending blood
   Through all the widespread veins of endless good."

VII.

IN FANEUIL HALL.

MR. PHILLIPS and Miss Greene were married on October 12th, 1837.[1] He wedded an invalid—a lifelong invalid, as it turned out. Through some defect of nervous organization[2] the lady, even as a child, was frequently shut up and closed in, being often, and as the time passed increasingly confined to her room. Beginning as lovers, they remained lovers to the end. Their honeymoon stretched from the altar to the grave. Because of his wife's ill-health the husband from the start added to the lover the tender nurse. And this function, also, was to find exercise until the final scene. Mrs. Phillips was inordinately fond of reading. When, as was often the case, she was too sick to hold a book, Mr. Phillips would be her eyes. This was her greatest treat. Those who have heard him read will know why, for in this delightful, and, strange to say, rare accomplishment he had no rival. She had then and ever retained a singular transparent beauty—blue eyes, magnificent long hair, Hebe's complexion, and the form of Juno. In the face of pain, and of the deprivation that comes from pain, she was joyous in

---

[1] Miss Mary Grew, Mrs. Phillips's cousin and life-long intimate, confirms this date.

[2] So says Dr. David Thayer, the family physician.

disposition, with unfailing good spirits, and fond of fun and stories, in which respect her husband matched her, so that hilarity was with them an abiding guest. "My better three quarters," was her favorite descriptive phrase of him. And, evidently, it had been love at first sight on her side as on his, for she confesses: "When I first met Wendell I used to think, 'It can never come to pass; such a being as he is could never think of me.' I looked upon it as something as strange as a fairy-tale."[1]

To a relative, on her first birthday after marriage, she further expresses her feelings with a *naïve* pen:

"November 19, 1837.

"Do you remember it is Ann Terry's birthday, and that I am so aged? Only last year I thought I should never see another birthday, but must leave *him* in the infancy of our love, in the dawn of my new life; and how does to-day find me?—the blessed and happy wife of one whom I thought I should never perhaps live to see. Thanks be to God for all His goodness to us, and may He make me more worthy of my Wendell. I cannot help thinking how little I have acquired, while Wendell, only two years older, seems to know a world more; so

"'. . . that still the wonder grew,
How one small head could carry all he knew.'"[2]

In the midst of their new-born gladness, long before the orange-blossoms had time to shrivel, an event occurred which was the occasion of Mr. Phillips's *début* as an orator, and which gave him the world for an audience.

The essential blasphemy of slavery lay in this, that it broke into and desecrated the temple of the Holy Ghost by reducing a man to be a chattel. It

---

[1] "Ann Phillips," by Mrs. Alford, p. 5.   [2] *Ib.*, pp. 5, 6.

dealt in men and women as a drover trades in cattle. It changed marriage into prostitution, and made every plantation a nest of brothels. It herded negroes together as swine herd. It sold their offspring as hogs are sold. John Wesley, after living two years in the midst of slavery in Georgia, shook the dust from his feet against it and sailed from Savannah back to England, crying out as he left, "Slavery is the sum of all villainies." The truest, tersest, strongest half dozen words ever tabled against it. Well he knew that language had no word that could fitly name such a system. So in despair of naming it, he could only define it. As he gazed at it no wonder his eyes filled, his sight grew dim, his brain grew dizzy. He listened till shrieks stunned him. He pondered the ghastly horror till the breath he drew steamed rank with scent of blood![1] We have learned in a previous chapter what befell the humane spirits who, in the land of liberty, ventured to repeat the definition of the great apostle of Methodism. Slavery now went a step further and proceeded from persecution to martyrdom. On November 7th, 1837, it murdered the Rev. Elijah P. Lovejoy, at Alton, in Illinois. The story of his death has been often told. It cannot be told too often. The fact and the lesson of it, Americans are bound to reiterate in words of fire until "the deep damnation of his taking off" shall be burned into the indignant consciousness of every freeman.

Mr. Lovejoy was a Presbyterian clergyman, a graduate of Waterville College, in the State of

---

[1] Weld's "Eulogy on Wendell Phillips," p. 25.

Maine, where he was born, and of Princeton Theological Seminary. He went to the West after completing his studies and made a home in St. Louis. Here his sect made him the editor of their local organ, the *Observer*. He was not an Abolitionist. He had not grown up to that as yet. But he saw enough, heard enough, felt enough in that slave-holding community to make him hate slavery. One day a negro killed an officer in attempting to avoid arrest. He was seized in jail by a gang of lynchers, taken out, chained to a tree, and burned to death. Mediæval barbarism! Efforts were made to punish the murderers. The judge (whose suggestive name was Lawless) charged the Grand Jury substantially as follows: "When men are hurried by some mysterious, metaphysical, electric frenzy to commit a deed of violence, they are absolved from guilt. If you should find that such was the fact in this case then act not at all. The case transcends your jurisdiction; it is beyond the reach of human law."[1] Of course they did not bring in an indictment. Mr. Lovejoy commented in the *Observer* upon this outrageous charge as it deserved. Then the "mysterious, metaphysical, electric frenzy" again found expression, and his printing-office was gutted. The editor decided to remove his headquarters to Alton, in Illinois, ten miles up the Mississippi, on the free-soil side of the river. He was now on free soil, but, alas, not among free men! No sooner was his press landed than a mob destroyed it. He procured a new one. This also was ruined.[2] Then he appealed to the mayor for protection. This magistrate affirmed

---

[1] "Garrison and his Times," by Oliver Johnson, p. 223. [2] *Ib.*

his inability to shield the victim, saying : " I have
no police force." To this Mr. Lovejoy replied :
" Very well, I will get another press, and with your
consent I will enroll a special police force in the interest of law and order." The mayor assented.
The defenders were marshalled. The third press
arrived. The next night the grog-shops vomited
forth their bloats, the building where the press was
sheltered was assailed with incendiary torches and
seditious muskets, and in the act of protecting his
property, with the mayor's sanction, Mr. Lovejoy
was shot down like a mad dog. As he fell, his huddle of supporters scattered amid a fusillade of bullets,
the house was fired, and the press was for the third
time flung into the Mississippi.[1]

The news from Alton convulsed the continent.
The South openly exulted. The North condemned
the mob, but lamented the " imprudence" of the
victim ; which reminds one of the man down in
Maine who, in speaking of the prohibitory liquor law,
said, " He was in favor of the law, but agin its execution !" Only the more thoughtful recognized the
tragedy for what it was, and saw in it the burial of
a bravo's dagger in the heart of liberty.

Strangely enough Boston, which was farthest off,
was most moved. It is greatly to the credit of the
old town. A number of eminent citizens, headed by
the Rev. Dr. Channing, applied for the use of Faneuil
Hall in which to denounce the outrage ; not as
Abolitionists, with whom few were affiliated, but as
believers in free speech and a free press. The mayor
and aldermen refused the hall on the ground that the

---

[1] "Garrison and his Times," by O. Johnson, p. 226.

country might regard the meeting "as the public voice of the city."[1] This denial increased the agitation. Dr. Channing appealed to Boston in an open letter, which resulted in another application, signed by an enlarged number of influential names. Now the municipal authorities heard and obeyed; the hall was opened.[2]

What place could be so conspicuously fit for the rebuke of an attack on freedom as the "Cradle of Liberty?"

Faneuil Hall was built "at his own cost" and presented to Boston in 1742, by Peter Faneuil, a wealthy merchant of the city, whose Huguenot ancestors had been driven out of France by the tyranny of Louis XIV., when, at the instigation of a mistress, he revoked the Edict of Nantes;[3] just as the Pilgrims had been exiled from England by the inquisitive despotism of the Stuarts. Boston, in accepting the gift, named it after the generous donor.[4] Hence it belonged to liberty in its very origin. It received a further consecration when, in the days which ushered in the Revolution, the "Sons of Liberty" were wont to meet within its walls to cheer James Otis in his defiance of George III. and Lord North. "Cra-

---

[1] "Garrison and his Times," by O. Johnson, p. 227.

[2] *Ib.* With Mr. Johnson all other authorities agree.

[3] See a curious book, "Dealings with the Dead," published in Boston in 1856, in which the descent and life of Peter Faneuil are more elaborately traced than anywhere else.

[4] *Ib.* This was voted at a town meeting held in 1742. The hall was burned January 13th, 1761, nothing but the walls remaining. The town rebuilt it in 1762—P. Faneuil having died soon after its first erection. In 1806 it was enlarged, its area being doubled on the ground, and another story was added. Since then it has remained as it now stands.

dle of Liberty," indeed! And now about to rock the lusty child again, and to become the cradle of freedom, not for one race, but for all—to rock the genius of universal emancipation.

Having obtained the hall, the managers of the meeting determined to use it in the daytime, their prudence leading them to fear lest the Alton mob might reappear in Boston under cover of the congenial darkness.[1] The behavior of the Abolitionists, too, was admirable at this crisis. Although indignant beyond all others, their souls aflame, they carefully abstained from appearing in connection with the meeting, and their names were conspicuous only by their absence from the published call and the various preliminaries, like the images of Brutus and Cassius in the imperial procession in ancient Rome.[2] In fact, they had no wish to add to the prevailing excitement, and were willing enough to have their places filled by more "respectable" citizens, if these would act. But they meant, of course, to go to Faneuil Hall.

On December 8th, 1837, in the morning, the meeting was called to order. The old hall, used to crowds, was full to suffocation. The throng was divided into three factions: one third being free discussionists, among whom were sprinkled here and there an Abolitionist (the salt which was to give savor to the hour); another third being mobocrats, present to make mischief; while the remaining third were indifferent, idle spectators, attracted by curiosity and swayed to and fro by each speaker in turn, but hold-

---

[1] "Garrison and his Times," p. 227.
[2] "William Lloyd Garrison," by his sons, vol. ii., p. 189.

ing the balance of power.[1] The proceedings opened quietly and decorously. The Hon. Jonathan Phillips, a wealthy Bostonian, a warm friend of Dr. Channing, and a kinsman of Wendell Phillips, took the chair. Dr. Channing made a brief but impressive address, speaking from a lectern set in front of the platform and well out toward the centre of the hall ; a position which he selected because he feared he might not be heard amid the rush and crush if farther back.[2] Resolutions drawn by Dr. Channing were next offered and read by the Hon. Benjamin F. Hallet. These were seconded by George S. Hillard, Esq., in an incisive speech.

As Mr. Hillard concluded there was a stir, then an outburst of anticipatory applause, as the Attorney-General of Massachusetts was seen to elbow his way down toward the great gilded eagle in the gallery over the main entrance, with the evident purpose of making a speech not on the programme. Everybody knew this official—James Tricothic Austin. He was a parishioner of Dr. Channing, a popular politician, and a master of the art of captivating the crowd. With a red face and a bullying manner, thunder in his voice and demagogism on his lips, he at once, with practised skill, began an harangue clearly intended and adroitly adapted either to break up the meeting in a row or array it against the ob-

---

[1] So writes Mrs. Chapman in a letter to Harriet Martineau, and quoted by her in an article in the *Westminster Review*, December, 1838, on "The Martyr Age."

[2] Weld's "Eulogy," p. 34. There are no seats in Faneuil Hall. At great gatherings there the people stand. This, of course, increases the capacity of the hall, and also, in times of excitement, the difficulty of controlling the auditory.

ject of its callers. He claimed that there was "a conflict of laws" between Missouri and Illinois; compared the slaves to a menagerie, "with lions, tigers, a hyena and an elephant, a jackass or two, and monkeys in plenty," and likened Lovejoy to one who should "break the bars and let loose the caravan to prowl about the streets;" talked of the rioters of Alton as akin to the "orderly mob" which threw the tea into Boston Harbor in 1773, and declared their victim "died as the fool dieth;" and in direct and insulting allusion to Dr. Channing closed by asserting that a clergyman with a gun in his hand, or one "mingling in the debates of a popular assembly, was marvellously out of place."[1]

When he retired Faneuil Hall rocked indeed, but not in the old-time way. Hands of devils were rocking it. Friends of law and order were aghast. The indifferent were drawn over by the infectious enthusiasm to the side of the apologist for murder, and joined Austin's myrmidons in their roar of triumph. The foes of freedom had captured the hall! They were so sure of this that they did not care to precipitate a riot, but waited to vote down the resolutions and thus turn the protest into an indorsement.

At this wild moment, under the very shadow of the impending catastrophe, Wendell Phillips, who was standing on the floor, a mere auditor, with no thought of speaking,[2] leaped upon the lectern and

---

[1] *Vide* the Boston journals of December 9th, 1837.

[2] Mr. Weld, usually the most accurate of men, thinks he did intend to speak, though, of course, unaware of the need of replying to Austin. See his "Eulogy," p. 34. He is mistaken. The testimony is the other way. The speech itself is the proof, for it is throughout a reply

confronted the raging multitude, himself an embodied Vesuvius. But the fire was as yet smothered, the lava did not at once begin to flow; the eruption was in reserve. His easy attitude, his calm dignity, the classic beauty of his face, challenged attention and piqued curiosity. Suddenly the turbulence hushed itself into silence. Then that marvellous voice, sweet as a song, clear as a flute, was heard for the first time by a vast audience and completed the charm which his masterful bearing had begun to work. It was the opportunity of a lifetime. It meant renown or discomfiture, with a nation for the witness. Would, could this stripling of twenty-six lift himself to the level of the lofty occasion and dominate the scene? All fears were soon and happily dispelled. Mr. Phillips, however, was too full of his subject to be self-conscious. He spoke not for fame, but for freedom. "My purpose," said he, in referring to the occasion, "was to secure the passage of Dr. Channing's resolutions." He commenced in that quiet, dulcet tone with which all America was erelong to become familiar:

"MR. CHAIRMAN: We have met for the freest discussion of these resolutions, and the events which gave rise to them (cries of 'Question!' 'Hear him!' 'Go on!' 'No gagging!' etc.). I hope I shall be permitted to express my surprise at the sentiments of the last speaker—surprise not only at such sentiments from such a man, but at the applause they have received within these walls. A comparison has been drawn between the events of the Revolution and the tragedy at Alton. We have heard it asserted here, in Faneuil Hall, that Great Britain had a right to tax the Colonies, and we have heard the mob at Alton, the

---

to Austin. Of course he had thought deeply on the subject, so that, while speaking extemporaneously, he spoke out of knowledge as well as out of conviction.

drunken murderers of Lovejoy, compared to those patriot fathers who threw the tea overboard! (*Great applause.*) Fellow-citizens, is this Faneuil Hall doctrine? ('No, no!') The mob at Alton were met to wrest from a citizen his just rights—met to resist the laws. We have been told that our fathers did the same; and the glorious mantle of Revolutionary precedent has been thrown over the mobs of our days. To make out their title to such defence, the gentleman says that the British Parliament had a right to tax these Colonies. It is manifest that, without this, his parallel falls to the ground; for Lovejoy had stationed himself within constitutional bulwarks. He was not only defending the freedom of the press, but he was under his own roof, in arms, with the sanction of the civil authority. The men who assailed him went against and over the laws. The mob, as the gentleman terms it—mob, forsooth!—certainly we sons of the tea-spillers are a marvellously patient generation!—the 'orderly mob' which assembled in the 'Old South' to destroy the tea were met to resist, not the laws, but illegal exactions. Shame on the American who calls the tea-tax and stamp-act laws! Our fathers resisted, not the king's prerogative, but the king's usurpation. To find any other account, you must read our Revolutionary history upside down. Our State archives are loaded with arguments of John Adams to prove taxes laid by the British Parliament unconstitutional—beyond its power. It was not till this was made out that the men of New England rushed to arms. The arguments of the Council Chamber and the House of Representatives preceded and sanctioned the contest. To draw the conduct of our ancestors into a precedent for mobs, for a right to resist laws we ourselves have enacted, is an insult to their memory. The difference between the excitement of those days and our own, which this gentleman in kindness to the latter has overlooked, is simply this: the men of that day went for the right, as secured by laws. They were the people rising to sustain the laws and constitution of the province. The rioters of our day go for their own wills, right or wrong. Sir, when I heard the gentleman lay down principles which place the murderers of Alton side by side with Otis and Hancock, with Quincy and Adams, I thought those pictured lips (pointing to the portraits in the hall) would have broken into voice to rebuke the recreant American—the slanderer of the dead!"

As Mr. Phillips hurled this thunderbolt at the Attorney-General, and accompanied it with an electric glance and gesture, the arches of Faneuil Hall echoed with successive thunder-claps of approval, which the partisans of Austin were too dazed to do more than attempt to resent. As the plaudits subsided, the waiting orator, standing there in the attitude of fiery readiness, followed his last sentence and climaxed it with this volcanic flame-burst :

"The gentleman said he should sink into insignificance if he condescended to gainsay the principles of these resolutions. For the sentiments he has uttered, on soil consecrated by the prayers of Puritans and the blood of patriots, the earth should have yawned and swallowed him up !"

This was Vesuvius in full eruption, and as Pompeii was buried, so now the heaving earth seemed to swallow the patron of mobs and murderers. The scene beggars description. Men lost their reason. Enthusiasm became delirium. Anticipating defeat, as just before they had anticipated triumph, the riotous faction now attempted to precipitate violence. They pushed and howled vainly ; for Mr. Phillips had mesmerized the mere spectators who had cheered Austin's sophisms into complete sympathy with himself, and holding them under his eye and voice would not let them go. Waiting again with that serene composure always so characteristic of his style, and as marked at the start as at the close of his career, he paused only long enough to obtain so much of silence as might float his tones to the ears of the throng, and felt that then his voice and persuasions would enforce attention. In a moment those even, honeyed cadences once more filled the hall, and the crowd, entranced, bent with eagerness to hear. The gifted boy had conquered already, and from this point to the close he spoke without interruption, save such as punctuated his sentences with the approbation of the auditors. Having buried the Attorney-General out of sight, he proceeded to dissect his argument:

"Allusion has been made to what lawyers understand very well—the 'conflict of laws.' We are told that nothing but the Mississippi River runs between St. Louis and Alton; and the conflict of laws somehow or other gives the citizens of the former a right to find fault with the defender of the press for publishing his opinions so near their limits. Will the gentleman venture that argument before lawyers? How the laws of the two States could be said to come into conflict in such circumstances I question whether any lawyer in this audience can explain or understand. No matter whether the line that divides one sovereign State from another be an imaginary one or ocean wide, the moment you cross it the State you leave is blotted out of existence, so far as you are concerned. The Czar might as well claim to control the deliberations of Faneuil Hall, as the laws of Missouri demand reverence, or the shadow of obedience, from an inhabitant of Illinois.

"Sir, as I understand this affair, it was not an individual protecting his property; it was not one body of armed men assaulting another, and making the streets of a peaceful city run blood with their contentions. It did not bring back the scenes in some old Italian cities, where family met family, and faction met faction, and mutually trampled the laws under foot. No; the men in that house were regularly enrolled under the sanction of the mayor. There being no militia in Alton, about seventy men were enrolled with the approbation of the mayor. These relieved each other every other night. About thirty men were in arms on the night of the 6th, when the press was landed. The next evening it was not thought necessary to summon more than half that number; among these was Lovejoy. It was, therefore, you perceive, sir, the police of the city resisting rioters —civil government breasting itself to the shock of lawless men. Here is no question about the right of self-defence. It is, in fact, simply this : Has the civil magistrate a right to put down a riot ? Some persons seem to imagine that anarchy existed at Alton from the commencement of these disputes. Not at all. No one of us,' says an eye-witness and a comrade of Lovejoy, 'has taken up arms during these disturbances but at the command of the mayor.' Anarchy did not settle down on that devoted city till Lovejoy breathed his last. Till then the law, represented in his person, sustained itself against its foes. When he fell, civil authority was trampled under foot. He had 'planted himself on his constitutional rights'—appealed to the laws—claimed the protection of the civil authority—taken refuge under 'the broad shield of the Constitution. When through that he was pierced and fell, he fell but one sufferer in a common catastrophe.' He took refuge under the banner of liberty— amid its folds ; and when he fell, its glorious stars and stripes, the emblem of free institutions, around which cluster so many heart-stirring memories, were blotted out in the martyr's blood.

"If, sir, I had adopted what are called peace principles, I might lament the circumstances of this case. But all you who believe, as I do, in the right and duty of magistrates to execute the laws, join with me and brand as base hypocrisy the conduct of those who assemble year after year on the Fourth of July, to fight over the battles of the Revolution, and yet 'damn with faint praise,' or load with obloquy, the memory of this man, who shed his blood in defence of life, liberty, property, and the freedom of the press !

"*Imprudent* to defend the liberty of the press ! Why ? Because the defence was unsuccessful ? Does success gild crime into patriotism, and want of it change heroic self-devotion to imprudence ? Was Hampden imprudent when he drew the sword and threw away the scabbard ? Yet he, judged by that single hour, was unsuccessful. After a short exile, the race he hated sat again upon the throne.

"Imagine yourself present when the first news of Bunker Hill battle reached a New England town. The tale would have run thus : 'The patriots are routed ; the redcoats victorious ; Warren lies dead upon the field.' With what scorn would that *Tory* have been received, who should have charged Warren with imprudence ! who should have said that, bred as a physician, he was 'out of place' in the battle, and 'died as the fool dieth !'

(*Great applause.*) How would the intimation have been received, that Warren and his associates should have waited a better time? But, if success be indeed the only criterion of prudence, *Respice finem*—wait till the end.

"*Presumptuous* to assert the freedom of the press on American ground! Is the assertion of such freedom before the age? So much before the age as to leave one no right to make it because it displeases the community? Who invents this libel on his country? It is this very thing which entitles Lovejoy to greater praise, the disputed right which provoked the Revolution—taxation without representation—is far beneath that for which he died. (Here there was a strong and general expression of disapprobation.) One word, gentlemen. As much as *thought* is better than *money*, so much is the cause in which Lovejoy died nobler than a mere question of taxes. James Otis thundered in this hall when the king did but touch his *pocket*. Imagine, if you can, his indignant eloquence had England offered to put a gag upon his *lips*. (*Great applause.*)

"The question that stirred the Revolution touched our civil interests. This concerns us not only as citizens, but as immortal beings. Wrapped up in its fate, saved or lost with it, are not only the voice of the statesman, but the instructions of the pulpit and the progress of our faith.

"The clergy 'marvellously out of place' where free speech is battled for—liberty of speech on national sins? Does the gentleman remember that freedom to preach was first gained, dragging in its train freedom to print? I thank the clergy here present, as I reverence their predecessors, who did not so far forget their country in their immediate profession as to deem it duty to separate themselves from the struggle of '76—the Mayhews and the Coopers—who remembered they were citizens before they were clergymen."

Mr. Phillips closed with these words:

"I am glad, sir, to see this crowded house. It is good for us to be here. When liberty is in danger, Faneuil Hall has the right, it is her duty, to strike the key-note for these United States. I am glad, for one reason, that remarks such as those to which I have alluded have been uttered here. The passage of these resolutions, in spite of this opposition, led by the Attorney-General of the commonwealth, will show more clearly, more decisively, the deep indignation with which Boston regards this outrage."

When the whirlwind of applause which followed the orator's conclusion had rolled away, the chairman put the resolutions, and they were carried by an overwhelming vote.[1] Thus was defeat turned into victory by the genius of Phillips, as, years afterward, that other defeat at Winchester was turned into victory by the magnetism of Sheridan.

Where now and what was the Attorney-General? Nowhere and nothing. Transfixed by forked-lightning, *sic exit* Austin. Thus may all the foes of liberty be buried in shame and sepulchred in ignominy!

Oliver Johnson, who was one of Mr. Phillips's auditors that morning, remarks:

"I had heard him once before (in his first Anti-Slavery speech at Lynn[2]), as a few others in that great meeting probably had, and my expectations were high; but he transcended them all and took the audience by storm. Never before, I venture to say, did the walls of the old 'Cradle of Liberty' echo to a finer strain of eloquence. It was a speech to which not even the completest report could do justice, for such a report could not bring the scene and the manner of the speaker vividly before the reader. It was before the days of phonography, and the reporter caught only a pale reflection of what fell from the orator's lips."[3]

---

[1] So wrote Mr. Garrison to G. W. Benson on the following day. Mr. G. was present as an auditor. *Vide* his Life by his sons, vol. ii., p. 189, note.

[2] *Ante*, p. 81.   [3] "Garrison and his Times," p. 229.

Dr. Channing, too, then and ever afterward testified to his wonder and delight, and referred especially to the power which Phillips's voice exercised; catching and enchaining the riotous throng from the moment its delicious cadences were heard.[1]

When we remember all the circumstances—the momentous occurrence that led to the meeting, the public excitement, the mixed character of the throng in Faneuil Hall, the ability and reputation of the Attorney-General, who no doubt bellowed forth the real sentiments of the majority, the presence of his partisans there in great numbers for the purpose of breaking up or breaking down the protest, the youth of the orator and his lack of experience in handling a mob—certainly the success of Wendell Phillips that day was marvellous. It revealed him to himself as well as to the world and fixed his destiny. The orator sprang into being in the full possession, as it should seem, of all his powers—maturity in youth and experience ahead of knowledge—like Minerva from the brain of Jove. Not in American history is there such another precocious and dramatic oratorical *début*.

From that hour Faneuil Hall was to be identified with Wendell Phillips, as until that hour it had been identified with James Otis. The eloquence of Otis blossomed in the Declaration of Independence. The eloquence of Phillips was to flower in the Proclamation of Emancipation.

---

[1] "The Golden Age of American Oratory." By E. G. Parker. Notice of Wendell Phillips.

BOOK II.

NOON.

1838-1865.

I.

THE ABOLITIONISTS—MEN AND MEASURES.

The decree of social outlawry pronounced in blue-blood circles against Wendell Phillips when he became an Abolitionist, was confirmed and stamped with the unchangeableness of the laws of the Medes and Persians after the speech on Lovejoy's murder in Faneuil Hall. That was death; this was burial. The young man, however, refused to concede his decease, and certainly proved to be a lively corpse. More correctly, he did recognize his death to Fashion and rejoiced in his new life for Humanity.

Upon looking around he found himself in congenial company—few but fit. If the Abolitionists were not received in my lady's boudoir, they were eagerly welcomed by those ready to perish. If commerce averted its countenance from them and withheld its golden recompense, the great Proprietor of heaven and earth adopted them to be His heirs. If politics scorned and spat upon them in the 'thirties, the sycophant made haste to crown and then to kneel before them in the 'sixties. Great is Success, and Fashion is its prophet! Bless you, there is all the difference in the world between the John Wesley of 1729, whom the graceless scholars of Oxford nicknamed "methodist," and the *pontifex maximus* of the largest of the Christian sects in the nineteenth century. And there is the same difference between those whom 1837 pilloried as the "friends of the niggers," and 1863 garlanded as the "saviours of a race," and 1865 as the reconstructors of the continent. But our business at present is with the "friends of the niggers," not with the honored, because successful philanthropists.

Who were some of these Abolitionists? Chief among them was William Lloyd Garrison, least pliable, most persistent of men. His head was worth more than Georgia offered for it or than the South was able to give. A phrenologist would have pronounced firmness the ruling elder in the circuit of his faculties. His manner, however, not as combative as his nature, was composed and conciliatory. Of all phases of the question to which he had dedicated his life, he was a walking encyclopædia. As an organizer he was unexcelled. And he had self-fed fire enough to thaw the ice of the moral North Pole, and melt out and down a passage to the temperate zone—to the conscience and heart of America. Such was the director of the Abolition *Societas de Propaganda Fide:* not less protean than his namesake at Rome.

Around Mr. Garrison were grouped those who had already heard and heeded his bugle-call. There was the Rev. Samuel J. May, the St. John of the Garrisonians,[1] whose character is painted in that allusion to the apostle who learned his creed as he leaned on the breast of Jesus, a Unitarian clergyman who held and taught that man was more than money, and that Christianity was more important than creed.

---

[1] Mr. May was born, 1797; died 1871. Long settled in Syracuse, N. Y.

There was John G. Whittier, the poet of freedom, with the bashful manner of a girl and the moral courage of a hero, his eyes flashing out from beneath a beetling crag of brow, sure to attract attention and as sure to decline it. There was Charles C. Burleigh, most unique of men, in person *outré*, with long, flowing hair, unshorn beard, and "high-water" pantaloons that dangled above his ankles—an appearance which made him the inevitable laughing-stock of every audience until he began to speak ; then his Niagara rush and weight of utterance changed ridicule into admiration and carried opposition over to agreement. His life was an apostleship.[1]

> "Called in his youth to sound and gauge
> The moral lapse of his race and age,
> And, sharp as truth, the contrast draw
> Of human frailty and perfect law ;
> Possessed by the one dread thought that lent
> Its goad to his fiery temperament,
> Up and down the world he went,
> A John the Baptist, crying—Repent !"[2]

There was Francis Jackson, a successful merchant, who sold his goods, not his principles, and who at the time of the Garrison mob had made his own house a sanctuary of liberty by opening it to the heroines whom Mayor Lyman had driven out of doors[3]—a man unpretentious but magnificent, rich but philanthropic, a knight-errant of trade, and, like Bayard, *sans peur et sans reproche*. At his side stood another merchant, Henry G. Chapman (the cousin

---

[1] Mr. Burleigh was born in Connecticut, in 1801 ; died at Florence, Mass., in 1878.
[2] Whittier's "Preacher." Diamond edition, p. 306.
[3] *Vide* "Wendell Phillips's Speeches," p. 219.

of Mrs. Wendell Phillips), who moved in the best society, dwelt in a ceiled house, and fared sumptuously every day ; but who accepted the condemnation of his pastor, Dr. Channing, and of his business and social intimates, in order to become the treasurer of the Abolition cause—a moneyed man, but not a man of money. There were Ellis Gray Loring and Samuel E. Sewall, a brace of conscientious lawyers, fitted by legal attainments and judicial spirit to adorn the bench, but who read over the entrance to their Anti-Slavery career Dante's motto of the *Inferno:*

" All hope abandon, ye who enter here !"

and entered notwithstanding. The brace of merchants and the brace of lawyers were matched by a brace of Congregational ministers, the Rev. Moses Thatcher and the Rev. Amos Phelps, able and eloquent men, who felt for the slaves as though bound with them, and the latter of whom gave to the Abolitionists their earliest definition of slavery, viz., " Slavery is the holding of a human being as property." [1]

Nor was Mr. Garrison the only editor in the humanitarian coterie. At his side stood David Lee Child, a strong writer, a Harvard graduate, yet an honest man. Even professional scholarship was represented in this contracted circle, notably represented by Charles T. C. Follen, a liberty-loving German, who occupied the chair of German Language and Literature at Cambridge, which he was soon driven to vacate because of his connection with the Abolitionists. Thus was the son of Luther, who

---

[1] " Garrison and his Times," p. 73.

came to America in the same ship which bore Lafayette to these shores in 1823, requited for his passion on behalf of freedom.[1]

The tragedy at Alton brought into the Anti-Slavery camp another recruit destined to become a mighty man of valor—Edmund Quincy. His presence was especially welcome to Mr. Phillips, for he came out of the same social set,[2] snapped the same green withes of aristocracy, and showed the same heroic self-denial. He was the *littérateur* of Abolition, and wrote with the pen of Junius. Having gotten his eyes open he kept them open until he saw the glorious end.[3]

The women in those days, as in all days, averaged better than the men, and justified the saying of Luther : " I have oftentimes noted when women espouse a cause they are far more fervent in faith, they hold to it more stiff and fast than men do ; as we see in the loving Magdalen, who was more hearty and bold than Peter himself."[4] So here there was no dearth of heroines. Each one wears the nimbus with which the old painters crowned the Virgin. Some of them we shall have occasion to mention as we proceed. At the outset two stood forth in beautiful relief like the figures of saints in a cathedral. One of these was Lydia Maria Child, the wife of Editor David Lee Child, the earliest and most popu-

---

[1] May's " Anti-Slavery Recollections," p. 254. See also the " Life of Follen." He perished in the fire which destroyed the steamboat Lexington in the passage from New York to Stonington, January 13th, 1840.

[2] See p. 39 of this volume.

[3] Mr. Quincy was four years older than Mr. Phillips. He died in 1877.

[4] " Table Talk," Bohn's edition, p. 367.

lar of our female editors and authors ; "than whom," remarks the *North American Review*, in an issue of the period, "few women, if any, have done more or better things in literature, whether in its lighter or graver departments." She did not hesitate to sacrifice her literary prospects on the altar of Abolition, and at the cost of fame and fortune lent her wizzard pen to the slave until he ceased to need it.[1] Mrs. Child made the splendid beginning of an Anti-Slavery literature in her famous "Appeal in Favor of that Class of Americans called Africans," a book fit to

> ". . . Create a soul
> Under the ribs of death ;"[2]

and which worked that miracle in thousands of cases, Wendell Phillips being one.[3]

The other of these bas-relief women was Maria Weston Chapman, the wife of Henry G. Chapman, and the cousin by marriage of Mrs. Wendell Phillips. Of Mayflower lineage, dowered with woman's chief charm and snare—beauty—to which she added a rare intellect, which Europe had cultivated, she was the idol of the most exclusive circles and seemed certain to be a queen of fashion. When she espoused the righteous, but unpopular cause of the negro great was the amazement, unutterable the disgust of Boston. She at once made herself the *alter ego* of Mr. Garrison.

---

[1] This noble and gifted woman died in 1880.
[2] Milton's "Samson Agonistes," line 560.
[3] Mr. Phillips had his attention called to slavery by the "Appeal," before he openly espoused the Anti Slavery cause. This was one of his awakeners ; so says Mrs. Alford in her sketch of Mrs. Phillips. *Vide* p. 4.

As a writer she was only less gifted than Mrs. Child, and knowing the value of printers' ink, she published her thoughts in prose and verse. Wise in counsel and fertile in resources, she suggested ways and means in the darkest hours. Her graces of person and gifts of mind were exerted in unfriendly coteries to conciliate and attract, and always with a single object—the downfall of slavery. Lowell has hymned it all in five lines of poetic photography :

> "A noble woman, brave and apt,
> Cumæ's sibyl not more rapt,
> Who might, with those fair tresses shorn,
> The Maid of Orleans' casque have worn—
> Herself the Joan of our Arc." [1]

Surely, let Mrs. Grundy sneer as she might, Wendell Phillips, among these high souls, was not in the way greatly to miss estranged associates, who cut his acquaintance when he avowed himself the "friend of niggers." Such companionship was a moral tonic. Such a life-purpose fired his soul with generous aspirations. The service of God through the uplifting of man raised him above the frivolities which make the main business of what calls itself Society, freed him from the thraldom of petty pursuits, yardstick measurements and the selfish dicker in cotton and corn, and flashed a divine meaning into human life. As an intellectual stimulus and spiritual safeguard his new career was worth all he paid for it. Men unconsciously aggrandize themselves when they imitate the Christ.

How did this magnificent band, smaller than Gideon's army after it had been twice weeded, opposed

---

[1] Mrs. Chapman died in 1885.

to every element that was potent in America, to State and Church, to trade and society, to law and learning, to politics and art, propose to fight their battle? They deliberately chose the Christian methods. They distinctly disavowed carnal weapons and adopted moral suasion. They believed in reason, not passion; in conscience, not force; in ideas, not bullets. In the preamble to the constitution of the "New England Anti-Slavery Society" we find a statement of their principles:

"We, the undersigned, hold that every person, of full age and sane mind, has a right to immediate freedom from personal bondage of whatsoever kind unless imposed by the sentence of the law for the commission of some crime. We hold that man cannot, consistently with reason, religion, and the eternal and immutable principles of justice, be the property of man. We hold that whoever retains his fellowman in bondage is guilty of a grievous wrong. We hold that mere difference of complexion is no reason why any man should be deprived of any of his natural rights, or subjected to any political disability. While we advance these opinions as the principles on which we intend to act, we declare that we will not operate on the existing relations of society by other than peaceful and lawful means, and that we will give no countenance to violence or insurrection." [1]

In the constitution of the "American Anti-Slavery Society" these principles reappear in another form:

"ARTICLE TWO.—The object of this Society is the entire abolition of slavery in the United States. While it admits that each State in which slavery exists has, by the Constitution of the United States, the exclusive right to legislate in regard to its abolition in said State, it shall aim to convince all our fellow-citizens, by arguments addressed to their understandings and consciences, that slave-holding is a heinous crime in the sight of God, and that the duty, safety, and the best interests of all

---

[1] "Garrison and his Times," p 85.

concerned require its immediate abandonment, without expatriation. The Society will also endeavor, in a constitutional way, to influence Congress to put an end to the domestic slave trade, and to abolish slavery in all those portions of our common country which come under its control, especially in the District of Columbia—and likewise to prevent the extension of it to any State that may be hereafter admitted to the Union.[1]

"ARTICLE THREE.—This Society shall aim to elevate the character and the condition of the people of color, by encouraging their intellectual, moral, and religious improvement, and by removing public prejudice, that thus they may, according to their intellectual and moral worth, share an equality with the whites of civil and religious privileges; but this Society will never, in any way, countenance the oppressed in vindicating their rights by resorting to physical force."[2]

These were the earliest organizations. The great family of similar bodies domiciled throughout the free States reproduced these distinctive features of their parents as one after the other they were born.

Mr. Garrison was a non-resistant, as were many of his followers. Mr. Phillips was not. But he fully adopted the measures in vogue when he came into the movement, and his efforts for a quarter of a century were exerted persistently and consistently on the moral suasion platform, though when the war broke out he gave it a hearty support—all the more hearty because of his long moral advocacy.

Throughout this period the indictment of the Abolitionists had two contradictory counts. The slave-holders charged them with attempting to stir insurrection. Those who professed to abhor slavery, but who excused themselves from moving against it, accused them of impracticability. They answered

---

[1] The ultimate purpose of the Free Soil and Republican parties.
[2] "William Lloyd Garrison," by his sons, vol. i., p. 414.

the charge of sedition by pointing to their standards of faith and practice. They responded to the accusation of impracticability by proving that they were acting under the inspiration of Jesus Christ, and that they were, therefore, just as practical as the genius of His system would permit them to be. Did the Master preach immediate repentance? So did they preach immediate emancipation. Was it within the power of a sinner to let go of his sin? So was it within the power of a slave-holder to free his slaves.

Moreover, as a further and triumphant reply to this assertion that they were impracticables, they called attention to the recent success of the English Abolitionists, who, on the same basis, had assailed and at length abolished slavery in the British West Indies.[1] Why was not what had been practicable there, after years of agitation, equally practicable here? Were Clarkson and Wilberforce, Buxton and Macaulay, Brougham and O'Connell hotheads? Then they, too, were content to be known as fanatics. Was there any peculiarity in the American moral climate which could hocus-pocus success in Palestine and triumph in England and the West Indies into failure in the United States? Why should what was acknowledged to be statesmanship on one side of the Atlantic become fanaticism on this side? The Abolitionists waited long for an answer to these questions. Those who survive are waiting still.

Not at once did Mr. Phillips devote his whole time and attention to Abolition. He attended to what law business the Faneuil Hall meeting had left in his hands. Now, too, he commenced his wonder-

---

[1] On August 1st, 1834, 800,000 slaves were set free.

ful career as a public lecturer. From the moment he entered this field he was in continental demand. His literary productions, especially, were eagerly sought; each new lecture was an event. These he valued as so many introductions to audiences which would not permit him to discuss slavery at first, but which, once under the spell of the magician, gave him *carte blanche*. Hence he kept constantly on hand an assortment of lectures on science, of which he was fond, and biography (a department in which he was an adept), and through these won a hearing for the cause which lay nearest his heart. It was in this way that he was led to prepare his famous lecture on "The Lost Arts."[1] He began to deliver it in 1838. Thenceforth and for forty-five years he gave it again and again—over two thousand times in all—to fascinated crowds from Portland to St. Louis, until it netted him $150,000, the largest sum ever earned by a similar production.[2]

The boards of the Lyceum he continued to tread through life. But by and by he made the Lyceum an Anti-Slavery rostrum, and the movement absorbed him.

---

[1] This is given in full in the Appendix.
[2] So he informed the writer in 1883.

II.

A CONUNDRUM.

Woman is a conundrum which man is unwilling to give up. We write her with an interrogation mark. Mrs. Mary A. Livermore used to deliver an entertaining lecture entitled "What shall we do with our Daughters?" 'Tis a serious question even now. Fifty years ago it was a hopeless question. It might have been reversed and put in this form: "What will our daughters do with us?"

Woman has always been the power behind the throne. There has been the difficulty. She has been behind it when she should have been on it. Hers has been power without the sobering sense of responsibility. She has had her way; but in order to get it she has been obliged to cheat her male belongings into thinking they were having theirs. It has been finesse against force—the fox against the lion. In such a rôle there is no dignity and little credit. We have shut woman up in a doll-world, and then complained of her frivolity. "Why are you women such fools?" queried a crusty benedict. "I suppose," was the quick reply of the bright woman he addressed, "it is because God made us to match the men!"

As soon as the various Anti-Slavery societies, which now began to abound, were organized, they were confronted by a perplexity nearer and more exacting than slavery itself—woman! The ladies composed two thirds of the membership and did three fourths of the work. Yet when it came to the election of officers and the shaping of policies they had no vote and no voice. Some of them resented this. They insisted upon recognition as an act of justice to themselves on the part of societies pledged to win justice for others. They wanted to help in the choice of their leaders. They desired to share in the maturing of measures and methods. A few went further—they wished to go out and tell the community, as only women could, about the horrors of slavery, and to do this with the sanction and under the seal of one and another of the Anti-Slavery societies.

Well, these demands made a great ado. Oriental notions then prevailed regarding woman's seclusion. The Shah of Persia would not have been more shocked by a protest on the part of one of his wives against plural marriage than were some of the Abolitionists by such unheard-of claims. They were pronounced "unwomanly" and "unsexing." Nowadays it is laughable. But let us remember that those ladies by their persistence made the happy social change which gives us the right to laugh. They fought their battle bravely. They acknowledged their sex to be miraculously able, but said they did not go so far as to hold that one whom God had made a woman could make herself anything else. They begged to be informed why it was *en règle* for a woman to act on the stage and sing in public, but unwomanly for her to sit with men on committees and talk to a mixed company from the platform? Yet many of those who held up their hands in horror at the thought of this proposed outrage upon propriety, paid fabulous prices to hear Jenny Lind sing and to see Rachel act.

It is a suggestive fact that an effort at reform in one direction surely discloses the need of reform in other directions, and at the same time educates some who have acted in that one line to move in those other lines of amelioration. Thus it was that the crusade against slavery inevitably led first to the movement in behalf of woman and then to the movement in behalf of labor. For numbers of the reformers, their attention having been called to it, saw at once the reasonableness of the women's claim, and conceded it, Mr. Phillips among the foremost. In the matter of rights he could see no difference between a coat and a petticoat. Nor was he much disturbed when certain of the brethren assured him that the Bible had closed woman's mouth—in conventions—with a seal which bore the imprint of St. Paul. That bugaboo had been paraded so often in the case of slavery, through allusions to Abraham and Onesimus, it could no longer scare. "Since woman," said Mr. Phillips, "is interested equally with man in righting the wrongs of slavery; since among the blacks she suffers vitally as wife and mother, as daughter and sister, just as he does as husband and father, as son and brother; why is she not entitled to utter her indignation anywhere, everywhere, and most of all in Anti-Slavery committee-rooms and upon Anti-Slavery platforms?"[1]

This burning issue did not come up as an abstract question, but in an actual case. A couple of heroic

---

[1] So he writes in a letter to Arthur Tappan, in 1838 (MS.).

women, the sisters Sarah and Angelina Grimké, daughters of a celebrated jurist of South Carolina, Judge John F. Grimké, no longer able to endure the horrors they witnessed in the house of bondage, shook off the dust from their feet against their native State and made a home in Philadelphia. They had been members of the Episcopal communion. Finding it a hot-bed of Pro-Slavery sentiment, they came out again and united with the orthodox Quakers. Soon they began a house-to-house canvass among their own sex in the interest of Abolition. Their words were so incisive, their impeachment of slavery was so tremendous, their story of its immoralities was so pathetic, that the women who heard them were deeply moved. Presently the men, hearing of their successful advocacy, began to clamor for admission to these conferences, for women have no monopoly of curiosity. The surest way to attract a man anywhither is to bar him out—especially if women are barred in! Erelong, therefore, there was a demand for the public appearance of the Misses Grimké. Being Quakeresses they had no objection to a promiscuous audience. Accordingly, under the auspices of the various Anti-Slavery societies, they began to discuss slavery in public; always to the conviction and conversion of those who listened. Indeed, they proved to be the most effective of speakers.[1]

Marking this, the conservatives made haste to do two things: First, to shut in their faces the doors of every church which they controlled—the vast majority; and, secondly, to fulminate against them a

---

[1] Johnson's "Garrison and his Times," p. 261.

Protestant "bull," in which the faithful were exhorted not to countenance such caricatures upon true womanhood.

This "bull," which appeared in the summer of 1837,[1] called forth from Whittier one of his most pungent lyrics:

> "So this is all—the utmost reach
>   Of priestly power the mind to fetter!
> When laymen think, when women preach,
>   A 'War of Words'—a pastoral letter.
> But ye who scorn the thrilling tale
>   Of Carolina's high-souled daughters,
> Which echoes here the mournful wail
>   Of sorrow from Edisto's waters,
> Close while ye may the public ear,
>   With malice vex, with slander wound them;
> The pure and good shall throng to hear,
>   And tried and manly hearts surround them."[2]

These last lines were prophetic. For the measures taken to suppress only enlarged their meetings.[3] Other women began to exhort. More and more were the Anti-Slavery societies called upon to accord to the women the privileges enjoyed by men. More and more did Mr. Phillips insist that this be done; in which Mr. Garrison and many others joined him. The debate was hot. In various instances the rights demanded were accorded.

---

[1] This was the utterance of the General Association of the Massachusetts orthodox churches, in session at Brookfield, which met June 27th. The paper was drawn up by the Rev. Dr. Nehemiah Adams, of Boston, who soon earned for himself, by a book called "A Southside View of Slavery," the sobriquet of "Southside Adams."

[2] "Whittier's Poems, 'The Pastoral Letter.'" Diamond edition, p. 70.

[3] Angelina Grimké was married to Theodore D. Weld in 1838. She died some years ago. Sarah died earlier.

Reference is here made to this issue and to Mr. Phillips's position on it, because it belongs here in point of time; because soon afterward it divided the Abolitionists into two camps; and because in England and at home our knight-errant of freedom was to break many a gallant lance as the champion of the ladies.

III.

"VALE."

Boston has always been celebrated as an intellectual headquarters. It was markedly so when Wendell Phillips was young. There was then a circle of wide-awakes meeting at irregular intervals under the name of "The Friends," usually in the palatial apartments of Mr. Jonathan Phillips, a wealthy bachelor, who resided at the Tremont House, that relative of the orator who had presided over the gathering in Faneuil Hall where he spoke, and, like Byron, awoke the next morning to find himself famous. In this conclave the wits of the day were wont to discuss living questions of all sorts.[1] Here Dr. Channing might surely be found, and Bronson Alcott, a gentle philosopher with an orthodox training and a heterodox slant, and Theodore Parker, already known as an heresiarch, whose acquaintance Mr. Phillips thus early made at one of these symposiums, for the young lawyer was another of the "Friends." What hairs did they split! What fine distinctions between tweedle-dum and tweedle-dee! Mr. Phillips used to refer to it all as a rare school of dialectics. No doubt he often took occasion to remind the circle that inequity should properly be spelled iniquity.

---

[1] "Life of Theodore Parker," by O. B. Frothingham, p. 96.

Early in 1839 he was made General Agent of the Massachusetts Anti-Slavery Society, of which Francis Jackson was the President and William Lloyd Garrison was the Corresponding Secretary. Into this work Mr. Phillips threw himself with the ardor of an enthusiast and the success of a man of affairs. He organized a school-house campaign, held meetings from the sands of Cape Cod to the hills of Berkshire, made every cross-roads a hustings, created lecturers by the score, and set on two feet a protean discussion. He spoke himself here, there, and yonder, and became ubiquitous. He hung out a new lantern and started another Paul Revere's ride, to give warning of a more dangerous invasion than the old one by the redcoats. Soon he had the State agog, this aristocrat turned democrat who was not yet thirty ![1]

To the perturbations of his official position (which he held without pecuniary recompense)[2] he added, in these early years of his married life, an increasing anxiety for his wife. She grew frail apace. The cradle of their happiness seemed destined to be its grave. As a *dernier ressort* the nonplussed physicians advised a European trip. Mr. Phillips's family eagerly coincided, hoping that time and distance might cure him of his "fanaticism" and her of her ailment. The thought of withdrawal, even for a time, was a cross to both. Their hearts were at one in the Anti-Slavery crusade. But health and strength might come from the tonic of new scenes and experiences, and so long years of usefulness. The unpalatable medicine was worth a trial. They decided to obey.

---

[1] *Vide Liberator*, vol. ix., p. 95.   [2] *Ib.*

At this moment the annual meeting of the New England Anti-Slavery Society was held, the place being Boston, and the date May 30th, 1839. The Convention unanimously adopted a series of resolutions referring in warm terms to Mr. Phillips's unselfish labors, and recommending him to the hospitality and confidence of Abolitionists on the other side of the water, as "a devoted, uncompromising and eloquent friend of the slave."[1]

After listening to this tribute he ascended the platform, evidently much affected, and was received with round on round of hearty plaudits. Speaking with emotion, he said :

"I thank you for your vote. I feel my responsibility as your representative abroad. I trust in the opinion of the civilized world whose thunder tones are beginning even now to sweep over the Atlantic, in the power of Christendom, awake, united, indignant, speaking in the voice of our fatherland and echoed by gallant and beautiful France. England has solved the 'vexed question,' and proved that emancipation is both safe and expedient, and has written that demonstration in letters emblazoned in lines of light

'On the blue vault of heaven,
'Twixt Orion and the Pleiades.'

. . . . .

"The Germans call enthusiasm *Schwärmerei*, as if its origin were amid a swarm or assembly of people. Let us rather keep to the old Greek definition—*the God within us*—and go hence to work as earnestly as we have *felt* in this crowded Convention."[2]

As Mr. Phillips resumed his seat the convention broke forth in a tornado of cheers.

Soon after this valedictory address the managers of

---

[1] *Liberator*, vol. ix., 2d week in June.   [2] *Ib.*

the Massachusetts Anti-Slavery Society bade him an affectionate and appreciative farewell in an open letter, which recited in detail his birth, sacrifices, talents, and services, and commended him to the friends of humanity everywhere. These references were followed by a remarkable summing up of the Anti-Slavery progress within a decade :

"Ten years ago a solitary individual stood up as the advocate of immediate and unconditional emancipation. Now, that individual sees about him hundreds of thousands of persons, of both sexes, members of every sect and party, from the most elevated to the humblest rank in life. In 1829 not an Anti-Slavery society of a genuine stamp was in existence. In 1839 there are nearly two thousand such societies swarming and multiplying in all parts of the free States. In 1829 there was but one Anti-Slavery periodical in the land. In 1839 there are fourteen. In 1829 there was scarcely a newspaper of any religious or political party which was willing to disturb the 'delicate' question of slavery. In 1839 there are multitudes of journals that either openly advocate the doctrine of immediate and unconditional emancipation, or permit its free discussion in their columns. Then, scarcely a church made slave-holding a bar to communion. Now, multitudes refuse to hear a slave-holder preach, or to recognize one as a brother. Then, no one petitioned Congress to abolish slavery in the District of Columbia. Now, in one day, a single member of the House of Representatives (John Quincy Adams) has presented one hundred and seventy-six such petitions in detail ; while not less than seven hundred thousand persons have memorialized Congress on that and kindred subjects. . . . Tell our British brethren that the apathy which once brooded over the land like the spell of death is broken forever." [1]

Accompanied by these good wishes and with such credentials, the Phillipses said good-by to their country with tolerable composure, and set sail from New York for London in the packet "Wellington" on June 6th, 1839.[2] No steam, no electric lights, no hotels afloat at that time. But the "Wellington" was the best ship up to date on the vast ferry between the continents. Hence our travellers esteemed themselves fortunate in securing a passage on her; and were so, for she carried them safely, and conquered Neptune as her namesake did Napoleon.

---

[1] *Liberator*, vol. ix., p. 95.   [2] *Ib.*

IV.

SCENES AND EXPERIENCES IN EUROPE.

The two Bostonians reached London in July. Here they tarried only long enough to take their sea-legs off and put their land-legs on. Their purpose was to pass the approaching winter in Rome and to return to Great Britain for the summer of 1840. Hence they did not regret the hasty exit, but realized the need of "movin' on," like poor Joe in Dickens's story, since the long journey on the Continent must be made by easy stages and in the clumsy *diligence*, which represented the rapid transit of the period. In September they were in Lyons, whither they went from Paris *en route* for Italy. Before the snows fell they were in the Eternal City, whence Mr. Phillips wrote, under date of January 5th, 1840, to a relative at home:

"It seems useless to catalogue interesting objects, so numerous are they here; yet catalogues are more eloquent than descriptions. The Cæsars' palace speaks for itself. To stand in the Pantheon, on which Paul's eyes may have rested, what needs one more to feel? We have been up Trajan's Pillar by the very steps the old Roman feet once trod; rode over the pavement on which Constantine entered in triumph; seen the Colosseum (I by moonlight, and heard the dog bay, though not 'beyond the Tiber' that I know of); lost ourselves in that little world of dazzling, bewildering beauty, the Vatican, where the Laocoon breathes in never-ending agony, and eternal triumph beams from the brow of the Apollo. We have dived into Titus's baths and the half-buried ruins of Nero's 'golden house, where the frescoes are blooming and fresh after eighteen hundred years." [1]

Amid these scenes they learned that a World's Anti-Slavery Convention had been called to meet in London, June 12th, 1840; that the Massachusetts and Pennsylvania societies had accredited a number of well-known men and women as delegates, themselves included, and that they were expected to report for duty there and then. Returning to England they duly reached the metropolis. Their letters of introduction were an "open sesame." They met all the high mightinesses of the day—the Duchess of Sunderland, a great beauty and next in rank to the Queen, her daughter, afterward the Duchess of Argyle, Lady Byron, wife of the poet, Lord Brougham, and, best of all, Daniel O'Connell, the Irish liberator, between whom and Mr. Phillips a great friendship sprang up. Now, too, the Phillipses first met George Thompson, the orator of the West Indian emancipation, who had been publicly crowned in the House of Commons as the foremost and most eloquent pleader for negro liberty in England,[2] but whom America had scorned and sought to crucify, when, on the invitation of Mr. Garrison, he had visited us in 1834.[3] The meeting between these two was cordial. Mr. Thompson was a Scotsman, a resident of Edinburgh, a wit and a genius, now in the prime of life. "Ann and I," said Mr. Phillips, "went laughing through England and Scotland with this prince of *raconteurs*. One of his stories, especially,

---

[1] "Memorial of Ann Phillips," by Mrs. Alford, p. 7.
[2] "Garrison and his Times," p. 134.
[3] *Ib.* Also "William Lloyd Garrison," vol. i., pp. 432–67.

always convulsed us, told as it was with inimitable drollery : The story of an East Indian Rajah who had been persuaded to take a seidlitz-powder by some wag, and to take it in sections, swallowing first the contents of the blue paper and instantly afterward the contents of the white, so that the effervescence took place internally, throwing the astounded Rajah into volcanic eruption, with his mouth and nostrils for craters."[1]

In attendance upon the convention were a couple of Abolitionists to whom they were instantly drawn as by a kinship of soul. The first of these was Miss Elizabeth Pease, a young Quaker lady, of Darlington, England, a lovely character; in whose society they spent many delightful days, and with whom they continued an intimate correspondence for years after their return to America.[2] The other was Richard D. Webb, of Dublin, a rich Quaker printer, one of the most genial and witty of men, whose Irish blood showed itself, spite of his Quakerism, in an unconscious and irrepressible love for a "scrimmage ;" as is evident from the fact that he struck off on his presses an edition of non-resistant pamphlets, "just to raise a little bit of a row !"[3]

The World's Convention opened on Friday, June 12th, 1840, in Freemason's Hall, with five hundred delegates on the floor,[4] many of them Americans. In the preceding year the British and Foreign Anti-Slavery Society had been organized by an eminent

---

[1] Letter from Mr. Phillips to a relative (MS.).

[2] "Memorial of Ann Phillips," by Mrs. Alford, p. 7.

[3] Quoted from a letter written by Richard D. Webb to George Thompson, in "William Lloyd Garrison," vol. ii., p. 403.

[4] "William Lloyd Garrison," by his sons, vol. ii., p. 367.

member of the Society of Friends, Joseph Sturge.[1]
This body had issued a call for a General Conference
and addressed it to "Friends of the slave of every
nation and of every clime."[2] Accordingly, the various
American societies met and appointed delegates.
Pennsylvania and Massachusetts, in agreement with
their recent rules, had, as we have stated, sent mixed
delegations, among the men, William Lloyd Garrison,
Wendell Phillips, and William Adam, Professor
of Oriental Languages at Harvard College ; among
the women, Harriet Martineau (who, though an
Englishwoman and a non-resident of America, was
an honorary member of the Massachusetts Anti-
Slavery Society, and already on the ground), Mrs.
Wendell Phillips, Mrs. Henry G. Chapman, and
Lucretia Mott, by odds the ablest and most distinguished
Quakeress in the world.

These ladies were now in London, and they requested
Wendell Phillips to present their credentials.
Upon doing so, a day or two before the first session
of the Convention, he was waved off to the Executive
Committee of the British and Foreign Society,
which had assumed authority to determine who
were eligible for membership. This cabal refused
to admit women. From their star-chamber decision,
Mr. Phillips appealed to the convention itself. As
soon, therefore, as the venerable Thomas Clarkson,
the father of the West India emancipation, who presided,
had concluded his address of greeting, the
young American rose and offered this resolution :

"That a committee of five be appointed to prepare a correct

---

[1] "William Lloyd Garrison," by his sons, vol. ii., p. 352.
[2] *Ib.*

list of the members of this Convention, with instruction to include in such list all *persons* bearing credentials from any Anti-Slavery society."

The resolution stirred a hubbub. It shifted the question as to who should and who should not be considered as delegates from the committee-room to the Convention, and bluntly put the decision as to whether it was a self-constituting body where it belonged, with the body. When quiet was restored Mr. Phillips, calm, debonair, in London as in Boston, proceeded to argue the case:

"When the call reached America, we found that it was an invitation to the 'friends of the slaves of every nation and of every clime.' Massachusetts has for several years acted on the principle of admitting women to an equal seat with men in the deliberate bodies of Anti-Slavery societies. When the Massachusetts Anti-Slavery Society received that paper, it interpreted it, as was its duty, in its broadest and most liberal sense. We stand here in consequence of your invitation; and, knowing our custom, as it must be presumed you did, we had a right to interpret 'friends of the slaves' to include women as well as men. In such circumstances we do not think it just or equitable to that State, nor to America in general, that after the trouble, the sacrifice, the self-devotion, of a part of those who left their families and kindred and occupations in their own land, to come three thousand miles to attend this World's Convention, they should be refused a place in its deliberations." [1]

English habits and customs felt outraged. Women sitting with men in a convention—shocking! They might sit together at home, in church, at theatres, in the ball-room, at a concert, in the public conveyances, anywhere, everywhere, except in a convention. In the interest of decency and in the interest

---

[1] "The Life and Times of Wendell Phillips," by George L. Austin, p. 97.

of harmony, the New Englander was besought on all sides to withdraw his motion. He rose again and said:

"I would merely ask whether any man can suppose that the delegates from Massachusetts or Pennsylvania can take upon their shoulders the responsibility of withdrawing that list of delegates from your table, which their constituents told them to place there, and whom they sanctioned as their fit representatives, because this Convention tells us that it is not ready to meet the ridicule of the morning newspapers, and to stand up against the customs of England? In America we listen to no such arguments. If we had done so, we had never been here as Abolitionists. It is the custom there not to admit colored men into respectable society; and we have been told again and again that we are outraging the decencies of humanity when we permit colored men to sit by our side. When we have submitted to brickbats and the tar-tub and feathers in New England rather than yield to the custom prevalent there of not admitting colored brethren into our friendship, shall we yield to parallel custom or prejudice against women in Old England?

"We cannot yield this question if we would, for it is a matter of conscience. But we would not yield it on the ground of expediency. In doing so, we should feel that we were striking off the right arm of our enterprise. We could not go back to America to ask for any aid from the women of Massachusetts if we had deserted them when they chose to send out their own sisters as their representatives here; we could not go back to Massachusetts and assert our unchangeableness of spirit on the question. We have argued it over and over again, and decided it time after time, in every society in the land, in favor of the women. We have not changed by crossing the water. We stand here the advocates of the same principle that we contend for in America. We think it right for women to sit by our side there and we think it right for them to do the same here. We ask the Convention to admit them; if they do not choose to grant it, the responsibility rests on their shoulders. Massachusetts cannot turn aside or succumb to any prejudices or customs, even in the land she looks upon with so much reverence as the land of Wilberforce, of Clarkson, and of O'Connell. It is a matter of conscience, and British virtue ought not to ask us to yield." [1]

The result was that, after a gallant struggle, the ladies were denied admission to the floor as delegates and shunted off into the galleries as spectators.[2] Negroes were admitted; but women, gracious, no! It was when Mr. Phillips left her to conduct this case that Mrs. Phillips addressed him in the oft-quoted words:

"Wendell, don't shilly-shally."[3]

Well, he did not. And though immediately defeated, he opened then and there the broadest and profoundest of all agitations, that which contemplates the emancipation of the larger and better half of the human race. The World's Convention straightway shrank into a conclave of men—a sex convention. It was its ironical fate to stand rather as a landmark in the history of woman's rights than in that of Abolition.[4]

This action set tongues a-wagging from Land's End to John o'Groat's house; yes, and across the continent of America. It was a better advertisement for fair play than a dozen unchallenged admissions would have been.

Unfortunately Mr. Garrison, detained by storms on the ocean, did not reach London until the Convention was nearing its end. When he arrived he refused to enter the body, and took his place yonder in the galleries among the excluded and disfranchised

---

[1] "Life and Times of Wendell Phillips." by George L. Austin, pp. 98, 99.
[2] "Life and Letters of J. and L. Mott," *in loco.*
[3] "Memorial of Ann Phillips," p. 8
[4] "William Lloyd Garrison," vol. ii., p. 381.

delegates. In a letter to the *Liberator* he gives his reason :

"The Convention had but three days more to sit, and therefore we would not disturb it by renewing the agitation of the subject already decided, but so decided as to prevent us also from entering without renewing its discussion. Another reason was that, after having called every friend of the oppressed from all parts of the globe, the Convention was not an open one, but resolved itself into a delegated body. Another was that, being a delegated body, the delegates were not all received. Why, which of the delegates had the right to reject the rest? As well might the women have conspired to vote out the men, as the men have undertaken to exclude the women."[1]

The action of the World's Convention was pitiful ; all the more inexcusable because it was, in its inception, and largely in its management, a Quaker conference, and, as everybody knows, the Quakers have given to women the largest recognition. Now they poured contempt upon their own traditions and borrowed the manners of the "world's people."

Two names stand out in honorable prominence upon the record. They are the names of two Roman Catholics—one the foremost priest of his age, the other the most illustrious layman in the Pope's communion. Father Mathew, the great apostle of temperance, who revolutionized Ireland on that question, expressed his deep regret at the exclusion of the women delegates.[2] And Daniel O'Connell, in a letter to Lucretia Mott, dated London, June 20th, wrote :

"I readily comply with your request to give my opinion as to the propriety of the admission of the female delegates into the Convention.

---

[1] *Vide Liberator*, vol. x., p. 165.   [2] *Ib.*, p. 139.

"I should premise by avowing, that my first impression was strong against that admission; and I believe I declared that opinion in private conversation. But when I was called upon by you to give my personal decision on the subject I felt it my duty to investigate the grounds of the opinion I had formed; and upon that investigation I easily discovered that it was founded on no better grounds than an apprehension of the ridicule it might excite, if the Convention were to do what is so unusual in England—to admit women to an equal share and right of discussion. I also, without difficulty, recognized that this was an unworthy, and, indeed, a cowardly motive, and I easily overcame its influence.

"My mature consideration of the entire subject convinces me of the right of the female delegates to take their seats in the Convention, and of the injustice of excluding them. I do not care to add, that I deem it also impolitic; because, that exclusion being unjust, it ought not to have taken place even if it could also be politic.

"I have a consciousness that I have not done my duty in not sooner urging these considerations on the Convention. My excuse is, that I was unavoidably absent during the discussion of the subject!"[1]

For their part in the Convention, the controlling spirits sent Messrs. Phillips and Garrison to Coventry. When a monster meeting was held in Exeter Hall, as a *grand finale*, neither of them was invited to speak, though one was the originator and the other was the orator *par excellence* of the Abolition movement in America. Two lesser lights represented this country on the platform that night; while O'Connell spoke, as only he could, for Europe, gathering into one tremendous thunder-tone the old world's rebuke of the recreant Republic. This was

---

[1] *Liberator*, vol. x., p. 119. Compare "William Lloyd Garrison," vol. ii., p. 382.

the occasion when the eloquent Irishman uttered the sentence which Phillips never tired of repeating :

"I send my voice across the Atlantic, careering like the thunder-storm against the breeze, to tell the slave-holder of the Carolinas that God's thunder-bolts are hot, and to remind the bondman that the dawn of his redemption is already breaking!"[1]

In commenting upon this, Mr. Phillips said : "You seemed to hear the tones come echoing back to London from the Rocky Mountains."[2]

He went with Garrison soon after to call on O'Connell. The Irishman had just begun to agitate for the repeal of the union with England. He was to make a speech that night in the House of Commons on that very issue. The two friends intruded with fear and trembling, expecting to find him in the throes of preparation. On the contrary, he was stretched upon a sofa enjoying one of Charles Dickens's novels![3] After the manner of great minds he sought recreation on the eve of conflict and left his opponents to do the agony.

The Convention adjourned on June 23d.[4] There-upon social enjoyments, which the session had interrupted, resumed their sway. It was here, there, or yonder from daybreak to midnight, an unceasing round of *fêtes* and pleasures. Into them Mrs. Phillips entered as deeply as her strength would allow,

---

[1] See Phillips's lecture on O'Connell in the Appendix of this volume.

[2] *Ib.*

[3] For one interesting parallel case the reader is referred to Edward Everett's account of Webster's manner the night previous to his crushing response to Hayne. *Vide* Everett's "Orations and Speeches," vol. iv., p. 205.

[4] "William Lloyd Garrison," vol. ii., p. 373, note.

and often when she was spent she urged her devoted
"better three-quarters," as she persisted in calling
him, to go and represent the remaining quarter,
finding it difficult, however, to enforce obedience in
this from the usually submissive husband. What
were scenes and experiences of gayety to him with
her absent and in pain?

Finding that the social pace was harmful to her,
and mindful of the purpose of their exile, he hurried
off with her against the protests of his British friends,
and in July, 1840, set out, by way of Belgium and
the Rhine, for Kissingen, in Bavaria, in the vain
hope that the medicinal waters of the spa would
prove beneficial. In a letter to Miss Elizabeth Pease,
written from Kissingen, in August, he gives a hint
of what they saw:

"To Americans it was especially pleasant to see at Frankfort
the oldest printed Bible in the world and two pairs of Luther's
shoes, which Ann would not quit sight of till I had mustered
German enough to ask the man to let the 'little girl' feel of
them. So, after being permitted to hold the great man's slippers
in her own hands, the man watching to see she did not vanish
with them, the 'delegate from Massachusetts' was content to
leave the room. But she'll speak for herself."

Then, in the same letter, Mrs. Phillips adds:

"We are settled down in this quiet little village, and strange
indeed it is after the busy London hours. How much we enjoyed there! Even I have a world to look back upon, though
I was able to take but little share in the rich feast of heart and
mind. It was the remark of the great physician Hunter that he
should be happy through eternity if God would but let him muse
upon all he had seen and learned in this world. So what a
never-ending store of recollections you will have in this visit
from those you have so long known (though not face to face).
How hallowed will be to you the memory of those hours of com-

munion with such a being as Garrison! I thought you could not but love him."[1]

As Kissingen did not answer their expectations, they next tried Brückenau, another Bavarian spa. Meeting with continued disappointment, they devoted the autumn, which was a delightful one, to leisurely travel in Switzerland and Northern Italy. Leaving Germany *via* Heidelberg, they visited in succession the Falls of the Rhine, Zurich, Lucerne, Berne, Interlaken ("over that gem of a lake by Thun"), the Staubbach and Wengern Alps, and Lausanne, and in October they crossed the Simplon to Milan.[2] On reaching Florence, which they did in November, Mr. Phillips wrote:

"After a fortnight of glorious weather, we came hither by Bologna, that jewel of a city, . . . for she admits women to be professors in her university, her gallery guards their paintings, her palaces boast their sculptures. I gloried in standing beside a woman-professor's monument set up side by side with that of the illustrious Galvani."[3]

At the same time he wrote an interesting descriptive letter to his wife's cousin and his own devoted friend, Miss Mary Grew, of Philadelphia, who had been among the rejected delegates at the World's Convention, one of the most gifted and indefatigable of the Anti-Slavery band:

"FLORENCE, ITALY, November 19, 1840.

"DEAR COUSIN: I have remembered well my promise to write to you, but a thousand things have pushed the August which should have been into the November which stares at me rather reproachfully from my dating. This, however, is not the only plan for this second year abroad which has not come to

---

[1] "Memorial of Ann Phillips," p. 9.   [2] *Ib.*, p. 10.   [3] *Ib.*

reality ; and, though we are very happy, and mean to be under all circumstances, still, when we look back on all the things we meant to do—sights to see, scenes to explore, curiosities to gloat over, we feel something as Johnson did when, after printing the glorious plan he had at first drawn for his dictionary, he ludicrously says, ' Such were the dreams of a poet destined to awake a lexicographer.'

"We had dreamed of seeing all the Alps, Chamouni, climbing hundreds of hills, roaming over the Simplon and the Splügen and lakes innumerable, being drenched in the mist of every waterfall which boasts a name, and topping off with Venice— half-Eastern, half-Gothic, and all romance. But such were the dreams of a traveller destined to awake an invalid.[1] I'll not stop to tell you of the London days after you left us. You shall go on board with us and sail over that rough, chopping Channel to Ostend ; passing mournfully, because too rapidly, by those rich old places full of pictures and churches and town halls (these last the scenes of the first struggle of municipal freedom) ; *i.e.*, by Liège, Brussels, Namur, Aix-la-Chapelle, we come to spend Sunday at Cologne. I do not deem myself ill employed in spending some few hours in wandering around that miracle of art, that half-finished cathedral, number one in Gothic architecture the world over ; and staring rather stupidly at that romance-known and queer old chapel which boasts of having the skulls of the three kings who saluted Mary and the Child. I would I could stop to catalogue the strange list of relics they pretend to show in Catholic shrines, from the Saviour's blood downward. It is certainly shocking, the manner in which they have ransacked the Gospel and marked the slightest things—and sometimes ludicrous, though the blind devotion which they inspire can only and always be melancholy. But, if you trust them, you can see almost any article named in Holy Writ, and sometimes, unfortunately, two of the same things.

"The next day we launched on the Rhine—river ever-varying, always grand and noble ; while we just set foot for the night at Coblenz. Come with me, and I'll show you the house where Metternich was born ; and in that little church yonder the sons of Charlemagne met to divide his empire.

---

[1] This refers to his wife.

"In the Frankfort library, they show you the first printed Bible, 1450 or 1455, by Gutenberg, at Mayence (no date in it, though), on paper which is as rare as many of these earliest prints were on parchment—perhaps the oldest printing in the world, and seen almost in its cradle. We have seen here, at Florence, many ancient stamps for pottery, etc., made of one piece of iron, and with over thirty letters cut upon them, just like a stereotype plate, to stamp the maker's name on bread or burned ware. Strange that they were thus in sight of this glorious invention— only one step, and to take that step cost fifteen hundred years !

"Look here, and you may take into your hands the very shoes Luther wore (always provided the librarian holds on to the other end to see you do not vanish with them), just such sandals as one sees now every day on the monks' feet in Italy. 'Tis strange how alike the human mind is, all nations and both sexes through. I have found one vein of defect running through Catholicism into Quakerism. For instance, the monks dress in the fashion of five hundred years ago ; these shoes might be mated in any Italian town now, and could have been in the days of Petrarch.

"Yet St. Benedict, when he laid down the rules of his order, commanded only plainness, and cautioned against singularity. How like broad-brim and straight collars !

"But a truce to prosing. Like the Scotsman 'back agen,' we came to Frankfort, made acquaintance with Mr. Woodbridge—a very pleasant one—he was very civil and kind, as Americans always ought to be to each other in strange countries ; and then down to Switzerland, to Schaffhausen, with its falls, the boast of Europe ; so-so to an American, though, to be sure, they are beautiful. But when I see falls here, I always think of the story of a cockney who was visiting in the country, and on being requested to observe a fine river exclaimed, ' Yes, fine, very fine for a *country* river.' So it is with the European falls ; not so, though, with the beautiful shoot of the Staubbach, which falls some eight or nine hundred feet into a fearful valley hemmed in by precipices of black rock on both sides thousands of feet high ; on one side the falls, and on the other, peering over the lowering black rocks, you see the glistening white of the eternal snow of the glaciers reflecting the sunset. Oh, those glaciers ! surely next to the ocean they are the sublimest natural objects in the world. Perhaps I ought to except Niagara, but am not sure. Winter—not in the lap of spring, but of summer; roses at your feet, blue-cold ice, dazzling snow over your head; and, far up in the sky, towering above the barren piles of rock, perfect wildernesses of snow—heaps on heaps.

"At Milan we received a letter from Elizabeth Pease. She is a noble woman, worth coming to a 'World's Convention,' and not finding one, to make her acquaintance.

"Remember us and pray for us, that we may be kept forever watching the will of God and doing it with hearts pure and raised above every worldly motive or temptation.

"Yours most truly,
"WENDELL PHILLIPS."

Wendell Phillips in Florence! The swift radical for once at rest among conservatives! The architect of the future in the city of the past! The contrast was sharp. Yet there was in him a singular combination of radicalism and conservatism. Mentally he believed in and worked for a nobler to-morrow. In sentiment he was reminiscent, and delighted to think and speak of the fated yesterday. Hence, he found Florence a place of enchantments.

Such landscapes as might be viewed

"At evening from the top of Fesole,
   Or in Val d'Arno;"

such dark piles of mediæval architecture as frowned down upon him on every side, a romance in each stone; such museums filled with the medals and coins of every age, and populous with the breathing marbles and the inspired canvas of the master artists; such libraries stored with the choicest texts of ancient letters; such gardens—rose, orange, pomegranate, myrtle—bewitching the air with fragrance—

where else would a scholar so willingly live or die?[1]

Many and lingering were his visits to the Church of Santa Croce; to the house of Michel Angelo; to the stone where Dante stood to gaze on the Campanile. Nor did this latest struggler for truth omit to go where Milton, also a wanderer amid these kindling scenes, went, to the house where Galileo lived and died—half-villa and half-prison, where the English poet (another of those " of whom the world was not worthy") found the great Italian, who first beheld the heavens through a telescope and saw Venus crescent like the moon, grown old and blind, and held a " prisoner to the Inquisition for thinking on astronomy otherwise than as the Dominican and Franciscan licensers thought."[2]

From Florence the Phillipses turned with a sigh of regret and sought Leghorn for the sea-breezes. Here they welcomed the birth of the year 1841.[3] Here, too, they learned of another birth, that of a young son of Mr. Garrison, away off in Boston, whom the parents had honored one of the wanderers by naming Wendell Phillips.[4] Writing from Leghorn in recognition of it, he says to a relative: " What shall I say of William Lloyd Garrison's touching mark of kindly feeling? I ask you to thank

---

[1] These points are variously touched in letters which he wrote and which we thus summarize.

[2] "Milton's Prose Works," vol. i., p. 313.

[3] "Memorial of Ann Phillips," p. 10.

[4] This gentleman has reflected credit upon his name. He was educated (by his namesake) at Harvard College, and has been for years prominent and useful in connection with the New York press; and latterly has given to the world a voluminous record of his father's life and work, aided by a brother.

him for this new token of his love and to pet the little one until I return to do it !" [1]

Three months later the travellers reached Naples, ascended Vesuvius, wandered through the once-buried Pompeii and Herculaneum, "adored the bay," and laughed at the lazy lazzaroni as they sunned themselves at full length on the sidewalks. On April 12th Mr. Phillips wrote to Mr. Garrison, with Naples for a writing-desk.

His letter is so characteristic and reveals his artistic and humanitarian instincts—two selves in one—so remarkably, that we must quote some portions of it :

" 'Tis a melancholy tour, this through Europe ; and I do not understand how any one can return from it without being, in Coleridge's phrase, ' a sadder and a wiser man.' Every reflecting mind must be struck at home with the many social evils which prevail ; but the most careless eye cannot avoid seeing the powerful contrasts which sadden one here at every step ; wealth beyond that of fairy tales, and poverty bare and starved at its side ; refinement face to face with barbarism ; cultivation, which hardly finds room to be, crowded out on all sides by such debasement. . . . Europe is the treasure-house of rich memories, with every city a shrine. Mayence, the mother of printing and free trade ; Amalfi, with her Pandects, the fountain of law—her compass of commerce—her Masaniello of popular freedom ; Naples, with her buried satellite of Pompeii ; Florence, with her galaxy of genius ; Rome, whose name is at once history and description, must ever be the ' Meccas of the mind.' One must see them to realize the boundless wealth, the refinement of art, the luxury, to which the ancients had attained. The modern world deems itself rich when it gathers up only the fragments.

"'But all the fascinations of art and the luxuries of modern civilization are no balance to the misery which bad laws and

---

[1] "William Lloyd Garrison," vol. ii., p. 413, note.

bad religion alike entail on the bulk of the people. The Apollo himself cannot dazzle one blind to the rags and want which surround him. Nature is not wholly beautiful. For even when she marries a matchless sky to her Bay of Naples the impression is saddened by the presence of degraded and suffering humanity. When you meet in the same street a man encompassed with all the equipage of wealth and the beggar on whose brow disease and starvation have written his title to your pity, the question is involuntary, Is this a Christian city? To my mind the answer is, No. In our own country the same contrasts exist, but they are not yet so sharply drawn as here. I hope the discussion of the question of property will not cease until the Church is convinced that, from Christian lips *ownership means responsibility for the right use* of what God has given; that the title of a needy brother is as sacred as the owner's own, and infringed upon, too, whenever that owner allows the siren voice of his own tastes to drown the cry of another's necessities. . . .

"The moral stagnation here only makes us value more highly the stirring arena at home. None know what it is to live till they redeem life from monotony by sacrifice. There is more happiness in one such hour than in dwelling forever with the beautiful and grand which Angelo's chisel has shaped and vitalized from the 'marble chaos,' or the pencil of Raphael has given to immortality. . . .

"Nothing brings home so vividly to Ann as the sight of an occasional colored man in the street; and so you see we are ready to return to our posts in nothing changed. . . . In one way, I have learned to value my absence. I have found difficulty in answering others—however clear my own mind might be—when charged with taking steps which the sober judgment of old age would regret, with being hurried recklessly forward by the enthusiasm of the moment and the excitement of heated meetings. I am glad, therefore, to have had this space aside, this opportunity of holding up our cause, with all its bearings and incidents, calmly before my mind—of having distance of place perform, as far as possible, the part of distance of years —of being able to look back from other scenes and studies upon the course we have taken the last few years. Having done so, I rejoice now to say, that every hour of such thought convinces me, more and more, of the overwhelming claims our cause has on the lifelong devotion of each of us—of the rightfulness and expediency of every step we have taken; and I hope to return to my place prepared to urge its claims with more earnestness, and to stand fearlessly by it without a doubt of its success.

"Paul's 'appeal to Cæsar' brought him into this Bay of Naples, and he must have seen all its fair shores and jutting headlands covered with baths and villas, imperial palaces and temples of the gods. A prisoner of a despised race, he stood in the presence of the pomp and luxury of the Roman people. Even amid their ruins, I could not but realize how strong the faith of the Apostle to believe that the message he bore would triumph alike over their power and their religion. Struggling against priests and people may we cherish a like faith." [1]

The travellers returned to England by way of Paris (another city which charmed them both—a second visit), and went thence again to London, where they spent the last fortnight in June with Elizabeth Pease.[2] Mr. Phillips found his friend George Thompson busily engaged in organizing a British-India agency for the cultivation of cotton, the object being to compete with the South in the markets of the world, in the hope of superseding slave labor in the production and sale of that staple. He wrote and published an open letter to Mr. Thompson, from which we quote:

"How shall we address that large class of men to whom dollars are always a weightier consideration than duties, prices current stronger argument than proofs of Holy Writ? Our appeal has been entreaty; for the times in America are those 'pursy times' when,

"'Virtue itself of Vice must pardon beg,
    Yea, curb and woo for leave to do him good.'

"But from India a voice comes clothed with the omnipotence

---

[1] Published in *Liberator*, vol. xi., p. 87.
[2] "Memorial of Ann Phillips," p. 10.

of self-interest ; and the wisdom which might have been slighted from the pulpit, will be to such men oracular from the market-place. Gladly will we make a pilgrimage and bow with more than Eastern devotion on the banks of the Ganges, if his holy waters shall be able to wear away the fetters of the slave. God speed the progress of your society ! May it soon find in its ranks the whole phalanx of scarred and veteran Abolitionists— no single divided effort, but a united one to grapple with the wealth, influence, and power embattled against you ! Is it not Schiller who says, ' Divide the thunder into single tones, and it becomes a lullaby for children ; but pour it forth in one quick peal, and the royal sound shall shake the heavens ' ? So may it be with you ! And God grant that, without waiting for the United States to be consistent, before we are dust, the jubilee of emancipated millions may reach us from Mexico to the Potomac, and from the Atlantic to the Rocky Mountains." [1]

No lasting good resulted from the British-India endeavor, which enlisted the co-operating efforts of American Abolitionists,[2] though for a space it threw the Pro-Slavery interest into spasms of apprehension.[3]

After an absence of a little more than two years the Phillipses embarked from Liverpool for home on July 4th, 1841,[4] crossing by steamer, then thought hazardous, but taken, notwithstanding, by these friends of progress. Unhappily their chief purpose was not achieved, the wife returning as she had departed, a chronic sufferer. But they had seen and

---

[1] *Vide* " Wendell Phillips and his Times," by George L. Austin, pp. 103, 104.

[2] Compare a letter written by William Lloyd Garrison to Joseph Pease (brother of Elizabeth), of Darlington, England, on the same subject, in " William Lloyd Garrison," vol. ii., pp. 391-94.

[3] " William Lloyd Garrison,' vol. ii., p. 393, note.

[4] " Memorial of Ann Phillips," p. 10

felt much, storing a wealth of new emotions and bearing back a mass of classic spoil as the criteria of endless comparison and illustration. In so far as the completion of his outfit as a reformer and orator is concerned, Wendell Phillips could not have spent those years more admirably.

V.

NO. 26 ESSEX STREET.

THE Phillipses reached Boston about the middle of July.[1] Their return was commemorated by a formal reception and collation, at which the entire Abolitionist community was present, with the grateful colored people in the rôle of host. Slavery and salads were discussed with equal gusto; and the absentees were told how sadly they had been missed and how gladly they were welcomed back.[2] Having been thus dined (but not wined), they went to the summer house of Mr. Phillips's mother in Nahant, a resort of the *élite*, within half an hour of town, where they passed two or three months, meanwhile arranging for a home of their very own. Mrs. Phillips paints their temporary refuge in one of the rare letters traced by her pen, and addressed to her dear friend in England, Miss Elizabeth Pease:

"Picture to yourself a great wooden house, with doors and blinds as usual, a mile from any other habitation, little grass and fewer trees, and you have 'Phillips's Cliff.' The village of Nahant is about a mile from our house; there Dame Fashion struts about three months of the summer, but we have the blessing of being out of her way and doing as we please. Here dwells, in summer, Wendell's mother; one of her daughters, with five children, one side of the house, we with her in the

---

[1] On the 17th.
[2] "William Lloyd Garrison," vol. iii., pp. 17, 18. See note also.

other. What with fifteen children and twenty grandchildren at intervals dropping in upon her, you see she is not alone. We rise about seven, breakfast at half-past. Wendell rows the boat for exercise; bathes. I walk with him in the morning; dine at two; in the afternoon we ride with mother; tea at seven; in the evening we play chess or backgammon with her, or some brother or sister comes to pass the night, and we dispute away on the great questions. We are considered as heretics and almost infidels, but we pursue the even tenor of our way undisturbed. Sometimes Wendell goes off abolitionizing for two or three days, but I remain on the ground."

In October, '41, Mr. Phillips bought a tiny brick house of the English basement style on Essex Street, No. 26. Here the young couple decided to make their home. A dining-room and a kitchen on the ground floor; a double parlor facing south (unlike the occupants), small, but suitable for a literary workshop, on the second floor; front and back chambers (destined to form Mrs. Phillips's realm) on the third floor, with attic accommodations for the servants; such, in its *ensemble*, was the snuggery in which they were to reside for forty years.[1] It was as contracted as their sympathies were expanded. Knowing their own social gravitation, they selected this robin's nest precisely in order to make entertainment impossible. It was to be the abode of an invalid—a domestic sanitarium.

The house stood, however, in the midst of the Anti-Slavery colony—the Garrisons, the Chapmans, the Jacksons, the Lorings, within five minutes' walk.[2] It was a time when companionship was needed. Abolitionists might well huddle together for association, as the early settlers used to for protection when the Indians were prowling about.

---

[1] "Memorial of Ann Phillips," pp. 10, 11.   [2] *Ib.*, p. 18.

Just as soon as they were settled Mr. Phillips wrote to Miss Pease:

"November 25, 1841.

"I am writing in our own parlor—wish you were in it—on 'Thanksgiving Day.' Did you ever hear of that name? 'Tis an old custom in New England, begun to thank God for a providential arrival of food from the mother-country in sixteen hundred and odd year, and perpetuated now wherever a New Englander dwells, some time in autumn, by the Governor's appointment. All is hushed of business about me; the devout pass the morning at church; those who have wandered to other cities hurry back to worship to-day where their fathers knelt, and gather sons and grandsons, to the littlest prattler, under the old roof-tree to—shall I break the picture?—cram as much turkey and plum-pudding as possible; a sort of compromise by Puritan love of good eating for denying itself that 'wicked papistrie,' Christmas."

A humorous account follows of the first trials of the young housekeepers with unpromising servants, and there is a mention of a friend's calling and finding him sawing a piece of soapstone:

"I set to work to fix a chimney, having a great taste for carpentering and mason-work. (When I set up for a gentleman, there was a good mechanic spoiled, Ann says.) . . . Ann's health is about the same. She gets tired out every day trying to oversee 'the keeping house,' as we Americans call it when two persons take more rooms than they need, buy double the things that they want, hire two or three others, just, for all the world, for the whole five to devote themselves to keeping the establishment in order. I long for the time when there'll be no need of sweeping and dusting, and when eating will be forgotten."[1]

A little later Mrs. Phillips gives the same friend "some little insight into indoor life at No. 26 Essex Street:"

---

[1] "Memorial of Ann Phillips," p. 12.

"There is your Wendell seated in the arm-chair, lazy and easy as ever, perhaps a little fatter than when you saw him, still protesting how he was ruined by marrying. Your humble servant looks like the Genius of Famine, as she always did, one of Pharaoh's lean kine. She laughs considerably, continues in health in the same naughty way, has been pretty well, for her, this winter. Now what do you think her life is? Why, she strolls out a few steps occasionally, calling it a walk; the rest of the time, from bed to sofa, from sofa to rocking-chair; reads, generally, the *Standard* and *Liberator*, and that is pretty much all the literature her aching head will allow her to peruse; rarely writes a letter, sees no company, makes no calls, looks forward to spring and birds, when she will be a little freer; is cross very often, pleasant at other times, loves her dear L— and thinks a great deal of her; and now you have Ann Phillips.

"Now I'll take up another strain. This winter has been marked to us by our keeping house for the first time. I call it housekeeping; but, alas! we have not the pleasure of entertaining angels, awares or unawares. We have a small house, but large enough for us, only a few rooms furnished—just enough to try to make me more comfortable than at board. But then I am not well enough even to have friends to tea, so that all I strive to do is to keep the house neat and keep myself about. I have attended no meetings since I helped fill ' the negro pew.' What Anti-Slavery news I get, I get second-hand. I should not get along at all, so great is my darkness, were it not for Wendell to tell me that the world is still going on. . . . We are very happy, and only have to regret my health being so poor and our own sinfulness. Dear Wendell speaks whenever he can leave me, and for his sake I sometimes wish I were myself again; but I dare say it is all right as it is."[1]

And now, with a fireside of his own, and so far, tried by the most orthodox canons, a "respectable" and responsible citizen, the "vagabond Abolitionist" was ready to buckle on his armor.

---

[1] "Memorial of Ann Phillips," p. 13.

VI.

THE IRISH ADDRESS.

During Mr. Phillips's long absence the controversy over the status of women in the Anti-Slavery societies[1] had torn these bodies asunder, so that, like the patriarch Jacob, Mr. Garrison could say: "With my staff I passed over this Jordan, and now I am become two bands." National, State, county, city bodies—all were divided, and everywhere there were two instead of one.[2] The doubling of names, however, did not denote a doubling of forces. When the schism occurred, the Garrisonians, having outvoted the schismatics, retained possession of the original organizations. But they lost their national organ, which eloped with the retiring faction, so that they were compelled to establish a new one, the *Standard*, which was published in New York and was a sort of twin of the *Liberator*, Mr. Garrison's personal mouthpiece.

Among the Garrisonians the women were enfranchised, and continued to render the most unselfish and successful service. Being free now from disturbing elements they compacted themselves and reaffirmed their purpose to conduct a purely moral

---

[1] *Ante*, p. 116 *sqq*.
[2] See this whole question elaborately treated in "William Lloyd Garrison," vol. ii., *passim*.

war against slavery, avowing their confidence in conscience and reason and discussion as the surest means wherewith to pull down the strongholds of oppression.[1] On the other hand, the seceding brethren tended increasingly to adopt political methods, and were soon drawn into parties which rallied to stone slavery with ballots.

As all the world knows, Mr. Phillips sided in this division with the Garrisonians and remained to be their attorney-general. In common with Abolitionists of every faction, he was incensed at this hour by the recent action of Congress in denying the right of petition—a right as old as Anglo-Saxon liberty and embalmed in the Magna Charta. Congress had been bombarded for years with petitions for emancipation in the District of Columbia. In January, 1841, the House of Representatives passed a gag law :[2] "That no petition praying the abolition of slavery in the District of Columbia or any State or any Territory, or the slave trade between the States or Territories of the United States, in which it now exists, shall be received by this House." The obsequious Senate made haste to concur.[3] Nor was this all. Ex-President John Quincy Adams, a Representative of Massachusetts, who had been honorably active in presenting these petitions, and who in eminence and value of public service was easily the foremost statesman in America, was menaced with expulsion for his "impudence."

---

[1] "William Lloyd Garrison," vol. ii., p. 391.

[2] By a vote of 114 yeas to 108 nays. A close vote. But slavery could say with Mercutio, in the play : "'Tis not so deep as a well, nor so wide as a church door ; but 'tis enough."

[3] *Vide* "Rise and Fall of the Slave Power," by Henry Wilson.

In the autumn after his return from Europe an event occurred which Mr. Phillips eagerly seized and used as a sword with which to smite this defiant aggression, this twofold assault upon freedom.

There came from Ireland a monster appeal signed by seventy thousand Irishmen, with Daniel O'Connell and Father Mathew at their head, condemning slavery and urging the Irish in America to identify themselves with the Abolitionists.[1] At this crisis the Irish were, almost without exception, on the side of slavery. They belonged to the laboring class. They were thus brought into competition with the negroes. Their freedom and their color alone distinguished those from these. All the more strongly, therefore, did they prize and seek to emphasize the marks of distinction. Moreover, finding, as they did, the wealth and fashion and political power of the country arrayed against the Abolitionists, and hungry themselves for the flesh-pots of Egypt, they naturally hurrahed for Pharaoh and went where they could fill their stomachs and their pockets. It is only a saint who can prefer a lean right to a fat wrong, truth out-at-the-elbow to error in broadcloth.

The Abolitionists hailed the Irish petition with enthusiasm. They hoped it might prove the fulcrum on which to rest their Archimedes-lever and move over the Irish in America from that side to this. They secured Faneuil Hall. They opened it on the evening of January 28th, 1842, and filled it as it had not been filled since the Lovejoy meeting in 1837. Wendell Phillips now as then was the orator of the

---

[1] *Vide Liberator*, vol. xii., p. 39, for the full text.

occasion. Fresh from the old world, with the rich Irish brogue of O'Connell still in his ears, he mounted the rostrum and delivered an address which captivated the assemblage, the Irish, especially, who were present in crowds, going wild over it. This is what he said :

"I hold in my hand, Mr. Chairman, a resolution expressive of our thanks to the seventy thousand Irishmen who have sent us that token of their sympathy and interest, and especially to those high and gallant spirits who lead the noble list. I must say that never have I stood in the presence of an audience with higher hopes of the rapid progress and success of our cause than now. I remember with what devoted earnestness, with what unfaltering zeal, Ireland has carried on so many years the struggle for her own freedom. It is from such men—whose hearts lost no jot of their faith in the grave of Emmet, over whose zeal the loss of Curran and Grattan could throw no damp, who are now turning the trophies of one field of victory into weapons for new conquests, whom a hireling press and prejudiced public could never sever a moment from O'Connell's side —it is from the sympathy of such that we have a right to hope much.

"The image of the generous isle comes to us, not only 'crowned with the spoil of every science, and decked with the wreath of every muse,' but we cannot forget that she lent to Waterloo the sword which cut the despot's 'shattered sceptre through;' and, to American ears, the crumbled walls of St. Stephen's yet stand to echo the eloquence of her Burke, when, at the foot of the British throne, he took his place side by side with that immortal rebel (pointing to the picture of Washington).

"From a priest of the Catholic Church we might expect superiority to that prejudice against color which freezes the sympathies of our own churches when humanity points to the slave. I remember that African lips may join in the chants of the Church, unrebuked, even under the dome at St. Peter's ; and I have seen the colored man in the sacred dress pass with priest and student beneath the frowning portals of the Propaganda College at

Rome, with none to sneer at his complexion, or repulse him from society.

"I remember that a long line of popes, from Leo to Gregory, have denounced the sin of making merchandise of men; that the voice of Rome was the first to be heard against the slave-trade, and that the bull of Gregory XVI., forbidding every true Catholic to touch the accursed thing, is yet hardly a year old.

"Ireland is the land of agitation and agitators. We may well learn a lesson from her in the battle for human rights. Her philosophy is no recluse; she doffs the cowl and quits the cloister, to grasp in friendly effort the hands of the people. No pulse beats truer to liberty, to humanity, than those which in Dublin quicken at every good from Abolition on this side of the ocean. There can be no warmer words of welcome than those which welcome the American Abolitionists on their thresholds. Let not any one persuade us, Mr. Chairman, that the question of slavery is no business of ours, but belongs entirely to the South.

"I trust in that love of liberty which every Irishman brings to the country of his adoption, to make him true to her cause at the ballot-box, and throw no vote without asking if the hand to which he is about to trust political power will use it for the slave. When an American was introduced to O'Connell in the lobby of the House of Commons, he asked, without putting out his hand, 'Are you from the South?' 'Yes, sir.' 'A slave-holder, I presume?' 'Yes, sir.' 'Then,' said the great liberator, 'I have no hand for you!' and stalked away. Shall his countrymen trust that hand with political power which O'Connell deemed it pollution to touch?

"We remember, Mr. Chairman, that, when a jealous disposition tore from the walls of the City Hall of Dublin the picture of Henry Grattan, the act but did endear him the more to Ireland. The slavocracy of our land thinks to expel that 'old man eloquent,' with the dignity of seventy winters on his brow (pointing to a picture of J. Q. Adams), from the halls of Congress. They will find him only the more lastingly fixed in the hearts of his countrymen.

"Mr. Chairman, we stand in the presence of at least the name of Father Mathew. We remember the millions who pledged themselves to temperance from his lips. I hope his countrymen will join with me in pledging here eternal hostility to slavery. 'Will you ever return to his master the slave who once sets foot on the soil of Massachusetts?' ('No, no, no!') 'Will you ever raise to office or power the man who will not pledge his utmost effort against slavery?' ('No, no, no!')

"Then may we not hope well for freedom? Thanks to those noble men who battle in her cause the world over. The 'ocean of their philanthropy knows no shore.' Humanity knows no country; and I am proud, here in Faneuil Hall, fit place to receive their message, to learn of O'Connell's fidelity to freedom and of Father Mathew's love to the real interests of man."[1]

Amid thunders of applause Mr. Phillips retired and the meeting adjourned. Many Irishmen drew their first Anti-Slavery breath as the result of that speech, and threw themselves thenceforward into the movement with the ardor of their race. When O'Connell read it he pronounced it the most classic short speech in the English language, and said: "I resign the crown. This young American is without an equal."[2]

On this occasion resolutions denouncing Congress for tolerating the existence of slavery under the shadow of the Capitol, and demanding its abolition in the District of Columbia, were adopted with a roar which might have moved the envy of Niagara —a genuine Irish roar.

"Well," remarked Mr. Phillips, as he left the hall, "we will send our resolution to Washington spite of the gag law. And we say, as Patrick Henry did in the House of Burgesses, when he spoke to George III. across the ocean: 'If this be treason, make the most of it!'"[3]

---

[1] *Vide Liberator*, vol. xii., p. 18.
[2] Letter from George Thompson to Wendell Phillips (MS.).
[3] Letter to a relative (MS.).

The purpose of O'Connell and Father Mathew was not accomplished by their address. The Irish press in America unanimously condemned it. The hierarchy here, through the lips of Bishop Hughes, of New York, impugned its genuineness; and, genuine or not, declared it the duty of every naturalized Irishman to resist and repudiate it with indignation as a foreign interference. The various Irish repeal associations, although organized to interfere in British affairs from this side of the water, with characteristic inconsistency echoed the tone of Bishop Hughes toward O'Connell and Mathew for their interference in American affairs from the other side. To illustrate by a current reference, the Irish address met precisely the fate which a similar appeal would meet to-day headed by Parnell, and urging the Irish in the United States to abjure the "spoils system," and adhere to the civil service reformers.[1] Individuals here and there heard and heeded. The race continued to cheer for slavery and "damn the niggers."

---

[1] "William Lloyd Garrison," vol. iii., p. 45.

VII.

A NEW BATTLE OF CONCORD.

The town of Concord, some twenty miles distant from Boston, and the twin scene with Lexington of the first battle in the Revolution, was a stronghold of conservatism in the 'forties. Half a dozen prominent and elderly squires dominated it, insomuch that it was known far and wide as Squireville. The squirocracy naturally sympathized with the slavocracy. In the winter of 1842-43 the Lyceum out there invited Wendell Phillips to come and give his lecture on "Street Life in Europe"—an outcome of his travels. He did so, confining himself in the main to sights abroad, but managing to give slavery a number of sharp thrusts as he trod along. These passing references piqued curiosity, and he was invited to come again the next winter and speak on slavery. He gladly accepted, and the date fixed was January 17th, 1844. On January 10th a prominent citizen moved in the Lyceum (which then met weekly for debate), that Mr. Phillips be asked to choose some other topic, adding that his sentiments on slavery, expressed the year before, were "vile, pernicious, and abominable." A large majority voted to hear him on slavery and nothing else. So he came according to agreement, January 17th, and spoke for an hour and a half in a strain of invective eloquence very galling to the squires, especially to two of them, Squire Keyes and Squire Hoar—father of the present Senator Hoar. He charged the sin of slavery upon the religion of the country, with its twenty thousand pulpits, all dumb, or advocating the iniquity. The church, he said, had accused the Garrisonians of infidelity, and there was some truth in it; they were infidels to a religion that sustained human bondage. As for the State, the curse of every honest man should be upon its Constitution; could he say to Jefferson, Adams, and Hancock, after the experience of fifty years: "Look upon the fruits of your work!" they would bid him crush the parchment beneath his feet.

These utterances were worse than those of the year before, and so the next week the conservatives in the Lyceum began to debate Phillips's lecture and to denounce him. Word had been sent to Phillips by his friends, and he came into the meeting while Squire Keyes was jeering at him for "leading captive silly women." Squire Hoar then took up the testimony against the audacious "stripling" who had proclaimed such monstrous doctrines, complimented him on his eloquence, but warned the young against such insidious and exciting oratory. About nine o'clock Phillips stepped forward from the rear of the hall and asked permission to reply. He said:

"I do not care for criticisms upon my manner of assailing slavery. In a struggle for life it is hardly fair for men who are lolling at ease to remark that the limbs of the combatants are not arranged in classic postures. I agree with the last speaker that this is a serious subject; had it been otherwise I should not devote my life to it. Stripling as I am, I but echo the voice of the ages, of our venerable forefathers—of statesmen, poets, philosophers. The gentleman has painted the dangers to life, liberty, and happiness that would be the consequence of doing right. These dangers now exist by law at the South. Liberty may be bought at too dear a price ; if I cannot have it except by sin, I reject it. But I cannot so blaspheme God as to doubt my safety in obeying Him. The sanctions of English law are with me ; but if I tread the dust of law beneath my feet and enter the Holy of Holies, what do I find written there ? ' Thou shalt not deliver unto his master the servant which is escaped to thee ; he shall dwell with you, even among you.' I throw myself then on the bosom of Infinite Wisdom. Even the heathen will tell you, ' Let justice be done though the heavens fall ;' and the old reformer answered when warned against the danger of going to Rome, ' It is *not* necessary that I should live ; it *is* necessary that I go to Rome.' But now our pulpits are silent—whoever heard this subject presented until it was done by ' silly women ' and ' striplings ' ? The first speaker accused me of ambition ; let me tell him that ambition chooses a smoother path to fame. And to you, my young friends, who have been cautioned against exciting topics and advised to fold your hands in selfish ease, I would say, Not so—throw yourselves upon the altar of some noble cause ! To rise in the morning only to eat and drink, and gather gold—that is a life not worth living. Enthusiasm is the life of the soul."

Never was an oratorical triumph more complete. The audience applauded heartily ; the meeting, which was to vote Phillips down, was hastily adjourned, and from that day forward he was the favorite speaker in Concord. It was in the next year (March, 1845) that he gave the thrilling address there which Thoreau has commemorated, containing a prayer which concluded, says Thoreau, " Not like the Thanksgiving proclamations, with ' God save the Commonwealth of Massachusetts,' but with ' God dash it into a thousand pieces, till there shall not remain a fragment on which a man who dare not tell his name can stand.' " The reference here was to Frederick Douglass, who had then newly escaped from slavery, who in Boston was in momentary danger of arrest and rendition, and whose liberty was conditioned upon his denial of his identity.

This was the day of extreme statements, for in that same year—1845—Emerson said, in an emancipation address at Waltham (one of his earliest):

"If the Creator of the negro has given him up to stand as a victim of the white man beside him, to stoop under his pack and to bleed under his whip—if that be the doctrine, then I say, 'If He has given up his cause, then He has also given up mine, who feel his wrong and ours, who in our hearts must curse the Creator who has undone him.'"[1]

Of course in these utterances Emerson did not mean to curse the Creator, nor did Phillips mean to curse civil government. In both cases it was the pretence of God and the pretence of law that was denounced—that worst form of atheism, which worships the devil in the name of Christ. The real infidels of those days were in the churches, and the real anarchists were in office at Washington.

All professional lecturers meet with some humorous and comical incidents which relieve some of the drudgery of their work. Perhaps a larger proportion fell to the lot of Anti-Slavery lecturers than to others. Certainly Mr. Phillips had a keen sense of humor. Shortly after the Concord episode he was invited to lecture before a Lyceum in a neighboring country town. Arriving at the place he went directly to the church in which the Lyceum was assembled, and was ushered into a pew with the President and Secretary. The latter asked him if he had brought his lecture on Europe, and he replied that he had. This information the Secretary imparted

---

[1] "Recollections of Wendell Phillips," by F. B. Sanborn (MS.).

to the President, who received it with an intimation of displeasure, and he, turning to Mr. Phillips, asked : " Did we invite you here to lecture on Europe?" "No," replied Mr. Phillips, "you invited me here to lecture. The subject was not specified. I told the Secretary that I brought my lecture on Europe with me. I carry all my lectures in my head." " Didn't the Secretary write to you that we wanted a lecture on slavery ?"

"No, he did not," rejoined Mr. Phillips. The somewhat irate President took his official seat, and calling the meeting to order announced that the Lyceum had instructed its Secretary to write to Mr. Phillips to lecture to them upon the subject of slavery, and added, "There's Mr. Phillips, and he says he was not invited to lecture on any specified topic ; and there's the Secretary." Whereupon the Secretary responded : " I wasn't going to have Anti-Slavery crammed down my throat!" "Nor," rejoined the President, "are we going to have you crammed down our throats !"

The members of the Lyceum then discussed the question, and by a large majority decided to have an Anti-Slavery lecture. The most amusing part of the discussion, to him, was a remark made by a member that he "supposed Mr. Phillips would as lief lecture on slavery if he were paid the same." [1]

---

[1] Recollections of Miss Mary Grew (MS.).

VIII.

THE "COVENANT WITH DEATH."

In following to an end the Concord incident we have stolen a march upon time. We must now retrace our steps and go back to the autumn of 1842, and to the succeeding months, in order to observe certain occurrences of a broader and more essential nature—events in which Mr. Phillips was far more vitally concerned.

In October a mulatto named Latimer came to Boston from Norfolk, Va. He was arrested and thrown into jail on a charge of theft. Presently it was shown that he was indeed a thief—he had stolen himself! Friends rallied to his side and demanded a trial by jury. "No," replied Judge Shaw, "he is a fugitive slave. The Constitution of the United States authorizes the owner of such an one to arrest him in any State to which he may have fled." [1]

The city was wild with excitement. The Abolitionists thronged to Faneuil Hall—the trysting-place of liberty. It was on a Sunday night. No matter. Did not Christ maintain that acts of mercy were acts of worship? And what act of mercy so supreme as the rescue of a man from slave-hounds? Mr. Phillips spoke. Referring to Judge Shaw's ruling, he exclaimed: "We presume to believe the Bible out-

---

[1] See the ruling in the Massachusetts court records of the period.

weighs the statute-book. When I look on those crowded thousands and see them trample on their consciences and on the rights of their fellowmen, at the bidding of a piece of parchment, I say, my curse be on the Constitution of these United States!"[1] This was his first direct collision with the Constitution. The case of Latimer opened his eyes to a clear perception of the fact that in advocating the rights of the blacks his real antagonist was the Union. It was a moment like that when Luther realized that in undertaking to reform the Romish Church he was assailing the Papacy ; like that when the Revolutionary sires were startled to find that in defending their charters they were committing treason—an earthquake experience full of destiny. But as Luther composed himself and said : " Here I must stand ; God help me, I can do nothing else !" as the fathers said : " If this be revolution, let it come !" so he said : " If I must choose between the Union and liberty, then I choose liberty first, Union afterward !"

Happily Latimer was saved, an offer being made and accepted to pay four hundred dollars for his release, with free papers ; whereupon the " chattel" became a man, and the free papers were surrendered instead of the fugitive.[2] But from this moment Wendell Phillips began to denounce the Constitution, that old Pro-Slavery Constitution which the Civil War so magnificently amended. He went further. He personally seceded from the Union and refused all voluntary action under it. His law office—this he closed, for an attorney had to take an oath to

---

[1] *Vide Liberator*, vol. xii., p. 178.   [2] *Ib.*, p. 205.

support the Constitution. The ballot-box—this he forswore, for a voter was an active participant in governmental affairs. Thus he stood—until the outbreak of the Rebellion, which changed the whole situation—a man without a country. He became a political Ishmael, his hand against every man and every man's hand against him. Whatever may be thought of his wisdom, no one can deny his self-sacrifice. It was an act of conscience as sublime as Luther's, as heroic as the penmanship of John Hancock on the Declaration of Independence, which George III. read and understood across the Atlantic.

Nor did Mr. Phillips take this step in a passion. He took it calmly, soberly, as he did everything else, and with a perfect knowledge of what and all it meant. He deliberately counted the cost. "He chose rather to suffer affliction with the people of God than to enjoy the pleasures of sin for a season" —a modern version of Moses quitting the palace of Pharaoh for the brick-yard. The contemporary world hissed both, but heaven and history commend. Anyhow, what is the opinion of man compared with a good conscience and the approbation of God?

When he came to study the Constitution, and, more significantly, when he analyzed it in the light of its consistent interpretation for half a century, he straightway discovered that it was a "covenant with death and an agreement with hell." It erected the negation of God into a system of government. For consider, here was the clause which legalized the slave-trade for twenty years from the date of its adoption; here was the clause which allowed the slave-masters to count three fifths of their slaves in the basis of national representation; and here was the clause which made provision for the return of fugitives throughout the Union—a trinity of evil as satanic as the orthodox trinity was divine. Then, when he lifted his eyes from the parchment, and looked back into the Convention which framed it, he saw—what? Why, that these provisions expressed the exact purpose of its authors.[1] And when he glanced at the successive administrations since that time, at the decisions of the courts, at the practice of the country, at the existing situation, he was driven to the conclusion that consistent Abolitionism was impossible under that document, and that slavery was intrenched in the fundamental law of the nation.

Accordingly, he was indignant but not surprised to observe that the liberty of speech and the freedom of the press were not tolerated in the Southern half of the Union, and were only exercised in the Northern half at the peril of the free speakers and free printers; that the right of trial by jury was denied to any colored man in any State who might be claimed as a slave;[2] that the right of petition was struck down on the floor of Congress;[3] that slavery was declared to be the supreme law of the land.

Mr. Phillips was amazed at his own blindness in not sooner discovering all this. Well, he saw it now, and without waiting to ask what others would do, he did as his Puritan ancestors had done under the despotism of Charles I. and Archbishop Laud— he came out.

---

[1] *Vide* the Proceedings of the Convention. Compare "The Constitution a Pro-Slavery Compact," by Wendell Phillips.

[2] Case of Prigg *vs.* the Commonwealth of Pennsylvania.

[3] *Ante*, p. 153.

Soon he was gratified to find that he was not alone. Others of the Abolitionists saw what he saw, felt as he felt, acted as he acted. There was a band of come-outers, among them his friends and co-laborers, Garrison and Quincy. The months that followed were weary, anxious, tumultuous. There was a pang in every hour. This question was the topic of debate at every Anti-Slavery meeting, in every Anti-Slavery society. In 1843 the Massachusetts Society adopted "come-outer" resolutions.[1] In 1844 the New England and National societies did likewise.[2] One by one the kindred organizations throughout the free States wheeled into line.[3] Soon the entire Garrisonian phalanx presented a united front. In the consciences and the platforms of these bodies the Pro-Slavery Union was dissolved. But these few sentences coldly, feebly summarize convulsive debates and torturing deliberations. How can Gutenberg's types depict heart agonies? Remember what that old Constitution was: the ark of the political covenant, as sacred in the reverence of the American people as its prototype was in the feelings of the ancient Israelites. Reflect upon the prejudices of education and habit which these men had to conquer in themselves. Recall the rage which their renunciation and denunciation provoked in the North as well as in the South, the blasphemy they were charged with, and then estimate the depth of their regard for those who were bound, and their passion for liberty!

They were true to their convictions. They cried

---

[1] *Liberator*, vol. xiii., p. 19. [2] *Ib.*, vol. xiv., pp. 82 and 91.
[3] "Garrison and his Times," p. 338.

aloud and spared not. The Anti-Slavery organs in Boston and in New York displayed in bold head-lines the obnoxious motto : " No Union with Slave-holders." The resolutions at Anti-Slavery meetings bristled with aggressive defiance.

Meantime those Abolitionists who had withdrawn in 1840 from the Garrisonian organizations, because they could not believe that a coat and a petticoat had equal rights, now made haste to identify themselves with a political movement just started, and called the " Liberty party." [1] This party participated in State and national elections with all the machinery of Conventions and candidates. It was small but well organized, earnest and alert. Professedly it was actuated by the same motives as the Garrisonians. In reality it was

" —— cabined, cribbed, confined, bound in
To saucy doubts and fears,"

by the inevitable limitations of politics. More, the " Liberty party," as an Anti-Slavery party, was fatally hampered by the compromises of the Constitution. It could only propose such measures as the Constitution would sanction. When the National Government had exhausted its whole power, that which the Abolitionists hated and meant to destroy, the *slave system*, would remain intact. Under a Pro-Slavery Constitution what chance had an Anti-Slavery crusade ?

Recognizing this difficulty, the Liberty party claimed sometimes that the Constitution had been fatally misinterpreted, that the text was blameless,

---

[1] *Vide* Richard H. Dana's article on the Republican party, in Johnson's *New Universal Cyclopædia, in loco.*

that it was, in fact, an Abolition document. This was the view of William Goodell, and Gerrit Smith, and George B. Cheever—honest and able men. At other times, and by other exponents, it was asserted that the Constitution could be amended and made Anti-Slavery if it were not so. At all times the political Abolitionists derided and belittled the moral-suasion school and cried for action. Many haters of slavery became impatient and wanted to grapple the evil in a hand-to-hand encounter—gladiator fashion—with the ballot-box for an arena. With revolution in the air they esteemed an agitation that was educative and moral alone as inadequate. This it was that led Whittier and Sumner and Wilson and Hale and Chase to adopt political expedients.

All through these years a fierce controversy was carried on between these two wings of the Abolition host—the moral suasionists and the political actionists, each appealing for recruits on the ground of superior facilities, each emphasizing the defects of the other, but both doing a grand work for truth and righteousness, though in different, and, as it often appeared, antagonistic ways.

Mr. Phillips, of course, participated in the discussions of the hour. Indeed, he was preternaturally active—a White Plume of Navarre in this Ivry. It was largely owing to his skill as an organizer, and even more to his eloquence on the platform, that the Garrisonians had been held together, despite the disintegrating influence of the Liberty party, and were led to take and hold the tremendous position of disunion. In 1845 he wrote and published an argument entitled, "The Constitution a Pro-Slavery Compact." With masterly and unanswerable logic he proved—what everybody now admits, and what the amendments, which the Civil War made possible, conclusively avouch—that the Constitution as it then stood was the Gibraltar of human bondage. He also published anonymously in the same year a pamphlet, "Can Abolitionists Vote or take Office under the United States Constitution?" Here he marshalled the pros and cons in successive order under the title of objections and answers. The brochure is a model of argumentative skill, and is full of wit and pat applications. As it was intended to defend and elucidate his position as a "come-outer," let us blow the dust from it and sample it; no danger of falling asleep in the task!

"My object," he says, "in becoming a disunionist is to free the slave, and meantime to live a consistent life. I want men to understand me. And I submit that the body of the Roman people understood better and felt more earnestly the struggle between the people and the princes, when the little band of democrats left the city and encamped on Mons Sacer, outside, than while they remained mixed up and voting with their masters. Dissolution is our Mons Sacer. God grant it may become equally famous in the world's history as the spot where the right triumphed."

To the objection that his course was Pharisaical, he replied:

"Because we refuse to aid a wrongdoer in his sin we by no means proclaim that we think our whole character better than his. It is neither pharisaical to have opinions nor presumptuous to guide our lives by them. He would be a strange preacher who should set out to reform his circle by joining in all their sins. This reminds me of the tipsy Duke of Norfolk, who, seeing a drunken friend in the gutter, hiccoughed: 'My dear fellow, I can't help you out, but I'll do better—I'll lie down by your side!'"

In noticing the objection that by the payment of taxes he recognized and supported the State practically while renouncing it in theory, he answered :

"We are responsible only so far as our ability and willingness go. Any evil which springs from our acts incidentally, without our ability or will, we are not responsible for. Such responsibility reminds me of that principle of Turkish law which Dr. Clark mentions in his travels, and which they call ' homicide by an intermediate cause.' The case he relates is this : A young man in love poisoned himself because the girl's father refused his consent to the marriage. The Cadi sentenced the father to pay a fine of eighty dollars, saying : ' If you had not had a daughter, this young man would not have loved ; if he had not loved, he had never been disappointed ; if he had not been disappointed, he would not have taken poison.' It was the same Cadi, possibly, who sentenced the island of Samos to pay for the wrecking of a vessel, because, if the island had not been in the way, the vessel would not have been wrecked ! "

He thus refers to the assertion that the Constitution, though Pro-Slavery now might be amended, and that he could vote meanwhile in that hope :

"It is necessary to swear to support it *as it is*. What it may become we know not. We speak of it as it is and repudiate it as it is. We will not brand it as Pro-Slavery after it has ceased to be so. This objection to our position reminds me of Miss Martineau's story of the little boy who hurt himself and sat crying on the sidewalk. ' Don't cry,' said a friend, ' it won't hurt you to-morrow.' ' Well, then,' whimpered the child, ' I won't cry to-morrow ! ' "

To the common statement that his position was that of a hot-head and a zealot, he responded :

"History, from the earliest Christians downward, is full of instances of men who refused all connection with government and all the influences which office could bestow rather than deny their principles or aid in wrong-doing. Sir Thomas More need never have mounted the scaffold, had he only consented to take the oath of supremacy. He had only to tell a lie with solemnity, as we are asked to do, and he might not only have saved his life, but, as the trimmers of his day would have told him, doubled his influence. Pitt resigned his place as Prime Minister of England rather than break faith with the Catholics of Ireland. Should I not resign a ballot rather than break faith with the slave?"

Further, and in the same connection, he adds:

"An act of conscience is always a grand act. Whether right or wrong it represents the best self of our nature. While an under-clerk in the War Office, Granville Sharp, that patriarch of the Anti-Slavery enterprise in England, sympathized with America in our struggle for independence. Orders reached his office to ship munitions of war to the revolted Colonies. If his hand had entered the account of such a cargo it would have contracted, in his eyes, the stain of innocent blood. To avoid this pollution, he resigned his place and means of subsistence at a period of life when he could no longer hope to find lucrative employment. As the thoughtful clerk of the War Office takes down his hat from the peg where it had hung for twenty years, methinks I hear one of our critics cry out: 'Friend Sharp, you are absurdly scrupulous; you may innocently aid Government in doing wrong.' While the Liberty party yelps at his heels: 'My dear sir, you are losing your influence!' And indeed it is melancholy to reflect how, from that moment, the mighty under-clerk of the War Office (!) dwindled into the mere Granville Sharp of history! the man of whom Mansfield and Hargrave were content to learn law, and Wilberforce philanthropy."

These are hap-hazard snatches made in turning the pages of Mr. Phillips's "Anti-Slavery Catechism." Those who would get a clear insight into the moral situation in the 'forties should read it from cover to cover. It is more than a polemic—it is a picture.

IX.

INFIDELITY IN THE 'FORTIES.

At the period now under review, with one or two small but honorable exceptions, like the Freewill Baptists and the Free Presbyterians, the churches were all the apologists and often the defenders of man-stealing. Thus the Christianity of America was three thousand years behind the Judaism of Moses, which denounced man-stealing. Individual pulpits and individual church-members, shining lights in this dreary midnight, were found in all the historic denominations refusing to quench their beams. But exceptions do not break—they prove the rule. As organized bodies, the churches admitted slave-holders to their communion, installed them in their pulpits, and screened their sin with palliative resolutions. At the same time they branded the Abolitionists as fanatics, meddling with what did not concern them, and anathematized them as infidels, assaulting the administration of Providence.

For example, the Rev. Wilbur Fisk, the leader of New England Methodism, declared that "the general rule of Christianity not only permits, but in supposable circumstances enjoins a continuance of the Master's authority." A New England Methodist bishop maintained that the right to hold slaves is founded on this *dictum:* "'Therefore all things whatsoever ye would that men should do to you, do ye even so to them.'"

The Inquisitors used to torture their victims into confessing whatever they chose to extort. But the worst instance of Inquisitorial torture on record is this which wrings a justification of slavery from the Golden Rule. Oh sapient commentator, go into history as Bishop Columbus, for you discovered what no one else ever dreamed of, that the Golden Rule, which seems to teach that men should do as they would be done unto, teaches instead the right of men to do as they would not be done unto!

The Rev. Dr. Wayland, President of the Brown University, the Coryphæus of the Baptists, published a book in which he taught that "the people of the North are in such relation to the people of the South that they ought not to agitate the question of slavery, and that it would be an act of bad faith for Congress to abolish slavery in the District of Columbia." Among the Congregationalists Professor Moses Stuart, at Andover Seminary, and President Lord, at Dartmouth College, were the thick and thin defenders of slavery; while their most prominent and influential pulpits were occupied by pastors who preached Christ at the North so as not to offend the devil at the South. The Presbyterians, the Episcopalians, the Unitarians, the Universalists, the Quakers, wide apart as the poles, and swearing prayers at one another, on other points, were cordially at one in this, and in the contemplation of the Southern "form of economic subordination" were drawn into a brotherhood of wonder and delight.

If such was the feeling among the churches in the free States, the situation in the slave States may be imagined. There, with absolutely no exceptions, pastors and laymen preached and practised the Gospel according to St. John—C. Calhoun. A certain prominent pulpiteer of South Carolina died one day—for even slave-holding saints were not immortal—his estate was sold at auction, and was advertised in the following terms:

"A plantation on and in Wateree Swamp (a good place for a slave plantation); a library, chiefly theological; twenty-seven negroes, some of them very prime; two mules, one horse, and an old wagon."[1]

Well, in these circumstances, as the Abolitionists had not hesitated to attack the State, so neither did they hesitate to attack the Church. They recognized in these twain one flesh. It was the Siamese twins over again. The State was *Chang* and the Church was *Eng*. Many of the Anti-Slavery apostles, who had set out in orthodox standing, were disgusted into unbelief, Garrison himself among the rest. Mr. Phillips held fast to his ancestral faith. He denounced the Church as it existed precisely as he denounced the State. But he saved his Christian creed by making a distinction which will bear examination, and which may be needed again some time. He distinguished between *Christianity* and *Churchianity*. While he held that the one was divine, he perceived that the other was human. Christ was God manifest. The Church was an institution which accepted so much of His spirit and works as it could or would embody. As Phariseeism, when the Nazarine was in Judea, had formal-

---

[1] See this whole subject treated in detail in "Garrison and his Times," *passim*, but particularly in chap. xiv.

ized the life out of religion and represented the show, not the substance of the divine in the human, so now he held that the nominal Christianity around about him was a body out of which the soul had gone. And he comforted himself with the reflection that the true Church, always and everywhere, is composed of those who are likest and nearest to Christ. Hence he made a solitude in his own heart and set up an altar and worshipped there apart.[1] Meanwhile he drew his ideals and borrowed his methods from Jesus of Nazareth, "in whom lives the moral earnestness of the world."[2] He said: "The men who have learned of him most closely— Paul, Luther, Wesley—have marked their own age and moulded for good all after-time."[3]

Holding these views he was nothing disturbed by the charges of infidelity with which the churches pelted him, no more than he was by the State's indictment of him as a traitor. Treason to a Pro-Slavery Constitution and infidelity to a Pro-Slavery religion he considered the highest patriotism and the truest Christianity. As James Otis thundered against the despot in England, so he thundered against the tyrant in America. As the Master Himself smote Phariseeism eighteen hundred years ago, so he "spoke daggers" against the Pharisees of the nineteenth century. Thus, in one of his most trenchant speeches, he exclaimed:

"When the pulpit preached slave-hunting, and the law bound

---

[1] For Mr. Phillips's own statement of his religious convictions, see pp. 431-439.

[2] "Sketches and Reminiscences of the Radical Club," by Mrs. J. T. Sargent, p. 81.

[3] *Ib.*, p. 147.

the victim, and Society said, 'Amen! this will make money,' we were 'fanatics,' 'seditious,' 'scorners of the pulpit,' 'traitors.' Genius of the past, drop not from thy tablets one of those honorable names! We claim them all as our surest title-deeds to the memory and gratitude of mankind. We, indeed, thought man more than Constitutions, humanity and justice of more worth than law. Seal up the record! If America is proud of her part, let her rest assured we are not ashamed of ours!"[1]

---

[1] The Sims Anniversary, "Speeches and Lectures," pp. 75, 76.

X.

THE AGITATOR.

Mr. Phillips was now the loneliest man on the continent—almost as "solitary" as G. P. R. James's famous horseman in the novel. He had discarded the State and had left the Church, not, like some of his friends, because of any disagreement with the philosophy of Government, or of any quarrel with Christianity, to which he stoutly adhered, but as a protest against the prostitution of State and Church to wicked ends and unholy uses.

In reflecting upon his ways and means of life and usefulness in these days, he was obliged to acknowledge that all the old arenas were closed against him — the Court, the State House, the Sanctuary. Providentially he had an independent income, so that poverty was not an added discomfort. But desiring and fitted to influence the world for good, along what lines should he exert himself? Surrounded by mountainous oppositions, how should he level them? Face to face with triumphant majorities on the wrong side, how could he swing them over to the right side?

These self-communings led Mr. Phillips to invent and adopt his characteristic method of *agitation*. He was the first and greatest American agitator. He made a platform outside of the State, outside of the Church, untrammelled by any limitations save those which inhere in human nature, with no political and no ecclesiastical creed to guard, a platform devoted to the freest, broadest, most critical discussion of questions and issues ; and this platform he put on wheels and moved from Maine to California, himself its central and commanding figure. This was his place of business, his Senate, his Rialto, his temple. And he made a business of summoning parties, sects, trades, social usages, for judgment to his peripatetic Faneuil Hall. Others for a special purpose dipped into agitation, as a bather wades into the surf, and then returned to their wonted vocations. He had no other calling, but trod the platform as king in a realm unique.

Mr. Phillips expected that the throne he first founded and filled would survive him and find an endless succession of occupants, because he claimed for this function of outside observation and criticism an essential and permanent place in American life, and he based this claim upon a profound philosophy. This philosophy embraced five cardinal principles. Let us consider these principles, for a clear understanding of them is necessary in order to an intelligent appreciation of his character and career :

1. He believed absolutely in the supreme power of ideas. Charge these with the dynamite of righteousness and conscience and they would blow any and every form of opposition to atoms. " The man who launches a sound argument," he said, " who sets on two feet a startling fact and bids it travel across the continent, is just as certain that in the end he will change the government, as if to destroy the Capitol he had placed gunpowder under the Senate

Chamber."[1] Hence he discountenanced force in a republic. Why resort to bayonets when ideas are stronger? He had no patience with anarchy and anarchists. "Agitation," said he, "is an old word with a new meaning. Sir Robert Peel defined it to be 'the marshalling of the conscience of a nation to mould its laws.' It is above-board—no oath-bound secret societies like those of old times in Ireland and of the Continent to-day. Its means are reason and arguments; no appeal to arms. Wait patiently for the slow growth of public opinion. The Frenchman is angry with his government: he throws up barricades and shots his guns to the lips. A week's fury drags the nation ahead a hand-breadth, reaction lets it settle half-way back again. As Lord Chesterfield said, a hundred years ago: 'You Frenchmen erect barricades, but never any barriers.' An Englishman is dissatisfied with public affairs: he brings his charges, offers his proofs, waits for prejudice to relax, for public opinion to inform itself. Then every step taken is taken forever; an abuse once removed never reappears in history."[2]

2. Next to ideas Mr. Phillips believed in the people—in the average common-sense and capacity of the millions. He never wearied of appealing from the people ill-informed to the people well-informed. This was the root of his republicanism, and the reason why he claimed for the most ignorant the ballot and the school, and all other educational appliances. Listen to him on this point:

"' *Vox populi, vox Dei.*' I do not mean this of any single

---

[1] Speech on Public Opinion, "Speeches and Lectures," p. 45.
[2] Lecture on Daniel O'Connell, see Appendix.

verdict which the people of to-day may record. In time the selfishness of one class neutralizes the selfishness of another. The people always mean right, and in the end they will do right. I believe in the twenty millions—not the twenty millions that live now, necessarily—to arrange this question of slavery, which priests and politicians have sought to keep out of sight. They have it locked up in the Senate Chamber; they have hidden it behind the communion-table; they have appealed to the superstitious and idolatrous veneration for the State and the Union to avoid this question, and so have kept it from the influence of the great democratic tendencies of the masses. But change all this, drag it from its concealment, and give it to the people; launch it on the age and all is safe. It will find a safe harbor." [1]

3. These words suggest another point in Mr. Phillips's philosophy of agitation, viz., the moral timidity of men under free institutions. He remarks:

"It is a singular fact that, the freer a nation becomes, the more utterly democratic the form of its institutions, this outside agitation, this pressure of public opinion to direct political action, becomes more and more necessary. The general judgment is, that the freest possible government produces the freest possible men and women, the most individual, the least servile to the judgment of others. But a moment's reflection will show any man that this is an unreasonable expectation, and that, on the contrary, entire equality and freedom in political forms almost inevitably tend to make the individual subside into the mass and lose his identity in the general whole. Suppose we stood in England to-night. There is the nobility and here is the Church. There is the trading-class and here is the literary. A broad gulf separates the four, and provided a member of either can conciliate his own section, he can afford in a very large measure to despise the judgment of the other three. He has to some extent a refuge and a breakwater against the tyranny of what we call public opinion. But in a country like ours, of absolute democratic equality, public opinion is not only omnipotent, it is omnipresent. There is no refuge from its tyranny; there is no

---

[1] 'Speeches and Lectures,'' pp. 45, 46.

hiding from its reach ; and the result is that, if you take the old Greek lantern and go about to seek among a hundred you will find not one single American who really has not, or who does not fancy at least that he has, something to gain or lose in his ambition, his social life, or his business from the good opinion and the votes of those around him. And the consequence is that, instead of being a mass of individuals, each one fearlessly blurting out his own convictions, as a nation, compared with other nations, we are a mass of cowards. More than all other people we are afraid of each other."[1]

The great agencies through which public opinion here finds expression are, the pulpit, parties, and the press. These he thought inadequate to deal with what the French call "burning questions," like slavery, woman suffrage, temperance, and labor, with issues ahead of public opinion, partly from preoccupation, but chiefly because, in the nature of the case, they voice and are bound by the average sentiment. Hear him again :

"The pulpit, for instance, has a sphere of its own. It is too busy getting men to heaven to concern itself with worldly duties and obligations. And when it tries to direct the parish in political and social ways, it is baffled by the fact that among its supporters are men of all parties and of all social grades, ready to take offence at any word which relates to their earthly pursuits or interests, and spoken in a tone of criticism or rebuke. As the minister's settlement and salary depend upon the unity and good-will of the people he preaches to, he cannot fairly be expected, save in exceptional and special cases, to antagonize his flock. If all clergymen were like Paul, or Luther, or Wesley, they might give, not take orders. But as the average clergyman is an average man he will be bound by average conditions."[2]

---

[1] Lecture on O'Connell, see Appendix.
[2] Extract from a lecture on Agitation which Mr. Phillips delivered far and wide for many years, but of which no extended report is now available.

The defect thus indicated in the Church, Mr. Phillips also discovered in parties and the press:

"If you were a caucus to-night and I were your orator, none of you could get beyond the necessary and timid limitations of party. You not only would not demand, you would not allow me to utter one word of what you really thought and what I thought. You would demand of me—and my value as a caucus-speaker would depend entirely on the adroitness and the vigilance with which I met the demand—that I should not utter one single word which would compromise the vote of next week. That is politics. So with the press. Seemingly independent, and sometimes really so, the press can afford only to mount the cresting wave, not go beyond it. The editor might as well shoot his reader with a bullet as with a new idea. He must hit the exact line of the opinion of the day. I am not finding fault with him; I am only describing him. Some three years ago I took to one of the freest of the Boston journals a letter, and by appropriate consideration induced its editor to print it. As we glanced along its contents and came to the concluding statement, he said: 'Couldn't you omit that?' I said, 'No; I wrote it for that; it is the gist of the statement.' 'Well,' said he, 'it is true; there is not a boy in the streets who does not know that it is true; but I wish you could omit that.' I insisted, and the next morning, fairly and justly, he printed the whole. Side by side he put an article of his own in which he said: 'We copy in the next column an article from Mr. Phillips, and we only regret the absurd and unfounded statement with which he concludes it.' He had kept his promise by printing the article; he saved his reputation by printing the comment. And that, again, is the inevitable, the essential limitation of the press in a republican community. Our institutions, floating unanchored on the shifting surface of popular opinion, cannot afford to hold back or to draw forward a hated question, and compel a reluctant public to look at it and to consider it. Hence, as you see at once, the moment a large issue, twenty years ahead of its age, presents itself to the consideration of an empire or of a republic, just in proportion to the freedom of its institutions is the necessity of a platform outside of the press, of politics, and of the Church, whereon stand men with no candidate to elect, with no plan to carry, with no reputation to stake, with no object but the truth, no purpose but to tear the question open and let the light through it." [1]

4. Another principle in Mr. Phillips's theory touched the reign of public opinion in a republic like ours, whose sceptre is at once omnipotent and irresolute:

"Each man here, in fact, holds his property and his life dependent on the constant presence of an agitation like this of Anti-Slavery. Eternal vigilance is the price of liberty; power is ever stealing from the many to the few. The manna of popular liberty must be gathered each day or it is rotten. The living sap of to-day outgrows the dead rind of yesterday. The hand intrusted with power becomes, either from human depravity or *esprit de corps*, the necessary enemy of the people. Only by continual oversight can the democrat in office be prevented from hardening into a despot; only by unintermitted agitation can a people be kept sufficiently awake to principle not to let liberty be smothered in material prosperity. . . .

"Some men suppose that, in order to the people's governing themselves, it is only necessary, as Fisher Ames said, that the 'Rights of man be printed and that every citizen have a copy;' as the Epicureans two thousand years ago imagined God a being who arranged this marvellous machinery, set it going, and then sunk to sleep. Republics exist only on the tenure of being constantly agitated. The Anti-Slavery agitation is an important, nay, an essential part of the machinery of the State. It is not a disease nor a medicine. No; it is the normal state—the normal state of the nation. Never, to our latest posterity, can we afford to do without prophets like Garrison, to stir up the monotony of wealth and reawake the people to the great ideas that are constantly fading out of our minds—to trouble the waters that there may be health in their flow." [2]

5. Mr. Phillips's final axiom as an agitator was,

---

[1] Lecture on O'Connell, see Appendix.
[2] "Speeches and Lectures," p. 52, 53.

"The truth, the whole truth, and nothing but the truth." That is, he acted on the platform as a witness acts who is put under oath to testify in a case at law. "No concealing half of one's convictions to make the other half more acceptable ; no denial of one truth to gain a hearing for another ; no compromise ; or, as O'Connell phrased it, ' Nothing is politically right which is morally wrong :' " such was his *dictum*. Under this rule he used a plainness of speech which appalled because it was unusual. He was the one outspoken man in a nation of euphemizers. He called a spade a *spade*, not " an agricultural instrument." He insisted that debts were *debts*, not " pecuniary obligations." He said slavery is *slavery*, not " a form of economic subordination." The wisdom of this is clear when we remember how a soft name softens a sin, and how the bare, hard name reveals and brands a sin and sometimes alarms and convicts the sinner. Said he :

"What is the denunciation with which we are charged ? It is endeavoring, in our faltering human speech, to declare the enormity of the sin of making merchandise of men—of separating husband and wife, taking the infant from its mother, and selling the daughter to prostitution—of a professedly Christian nation denying, by statute, the Bible to every sixth man and woman of its population, and making it illegal for ' two or three ' to meet together except a white man be present ! What is this harsh criticism of motives with which we are charged ? It is simply holding the intelligent and deliberate actor responsible for the character and consequences of his acts. Is there anything inherently wrong in such denunciation or such criticism ? This we may claim—we have never judged a man but out of his own mouth. We have seldom, if ever, held him to account, except for the acts of which he and his own friends were proud. All that we ask the world and thoughtful men to note are the principles and deeds on which the American pulpit and American public men plume themselves. We always allow our opponents to paint their own pictures. Our humble duty is to stand by and assure the spectators that what they would take for a knave or a hypocrite is really, in American estimation, a Doctor of Divinity or Secretary of State." [1]

In vindicating Daniel O'Connell's kindred plainness of speech at a later day, he applies his words to his own position :

"O'Connell has been charged with coarse, violent, and intemperate language. The criticism is of little importance. Stupor and palsy never understand life. White-livered indifference is always disgusted and annoyed by earnest conviction. Protestants criticised Luther in the same way. It took three centuries to carry us far off enough to appreciate his colossal proportions. It is a hundred years to-day since O'Connell was born. It will take another hundred to put us at such an angle as will enable us correctly to measure his stature. Premising that it would be folly to find fault with a man struggling for life because his attitudes were ungraceful, remembering the Scythian king's answer to Alexander, criticising his strange weapon : 'If you knew how precious freedom was, you would defend it even with axes,' we must see that O'Connell's own explanation is evidently sincere and true. He found the Irish heart so cowed and Englishmen so arrogant, that he saw it needed an independence verging on insolence, a defiance that touched the extremest limits, to breathe self-respect into his own race, teach the aggressor manners, and sober him into respectful attention. It was the same with us Abolitionists. Webster had taught the North the bated breath and crouching of the slave. It needed with us an attitude of independence that was almost insolent ; it needed that we should exhaust even the Saxon vocabulary of scorn, to fitly utter the righteous and haughty contempt that honest men had for man-stealers. Only in that way could we wake the North to self-respect, or teach the South that at length she had met her equal, if not her master. On a broad canvas meant for the public square the tiny lines of a Dutch interior would be invisi-

---

[1] Speeches and Lectures," pp. 107, 108.

ble. In no other circumstances was the French maxim, 'You can never make a revolution with rose-water,' more profoundly true. The world has hardly yet learned how deep a philosophy lies in Hamlet's—

> 'Nay, and thou'lt mouth,
> I'll rant as well as thou.' "[1]

Thus, as far as possible, in the Agitator's own language have we outlined his philosophy of agitation. It cannot be denied that he gave a reason for the faith that was in him, and that he opened a school whose influence was continental when he was at the head of it. Whether it shall last, as he supposed it would, it is for the future to decide.

---

[1] See the Address on O'Connell in the Appendix.

XI.

EGERIA.

It was the peculiar good fortune of Mr. Phillips, in his public isolation, to have a congenial home. The modest dwelling on Essex Street was more than his castle—as the British orator declared every Englishman's house to be—it was his sanctuary. When Numa, the second King of Rome, undertook to pacify the turbulency and refine the manners of the ancient city (so runs the legend), he visited a secret grotto and held converse with a hidden goddess named Egeria, whom he proclaimed his counsellor and inspiration and by whose authority he reinforced his own. The wife of the democratic monarch of the American forum was his Egeria. Few saw her —almost as invisible, through illness, as the old Roman divinity. The world felt her through him. Among his intimates Mr. Phillips was never tired of quoting her wise opinions and clever sayings. He proudly acknowledged his dependence upon her for moral guidance and initiative. Thus, in a letter to Elizabeth Pease, he writes:

"Ann is as usual: little sleep; very weak; never goes downstairs; interested keenly in all good things, and sometimes, I tell her, so much my motive and prompter to everything good that I fear, should I lose her, there'd be nothing left of me worth your loving." [1]

---

[1] "Memorial of Ann Phillips," pp. 14, 15.

Never was there a more genial and intellectual atmosphere than that in the chamber of the charming Egeria of Wendell Phillips. Her broad, modern culture, joined to a deep knowledge of classic lore, and stored in a brilliant mind, made her companionship an education to the favored few who penetrated into that rare sick-room, and, as he was always avowing, an inspiration to her husband.

Strange to say, considering the nature and length of the sufferer's complaint, the tone was never morbid at this fireside. Comedy, not tragedy, held the stage there, for these two were famous laughers. It was a saying of his that "there was more sun and fun in Essex Street than anywhere else in Boston."[1] Of course the laugh faded into seriousness when deep topics were considered, when she was to be comforted in pain and he was to be strengthened for duty. Unceasing were their mutual thoughts, constant their acts of self-sacrifice for one another, never-ending the counsel they took. She habitually discussed with him, before he left home to attend a convention or to deliver an important address, those aspects of current questions which she thought he ought specially to urge or emphasize.[2] The two were united in their views, or only so much at difference as gave added charm and piquancy to their intercourse. And he cared more for her approval than for all the plaudits of the admiring thousands who thrilled beneath his electric speech.[3]

To a relative who was familiar with the household economy of the Phillipses, we are indebted for a

---

[1] So says Dr. Samuel A. Green, ex-Mayor of Boston, an old friend and neighbor of Mr. Phillips.
[2] "Memorial of Ann Phillips," p. 6.   [3] *Ib.*

glimpse into it, as attractive as an interior by Rembrandt :

"To those whom Mrs. Phillips admitted to visit her freely there was seldom any symptom of depression or despondency visible. The sunny south chamber, having an outlook down Harrison Avenue, was bright with flowers, of which the invalid was passionately fond. In midwinter she would have nasturtiums, smilax, and costly exotics, later the brilliant tulips, and then the blossoms of spring, the May-flowers and anemones, until the garden rose and sweetbrier appeared. All these were supplied by loving hands and caused her unceasing delight. Nor did her personal appearance often betoken invalidism. She had a good color, a strong voice, and a hearty laugh, so that it was difficult to think her ill. Conversation never flagged. She was eager to hear about and discuss the news of the day, especially in Anti-Slavery and reformatory lines ; she took the warmest interest in the affairs of her friends, and to the poor and needy, who brought stories of sorrow and suffering and wrongs endured, her sympathy and aid were freely given, as were her husband's. There was no lack of cheer and merriment and sparkling humor from husband and wife, when two or three chosen friends were gathered in the sick-room, and shouts of laughter from it resounded through the house. ' Gay as the gayest bird is Ann T. Greene,' was written of her by a rhyming schoolmate when she was a girl, and she continued to merit the characterization. She was very fond of music, as was her father before her, and, debarred from going to concerts, she found pleasure in listening to the strains of the hand-organs which were frequently played beneath her window." [1]

When Mr. Phillips was going out his wife habitually said :

"Wendell, don't forget the organ money !"

This was as surely left, and as confidently expected by the musical mechanic who ground out the arias of sunny Italy in these daily serenades, as the sunrise.[2]

---

[1] "Memorial of Ann Phillips," pp. 15, 16.
[2] So the author was told by Mrs. Bannard, of Long Branch, N. J.

Mr. Phillips personally visited the markets every morning in search of delicacies to gratify the invalid's appetite, and might be seen wending his way homeward with his hands full of parcels "for Ann."[1] In the Phillips snuggery the meals were always served in the wife's apartment, he on this side she on that of a tiny table.

"We eat in French," said Mr. Phillips, referring to a habit they had of always conversing at such time in the language of Molière.

He was a good eater and a good sleeper, capital sanitary points, and the secret, no doubt, of his excellent health and spirits. He often quoted and commended the saying of Cobbett, the English political economist, that "the seat of civilization is the stomach;" to which he would tack on by way of climax, "add an easy conscience and a pillow steeped in poppy juice."

As the colonial women abjured tea in the pre-Revolutionary days and discountenanced the king by banishing the teapot, so Mrs. Phillips would use neither cane sugar on her table nor employ cotton fabrics in her household, so long as these were the product of slave labor. This was what she called an *argumentum ad hominem*—logic that would percolate through the pockets into the heads of the labor-stealers.

Mr. Phillips was constantly out in the thick and throng of the world. He saw everybody; had all sort of adventures. As his wife could not share his experiences at first hand, he made her his companion at second-hand. He was eyes and ears for her, and

---

[1] "Memorial," p. 16.

retailed at home what he got at wholesale abroad. No story ever lost anything in his telling of it, and in this way he twice enjoyed the manifold events of his stirring life.

Both were passionately fond of children. Deprived of any of their own, they adopted the children of their friends, with whom their house often ran over. Mrs. Phillips would see them when she denied herself to their elders. And Mr. Phillips had a rare faculty of opening or preparing his mail, and even of conducting his reading, while simultaneously carrying on an animated conversation with these little friends, always adapting himself to their level of interests and pursuits.[1] There are many now in middle life who held the love of this couple from early childhood, and whose gratitude for the bestowment grows with the lapse of time. That they were wise counsellors, the following half-sportive lines, written by Mr. Phillips at a later day, on the cars, while he was returning with a party from a visit to New York, will attest. They were pencilled on the fly-leaf of a little book for children called "Spectacles for Young Eyes," which had been requested as a souvenir of the jaunt by him (now an honorable and useful man) to whom the lines were addressed:

TO F. H. S.

   Frank
      Better loves to read
         Than to play.
  Hear him with mother plead,
 "Bring me a book from far away."
   Books—

---

[1] Mrs. Bannard is authority for this.

>   The mind's food—
>   Are good.
>   But never clutch
>   Too much.
> Good soul, sound stomach, sound brain,
>   These are the chain
> Which holds the world in your hand,
>   And govern the land.
>   These serve God the best,
>   "Till He gives you rest."
>   If you'd fill life with true joy,
>   My boy,
> While you use these "Spectacles
>   For Young Eyes,"
>   Remember to get strong
>   As well as wise.[1]

In the summer the town house was invariably exchanged for two or three months of country air and green meadows and bright birds, and the time was devoted to experimenting with various methods of treatment for Mrs. Phillips, all of which proved futile.[2] One of these was mesmerism, and, referring to the difficulty of securing a good operator and to her husband's being the best she had, the wife writes humorously to her English friend, Miss Pease:

"January 31, 1846.

"So the poor, devoted Wendell is caught one hour of his busy day and seated down to *hold my thumbs*. I grow sicker every year, Wendell lovelier; I more desponding, he always cheery, and telling me I shall live not only to be 'fat and forty,' but fat and scolding at eighty!"

---

[1] Given to the writer by Mrs. J. T. Sargent, whose son is the one referred to.
[2] "Memorial of Ann Phillips," p. 16.

The letter concludes:

"Dear Wendell has met with a sad affliction this fall in the death of his mother, who left us in November. She was everything to him—indeed, to all her children; a devoted mother and uncommon woman. . . . So poor unworthy I am more of a treasure to Wendell than ever, and a pretty frail one. For his sake I should love to live; for my own part I am tired, not of life, but of a sick one." [1]

On the same sheet Mr. Phillips speaks of his bereavement:

"Dear Ann has spoken of my mother's death. My good, noble, dear mother! We differed utterly on the matter of slavery, and she grieved a good deal over what she thought was a waste of my time and a sad disappointment to her; but still I am always best satisfied with myself when I fancy I can see anything in me which reminds me of my mother. She lived in her children, and they almost lived in her, and the world is a different one now she is gone." [2]

With such a mother and such a wife, no wonder Wendell Phillips thought highly of women. A man's judgment of women is the infallible index not only of his own refinement, but even more of the character of his feminine belongings. A mother moulds her son, a wife moulds her husband either into respect or into disrespect for her whole sex. Motive how powerful for lofty thought and a life above frivolity!

On the death of his mother, Mr. Phillips installed in a place of honor among the servants in his house, the dearly loved nurse of his childhood,[3] who now became his cook. This woman loved him in return with a passionate devotion. She habitually left the

---
[1] "Memorial of Ann Phillips," pp. 16, 17.
[2] *Ib.*, p. 17
[3] *Ante*, p. 12.

door into the kitchen open that she might hear him pass and repass, and said :

"Bless him, there is more music in his footfall than in a cathedral organ!"

Long afterward when she was too old for work he placed her in a home of her own, went to see her every Saturday with his arms full of remembrances, and took care of her until she died.[1]

Affairs in this house moved with the precision of machinery. At ten o'clock all was whist. When, as was often the case, a lecture engagement or a public meeting kept him out beyond that hour, he let himself in quietly and soon retired. Rising at seven in the morning, breakfast was ready at half-past seven, dinner was served at two o'clock, and a plain supper relieved the kitchen at half-past six.

Mr. Phillips was never happier than when engaged in tinkering. His mechanical tastes have been already referred to. When a door was to be eased, a fireplace to be overhauled, a window to be tightened, he went about hammer or saw in hand supremely satisfied. Of the kitchen, however, he stood in awe, never intruding there. Nor did he meddle with the "help." Characteristically he was on hand for service, never for interference. He was always amiable and easy about the house. No one ever heard him scold—a gentleman off as well as on parade, and he was appreciative of all that was done for him and was never exacting. Hence the servants idolized him and remained for years. He paid the best wages of anybody in the neighborhood, and contended that this was the best policy, as it

---

[1] Recollections of Mrs. John T. Sargent (verbal).

promoted contentment and secured a prompt response to all calls. "Good pay, good service," was his oracular remark.

Mrs. Phillips was a fitful sleeper. Her husband occupied a room just back of hers, and she frequently aroused him a dozen times in the course of the night. The family physician testifies that when calling in the early morning he often counted fifteen burned matches strewn about, mute witnesses to the number of her calls and his answers![1] And this continued more than forty-six years without a murmur on his part!

He was not a great talker at home. Indeed, Mrs. Phillips used to say that "Silence would reign at 26 Essex Street unless she broke it." When he came in from without, however, and had a budget of news to open, he would be all animation. These were the occasions when "laughter, holding both his sides," made the house merry.

Mr. Phillips was a constant student. When he was not with his wife, or was not engaged in one or another of those pottering excursions, he was busy with his books or devouring the newspapers, of which he took a vast number of all shades of opinion. In preparing his speeches he went down to the second floor, entered his "den," as he called the room where he kept his intellectual belongings, locked the door, and denied himself to every one, sometimes for days, only emerging to eat and sleep. His favorite position when so engaged was to lie on the sofa, where on his back he thought his way through and

---

[1] So Dr. David Thayer, of Boston, the physician referred to, informed the writer.

out.[1] He disliked the pen, and a letter from him was a supreme token of his regard. "Writing," he used to say, "is a mild form of slavery—a man chained to an ink-pot."

Such was the orator at home.

---

[1] The author had these details from the lips of one who passed many years under Mr. Phillips's roof.

XII.

CONCERNING A SINGULAR EPIDEMIC.

It is the judicious remark of one of the annalists of the Anti-Slavery movement, that "at the bottom of all the wretched casuistry by which men silenced the demands of justice in their hearts was this one fact—the slaves were black; or, to use the word more deeply freighted with atheistic contempt of human nature than any other, 'niggers.' If by a miracle the slaves had been suddenly made white, all excuses for slavery would have been overthrown, and the whole people would have risen up as one man to demand its instant abolition. The primary fault of the Abolitionists, in popular estimation, was their belief in the absolute humanity of the negroes." [1]

Colorphobia was now epidemic. A black skin dehumanized the wearer of it. Negroes were held to be cattle, and they were treated like cattle. If a black presumed to take the position of a man, or to claim any human rights at a hotel, in travelling, in business, or even at church, he was pelted back with insults and trampled down with oaths. "Jim Crow" cars were set apart for them on the railroads, and "negro pews" in the house of Him who said, "God hath made of one blood all nations of men to serve Him."

---

[1] "Garrison and his Times," pp. 36, 37.

The author just quoted tells the following story:

"A colored merchant from Liberia, a man of intelligence as well as wealth, and highly esteemed by Colonizationists, being on a visit to Boston, took the opportunity of making the acquaintance of the Abolitionists As he wished to hear Dr. Beecher preach, I invited him, as an act of courtesy to a distinguished foreigner, to take a seat in my pew. On my way out of church I encountered the indignant frowns of a large number of the congregation, but it was amusing to witness the change of countenance that fell upon the advocates of colonization as I introduced to them ' Mr. ——, of Liberia.' They really seemed to think his odor was not quite so offensive, after all, as they had suspected. The air of Liberia was such a powerful disinfectant! The slave-holders used to think the atmosphere of their home was perfectly delectable when slaves in kitchen, dining-room, parlor, and boudoir were as all-pervading as flies; but there was no odor so offensive to them as that imparted to a negro when he was set free; and Northern people in the days of slavery, while they required the free negro to occupy a separate apartment on steamboat and rail-car, as being personally offensive to white olfactories, never thought of remonstrating when the slave-holders (in the hot summer weather, too!) claimed for their slaves all the privileges of first-class travellers. Strange that in a republican country freedom was so offensive, while slavery was so fragrant!"[1]

All this was infinitely hateful to Wendell Phillips. He set himself to resist it by word and deed with tireless energy. "Emerson," remarks Mr. Higginson, "while thoroughly true to the Anti-Slavery movement, always confessed to feeling a slight instinctive aversion to negroes; Theodore Parker uttered frankly his dislike of the Irish. Yet neither of these had distinctly aristocratic impulses, while Phillips had. His conscience set them aside so imperatively that he himself hardly knew that they

---

[1] "Garrison and his Times," pp. 100, 101.

were there. He was always ready to be identified with the colored people; always ready to give his oft-repeated lecture on O'Connell to the fellow-countrymen of that hero; but in these and all cases his democratic habit had the good-natured air of some kindly young prince; he never was quite the equal associate that he seemed. The want of it never was felt by his associates; it was in his dealings with antagonists that the real attitude came out. When he once spoke contemptuously of those who dined with a certain Boston club which had censured him, as 'men of no family,' the real mental habit appeared. And in his external aspect and bearing the patrician air never left him—the air that he had in college days, or in that period when, as Edmund Quincy delighted to tell, an English visitor pointed out to George Ticknor two men walking down Park Street, and added the cheerful remark, 'They are the only men I have seen in your country who look like gentlemen.' The two men were the Abolitionists Quincy and Phillips, in whose personal aspect the conservative Ticknor could see little to commend."[1]

To return to Mr. Phillips's treatment of the satanic caste spirit of those days: he brought the question before the School Committee of his native city in 1846. Colored children were not allowed to study the three R's with white children, but were sent off into hovels and herded in exclusion, to catch their learning from the lips of inferior teachers. The very text-books seemed to protest against this wickedness; for they were printed on *white* paper in *black*

---

[1] Obituary notice of Wendell Phillips, p. 15.

ink—every one of them an object-lesson on the subject of equality. To the petition he stirred, and which prayed for abolition of the caste schools, the Committee returned a brutal denial. They were indiscreet enough to assign what they called their "reasons," which were utterly unreasonable, and the city solicitor accompanied their response with a confirmatory opinion. This gave Mr. Phillips an opportunity which he eagerly embraced to dissect the attorney's argument, and to rub red pepper in the wounds made by his knife.[1] Nor did he permit the matter to rest here. He brought it up again and again, made it the "Banquo's ghost" of the School Committee, until a few years later they were driven to yield the point, and the free schools of Boston became free indeed. At the annual meeting of the Massachusetts Anti-Slavery Society, which occurred soon afterward, the pertinacious Abolitionist published his victory in this resolution:

"*Resolved*, That this society rejoices in the abolition of the separate colored schools in the city of Boston as the triumph of law and justice over the pride of caste and wealth, and recognizes in it the marked advance of the Anti-Slavery sentiments of the State."[2]

At the same time he appealed to the Legislature of Massachusetts to compel the railroads as common carriers to admit colored men to the cars their tickets demanded, and, in the end, with equal success. Meanwhile, he made it a habit to share with any black man in whose company he found himself whatever accommodations the unfortunate was forced to occupy. Frederick Douglass mentions several in-

---

[1] *Vide Liberator*, vol. xv.   [2] *Ib.*, vol. xxv.

stances in which he had this gracious companionship :

"On one occasion, for instance, after delivering a lecture to the New Bedford Lyceum before a highly cultivated audience, when brought to the railroad station (as I was not allowed to travel in a first-class car, but was compelled to ride in a filthy box called the 'Jim Crow' car), he stepped to my side in the presence of his aristocratic friends, and walked with me straight into this miserable dog-car, saying, 'Douglass, if you cannot ride with me, I can ride with you.' On the Sound, between New York and Newport, in those dark days a colored passenger was not allowed abaft the wheels of the steamer, and had to spend the night on the forward deck, with horses, sheep, and swine. On such trips, when I was a passenger, Wendell Phillips preferred to walk the naked deck with me to taking a stateroom. I could not persuade him to leave me to bear the burden of insult and outrage alone." [1]

Acts like these admit us to look into Mr. Phillips's soul and reveal his moral grandeur.

---

[1] Oration on Wendell Phillips, delivered before the colored people of Washington, D. C., in 1884.

XIII.

MR. CALHOUN'S IDEA OF EQUILIBRIUM.

Mr. Garrison happily named John C. Calhoun "The Napoleon of Slavery," and he also foretold his Waterloo.[1] The great South Carolinian was a man of irreproachable private and infamous political character. He was not a demagogue. He never blustered; and he had the courage of his convictions. A believer in slavery, he claimed for it a divine warrant, and, with far more reason, a Constitutional sanction. His theory of the Union made it a mere confederacy formed by sovereign States for certain specified purposes, the States continuing to be sovereign and reserving all rights not expressly delegated.[2] Out of this doctrine, under which the South was conscientiously tutored, came secession. He spelled Nation with a small n, while the two other members of the historic senatorial trio—Clay and Webster—spelled it with a capital—an orthography which the march of Sherman to the sea and the success of Grant at Appomattox eventually enforced.

But while Mr. Calhoun lived he did two things.

---

[1] "William Lloyd Garrison," vol. iii., p. 217.

[2] For an admirable summary of his theory see the article on Calhoun by the late Vice-President of the defunct Southern Confederacy, Mr. A. H. Stephens, in Johnson's *New Universal Cyclopædia*.

He provided the South with a Constitutional door of escape from the Union, in case it should lose its supremacy. Meanwhile he strove, with magnificent energy, to hold the balance of power where it was—in the hands of the slave-masters. Had the Republic been confined to the thirteen States which formed it, this had been an easy task. But it was constantly and variously acquiring new Territories of vast extent and beyond the original limits. These Territories were rapidly peopled, and would surely in the near future exert a controlling influence in national affairs. What should be the character of the new States into which they were to be mapped out? Should they be slave States or free States? From the very start this issue forced itself into Congressional discussion. It became angrier and angrier with the lapse of time and the development of sectional interests. Efforts were always being made to quiet and end the discussion, and always vainly, because always by compromise rather than by justice. Thus, when the immense domain, then known as Louisiana, was acquired from France, just as soon as the portion of it which had St. Louis for a capital, had been colonized by slave-holders, it applied for admission into the Union under the name of Missouri, with a State constitution which not only established slavery, but prohibited its abolition. The free States protested. The strife raged during two bitter years. The South won the battle, but tossed to the sulky North a sop of comfort in the shape of the "Missouri Compromise," by which slavery was prohibited in so much of the outlying French purchase as lay north of latitude 36° 30'.

That was in 1820. For a quarter of a century it secured for the oligarchy the undisputed possession of the Government. All this while, however, immigration was pouring into the Northern States, increasing their population and wealth, which were further enlarged by natural growth, while the domestic economy of the Southern States cramped them and kept them stationary. Moreover, the Territories were constantly pre-empted, mainly from the more enterprising North and by settlers who had no objection to slavery in the South, but did object to the introduction of the system into their new abode, because it brought them, as working people, into juxtaposition with a servile class. This again transformed the Territories into a debatable ground. The South feared that the North would soon predominate. To preserve the political equilibrium (a convenient phrase which meant the concentration of power in the slavocracy), Mr. Calhoun began to scheme for the addition of new slave territory, and Texas, an empire in itself, was demanded.

The North, and the Whig party in particular, protested. Conventions were held here, there, everywhere. The annexation of Texas was pronounced unconstitutional and revolutionary. Statesmen like John Quincy Adams, merchants like Abbott Lawrence, asserted that the success of the plot would be equivalent to a dissolution of the Union, and advised forcible resistance.[1] Conservatives suddenly became radicals and Unionists clamored for contingent disunion. The nation was a great debating society,

---

[1] *Vide* Morse's "Life of John Q. Adams," *in loco*, and Hill's "Memoir of Abbott Lawrence," p. 21.

and the subject which no one was to talk about became everybody's theme.

At this crisis the Abolitionists were neither silent nor idle. Their presses struck off tons of matter. Their meetings attracted universal attention. Their speeches were cheered to the echo. Their aggressive spirit, their policy of carrying the war into Africa, their logical position, in noble contrast with the contortions of professional politicians, blowing hot and blowing cold, extorted the admiration of their bitterest opponents. They were the only persons at the North who clearly saw the nature of the contest, who recognized the impossibility of lasting union on the present basis, and who distinctly announced their purpose never to intermit their efforts until slavery, the prolific cause of all the disturbance, should be overthrown.

"As to disunion," remarked Mr. Phillips, "it must and will come. Calhoun wants it at one end of the Union, Garrison wants it at the other. It is written in the counsels of God. Meantime, let all classes and orders and interests unite in using the present hour to prevent the annexation of Texas."[1] For he knew that if Texas was not admitted the South would secede and thus relieve the North from all complicity. And he hoped that if Texas were admitted, the North would act as it now talked and declare the Union at an end. This was the motive of his course at this moment. Besides, the very controversy was a public education. The country was awakened to see the drift of affairs. Every speech on either side was another nail driven in the

---

[1] *Vide Liberator*, vol. xv., p. 177.

coffin of the system he hated. For tne one thing that slavery could not abide was examination. There was a widespread feeling at the North that the South would retreat before the storm of words which beat upon the plot and the plotters. Perhaps this was the explanation of the brave attitude of the Whig leaders—they did not believe they would be called to transmute words into deeds. They little knew the South!

Mr. Phillips did know it. Being swayed by positive convictions himself, he recognized the conscientious deviltry of Mr. Calhoun. Men of positive convictions die—they never yield. Therefore, judging the Southern leader by himself, he foresaw his persistence and foretold his success. He had the power, why should he not have his way? Early in 1845 Mr. Phillips wrote Elizabeth Pease: "Well, Texas you'll see is coming in. We always said it would and were laughed at." [1]

The prophecy was fulfilled. On the last day of February, only a few days after the date of Mr. Phillips's letter, Mr. Calhoun, having failed to carry the Treaty of Annexation through the Senate by the requisite two-thirds majority, accomplished his purpose by admitting the new slave State by the unconstitutional expedient of a joint resolution of the two Houses of Congress, and provided, besides, that it should have the option of subdividing its immense area into four slave States as soon as it should have sufficient population. Nay, while this legislation was pending, and in the face of the intense adverse feeling in the North, he engineered the admission of

---

[1] Quoted in "William Lloyd Garrison," vól. iii., p. 137.

Florida into the Union, side by side with Iowa, a slave State paired with a free State, and saw to it that the constitution of Florida, like that of Missouri, twenty-five years before, should contain a clause making slavery perpetual.

So, then, that had occurred which the chiefs of the Whig party had declared a sufficient reason for leaving the Union; nay, as *ipso facto* an act of dissolution. What did they do? They backed down and bowed their way out of the mighty presence with Eastern salaams. They ate their words, and went in for an era of "good feeling." Despite this craven behavior of trusted men, the agitation had aroused the North. The apparent success of the South was another step toward its ultimate destruction. It was a Bunker Hill victory. The Abolitionists gained and held a larger following than ever before. Mr. Phillips was almost as content with Mr. Calhoun's maintenance of his equilibrium as he would have been with his failure. For the new settlement would not stay settled. The war with Mexico followed the annexation of Texas. As the result additional Territories were acquired.[1] These at once raised the eternal question of Pro-Slavery and Anti-Slavery. Mr. Wilmot, of Pennsylvania, moved and carried through the House of Representatives a proviso (hence called the "Wilmot proviso") that slavery should never exist in any part of the domain just wrung from Mexico, which, however, the Senate refused to adopt.[2] In opposing the bill in this latter body, Mr. Calhoun rose and pointed out that the slave States

---

[1] Viz., New Mexico and California.   [2] In February, 1847.

were now in a minority in the Lower House and in the Electoral College, and that in the Senate they were evenly balanced against the free States—fourteen to fourteen. He added:

"Sir, the day that the balance between the two sections of the country—the slave-holding States and the non-slave-holding States—is destroyed, is a day that will not be far removed from political revolution, anarchy, civil war, and widespread disaster. The balance of this system is in the slave-holding States. They are the conservative portion, always have been the conservative portion, always will be the conservative portion, and, with a due balance on their part, may, for generations to come, uphold this glorious Union of ours. But if this policy should be carried out, woe, woe I say, to this Union!"[1]

Apparently this was the North's opportunity. Had the free States then stood together, one of two things would have happened: either the South would have precipitated secession, or slavery would have been hopelessly confined within the limits it then occupied. In one case the North would not have been ready for the issue; in the other, slavery would have been, as Charles II. apologized for being, "an unconscionable time in dying," and the whole nation would have been convulsed by its death-throes for a hundred years. Hindsight is better than foresight. God is wiser than man. The Almighty ruled and overruled, prolonging the struggle until the North was ripe for the tremendous crisis, and then administered to the hoary iniquity the death-stroke.

Hence the "furioso" utterance of Calhoun frightened the mercantile and political classes of the North into their wonted servility. They cringed and begged pardon, reminding one of Sterne's donkey,

---

[1] *Vide Liberator*, vol. xvii., p. 34.

whose attitude invited abuse, and seemed to say, "Don't kick me! but if you will you may; it is perfectly safe." But the renewed agitation rendered further service to liberty; it made more Abolitionists, and incensed many into the ranks of the rising political Anti-Slavery parties. There were indications that there would one day be a North.

XIV.

INCIDENTS.

THROUGH the years whose more public history we have outlined in the previous chapter, Mr. Phillips was variously active. As often as any fresh occurrence gave him a text he preached a sermon whose conclusion was sure to be *Delenda est Cathargo!* For instance, his whilom opponent at Concord, Squire Hoar,[1] had been sent by Massachusetts to South Carolina to test in the Federal courts in that State the constitutionality of a statute under which colored seamen of Massachusetts had been flung into jail for presuming to land at Charleston. When Mr. Hoar appeared on the scene he was insulted and expelled—as though he had been himself a "nigger." Mr. Phillips thereupon urged the Bunker Hill State to demand of the President an enforcement of Mr. Hoar's plain constitutional right to reside in the Fort Moultrie State: in default of which he asked the Legislature to authorize the Governor to proclaim the Union at an end, recall the Congressional delegation, and provide for the State's foreign relations.[2] Instead of adopting this heroic remedy, Massachusetts was content to bluster and—do nothing.

But alas! the State which did nothing officially to

---

[1] *Ante*, p. 129, sqq.   [2] *Vide Liberator*, vol. xv., p. 19.

resent an indignity, did much through certain of her recreant sons to aid and comfort the slave-masters. Slaves were constantly making their way to the North in ways which, if we could trace them, would transform these pages into martyrology. One of these black heroes secreted himself, in 1846, on board a Massachusetts vessel bound from New Orleans for Boston. He was discovered,—chained,—brought on to the Puritan City—transferred there to another Massachusetts ship, bound South,—carried back to New Orleans,—and remanded to slavery. Massachusetts vessels, Massachusetts ship-owners, and Massachusetts captains playing the part of slave-hounds![1]

But if the State had sons to stain, it also had sons to vindicate its outraged honor. Faneuil Hall was secured. The Abolitionists filled it. The venerable John Quincy Adams presided. The philanthropist, Dr. S. G. Howe, recited the abhorrent facts. John A. Andrew (afterward the great war governor) presented ringing resolutions. Charles Sumner (now enlisted for the war against slavery) made one of the speeches; and Wendell Phillips followed, and gibbeted the names of the miscreants, John H. Pierson, the owner, and James W. Hannum, the captain, to eternal infamy. "Let us proclaim," said he, "that law or no law, Constitution or no Constitution, humanity shall be paramount in Massachusetts. I would send a voice from Faneuil Hall that should reach every hovel in South Carolina, and say to the slaves, 'Come here and find in Massachusetts an asylum.'"[2]

---

[1] Austin's "Life and Times of Wendell Phillips," pp. 130, 131.
[2] *Ib.*, pp. 131, 132.

Daniel Webster was horrified at this. "You that prate of disunion," he said, "do you not know that disunion is Revolution?"

"Yes," retorted the Agitator, "we do know it, and we are for a revolution—a revolution in the character of the American Constitution!"[1] Well, it came.

The Church then said this was heresy, and the State then said this was treason. To-day both Church and State pronounce it magnificent—Christianity and patriotism combined.

Mr. Phillips found time amid these exciting happenings for other activities. One day he went, with Mr. Garrison, before a committee of the Legislature to argue against capital punishment. His speech is a masterpiece on that side of the question.[2] He believed with Bulwer, that "the worst use you can put a man to is to hang him." Another day, he bore witness to the superiority of phonography (then just come into use) over the old method of reporting: phonography, which snatched the words verbatim from his lips,[3] and then bade the telegraph flash the lightning he spoke around the globe. In the first of his speeches thus reported (a speech delivered on December 29th, 1846, at the Anti-Slavery Bazaar, in Faneuil Hall) occurs a passage in which he scores the Church:

"Is the pulpit forever to dwell in the graves of the Jews? The scepticism of Athens is not found in America—that special scepticism which Paul attacked, when he stood on Mars Hill. He directed his words against living sins. We ask of the suc-

---

[1] *Vide Liberator*, vol. xvii., p. 7.
[2] *Ib.*, vol. xiv., p. 23; xv., p. 3.   [3] *Ib.*, vol. xvii., p. 7.

cessors of Paul that they take his thunderbolt and hurl it, not at the graves of the Pharisees, but at the palaces of the tyrant."

He quotes approvingly the saying of Dr. Arnold that the Church exists " to put down all moral evils within or without her own body ;" and then proceeds :

" Anti-Slavery societies ought not to have any *raison d'être*. The Church should do our work. But she will have nothing to do with current sins. She has the sword of the Spirit, but glues it in the scabbard ! She puts on the breastplate of righteousness, but never goes into battle ! She has her feet shod with the Gospel of peace, but will not travel !" [1]

In January, 1847, Theodore Parker took a house in Exeter Place, directly in the rear of Mr. Phillips's residence—a happy occurrence for both. They differed radically in their religious views ; Parker being an ultra-Unitarian, while Phillips clung to the old faith. But they had much in common. With both liberty was a passion. They were alike, too, in their devotion to letters ; and still nearer akin in their pitiful ministry to every form of suffering and sorrow. Parker was a polyglot man—spoke or read fifteen languages. A wit of the day speaks of certain learned men " who know everything except how to apply it." Parker knew how to apply what he knew. He had a luxurious library and was never happier than when throned among his books—save when he was at work among and for his fellows. He was fond of animals—they were a hobby. *Bears* were his special pets. He said they were great, humorous children [Did he think them fit to hug ?] ; and imagined they had a wary Scotch vein in them.

---

[1] *Vide Liberator*, vol. xvii., p. 7.

His home was full of bears in plaster, ivory, wood (from Berne), and in seal metal. It was a short and economical way to his heart to fetch him an odder bear than usual. Mr. Phillips gave him a French caricature of the Revolution of 1848, representing the chief characters in the shape of bears—which he straightway raised conspicuously over his bureau.[1]

The intimacy between these men became as close as though they had been joined in the marriage relation—there was a union of souls. Mr. Phillips has told how often, as he looked from his own chamber window late at night, when some lecture engagement had brought him home in "the wee sma' hours ayont the twal'," he saw the unquenched light burning in Parker's study—"that unflagging student ever at work." Then he would turn away, murmuring: "The trophies of Miltiades will not let me sleep!"[2] Ah, Mr. Phillips, go to bed without envy in your heart! Those midnight carousals with books finally killed Theodore Parker. Late hours are as poisonous to students as the hemlock was to Socrates.

In the spring of the year when Parker became his neighbor, Mr. Phillips, at his own expense, published a pamphlet in which he reviewed with great acuteness and a lavish display of legal learning, an able book by Mr. Lysander Spooner, on "The Unconstitutionality of Slavery."[3] This was his third important contribution to the current discussion of the

---

[1] "Life and Correspondence of Theodore Parker," by John Weiss, vol. i., p. 287.

[2] "Memorial of Ann Phillips," p. 18.

[3] This pamphlet may be found in the Boston Public Library—the author's own copy.

character of that compact.[1] The large edition was soon disposed of, and others followed. Simultaneously his addresses treated the same issue, but in a less technical and more popular manner. As the ancients had a saying that all roads led to Rome, so now his utterances, whether from the press or the platform, all ended with the slogan: "No Union with Slave-holders."

It was at this period, also, that Mr. Phillips met Eliza Garnaut. She was one of those angels in human form who sometimes (alas! not often) come into our experience to renew our confidence in our kind, and to show us how nearly allied the human may be to the divine. This lady was of Welsh birth. She had married a Frenchman, and came with him to Boston. He soon died, leaving her with an only child, a girl. Without means, she managed to support herself and daughter; and in addition gave time and money to the destitute around about her—made herself a common mother. Wherever there was poverty,—misfortune,—grief,—downfall—there she stood, a modern good Samaritan. Some of the noblest people in Boston made her their almoner. Mr. Phillips loved her as a sister and looked up to her as a saint. He was always helping her with counsel and cash. When, in 1849, she fell a victim to the cholera, through her unselfish devotion to others, he adopted her daughter as his own, and Phœbe Garnaut became for a few delightful years to all concerned, Phœbe Phillips.[2] A relative

---

[1] *Ante*, pp. 143 *sqq*.
[2] "Memorial of Ann Phillips," p. 18. For a beautiful tribute to Mrs. Garnaut, from the pen of Mr. Phillips, see *Liberty Bell* for 1851.

of Mrs. Phillips speaks of the welcome the child, then twelve years old, met with : " She was a constant joy to both—' Ann busies herself with lessons and French exercises as when she herself went to school,' wrote Mr. Phillips ; who himself took pleasure in directing the girl's education, and found in her a bright and loving companion, until marriage took her away to another city, and finally to a foreign land." [1]

The hatred then felt for the Abolitionists among those who did not and would not understand their motives and aims is now incredible. After nearly twenty years of effort, and notwithstanding the always rising tide of Anti-Slavery sentiment, these pioneers of progress carried their lives in their hands within the shadow of their own homes. One day as Mr. Phillips turned the corner and walked toward his house, he passed two gentlemen—they seemed such in dress and carriage. One remarked to the other in a tone evidently meant to be overheard and with a jerk of his head in the direction of the orator :

" I would like to put a bullet through that man's heart !"

" Benevolent, wasn't it ?" was his comment in mentioning it to a friend.[2]

Adhering as he did to the religion of Christ, and feeling the need of communion with the divine Liberator, he was wont at this time to meet on Sundays with a few like-minded men and women in private

---

[1] " Memorial of Ann Phillips," p. 18. Miss Garnaut married, in 1860, Mr. George W. Smalley, the well-known London correspondent of the New York *Tribune*.

[2] The Rev. A. J. Gordon, of Boston, in New York *Independent*, April 17th, 1884.

houses, after the apostolic example, to observe the holy service of the Lord's Supper,[1]—this infidel! Thus he got fresh strength and courage to battle against overwhelming odds in behalf of the Golden Rule.

In 1848 an address to America against slavery came from Scotland, signed by forty thousand women. It played a prominent part in the various Anti-Slavery gatherings of the year. On one of these occasions, Mr. Phillips paid a tribute to this noble host, and, incidentally, as well to the faithfulness of their sisters on this side of the water :

"It was from a woman's lips (referring to Elizabeth Herrick) that the Abolitionists of the old world first heard the doctrine and learned the lesson of immediate emancipation. Women's voices, God bless them! have ever been clear in animating for the conflict and in pointing out the way."[2]

In January, 1849, Mr. Phillips made an aggressive speech at the annual meeting of the Massachusetts Anti-Slavery Society in which he reviewed the local history of the cause since his adhesion to it. He alluded to a gathering in Faneuil Hall, in 1837, which provoked the Garrison mob, when Harrison Gray Otis said that he had heard the Abolitionists in their madness, put the Bible above the Statute-book, and when Peleg Sprague endeavored to create Pro-Slavery feeling by pointing to the portrait of Washington, and calling him "that slave-holder." He referred to the encouragement given to the murderers of Lovejoy, at Alton, by "that infamous

---

[1] *Vide* Joseph Cook in his Monday lecture on Wendell Phillips, Boston, February 14th, 1884. Reported in New York *Independent*, February 14th, 1884.

[2] *Vide Liberator*, vol. xviii., p. 19.

attorney-general, James Trecothic Austin." He then proceeded to call the roll of the Boston churches:

"Where is Hubbard Winslow? Teaching that a minister's rule of duty, as to what he should teach and preach, is 'what the brotherhood will allow and protect.' Where is the pulpit of the 'Old South'? Sustaining slavery as a Bible institution. Where is Park Street? Refusing to receive within its walls, for funeral services, the body of the only martyr the Orthodox Congregationalists of New England have had, Charles T. Torrey,[1] and of whom they were not worthy. Where is Essex Street church? Teaching that there are occasions when the Golden Rule is to be set aside. Where is Federal Street church? Teaching that silence is the duty of the North with respect to slavery, and closing its doors to the funeral eulogy of the Abolitionist Follen, the bosom friend of the only man who will make Federal Street pulpit to be remembered, William Ellery Channing. And I might ask, where are the New South and Brattle Street? but *they are not!*"[2]

This speech made a sensation. It stabbed the ecclesiastical traitors to liberty with interrogation marks—no wonder they gasped out their rage.

The annexation of Texas and the successful war against ill-used Mexico had enlarged, actually and even more prospectively, the area of the South, and the value of the slaves was enhanced. According to the Richmond *Enquirer*, male negroes were now worth "seven hundred dollars around."[3] When seven hundred dollars funded in ebony took to its heels and ran away, the slave-masters felt in their

---

[1] Mr. Torrey was a Northern clergyman and Abolitionist who had been imprisoned and martyred at the South for aiding slaves to escape.

[2] *Vide Liberator*, vol. xix., 2d week in February.

[3] Compare *Liberator*, vol. xxvii., p. 1.

pockets a vacuum which they, like nature, abhorred. Their two-footed property kept doing this. And when the seven hundred dollars' worth of flesh and blood reached the North, the Abolitionists saw only the man or woman and could not see the property—no, not with a magnifying-glass. This tendency of this peculiar kind of value to scoot (always Northward), coupled with the poor eyesight of growing numbers up here, which disabled them from seeing the flight, kept the lords of the plantation in a condition of chronic fretfulness. Worse yet, there was a regular "underground railroad" in the North, with stations, conductors, and free cars, operated (so the South learned) for the very purpose of spiriting away as many embodiments of the aforesaid seven hundred dollars as cared to ride on it. Toward the end of May, 1849, several of these "chattels personal" suddenly appeared in Boston, *en route* for Canada, and stopped for refreshments at Faneuil Hall—the restaurant of liberty. One of these was "Box" Brown; so called, because he had escaped from Virginia in a box as merchandise—not a proper method of shipping live stock, for it nearly proved his coffin. Two others were William and Ellen Craft, husband and wife. She being almost white, had disguised herself in male attire as an invalid seeking medical treatment at the North, while her darker husband figured in the rôle of her negro "boy"—all of which was quite orthodox and constitutional, as it should seem. Well, Wendell Phillips fed them in Faneuil Hall, and amid thunders of approval cried:

"We say in behalf of these hunted beings, whom God created, and whom law-abiding Webster and Winthrop have sworn shall not find shelter in Massachusetts,—we say that they may make their little motions, and pass their little laws, in Washington, but that Faneuil Hall REPEALS them, in the name of humanity and the old Bay State!"'

With which defiance we ring down the curtain.

---

[1] *Vide Liberator*, vol. xix., p. 90.

XV.

THE DEVIL'S GOSPEL.

Mr. Phillips commenced the year 1850 by the delivery of a lecture before the Mercantile Library Association of Boston, on the "Philosophy of Reform." The audience was immense; the subject one with which the lecturer was *en rapport;* the result, the introduction of his sentiments where they had not been heard before.[1]

At this date the national situation may be thus summarized :

California stood knocking at the door of the Union for admission as a free State—a new danger to Mr. Calhoun's equilibrium. The "Free Soil party," child and successor of the old Liberty party, the latest political coalition against the extension and domination of slavery, had come into the field in 1848, when it cast an ominous vote for its Presidential candidate, and was now vigorously preparing to better the record in the approaching canvas of 1852. The Whig party was divided into two warring factions, the "Conscience" Whigs, who were unalterably opposed to the further spread of the "peculiar institution," and the "Cotton" Whigs, who put the desire to make money in the place of conscience, and went up and down crying "Peace, peace" when

---

[1] *Vide Liberator,* vol. xx., p. 7.

there was no peace. The Democratic party was animated and controlled by the South, and was composed of the slave-holders, booted and spurred to ride, and of donkey Northerners, saddled and bridled to be ridden. The Abolitionists were still few, but made up for their lack of numbers by their sleepless activity. They were the only consistent and uncompromising foes of slavery,—the only ones who contended not only for its restriction but for its destruction ; which they were enabled to do because they stood outside of all parties, untrammelled by Constitutional limitations ; and they were hated and feared because of their position on the morals of the case. The plantation barons were sulky. Their biped " property" had mastered enough astronomy to distinguish the North Star, and had mustered enough manhood to run for it. Meanwhile, large sections of the free States covertly co-operated with the fugitives, and openly refused to return them to the house of bondage. The scene was one of bewildering confusion—dizzy as a dance of dervishes.

In these circumstances, Mr. Clay stole a leaf from the devil's gospel—he proposed a compromise. This was the unfailing resource of the " Artful Dodgers" who substituted expedients for justice, and who imagined that statesmanship was shown by trimming. As though God could be hoodwinked by men ! As though the crater of Vesuvius could be stuffed up with a tuft of cotton ! Either Calhoun was right or Phillips was right. If Calhoun was right, slavery was a benign institution, and had a claim to be domesticated everywhere—like the cotton it produced. If Phillips was right, slavery was " the sum of all villanies," and had no claim to be tolerated anywhere. Between these two positions there was no logical standing-place. The turmoil of fifty years originated in the inability or unwillingness of this country to recognize this plain fact—in the attempt to make two and two count five instead of four. In questions of mere expediency, compromise is what Macaulay termed it, "the essence of politics." All parties agree to give up something to carry a common point. But when fundamental right and wrong are involved, compromise is a compounding of felony. It is like promising the burglar who has broken into your house and slain your children, that you will not prosecute him for murder if he will restore the family plate.

Mr. Clay's programme was, substantially, this: to admit California as a free State; to organize the Territories stolen from Mexico without raising the question of slavery, leaving them to decide that question for themselves; to gratify Northern sentiment, not by abolishing slavery in the District of Columbia, but by forbidding the sale of slaves in the Washington markets; and to satisfy Southern cupidity by the passage of a stringent law for the return of fugitive slaves. Like any other vendor of patent nostrums, he expatiated on the advantage of such a measure: It would kill the Free Soil party; for they only claimed what was now conceded,—the abolition of the slave-trade under the shadow of the Capitol, and the non-extension of slavery into the Territories under Governmental auspices; it would quiet the South; for their property was secured at the North as well as at home, while there were no exclusive fences in the Territories.

The great compromiser, after the habit of his kind,

forgot that God was not dead. He also ignored the Abolitionists, who were as hot against slavery in the slave States as they were against its introduction into the Territories. Of course, therefore, Mr. Phillips scouted the juggle. Nor was Mr. Calhoun much better pleased with it; for Mr. Clay's panacea did not preserve his equilibrium. With California admitted, there would be sixteen free, and only fifteen slave States. Besides, believing that slaves were legitimate property, he held, logically enough, that this kind of possession should go wherever a horse or a plough or a bond might be carried—had a right to the same protection. But before the uncompromising Southerner could develop his opposition, death snatched him away.[1]

While Clay's legislation was pending, all eyes were turned upon Daniel Webster. Would he throw the weight of his great name in the scale of compromise? Would he now lead the "Conscience" Whigs and create a North? It was an hour of hope and of fear. On March 7th, 1850, Mr. Webster slowly rose in the Senate, faced South instead of North, and, speaking with the ponderous deliberation characteristic of his oratory, advocated the Kentuckian's bill without an if or an and, and especially announced his purpose to carry out the fugitive-slave clause "with all its provisions, to the furthest extent."

It was the completest, saddest, most disastrous surrender ever made. The favorite son of New England thought to secure the Presidency by this act. In reality he committed both moral and political suicide. True, his advocacy carried the com-

---

[1] Mr. Calhoun died March 31st, 1850.

promise measure through the Senate and through
the House and made it law. True, he was thanked
for his course by the representatives of Massachusetts commerce, letters, theology, and law, in an
open letter which Rufus Choate, William Appleton,
George Ticknor, W. H. Prescott, Professor Moses
Stuart, and the Rev. Dr. Leonard Woods, signed,
with seven hundred other dough faces.[1] But he disgusted the South itself, which refused to give him
even the empty honor of a nomination at the Whig
Convention, a year or two later. And he alienated
those Anti-Slavery Whigs who had believed in him
and followed him, but who now swore *at* him instead
of *by* him. Clothed with shame and gnawed by
chagrin, he died not long afterward, and was sepulchred in dishonor. By a striking coincidence, his
colleague in infamy, Henry Clay, less enlightened and
therefore less guilty, by a few months preceded
him to the grave.[2] Unhappily their juggle "still
lived."

But the measure intended to quench only inflamed
the fire. It was popularly known by its most famous
(and infamous) provision, as the "Fugitive Slave
Law." This was the special feature that aroused
the wrath of the North. For this made slave-hunting a duty and sought to transform every freeman
into a slave-catcher. It placed the liberty of any
colored man who might be claimed and seized anywhere at the mercy of any commissioner, marshal,
or clerk of any Federal court; nay, of any collector
of customs, or any postmaster. It affixed to the res-

---

[1] *Vide Liberator*, vol. xx., pp. 55, 57, 62.
[2] Webster died October 24th, 1852; Clay, June 29th, 1852.

cue, or attempted rescue, or even to the harboring, of such an one, a fine of one thousand dollars, together with six months' imprisonment.[1]

This atrocious statute, and Mr. Webster's connection with it, were indignantly condemned in Faneuil Hall, on March 25th, 1850, by a vast concourse of citizens. The Hon. Samuel E. Sewall presided. Theodore Parker spoke, and was followed by Wendell Phillips, who riddled the recreant New England statesman, as years before in the same hall he had the smaller renegade who defended the Alton murderers.[2]

But the Abolitionists did not have it all their own way. The legislation at Washington resurrected the mob spirit, and 1850 repeated 1835. The annual meeting of the American Anti-Slavery Society, held in New York, in May, is an illustration. Its advent was heralded by a satanic outburst from the press of the city, invoking riot and instigating violence. A crowd of roughs, headed by one Captain Rynders, a typical bully, took possession of the galleries of the Broadway Tabernacle, where the opening session was held, and set disorder afoot. Amid constant interruptions and to an accompaniment of insults spiced with profanity the earlier speakers interjected their words. Then uprose a seedy-looking mobocrat, who undertook to prove that the negroes were not men but monkeys. Frederick Douglass came forward and said :

"The gentleman who has just spoken has undertaken to prove that the blacks are not human beings.

---

[1] The law is given in the *Liberator*, vol. xx., p. 153.
[2] *Vide Liberator*, vol. xx., 1st week in April.

He has examined our whole conformation, from top to toe. I cannot follow him in his argument. I will assist him in it, however. I offer myself for examination. *Am I a man?*"

The audience responded with a thunderous affirmative, which Captain Rynders sought to break by exclaiming : " You are not a black man ; you are only half a nigger." "Then," replied Mr. Douglass, turning upon him with the blandest of smiles, and an almost affectionate obeisance, " I am halfbrother to Captain Rynders !" He would not deny that he was the son of a slave-holder, born of Southern " amalgamation ;" a fugitive, too, like Kossuth —" another half-brother of mine" (to Rynders). He spoke of the difficulties thrown in the way of industrious colored people at the North, as he had himself experienced—this by way of answer to Horace Greeley, who had recently complained of their inefficiency and dependence. Criticism of the editor of the *Tribune* being grateful to Rynders, a political adversary, he added a word to Douglass's against Greeley. " I am happy," said Douglass, " to have the assent of my half-brother here," pointing to Rynders, and convulsing the audience with laughter. After this Rynders, finding how he was played with, took care to hold his peace ; but some one of Rynders's company in the gallery undertook to interrupt the speaker. " It's of no use," said Mr. Douglass, " I've Captain Rynders here to back me. We were born here," he said, finally, " we are not dying out, and we mean to stay here. We made the clothes you have on, the sugar you put into your tea. We would do more if allowed." " Yes," said a voice in the crowd, " you would cut our throats for us." "No," was the quick response, "but we would *cut your hair for you.*"

Douglass concluded his triumphant remarks by calling upon the Rev. Samuel Ward, editor of the *Impartial Citizen*, to succeed him. "All eyes," says an eye-witness, "were instantly turned to the back of the platform, or stage, rather, so dramatic was the scene ; and there, amid a group, stood a large man, so black that, as Wendell Phillips said, when he shut his eyes you could not see him. As he approached, Rynders exclaimed : ' Well, this is the original nigger !' ' I've heard of the magnanimity of Captain Rynders,' said Ward, ' but the half has not been told me !' And then he went on with a noble voice, and his speech was such a strain of eloquence as I never heard excelled before or since. The mob had to applaud him, too, and it is the highest praise to record that his unpremeditated utterance maintained the level of Douglass's, and ended the meeting with a sense of climax—demonstrating alike the humanity and the capacity of the full-blooded negro."[1]

The session ended before Mr. Phillips could speak. The fears of the owners of the building closed it against the Abolitionists thereafter, and they were mobbed out of the hall of the Society Library, whither they had betaken themselves for refuge. "Thus," remarked the New York *Tribune* the next morning, "closed Anti-Slavery free discussion in New York for 1850."

---

[1] The above account is taken from the report of the meeting written by the Rev. W. H. Furness, of Philadelphia, an eye-witness, and quoted in "William Lloyd Garrison," vol. iii., pp. 294, 295.

It was on this occasion that the Rev. Henry Ward Beecher, not then an Abolitionist, performed one of the bravest acts of his life by opening Plymouth Church to Wendell Phillips, and appearing with him on the platform, to signify his appreciation of free speech. " I was amazed," wrote he, referring to it, " at the unagitated Agitator,—so calm, so fearless, so incisive,—every word a bullet. I never heard a more effective speech than Mr. Phillips's that night. He seemed inspired, and played with his audience (turbulent, of course) as Gulliver might with the Lilliputians. He had the dignity of Pitt, the vigor of Fox, the wit of Sheridan, the satire of Junius,—and a grace and music all his own. Then for the first time did Plymouth Church catch and echo those matchless tones. I mean it shall not be the last time." [1]

At the anniversary of the New England Anti-Slavery Society, held in Boston, two weeks later, an attempt was made to re-enact the scenes in New York—with but partial success; for Parker, Garrison, and Phillips all had their say in splendid fashion, though their remarks were punctuated in a manner which no printer would have sanctioned.[2]

Mr. Phillips tossed out some of his most pungent sentences: this, for example: "Abolitionists risk bankruptcy for obeying commands which the pulpits preach, and then fine us for practising."

And this: "We have had here, in Massachusetts, Ellen Craft, a fugitive *from* slavery, and now Daniel Webster, a fugitive *into* slavery." [3]

He issued during this year a pamphlet in which

---

[1] Letter of Mr. Beecher to Oliver Johnson (MS.).
[2] *Vide Liberator*, vol. xx., pp. 89, 90.   [3] *Ib.*, p. 98.

he examined from the successive standpoints of law, ethics, history, and humanity, the position of Mr. Webster, and reached the conclusion which Whittier announced in the terrible title of his poem on the moral suicide—"Ichabod."[1]

On September 18th, in this memorable year, Millard Fillmore, who succeeded to the Presidency on the death of General Taylor,[2] signed the Fugitive Slave Bill, which thus became a law. Happy Taylor, relieved from this dreadful guilt! Unhappy Fillmore, pilloried forever in the curses of mankind!

The venerable Josiah Quincy[3] headed a call for a meeting in Faneuil Hall to consider the condition of the fugitive slaves and other colored people under the new statute. The meeting was held on October 14th, amid intense excitement. Charles Francis Adams (the son of John Quincy Adams, who had died in 1848) took the chair. Richard H. Dana, Jr., offered the resolutions which demanded the repeal of a measure repugnant to moral sense,—promised to defend the colored people,—and advised them to remain where they were. Theodore Parker, Frederick Douglass, and Wendell Phillips spoke in no uncertain tone, vocalizing and manufacturing public opinion.[4]

The result was seen in November, when the Whig party was snowed under by Massachusetts ballots; and yet more emphatically the next year, when (Webster having been called into President Fillmore's Cabinet) Charles Sumner was elected to re-

---

[1] The pamphlet is in the Boston Public Library.
[2] On July 9th, 1850.
[3] *Ante*, p. 22.
[4] *Vide Liberator*, vol. xx., p. 166.

place him in the Senate[1]—the high-water mark thus far of Anti-Slavery sentiment.

The following extract from a speech which Mr. Sumner delivered in Faneuil Hall upon the Fugitive Slave Law sharply contrasts the new senator with the old one, and bravely helped to lift him into the seat of Webster:

"The soul sickens in the contemplation of this legalized outrage. In the dreary annals of the past, there are many acts of shame—there are ordinances of monarchs, and laws, which have become a byword and a hissing to the nations. But, when we consider the country and the age, I ask fearlessly, What act of shame, what ordinance of monarch, what law can compare in atrocity with this enactment of an American Congress? (*None.*) I do not forget Appius Claudius, the tyrant Decemvir of ancient Rome, condemning Virginia as a slave; nor Louis XIV., of France, letting slip the dogs of religious persecution by the revocation of the Edict of Nantes; nor Charles I., of England, arousing the patriot-rage of Hampden by the extortion of ship-money; nor the British Parliament, provoking, in our own country, spirits kindred to Hampden, by the tyranny of the Stamp Act and the Tea Tax. I would not exaggerate; I wish to keep within bounds; but I think no person can doubt the condemnation now affixed to all these transactions, and to their authors, must be the lot hereafter of the Fugitive Slave Bill, and of every one, according to the measure of his influence, who gave it his support. (*Three cheers were here given.*) Into the immortal catalogue of national crimes this has now passed, drawing after it, by an inexorable necessity, its authors also, and chiefly him, who, as President of the United States, set his name to the bill, and breathed into it that final breath without which it would have no life. (*Sensation.*) Other Presidents may be forgotten; but the name signed to the Fugitive Slave Bill can never be forgotten. (*Never !*) There are depths of infamy, as there are heights of fame. (*Applause.*) I regret to say what I must; but

---

[1] By a vote of 193 out of 286—just enough to elect, and after a long struggle.

truth compels me. Better for him had he never been born! (*Renewed applause.*) Better far for his memory, and for the good name of his children, had he never been President!" (*Repeated cheers.*)[1]

With Phillips under Bunker Hill monument and Sumner in Washington, Massachusetts had reason to feel proud.

---

[1] *Vide* Works of Charles Sumner, speech on Fugitive Slave Law.

XVI.

THE WOMEN, AND A MAN.

THE feelings of Mr. Phillips with regard to women have been indicated,—his respectful admiration for them,—his chivalrous espousal of their cause when any Rebecca needed an Ivanhoe,—his profound belief in their capacity for a wider life than custom accorded them. Holding such views, he gave a warm indorsement to a proposal for a Women's Rights Convention, which was made in the summer of 1850, at one of the Anti-Slavery meetings, and with Mrs. Phillips signed the call. It was always a gratification to him that this cause should have been the issue of the Abolition movement—as Eve was taken from the side of Adam.

The Convention met at Worcester, in Massachusetts, on October 23d and 24th, 1850,[1] year of wonders! The attendance was large, the women being in the majority, but the men having fit representatives in Phillips and Garrison and Douglass, who stood for the Anti-Slavery interest, and in Sargent and Channing, from the liberal pulpit. No phonographic report of the proceedings was made. But enough is known of what was said and done to justify the statement that those present consciously and worthily launched the most magnificent reform ever under-

---

[1] *Vide Liberator*, vol. xx., p. 142.

taken,—an effort in behalf, not of a race (like Anti-Slavery), nor of a nation (like the revolt of the colonies), but of a sex.[1] The immediate result was the perfecting of an organization on a national basis, with the appointment of a central committee, of which Mr. Phillips was made treasurer.[2] Europe, too, answered to America. The *Westminster Review* noticed the Convention in an elaborate article written by Mrs. John Stuart Mill, and indorsed it: so that the women's cause dates in Old England as in New England from this gathering at Worcester.

The wits of the pot-house and the what-nows of society were equally and mightily amused. Those twanged their bow-strings and sped their arrows of ridicule at so plain a target. These coughed under the handkerchief, and ogled behind the door, and lamented the immodesty of "such brazen women." The "Hen Convention" was the name given it by the press. A certain Universalist clergyman (whose name it would be cruel to give) announced from his pulpit a meeting at which Lucy Stone was to speak in these words: "To-night, at the Town Hall, a hen will attempt to crow." This was wit in 1850—as the word "nigger" was humanity![3]

Early in the following year, Mr. Phillips wrote an account of his experiences at Worcester to his friend, Miss Pease, across the water:

"You would have enjoyed the Women's Convention. I think I never saw a more intelligent and highly cultivated audience, more ability guided by the best taste on a platform, more deep, practical interest, on any occasion. It took me completely by

---

[1] *Vide Liberator*, vol. xx., p. 181.   [2] *Ib.*

[3] Remarks of Mrs. H. H. Robinson, quoted in Austin's "Life and Times of Wendell Phillips," p. 155.

surprise ; and the women were the ablest speakers, too. You would have laughed, as we used to do in 1840, to hear dear Lucretia Mott answer me. I had presumed to differ from her, and asserted that the cause would meet more immediate and palpable and insulting opposition from women than from men—and scolded them for it. She put, as she so well knows how, the silken snapper on her whiplash, and proceeded to give me the gentlest and yet most cutting rebuke. 'Twas like her old fire when London Quakers angered her gentleness—and beautifully done, so that the victim himself could enjoy the artistic perfection of his punishment." [1]

Mr. Phillips adhered to his opinion, nevertheless ; and time has shown that he was correct. Women themselves have been the most heated and the most influential opponents of their own cause. Were they a unit, they could carry it to success in a week.

On October 29th, George Thompson,[2] the English orator, landed in Boston—his second visit to America. The first was in 1835, when he was mobbed out of the country for his Abolitionism. He found affairs much as he left them ; so that he might have rubbed his eyes and asked himself whether he had really been absent for fifteen years.[3] At a reception given him by the Abolitionists in Faneuil Hall, on November 15th, a throng of rowdies made themselves masters of ceremonies and howled so lustily that no one could get a hearing ; not more Wendell Phillips than George Thompson himself.[4] "No matter," said Mr. Phillips ; "the truth will float farther on the hisses of a mob than the most eloquent lips can carry it."

Shouted down in Boston, the Abolitionists with

---

[1] Quoted in "William Lloyd Garrison," vol. iii., p. 312, note.
[2] *Ante*, p. 102.
[3] "William Lloyd Garrison," vol. iii., p. 305. [4] *Ib.*, p. 306.

their guest went to Worcester—appealed from the pocket to the heart of the commonwealth. Here they enjoyed a feast of reason and a flow of soul. Thompson spoke magnificently, to sympathetic thousands, and so did Phillips. It was on this occasion that the latter uttered the famous sentence in which he laid a hand on the most prominent features of American geography. After referring to the failure of the European revolutionary movements in 1848, he burst forth :

"The Carpathian Mountains may shelter tyrants. The slopes of Germany may bear up a race more familiar with the Greek text than with the Greek phalanx. For aught I know, the wave of Russian rule may sweep so far westward as to fill once more with miniature despots the robber castles of the Rhine. But of this I am sure : God piled the Rocky Mountains as the ramparts of freedom. He scooped the Valley of the Mississippi as the cradle of free States. He poured Niagara as the anthem of free men." [1]

In the first month of the new year[2] there was a *soirée* in Cochituate Hall, in Boston, to celebrate the twentieth anniversary of Mr. Garrison's paper, the *Liberator*. It was an occasion of rare interest, and rallied the entire social and oratorical strength of local Abolitionism. In the course of the evening, George Thompson presented to Mr. Garrison a gold watch appropriately inscribed ; and amid delightful chat, interspersed with addresses from the various sons of thunder present, the hours sped. Mr. Phillips paints the scene—again for the delectation of Elizabeth Pease :

"You would have enjoyed the *soirée*, perfectly extempore—so much so that E. Q. did not know he was to be chairman until I

---

[1] *Vide Liberator*, vol. xx., p. 195.   [2] January 24th, 1851.

moved it, and then he filled the chair with the wit and readiness that is possessed by all the Quincys. It was unique—the heartiest Anti-Slavery gathering I ever saw. Thompson had been very ill in the country and was looking quite ghastly, fit for a sick-bed, but spoke gloriously ; and his presence was, in a great degree, an inspiration to the rest. Add to that, Garrison in tears—the occasion—and the company scarred with many a struggle—and you will easily see that we should feel deeply, and, like all times of deep feeling, it should be mingled of mirth and profound emotion. Such hours come rarely in life." [1]

From Mr. Phillips's own speech, which was largely in a sportive vein, we subjoin a serious sentence or two, as significant of his appreciation of the *Liberator* and of its editor :

"How many owe their reform alphabet to the *Liberator !* John Foster used to say, that the best test of a book's value was the mood of mind in which one rose from it. To this trial I am always willing the most eager foe should subject the *Liberator*. I appeal to each one here, whether he ever leaves its columns without feeling his coldness rebuked, his selfishness shamed, his hand strengthened for every good purpose ; without feeling lifted, for a while, from his ordinary life, and made to hold communion with purer thoughts and loftier aims ; and without being moved—the coldest of us—for a moment, at least, with an ardent wish that we, too, may be privileged to be co-workers with God in the noble purposes for our brother's welfare which have been unfolded and pressed on our attention ? Let critics who have time settle, after leisurely analysis, the various faults which, as they think, have marred our friend's course, and denounce, as suits them, the other topics which he has chosen to mingle with his main subject ; enough for us, in the heat of our conflict, to feel that it has always ' been good for us to have been ' with him. How can we ever thank him for the clear atmosphere into which he has lifted us ! If of the Abolitionists it may be said, with such exceeding measure of truth, that they have broken the shackles of party, thrown down the walls of

---

[1] Compare " William Lloyd Garrison," vol. iii., p. 313.

sect, trampled on the prejudices of their land and time, risen to something like the freedom of Christian men, something of that perfect toleration which is the fruit only of the highest intellectual and moral culture—how much is all this owing to the influence of such a leader! My friends, if we never free a slave, we have at least freed ourselves in the effort to emancipate our brother-man. (*Applause.*) From the blindness of American prejudice the most cruel the sun looks on; from the narrowness of sect; from parties, quibbling over words; we have been redeemed into full manhood—taught to consecrate life to something worth living for. Life! what a weariness it is, with its drudgery of education; its little cares of to-day, all to be lived over again to-morrow; its rising, eating, and lying down—only to continue the monotonous routine! Let us thank God that He has inspired any one to awaken us from being these dull and rotting weeds—revealed to us the joy of self-devotion—taught us how we intensify this life by laying it a willing offering on the altar of some great cause!"[1]

How did Mr. Thompson fare in America, beyond the congenial circle which bade him welcome? Mr. Phillips shall tell us, as he told Miss Pease, in a letter to that lady, from which we once more quote:

"His visit has had a wonderful effect; calling out into something of activity some who were alive during his former stay, but had fallen off, or fallen asleep, in the long and hard trials of the years since; and some who were awkwardly conscious of having ratted when trouble lowered, and longed for some occasion that would open the door for a return without imposing too palpable a confession of repentance. Then his name gathers immense audiences, the fame of his former achievements still haunting our towns, the plebeians of the cause (the converts since 1835) hankering after the sound of that voice whose echoes had reached them in the stirring tales of the nobles of earlier conversion. The rage, too, of opposition raises him into an object of universal attention.

"It is generally voted that he has not grown a day older since

---

[1] Compare "William Lloyd Garrison," vol. iii., pp. 319, 320.

1835, though the dissentients are not few. Then many scold, more laugh, at his snuff ; but his vivacity, brilliancy, and variety of accomplishments in private life charm every one that has the good luck to get near him. He is a universal idol. His project of lecturing upon general topics would, in my opinion, have been a failure even had no disturbance intervened to prevent it. Your English mode of lecture is so totally different from ours that, lacking the impetus of being abused, he would have go on but poorly in his voyage. As it is, he has delivered his course on 'British India' in five or six towns, and with tolerable success, owing to the extra exertion of friends, and the wish of many to hear the 'Great Unheard' without compromising their dignity by being seen in an Abolition meeting. In our Anti-Slavery gatherings his speeches have been grand and eloquent beyond all description. We hope that his visit will not have been wholly vain to him in a pecuniary point of view." [1]

Mr. Thompson, who was now a member of the British Parliament, prolonged his stay on these shores until his constituents began to murmur. Called home by these indications of English discontent, he sailed from Boston on June 26th, 1851, not, however, before his American friends (with Mr. Phillips among them) had *fêted* him at a farewell *soirée* at which a thousand plates were laid.[2]

Upon reaching England he addressed his constituents in explanation of his tarry. We clip a passage from his speech, as a specimen of his style :

"Allow me to say, that had I remained for ease, leisure, emolument, recreation, I should have condemned myself before I had appeared to receive your censure. I was not botanizing on the Himalayas ; I was not pursuing antiquarian researches on the banks of the Nile ; I was not gazing upon the sublimities of the Alps or the Andes ; I was not putting my legs under the tables of the bloated planters of the South, or truckling politicians of the North, of America. I was facing labors, perils, per-

---

[1] *Vide Liberator*, vol. xx., p. 18. [2] *Ib.*, vol. xxi., pp. 98, 101.

secutions, and obloquy, in the cause of the most oppressed and degraded of the human race. . . .

"Of all institutions of personal slavery, looked at in connection with its safeguards and its origin,—of all the institutions of slavery on the face of the earth, there are none so unmitigatedly bad, so inexcusably atrocious, so colossal in their felonious aspect, so diametrically opposed to the professions and practices of the people that encourage and support them, as the institution of slavery in the United States of America. There is no republicanism in America while slavery exists. The cause of liberty throughout the world is maimed and bleeding while slavery remains there. We preach democracy in vain in England while a Tory or Conservative can point us to the opposite side of the Atlantic, and say : ' There are nineteen millions of the human race, free, absolutely ; every man heir-apparent to the throne ; governing themselves—the government of all, by all, for all ; but, instead of being a consistent republic, it is one widespread confederacy of free men for the enslavement of an entire nation of another complexion.' While that institution lasts, the experiment of men to govern themselves has not been proved to be a successful one ; for there is no virtue in loving freedom for ourselves." [1]

While the Englishman was in this country, Mr. Phillips was with him as much as possible. The two orators spoke together on slavery at various places in the vicinity of Boston. What a pair ! What a treat ! Some who yet live remember to have heard them as they swung around this circle, and recall it as an experience of intellectual epicureanism.

---

[1] *Vide Liberator*, vol. xxi., p. 135.

XVII.

DISJECTA MEMBRA.

An ominous Pro-Slavery invasion of this country had been going on steadily through five decades. For it began in the administration of Jefferson, with the acquisition of Louisiana. It proceeded in constant encroachments, whose successive mile-stones were the Missouri Compromise, the annexation of Texas, the Mexican War, and now the Fugitive Slave Law. Thus far the inroads had been conducted by legislation. The South was soon to substitute rifles for constables.

Meantime, under the latest device of slavery, the condition of the colored people, even in the free States, was pitiable. They were without recourse. The Declaration of Independence was treason, and the Golden Rule was heresy. Senator Sumner estimated within a few months after the passage of the Fugitive Slave Law that " as many as six thousand Christian men and women, meritorious persons,—a larger band than that of the escaping Puritans,—precipitately fled from homes which they had established," to Canada.[1]

In Boston, on February 15th, 1851, Shadrach, a colored waiter in a coffee-house, was seized as an escaped slave. The court-room whither he had been

---
[1] *Vide Liberator*, vol. xxxiv., p. 70.

hurried was filled with a crowd of his own color, and, suddenly, Shadrach *disappeared* among them!'[1] Washington went into convulsions.

"'The head and front of the offending,' in this instance—what is it?" asked Mr. Garrison a week later. "A sudden rush of a score or two of unarmed friends of equal liberty—an uninjurious deliverance of the oppressed out of the hands of the oppressor—the quiet transportation of a slave out of this slavery-ruled land to the free soil of Upper Canada! Nobody injured, nobody wronged, but simply a chattel transformed into a man, and conducted to a spot whereon he can glorify God in his body and spirit, which are his!'"[2]

At this moment the authorities of the underground railroad resolved themselves into a Vigilance Committee for the purpose of giving aid and comfort to the flying bondmen. Mr. Phillips was a prominent stockholder in this corporation of humanity. Writing on March 9th, 1851, to Miss Pease, he gives that fair correspondent a graphic description of the operations of the Vigilance Committee:

"In Boston, all is activity—never before so much since I knew the cause. The rescue of Shadrach has set the whole public afire. We have some hundreds of fugitives among us. The oldest are alarmed. I had an old woman of seventy ask my advice about flying, though originally free and fearful only of being caught up by mistake. Of course, in one so old and valueless there was no temptation to mistake; but in others it is horrible to see the distress of families torn apart at this inclement season, and the working head forced to leave good employment, and seek not employment so much as the chance of it in the narrow, unenterprising, and overstocked market of Canada. Our Vigilance Committee meets every night. The escapes have been prov-

---

[1] *Vide Liberator*, vol. xxi., p. 30. [2] *Ib.*

idential. Since Shadrach's case, nigh a hundred have left the city. The way we get news of warrants is surprising. One officer was boasting to one of our members, whom he did not know to be such, that now they had a fellow in sight, and he would be arrested by one o'clock. Our friend lounged carelessly away, told what he'd heard, and by twelve the poor fellow described was steaming it on iron lines to Canada. Another, at work on a wharf, came out of his employer's store, saw his old master before him, heard him whistle, thought that was as much of such music as he cared for, dived into the cellar, up the back door, and 'has not been heard tell of,' as 'Baillie Nocol Jarvie' says, since.

"There have been several as close escapes as that, and there are still quite a number of Southerners here. It is said privately that all they want is *one* from Boston, to show the discontented ones at home that it can be done ; and our merchants groan at the trade they lose by the hatred the South bears us because she has not yet brought Boston under. Our business streets are markedly quiet. But we hope the same spirit is alive as laughed to scorn the mother country shutting up our harbor to starve us into compliance. Webster, too (like your Lord North), the infamous New Hampshire renegade, threatens to line our streets with soldiers. We've seen none, opposed to us, since the redcoats ; the Government, which wishes to succeed to the hatred they earned for their employers, had better send us their successors.

"I need not enlarge on this ; but the long evening sessions—debates about secret escapes—plans to evade where we can't resist—the door watched that no spy may enter—the whispering consultations of the morning—some putting property out of their hands, planning to incur penalties, and planning also that, in case of conviction, the Government may get nothing from them—the doing, and answering no questions—intimates forbearing to ask the knowledge which it may be dangerous to have—all remind one of those foreign scenes which have hitherto been known to us, transatlantic republicans, only in books. Yet we enjoy ourselves richly, and I doubt whether more laughing is done anywhere than in Anti-Slavery parlors." [1]

---

[1] Quoted in "William Lloyd Garrison," vol. iii., pp. 323, 324.

The next fugitive-slave case in Boston did not end so happily as had that of Shadrach. Thomas Sims, a colored refugee, was arrested, hustled into the court-house (which was surrounded by chains) ; and, with the police of the city and the militia of the State for an escort, was carried thence on shipboard and returned to Savannah.[1]

The better part of the community (but not the "respectability") bitterly opposed the atrocity. Bells were tolled in the country towns. In Boston, meeting after meeting was held, at which Phillips, Parker, Garrison, and Quincy spoke ; and there was a monster demonstration on the Common, where the orator addressed acres of excited people, and invoked the curse of the Almighty upon institutions which protected tyrants and immolated victims.

New York City being at this time dominated by Captain Rynders, the American Anti-Slavery Society was denied a hall there in 1851 in which to hold its annual May meeting, and found shelter in Syracuse, where Gerrit Smith, a Free Soil leader, bade it welcome.[2] The health of Mrs. Phillips was so precarious that her husband was held at home, and made himself notable at the session by his absence. He was able, however, to slip down to Worcester, on August 1st, to take part in the celebration, in that

---

[1] *Vide Liberator*, vol. xxii., p. 62. "Sims was severely whipped after arriving at Savannah, and for two months was kept closely confined in a cell. He was then sent to a slave-pen in Charleston, and thence to a slave-pen at New Orleans. He was purchased by a brick mason, and taken to Vicksburg, whence, in 1863, he escaped to the besieging army of General Grant, who gave him transportation to the North." Austin's "Life and Times of Wendell Phillips," p. 141, note.

[2] *Ib.*, vol. xxi., p. 81.

town, of West Indian emancipation. His speech was the feature of the day, and was devoted to a keen analysis of the condition of affairs in America.[1]

In October the second National Women's Rights Convention met, also in Worcester. Those who had attended it the previous year were present in 1851. Mr. Phillips there delivered the most elaborate and best-known of all his speeches on this theme. He sounded the depths and fixed the latitude and longitude of the reform with an accuracy which left no need for amendment. This was the powerful presentation of which George William Curtis has said : " In the general statement of principle nothing has been added to it; in vivid and effective eloquence of advocacy it has never been surpassed. All the arguments for independence echoed John Adams in the Continental Congress. All the pleas for applying the American principle of representation to the wives and mothers of American citizens echo the eloquence of Wendell Phillips at Worcester."[2] Happily, the address was harvested, and is easily accessible in the collected speeches of the orator. Those who would study this masterpiece are referred to it there.[3]

When Mr. Phillips met Theodore Parker, after returning from the Women's Rights Convention, the clergyman said to him :

"Wendell, why do you make a fool of yourself?"

"Theodore," was the reply, "this is the greatest question of the ages; you ought to understand it."

---

[1] *Vide Liberator*, vol. xxii., p. 130, for a full report.
[2] "Wendell Phillips. A Eulogy," by George William Curtis, p. 32.
[3] *Vide* "Speeches and Lectures," by Wendell Phillips, pp. 11-34.

Before the year had passed Parker had espoused the cause, and he preached four sermons upon it in warm advocacy of the whole claim.[1]

In December, 1851, Louis Kossuth came to America, seeking the intervention of the United States in behalf of Hungary, torn and bleeding in the talons of the Austrian eagle. This remarkable man had mastered the English language so completely that he could say with "Hamlet :"

" —— I am a native here,
And to the manner born."

Unfortunately, he had also acquired something else American—the national habit of ignoring slavery, and eulogizing our eagle as though it were not as cruel as the Hapsburg bird of prey. Slave-holders invited him here ; slave-holders entertained him while he remained ; and slave-holders profited by his silence regarding their sin and by his laudations of their government.

This was a bitter mortification to the Abolitionists. They were among his most ardent admirers. They deeply sympathized with his poor country. But as they watched his triumphal course, and saw him deliberately sacrifice the negro to aid the Hungarian, their indignation flamed. At the Anti-Slavery Bazaar,[2] in Boston, on December 27th, 1851, Wendell Phillips rebuked the illustrious Magyar in a Mont Blanc utterance, down whose side he shook loose

---

[1] Mrs. Lucy Stone is the authority for this story.

[2] An Anti-Slavery bazaar was annually held in Boston almost throughout the struggle against slavery ; at which articles contributed at home and abroad were offered for sale for the benefit of the Anti-Slavery treasury ; and at which Mr. Phillips and others were wont to make addresses.

avalanche after avalanche of condemnation. He told who Kossuth was—a fugitive from Austrian law ; he described this country, madly sensitive to foreign criticism, and hanging breathlessly upon the great fugitive's lips to catch what he should say ; he showed that Kossuth had been informed of the condition of the American struggle before he left the old world, so that he could not plead ignorance of the atrocities enacted here ; he quoted the unstinted eulogies pronounced by the nation's guest upon our institutions, with never a whispered exception of anything objectionable ; he contrasted this selfish patriotism of the Magyar, which consented to help Hungary at the expense of one sixth part of the population of America, meeted and peeled under iron heels which made Austria's seem merciful in comparison,—with the broad humanity of O'Connell, of Victor Hugo, of Lafayette, pleading not for one race but for all ; he disclaimed the expectation that the visitor would take a pronounced Anti-Slavery stand, but asserted that he might justly be called upon to guard his words and withhold such wholesale laudation ; and ended by quoting the words of Fletcher of Saltoun : " I would do much to help my country, but I would not do a wicked thing to save her !" [1]

The speech was made in Mr. Phillips's loftiest vein. It makes one's blood tingle even to read it. And it was prodigiously effective. In the delivery, the orator broke through his usual repose of manner. He seemed to feel the paradox involved in such a challenge of one reformer by another. He was de-

---

[1] *Vide Liberator*, vol. xxii., p. 3, for a full report of this speech, not elsewhere accessible.

clamatory beyond precedent. It was like one of Wagner's tenor *robustos* in "Lohengrin," singing with a full brass band accompaniment.

Kossuth's mission was a failure—and deserved to be. He asked the United States to do, what *he* distinctly refused to do—interfere in the domestic affairs of a foreign country. After parading as a nine days' wonder, he crept back to Europe to bury himself alive in chagrin, leaving behind him here only the memory of his marvellous oratory.

XVIII.

GOOD WORKS.

IN Boston, as in all large cities, there are many girls half or two thirds grown, women in their passions, children in their knowledge and self-control, afloat on the streets, whom idleness and vagrant habits expose to devilish temptations. They are in danger of becoming rotten before they are ripe. Mr. Phillips always interested himself in this class. With Theodore Parker, he assisted early in 1852 in the formation of a moral reform society for the rescue of such as had gone astray and for the protection of those as yet unfallen. The object of the organization was twofold: to instruct these waifs in the means of earning an honest livelihood, and then to remove them into a more wholesome environment beyond the town. One of Mr. Phillips's closest friends, the Rev. John T. Sargent, a gentleman of wealth and social prominence, a noble spirit, accepted the agency of the society, while Phillips and Parker were Aaron and Hur to hold up his hands.[1]

The anniversary of the Massachusetts Anti-Slavery Society always occurred in January. On the 28th of that month, Mr. Phillips addressed the Society in one of the ablest of his speeches, that on "Public

---

[1] "Life of Theodore Parker," by O. B. Frothingham, p. 365.

Opinion."[1] It is remarkable for its epigrammatic point, and also because of the absolute faith the speaker expressed in the republican principle—in the competency of the people, and in their ultimate certainty to right every wrong.

The sessions covered two days. In the evening of the third day, the 30th, the Abolitionists met in Faneuil Hall, and on this congenial platform the orator spoke upon the recent surrender of Sims.[2] Though opened by his friends, the hall was crowded by his foes. The meeting was stormy. Speaker after speaker was shouted down. Mr. Phillips himself had to fight for a hearing. Every mention of the exciting occurrences of the hour was hissed, every name he ventured to censure was cheered. But his wit, his satire, his repartee, so turned the laugh upon the interrupters that at last they were cowed into quietude. He mobbed the mob![3]

It was in March, 1852, that Mrs. Harriet Beecher Stowe's "Uncle Tom's Cabin" appeared—not so much a book as an event. Douglas Jerrold said, "the soil in Australia was so fertile that if you tickled it with a hoe it laughed with a harvest." "Uncle Tom" fell upon prepared ground. The crop of readers was wonderful—striking proof of the success of the Abolitionists in creating Anti-Slavery sentiment. Richard Hildreth's "White Slave," an equally dramatic work, first published in 1835, made no sensation because born out of due time. Mrs. Stowe's book, on the contrary, appearing seventeen

---

[1] *Vide* his "Speeches and Lectures," pp. 35-55.
[2] *Ib.*, pp. 55-70.
[3] *Vide* Higginson's "Wendell Phillips," p. 13.

years later, had the advantage of a ripened public conscience—wide awake enough to read if not to act. Twenty thousand copies of "Uncle Tom's Cabin" were sold within three weeks after it left the press. Eighty thousand copies were disposed of within three months.[1] Its success was even greater in England. George Thompson wrote Mr. Garrison, in the autumn of 1852, from London:

"'Uncle Tom' is doing a great work here. Between four and five hundred thousand copies (varying in price from sixpence to seven and sixpence) are already in circulation. Two of our metropolitan theatres are nightly crowded to overflowing by persons anxious to witness a representation of its striking scenes on the stage. Behold the fruit of your labors and rejoice."[2]

Not long afterward the book was dramatized in this country. In Boston and in New York, as in London, it proved a gold mine to the theatres; and slaves shot their hunters to slow music and loud applause.

God makes "the wrath of man to praise Him." Even the rendition of a fugitive slave created Anti-Slavery opinion. Realizing this (though sickened by the experience) and encouraged by the phenomenal popularity of Mrs. Stowe's novel, the Abolitionists decided to observe the anniversary of Thomas Sim's surrender. Accordingly, on April 12th, 1852, a great meeting was held in Boston, at which Mr. Phillips pronounced another of his masterpieces[3]— the third since the year broke. This is equal to either of the others; not in brilliancy, perhaps, but in a certain grave splendor and sustained majesty of

---

[1] "William Lloyd Garrison," vol. iii., p. 362.
[2] *Ib.*, pp. 362, 363.   [3] Phillips's "Speeches," pp. 71–97.

diction. It illustrates the variety and fertility of his style.

Mr. Phillips journeyed to Central New York in May, 1852, to attend the annual meeting of the American Anti-Slavery Society, which convened in Rochester.[1] He was warmly welcomed and eagerly listened to. Like Dante, exiled from Florence and driven to Ravenna, the absence of the Abolitionists from New York City made anniversary week stupid there, and raised the interior town into national prominence during the tarry of the Convention.

The nation was now in the throes of a Presidential canvass. Three parties divided the field—the Democratic, the Whig, and the Free Soil. When the votes were cast and counted in November, Franklin Pierce was chosen, the Whig party was routed never to rally again, and the Free Soilers were distanced in the race. It is a singular fact that, spite of the immense constituency of "Uncle Tom," the Anti-Slavery ballots only numbered one hundred and fifty-six thousand out of three millions—an actual falling off since 1848, when the Free Soil vote was two hundred and ninety thousand! And what did the election of Franklin Pierce mean? It meant the approval of the Pro-Slavery propaganda. It meant the disavowal of the Anti-Slavery protest. It showed how superficial the opposition to the lords of the plantation was, and how complete was their ascendency. The despotism of the Czar in Russia, the throne of the Hapsburgs in Austria, the privileges of the British aristocracy, did not seem as impregnable in 1852 as did the slave power in America.

---

[1] *Vide Liberator*, vol. xxii., pp. 82, 83.

As for Mr. Phillips, the result of the election only confirmed his views. As Milton said, "new presbyter is but old priest writ large," so he thought this latest and completest triumph of the South was but a new demonstration of old truth. The slave *Union* must be broken. There was no hope for liberty while it intrusted itself to slavery. It was "Little Red Riding-hood" led by the wolf. No man can serve two masters—neither can a country. What could be more unnatural than such a coalition? Freedom—coffle gangs; the nineteenth century—the twelfth century; republican institutions—despotism; ideas—ignorance; the Golden Rule—satanic selfishness; law—self-will; progress—stagnation! And these opposites and contradictions existing under one government, and administered by the worser part! Such a Union—what was it but the union of the shark with its prey? Therefore he redoubled his efforts to dissolve the Union,—to persuade the North to withdraw from such a hopeless partnership,—to win that section which furnished the strength and paid the bills to shake off the South and form a new Union, like attracting like.

Standing in isolation, with no party collar around his neck, and no sectarian padlock on his lips, he enjoyed the luxury of expressing his thought with uncompromising candor. He summoned the men and measures around him to judgment. He criticised freely and sharply. The Democratic and the Whig parties were the right and left hands of slavery. The Free Soil party, like its predecessor, the Liberty party, was inefficient because inconsistent. It was fatally hampered by the necessary limitations of a Pro-Slavery Constitution. The Free Soilers hated slavery, yet were forced as politicians to disclaim any purpose to interfere with it where it already existed. They wanted freedom throughout the Union, yet were obliged to content themselves with claiming it in the free States and the new Territories. They objected to engaging in a slave hunt, yet had to acknowledge that the return of fugitives was a Constitutional duty.

Mr. Phillips rejoiced in any increased Anti-Slavery sentiment which an enlarged political opposition to Calhounism might show. He recognized the good intentions and often the valuable services of the chiefs of political Anti-Slavery.[1] At the same time he remorselessly exposed their inconsistencies, and emphasized the inevitable limitations of their position inside of a slave Union. For himself, he kept reaffirming his purpose to oppose slavery not less in the slave States than in the Territories. While it actually existed anywhere in America it possibly existed everywhere. He hated the *system*, not merely the extension of it. Did the Constitution protect it? Then the Constitution must be revolutionized. Was the Union its bulwark? Then the Union must be overthrown, and a new Union must be constructed— a nineteenth-century Union—a Christian Union—a Union of liberty—a Union of progress—a Union in which the Declaration of Independence should *not* be treason, and in which the Golden Rule should *not* be heresy—a Union whose national emblem should no longer be a grand slave hunt, with the President as the foremost hound of the pack.

Such was Mr. Phillips's position throughout these

---

[1] *Vide* his "Speeches," pp. 120–48, *passim*, for instances.

years. Radical? Yes. Unpopular? Certainly. But logical, consistent, easily understood. The South said: "We will carry our slaves *everywhere*." Political Anti-Slavery said: "You must not take them into the *Territories*." Mr. Phillips said: "You shall hold slaves *nowhere*." He met the South in its own spirit, and replied to it with uncompromising boldness. He liked Southerners, personally. And politically, he admired their courage and directness. These qualities *he* likewise embodied, met frankness with frankness, and said "No" in the same tone in which Calhoun said "Yes."

Of course, the eloquent Abolitionist did not make many converts; that is, he did not persuade many to take his extreme position. But he leavened the whole lump. He made slavery hateful. He won multitudes to *start* on the crusade for freedom. He prepared the North to abolish slavery just as soon as it saw the way and got the opportunity. This he did. For the rest, he recognized the limitations of his own position. He was content to be a sower of seed. He knew, none better, that unless some one held up a high ideal, the loftiest and most outside conception of justice, in such an evil age, the situation would be hopeless. It was a part of his philosophy not to aim at immediate results,—at carrying the jury by a *coup de main;* but to educate public opinion. "My dear John," he wrote to a friend, "if we would get half the loaf, we must demand the whole of it."[1] These words summarized his philosophy of agitation. He looked at to-day from the

---

[1] Letter to Rev. John T. Sargent (MS.).

vantage-ground of to-morrow. He asked, not What is expedient? but What is right? He could afford to wait. He knew the world would catch up to him, sooner or later. So he kept ahead, made moral pioneering his function, and cried, "Excelsior."

XIX.

PORTRAITS.

THE rising tide of Anti-Slavery feeling was attributed, by those unfriendly to the Abolitionists, to anybody and everybody save Mr. Phillips and his colaborers. *They* were reckless, denunciatory, unreasonable, and obstructed the cause they professed to serve. Charles Sumner, Mrs. Stowe, Henry Ward Beecher, were the real influences that moved the swelling flood—such was the assertion.

At the meeting of the New England Anti-Slavery Society, on January 27th, 1853, Mr. Phillips considered these statements, which had just been ably repeated in detail in one of the English journals as a criticism upon the methods of the reformers. He went over the whole ground, staked out the boundaries between truth and falsehood, and mapped down the facts, luminously and voluminously. This speech he called "The Philosophy of the Abolition Movement."[1] It is, perhaps, the most exhaustive of all his efforts, and deserves the careful study of those who would see to the bottom of the subject. Personally, the orator was the least vain of men. He claimed nothing for himself, except the wish and purpose to do his duty. But he did feel the slight to the veterans who surrounded him, covered with honorable scars; and, most of all, the attempt by

---

[1] "Speeches and Lectures," by Wendell Phillips, pp. 98-153.

recent converts still in the "awkward squad," to court-martial Mr. Garrison. Said he:

"We are perfectly willing—I am, for one—to be the dead lumber that shall make a path for these men into the honor of the country. Use us, freely, in any way, for the slave. When the temple is finished the tools will not complain that they are thrown aside, let who will lead up the nation to 'put on the top-stone with shoutings.' But while so much remains to be done, while our little camp is beleaguered all about, do nothing to weaken his influence, whose sagacity, more than any other single man's, has led us up hither, and whose name is identified with that movement which the North still heeds, and the South still fears the most." [1]

As one result of this vindication, Mr. Phillips became involved in a prolonged controversy with Horace Mann, then a Free Soil member of Congress from Massachusetts. This gentleman was a prominent driller in the "awkward squad," and, with a brand new uniform on, set up for a veteran. He was a sharp fighter on paper, and with his pen for a sword was a formidable foe. The combat was fierce and angry on his part, calm and self-possessed on the part of Mr. Phillips. It was fought over the whole field of difference between the Free Soilers and the Abolitionists. It were needless at this late day to detail the respective thrusts and parries. Suffice it to say that it ended much as a certain famous duel in France did, between Floquet and Boulanger—with Mr. Phillips in the rôle of the former, and with Mr. Mann *hors de combat*, like the "brav' general." [2]

In the midst of this controversy, Mr. Phillips found

---

[1] Phillips's "Speeches," p. 138.

[2] For the *ipsissima verba vide Liberator*, vol. xxiii., pp. 42, 46, 54, 58, 66, 70.

time to address a Committee of the Constitutional Convention of Massachusetts, then in session, in advocacy of a numerously-signed petition of the women of the State asking for equal political rights with men. The Convention heard the orator, and then threw the petition into the waste-basket.[1] It was too far ahead. There was soft solder enough among those tinkers in the Convention—but they applied it to the women with their tongues and worked away at the Constitution with a calking-iron.

The month of May, 1853, found Mr. Phillips in New York City, whither the American Anti-Slavery Society had returned for its anniversary after its exile of two years. Baron Munchausen tells a story of a musician who, playing a tune in Russia, had it frozen, and who, being in Italy the following summer, was surprised to hear the balance of the tune come pealing forth—thawed out in that mild climate. So the orator resumed his speech at the point where Captain Rynders had stopped it, and poured it out triumphantly. In the course of his remarks, he referred to the offer of the Rev. Dr. Orville Dewey, an eminent Unitarian clergyman, to return (or as he afterward amended it, to *consent* to the return of) his mother into slavery if that were necessary to save the Union. Thereupon a hurricane of cheers and hisses, long-continued, broke forth. He paused blandly, and when the storm had subsided, said quietly : " For once I have the whole audience with me ; some of you are applauding me, and the rest are hissing Dr. Dewey !" This sally was followed by great laughter and loud cheers—no hisses ! [2]

---

[1] Austin's " Life and Times of Wendell Phillips," p. 159.
[2] *Vide Liberator*, vol. xxiii., last week in May.

The Woman Suffragists, who were in session at the same time, were not so fortunate as the Abolitionists. Their Convention was transformed into a Bedlam,—their speakers derided,—their proceedings parodied,—their earnest made a jest. Wendell Phillips spoke on their platform; but against a tempest and in interjections.[1]

In an address which he delivered in Boston, two weeks later, he gave a fine definition of the respective functions of the reformer and the politician. It is worth noting:

"The reformer is careless of numbers, disregards popularity, and deals only with ideas, conscience, and common-sense. He feels, with Copernicus, that as God waited long for an interpreter, so he can wait for his followers. He neither expects nor is over-anxious for immediate success. The politician dwells in an everlasting *Now*. His motto is 'Success'—his aim, votes. His object is not absolute right, but, like Solon's laws, as much right as the people will sanction. His office is, not to instruct public opinion, but to represent it. Thus, in England, Cobden, the reformer, created sentiment, and Peel, the politician, stereotyped it into statutes."[2]

It was in 1833, and in Philadelphia, that the American Anti-Slavery Society was organized.[3] It was now 1853—and the Abolitionists determined to celebrate the twentieth anniversary. Accordingly, they sped from all directions Quaker-Cityward and jubilated, with the pioneers to tell the story of yesterday, and with Phillips to speak for to-day.[4] "In the matter of voting," remarked Mr. Phillips, "I will be Mordecai at the gate." In another year the so-

---

[1] Austin's "Life and Times of Wendell Phillips," pp. 148–51.
[2] *Vide Liberator*, vol. xxiii., p. 97.
[3] *Ante*, p. 71.   [4] *Vide Liberator*, vol. xxiii., p. 192.

ciety would be twenty-one—old enough to vote! Phillips might get up and cast a ballot. But he never did, until he rose to see Haman hung!

In those times of excitement, the Anti-Slavery Convention, naturally enough, attracted cranks, as a magnet draws iron filings. A character of this sort was a certain Abigail Folsom. She was a harmless soul, sane on most subjects, but a monomaniac regarding free speech—which she esteemed a right on her part to silence everybody else in order to have her say in season and out of season. Emerson wittily nicknamed her "the flea of conventions." She was often removed from the halls she infected and afflicted by gentle force. As she was a non-resistant, she never struck back, save with her tongue, which was keen enough. One day, Mr. Phillips, with two others, placed her in a chair and were carrying her down the aisle through a crowd, when she exclaimed :

" I'm better off than my Master was ; He had but one ass to ride—I have three to carry me !" [1]

Abigail Folsom was with, not of, the Abolitionists. Oddities, however, abounded among them—men and women of the most original type. Individualism ran mad. There, for example, was Parker Pillsbury, who started for the pulpit, and brought up on the platform ; who set out orthodox, and ended in unbelief ; who had broad shoulders surmounted by an enormous head ; who carried "a crater in each eye," and rumbled like a human Ætna.

By his side stood a couple yet more unique— Stephen S. Foster and Abby Kelley, his wife. She,

---

[1] "Garrison and his Times," p. 304.

a "Judith turned Quakeress,"—he, a non-resistant in profession and a gladiator in practice, who smote his opponents with the olive branch ; she, courageous with the bravery of an indomitable purpose, —he, brave, too, but, like the Irishman at "Donnybrook Fair," carrying a chip on his shoulder which he dared any one to knock off, and inviting a row ; she, charged with the collection of the Abolition revenues, —he, by his pugnacious utterances, angering the half-friends who might have given into the wish to knock him down rather than contribute. Lowell, who knew and coworked with both, has portrayed them with exquisite fidelity. Of Abby he says :

"No nobler gift of heart or brain,
No life more white from spot or stain,
Was e'er on Freedom's altar laid
Than hers—the Simple Quaker maid."

Mr. Foster he hits off with rare humor :

"Hard by, as calm as summer even,
Smiles the reviled and pelted Stephen ;
Who studied mineralogy
Not with soft book upon the knee,
But learned the properties of stones
By contact sharp of flesh and bones,
And made the *experimentum crucis*
With his own body's vital juices ;
A kind of maddened John the Baptist,
To whom the harshest word comes aptest,
Who, struck by stone or brick ill-starred,
Hurls back an epithet as hard,
Which, deadlier than stone or brick,
Has a propensity to stick."

It was remarked of a well-known Baptist clergyman, of a controversial temper, that he baptized his converts in *hot* water. So did many of the Garrisonians. As the chronic invalid, when asked how he was, always said "he enjoyed poor health," so they seemed, some of them, to enjoy their unpopularity, and to court it.

There were those among the Garrisonians, too, who had adopted every *ism* of the day. These they sifted into their Anti-Slavery utterances, and thus produced the impression that Abolitionism was the nucleus of every scatter-brain theory and Utopian enterprise. Mr. Garrison himself was a sinner in this respect. He had now given up all his earlier religious views—was an anti-Bible man,—an anti-Sabbatarian,—a no-government exponent, as well as an Abolitionist. Because he held and taught such doctrines, the community naturally concluded that these were a normal part of Abolitionism—all the more because he mixed them. Of course, Mr. Garrison had a right to his opinions. But it was not good generalship to load down a cause already sufficiently odious by identifying it with other and unrelated issues which were yet more unpopular. "One war at a time," as Lincoln said. He should have emphatically distinguished between what was Abolitionism and what was not, in expressing his convictions, and should have made the line of demarkation broad as Boston Bay, high as Bunker Hill monument—unmistakable.

Mr. Phillips did not share in the vagaries of some of his friends. Nevertheless, he had to bear the odium; which he did uncomplainingly—too uncomplainingly. It was the glory of the Anti-Slavery platform that it made room for both sexes, all colors, and every creed. There was the more reason, therefore, that each should define his own position. But the cosmopolitan character of the Abolitionists was magnificent and sensible. If a general should call for volunteers to go into a forlorn hope, as one and another slipped out from the ranks, it would not occur to him to inquire into the religious ideas of this, and the home relations of that, and the financial condition of the other. In building railroads or organizing banks, Episcopalians, Baptists, Quakers, Presbyterians, Congregationalists, Roman Catholics, and atheists combine. They surrender nothing of their individual belief in doing so. They come together for a specific cause, and, reserving their separate interests for other hours, unite for the prosecution of the common purpose. Precisely so with the Abolitionists. Members of all sects and of none might consistently join in a movement against slavery. As soon, however, as a sifting in of outside opinions began, there was a necessity laid upon everybody to protest and define; while the result enabled the Pro-Slavery spectators to identify Anti-Slavery with Bedlam. We repeat, it was a disastrous error, and it robbed the Garrisonians of influence and a following which they might otherwise have held.

The contrast between Mr. Phillips and *some* of his *confrères* was so striking that audiences familiar with them but which had never heard him, were amazed when he appeared before them. His patrician bearing, his unobtrusive but self-evident scholarship, his common-sense uttered in such gorgeous sentences, —made him as "Hyperion to a satyr."

XX.

EXCITEMENT.

In 1854 Congress passed the Nebraska Bill—an apple of contention thrown by the goddess of discord. In effect, it repealed the Missouri Compromise, which had dedicated to freedom whatever territory lay north of 36° 30', and relegated to the inhabitants themselves the question as to whether slavery should be domesticated in the vast lands included under the name of Nebraska. That is to say, Kansas, Montana, and parts of Dakota, Wyoming, and Colorado, were opened to slavery, provided the South could colonize them. The section immediately concerned was Kansas, which the slave-holders had already entered in great numbers, and which might soon be expected to become a State. The other sections were, as yet, unpopulated, but were certain to be arenas of strife as fast as they were reached. The Compromise measures of 1850 had foreshadowed that which the Nebraska Bill made the permanent policy and deliberate practice of the Union. Such was the doctrine known as "Squatter Sovereignty."

To say that it revived and intensified sectional rivalry, is like speaking of the Civil War as an "unpleasantness." The country was aflame. A stupendous race into Kansas began in the South, and from the North, and Kansas itself was straightway transformed into a bloody battleground—the opening skirmish of the impending revolution.

With a host of others, Mr. Phillips exerted himself to expose and defeat the Nebraska Bill; and when it passed, he redoubled his efforts with voice and purse to hasten Northern immigration to Kansas in order to secure it for freedom. He no longer stood alone. His views of the Union,—of its Pro-Slavery character and tendency, were widely adopted,—and his remedy was more and more seriously considered. In February, 1854, he visited New York City and spoke in the Broadway Tabernacle on "Squatter Sovereignty," and in doing so treated the whole question of slavery. "Straws show which way the wind blows." That it was now blowing North is shown by the following notice of his lecture, taken from the conservative *Evening Post:*

"The distinguished orator of Abolitionism, Mr. Wendell Phillips, held forth on his favorite topic on Tuesday evening to an audience which completely crowded the Tabernacle, and it must be admitted that in all respects a more desirable audience could not have been selected from the population of the city. It marks a great change in the public sentiment, when a gathering like that of Tuesday night can sit for two hours and a quarter and listen, not merely with patience, but with manifest delight to a presentation of unadulterated Abolitionism. Mr. Phillips is certainly an orator of the highest order. In addition to rhetorical accomplishments that outrival those of Mr. Everett, he exhibits a sincerity and naturalness which his compeer is obliged to counterfeit. The lecture was a felicitous recast of Mr. Phillips's familiar views; but the untiring enthusiasm and graceful eloquence of the speaker constantly evoked expressions of approval from the listeners."

We know now, what men only surmised then, that the Southern leaders were confederated to rule or ruin. They were ruling at present. They were also deliberately preparing to ruin on the first evidence that the sceptre would depart from Judah. Meantime they omitted no opportunity to exasperate Northern sentiment. The Fugitive Slave Law was enforced with special and diabolical thoroughness, as a master measure of provocation.

The Anthony Burns case occurred in May, 1854. Burns had escaped from Richmond, Va., in the preceding February, and was now hiding in Boston. At eight o'clock in the evening he was arrested, on a false charge, as usual in such cases, hurried to the court-house and concealed—no one being admitted to see him but the slave-claimant, the United States Marshal, and the police.[1] The next morning, the fugitive, ignorant, confused, trembling, friendless, was hustled before the United States Commissioner, Edward G. Loring, who was also a Massachusetts Judge of Probate. This heartless judge was about to deliver him to his master (not God, but one Colonel Seattle), when by accident Richard H. Dana, Jr., entered the court-room. Grasping the situation, he rose, protested against the indecent haste, and secured an adjournment of the hearing for two days.[2]

It was anniversary week in Boston. The city was full of strangers in attendance upon the Anti Slavery, the Women's Rights, and other conventions. The news circulated like wild-fire. "Since the Revolution," wrote Mr. Garrison in the *Liberator* of that week, "Boston has never witnessed such a popular excitement,—the commonwealth has never been so

---

[1] Phillips's "Speeches," p. 185.   [2] *Ib.*, pp. 186-92.

convulsed."[1] Faneuil Hall was flung open and thronged. Phillips and Parker were the orators, and their words were thunderbolts. "I do not believe in Squatter Sovereignty in Kansas," declared the former, "and I hold Kidnapper Sovereignty to be more infamous in the streets of Boston."[2] He went on to quote the saying of Judge Harrington, of Vermont, away back in the first decade of the century, who, when asked to return a runaway slave, refused on the ground of insufficient evidence. "What would you regard as sufficient?" asked the claimant. "Nothing short of a bill of sale from Almighty God!" was the reply.[3]

While the "Cradle of Liberty" was being rocked, an effort was simultaneously made by an excited crowd to rescue Burns, but failed through a misunderstanding and the lack of concert. Parker knew of it—Phillips did not.[4]

In the meanwhile President Pierce and the Mayor of Boston concentrated all the military and civic powers within reach to overawe the New England capital—just as Lord North had done two generations before; Commissioner Loring delivered the unhappy black to his alleged owner; and an army carried him down State Street, over the very ground where Crispus Attucks, a colored man, fell as the first victim of British tyranny in resisting the redcoats; and Burns was flung manacled into the hold of a vessel bound for Virginia,—the latest, and, thank God! the last victim in Boston of American law.[5]

---

[1] *Vide Liberator*, vol. xxiii., p. 86.   [2] *Ib.*   [3] *Ib.*
[4] Higginson's "Obituary Notice of Wendell Phillips," p. 9.
[5] *Vide Liberator*, vol. xxiii., p. 91.

The *Liberator* painted the scene and called attention to the fact that the whole city hissed and jeered the infamous procession—the most conservative, even ; a great change in public opinion since the Sims case.[1] There was not yet enough Anti-Slavery feeling to prevent the rendition ; but the Abolitionists had been successful in making it despicable. Further proof of this was given when Wendell Phillips, who had been absent from the sessions looking after Burns, came into the Anti-Slavery Convention on the night of May 30th, and was received with tumultuous cheers, which were repeated again and again after he had spoken in the strains of his Faneuil Hall address.[2]

The Abolitionists were in the habit of celebrating the Fourth of July in a lovely grove, at Framingham, just out of Boston. At their gathering this year, Mr. Phillips related an incident in connection with the Burns case, which shows how much more strongly some men are influenced by sectarian than by humanitarian motives :

"I met a man a week after Burns was surrendered, and he asked me : ' Mr. Phillips, was Burns really a Baptist exhorter, regularly licensed ? ' Said I : ' He was, sir, a Baptist exhorter, regularly licensed.' ' Well,' said he, ' I didn't take much interest in the case : but when I heard that Major-General Edmunds had sent back a brother Baptist, I couldn't sleep ! ' He took no interest in the *man*—it was the *Baptist*. He heard the mere fact of a human being surrendered as a chattel—and went about his business. But when he learned that one Baptist had surrendered another Baptist,—*it disturbed his slumber !*"[3]

The Phillipses passed that summer in Milton : " One of the most delightful of our country towns

---

[1] *Vide Liberator*, vol. xxiii., p. 91.　　[2] *Ib.*, p. 94.　　[3] *Ib.*

(wrote the orator, on August 7th, to Miss Pease). Ann's brother has a place here, and we are with him."[1] He goes on to open his heart to his fair sympathizer:

"I would say something on the Burns case if I did not know you saw the *Standard* and *Liberator*, from whose columns you get so many particulars that a note like this can add little. 'Twas the saddest week I ever passed. Men talked of the good we might expect for the cause, but I could not think then of the general cause, so mournful and sad arose ever before me the pleading eyes of the poor victim, when he sat and cast his case on our consciences, and placed his fate in our hands. I could not forget the man in the idea. Time has passed since, and I begin to think more of the three millions and less of the individual. The effect of his surrender under this infamous law has been, like 'Uncle Tom' and all such spasms, far less deep and general than thoughtless folks anticipated. We always gain at such times a few hundred and the old friends are strengthened, but the mass settle down very little different from before.

"Indeed, the Government has fallen into the hands of the slave power completely. So far as national politics are concerned, we are beaten—there's no hope. We shall have Cuba in a year or two, Mexico in five; and I should not wonder if efforts are made to revive the old slave trade, though perhaps unsuccessfully, as the Northern slave States, which live by the export of slaves, would help us in opposing that. Events hurry forward with amazing rapidity: we live fast here. The future seems to unfold a vast slave empire united with Brazil, and darkening the whole West. I hope I may be a false prophet, but the sky was never so dark. Our Union, all confess, must sever finally on this question. It is now with nine tenths only a question of time."[2]

In the autumn, after safely bestowing his wife at No. 26 Essex Street, "dear, delightful, dusty spot," the Agitator went off on a lecturing tour, travelling

---

[1] "Memorial of Ann Phillips," p. 14.
[2] "William Lloyd Garrison," vol. iii., p. 410 *sq*.

through Central New York as far West as Detroit, Mich., and returning by way of Philadelphia. He spoke everywhere to enthusiastic multitudes.[1] His tone may be caught from these lines, penned by one of the fathers of Anti-Slavery, the Rev. Samuel May, of Syracuse, and published in the *Liberator:*

"Wendell Phillips delivered to a crowded audience in our City Hall, the ablest speech I ever heard, even from him—which is equivalent to saying the ablest I ever heard. He showed that we have little to hope from parties, but much from the moral and religious sentiment, which must be aroused to abhor slavery, as we abhor sheep-stealing, piracy, and murder."[2]

When he got home from this trip, Mr. Phillips was arrested. History has much to say of the "brace of Adamses," and nothing unworthy. Boston, in these years, held another brace, a brace of *Bens*, suggestive of the first only by dishonorable contrast,—Benjamin R. Curtis, of the United States Supreme Court, and Benjamin F. Hallett, United States District-Attorney. The two Bens were willing (for a consideration) to figure as legal hounds in the national slave hunt. Accordingly, they indicted Wendell Phillips and Theodore Parker for "obstructing the process of the United States," meaning the Fugitive Slave Law. It is not probable that they expected to accomplish much as against the defendants. They only wished to impress the Administration with a due sense of their official activity, and to secure preferment by licking the hand that could bestow it. Personally, they put the indictment on the ground of patriotism—forgetful of Dr. Johnson's apothegm: "Patriotism is the last refuge

---

[1] *Vide Liberator*, vol. xxiii., p. 183.   [2] *Ib.*, vol. xxiv., p. 194.

of a scoundrel." So Wendell and Theodore were each held in $1500 to answer. They were not much troubled to get bail. Phillips's sureties were six, viz., George William Phillips (his brother), the Rev. Samuel May, William I. Bowditch, Francis Jackson, Robert E. Althorp, and Charles Ellis.[1]

Parker, in a letter to Charles Sumner, jots down all this, and adds: "John Hancock was also once arrested by the British authorities, in October, 1768. Great attempts were made to indict Sam Adams, and Edes, and Gill, patriotic printers: but no grand jury *then* would find a bill."[2]

Sumner dashed back from Washington these lines in reply: "I regard your indictment as a call to a new parish with B. R. Curtis and B. F. Hallett as deacons, and a pulpit higher than Strassburg steeple."[3] At the same date he wrote to Mr. Phillips:

"Well, Wendell, your Faneuil Hall speech anent poor Burns, and your treasonable efforts to humanize those whom the United States chattelizes, have at last, it should seem, overtaxed the mercy of a long-suffering Government; and Franklin Pierce, by the worthy proxies of B. R. C. and B. F. H., has struck back. You are indicted! What a small mouse for so big a mountain to bring forth—and after such prolonged travail, too. All right. 'Everything helps us.'"[4]

These cases never came to trial. Through technical defects, the indictments were quashed.[5] The brace of Bens had shown the South that they proudly wore the collar,—their object was attained,—they were now in the line of promotion.

---

[1] *Vide Liberator*, vol. xxiv., p. 203.
[2] Weiss's "Life of Theodore Parker," vol. ii., p. 144.   [3] *Ib.*
[4] Letter to Wendell Phillips, December (MS.).
[5] Weiss's and Frothingham's biographies of Theodore Parker, *in loco.*

On December 21st Mr. Phillips lectured in Boston. Let the *Courier*, the most servile Pro-Slavery journal in Massachusetts, describe it:

"Tremont Temple was crowded to its utmost capacity on Thursday night. Wendell Phillips was the orator of the evening. His subject was 'The Nature and Extent of the Anti-Slavery Feeling in New England,' and never were the splendid abilities of this most accomplished and able fanatic more amply displayed than on this occasion. Sentiments the most repugnant to the feelings of every patriot were absolutely applauded when clothed in the magnificent diction of the Anti-Slavery Cicero. No pen can describe the gross injustice of the matter, nor the exquisite felicity of the manner of the Abolition orator."

This extract suggests Balaam, who set out to curse Israel, and blessed it instead.

XXI.

GREAT EVENTS.

ANTI-SLAVERY Massachusetts had now two objects at heart. One was the removal from the Probate Judgeship of Edward G. Loring, who as United States Commissioner had returned Anthony Burns to Virginia. The other was the making such acts impossible within her borders in future. Petitions praying for legislative intervention choked the mails and reached the State House in vast numbers, with signatures from Cape Cod to the Berkshire hills. Who should present them? Who should mature the needful action? The popular choice instinctively selected the fittest man alive—Wendell Phillips.

It was a task quite to his liking. On February 20th, 1855, he went before a designated committee of the Legislature, with the commonwealth for a client, and pleaded for the removal of Judge Loring. Competent legal critics pronounced his argument worthy to rank with the impeachment speeches of Burke and Sheridan, when Warren Hastings was on trial in Westminster Hall—with the loftiest forensic efforts of Brougham and Erskine.[1] Rufus Choate, a political opponent, said: "It is outrageously magnificent."[2] As it lies in the printed vol-

---

[1] Lawyers, for example, like Sumner, Richard H. Dana, Jr., Edward L. Pierce, and Samuel H. Sewall.
[2] His remark to Senator Sumner.

ume of the orator's speeches,[1] it is unnecessary to attempt a summary. The effect was electric. The Legislature voted to remove the disgraced official.[2] Temporarily the Governor checkmated the will of the people by a veto;[3] ultimately, the measure was signed and sealed, and Loring, judge no longer, stepped down and out.[4]

Simultaneously with these proceedings, Mr. Phillips presented and argued the question of a "Personal Liberty Act." It is enough to say of this argument that it takes rank with the other. It is remarkable for the same passion for freedom,—the same profound knowledge of the law,—the same exhaustive marshalling of authorities,—the same luminous reasoning. This, too, was successful—the act was adopted with an hurrah.[5] What were its provisions? Read:

"Habeas Corpus was secured to the alleged fugitive; no confessions of his were admissible, but the burden of proof was to be upon the claimant, and no *ex parte* affidavit was to be received. For a State office-holder to issue a warrant under the law was tantamount to a resignation; for an attorney to assist the claimant was to forfeit his right to practice in the State courts; for a judge to do either was to make himself liable to impeachment or removal by address. No United States Commissioner under the Fugitive Slave Law should hold any State office. No sheriff, jailer, or policeman should help arrest a fugitive, no jail receive him. The militia should not be called out on the claimant's behalf. The Governor should appoint

---

[1] *Vide* "Speeches," pp. 154–212.
[2] *Vide Liberator*, vol. xxv., p. 82.   [3] *Ib.*
[4] *Ib.*, vol. xxviii., pp. 42, 46, 50. The removal was finally made in the spring of 1858.
"Acts and Resolves of Massachusetts," p. 924.

County Commissioners to defend fugitives and secure them a fair trial."[1]

Thorough? Of course—was not Mr. Phillips substantially its author? Efficacious? Yes—no fugitive slave was ever afterward remanded from the old Bay State. And the example proved contagious. State after State made haste to copy it.[2]

The various Anti-Slavery societies held their anniversaries in New York and Boston in the May of 1855, the prevalent excitement and the famed vigor of their speakers making them the events of the week.

"The people," wrote Mr. Phillips to a friend, "never tire of listening to and applauding the most radical of our number. The Scotch proverb runs:

> 'The king said, "Sail!"
> The wind said, "No!"'

No need to ask whether there was a voyage. So now when slavery says, 'Sail!' let liberty say, 'No!'"[3]

An occurrence which interested him greatly was the celebration of the twentieth anniversary of the Garrison mob; which took place in October, in the very hall (Stacy Hall) out of which Mayor Lyman had driven the women of Boston who had assembled there to discuss the peculiar institution. Many of the heroines of 1835 were present in 1855. The scene was solemn and historic. Francis Jackson in the chair (the brave merchant who had made his house the asylum of free speech when the city tabooed it); Garrison on the platform; Phillips inside now, instead of on the street;[4] sympathy, in

---

[1] "William Lloyd Garrison," vol. iii., p. 416. [2] *Ib.*, pp. 459, 460.
[3] Letter from Wendell Phillips to Henry Ward Beecher (MS.).
[4] *Ante*, p. 57.

place of riot ;—what a change ! Mr. Phillips for the benefit of posterity, recited the story of the mob, and did it as only he could, in words that fell at first in a golden shower, deepening at last into a rain of fire.

"I thank these women," he said, in closing, "for all they have taught me. I had read Greek and Roman and English history ; I had by heart the classic eulogies of brave old men and martyrs ; I dreamed, in my folly, that I heard the same tone in my youth from the cuckoo lips of Edward Everett ;—these women taught me my mistake. They taught me that down in those hearts which loved a principle for itself, asked no man's leave to think or speak, true to their convictions, no matter at what hazard, flowed the real blood of '76, of 1640, of the hemlock-drinker of Athens, and of the martyr-saints of Jerusalem. I thank them for it ! My eyes were sealed, so that, although I knew the Adamses and the Otises of 1776, and the Mary Dyers and Ann Hutchinsons of older times, I could not recognize the Adamses and Otises, the Dyers and the Hutchinsons, whom I met in the streets of '35. These women opened my eyes, and I thank them and you (turning to Mrs. Southwick and Miss Henrietta Sargent, who sat upon the platform) for that anointing. May our next twenty years prove us all apt scholars of such brave instruction !" [1]

The autumn of 1855 was devoted by Mr. Phillips, after his custom, to lecturing. The Lyceum system was at its noon—that remarkable institution which gathered audiences throughout the free States to sit at the feet of the great speakers of the country. It was a kind of church without a creed, and with a constant rotation of clergymen ; a kind of party without a platform, and with orators of every opinion —neutral ground ; so that he who could give the best reason carried off the most honor. Beginning as

---

[1] "Speeches and Lectures," by Wendell Phillips, pp. 226, 227.

a literary recreation, it became a continental rostrum where questions of any and every sort were discussed. The political issues of the period were perpetually introduced. The utterances of the lecturers compromised no one save the lecturers themselves, and as the various lyceums endeavored to give all sides a hearing, the system filled an important place in American life. This was the special realm of Wendell Phillips. Here he was king; and his ministers of state were Chapin, Beecher, Gough, Curtis, and no end of others, a motley and often an insurgent multitude. The collision of opinions, the consequent sharpening of wits, and the toleration which resulted from hearing all sides, spiced these unconventional assemblies, made them amazingly popular, and gave them rare educational value.

The New Englanders, then as now, were in the habit of observing the landing of the Pilgrims and kissing the Yankee Blarney-stone. William H. Seward was the orator at Plymouth in December, 1855. His oration was a worthy tribute to the founders of empire on this side of the water. Phillips was present as a guest of the Plymouth Society, and spoke brilliantly at the dinner-table. Here is an illustrative story which he told:

"The Phillipses, Mr. President, did not come from Plymouth; they made their longest stay at Andover. Let me tell you an Andover story. One day, a man went into a store there, and began telling about a fire. 'There had never been such a fire,' he said, 'in the county of Essex. A man going by Deacon Pettingill's barn saw an owl on the ridge-pole. He fired at the owl, and the wadding somehow or other, getting into the shingles, set the hay on fire, and it was all destroyed,—ten tons of hay, six head of cattle, the finest horse in the country, etc. The deacon was nearly crazed by it.' The men in the store began

exclaiming and commenting on it. ' What a loss ! ' says one.
' Why, the deacon will well-nigh break down under it,' says another. And so they went on, speculating one after another, and the conversation drifted on in all sorts of conjectures. At last, a quiet man, who sat spitting in the fire, looked up, and asked, ' Did he hit the owl ? ' (*Tumultuous applause.*) That man was made for the sturdy reformer, of one idea, whom Mr. Seward described."[1]

Events hurried. After a parliamentary struggle prolonged through two months, on February 2d, 1856, the free States elected N. P. Banks Speaker of the Lower House of Congress—" the first gun at Lexington of the new revolution," said Mr. Garrison.[2] This victory was soon followed by an act which made a universal spectacle of the barbarism that masqueraded as chivalry by transplanting to Washington the manners and habits of the plantation. In May, Senator Sumner spoke in the Senate on " The Crime against Kansas." On the 22d of the month, for words spoken in debate, Preston S. Brooks, a representative from South Carolina, assaulted him. The attack was a blow at liberty ; the manner of it was an exposure of Southern " gallantry." While Sumner sat at his desk engaged in writing, Brooks crept up behind him, and, without warning, struck him again and again upon the head with a heavy gutta-percha cane. The senator, half stunned by the blows, strove to rise and free himself from the restraint of the desk. He succeeded in wrenching it from the floor to which it was screwed, but fell unconscious in the endeavor to rise. Keitt, Douglass, Toombs, and other members of Congress

---

[1] Phillips's " Speeches and Lectures," pp. 236, 237.
[2] *Vide Liberator*, vol. **xxvi**, p. 23.

looked on in silence—in that kind of silence which gave consent. Sumner's fall saved his life. Had he risen and turned, Brooks, who was armed, would have shot him. Mason, of Virginia, Jefferson Davis, of Mississippi, leading senators, the Southern press, and sections of the Northern, applauded the deed.[1]

So, then, the debate was to be one of bludgeons. The man-stealers and woman-whippers introduced into the halls of Congress their familiar home methods of discussion.

The wrath of the North was wide and hot. Indignation meetings abounded. Mr. Phillips regarded them with disgust. He held that the proper reply of Massachusetts would be to call home her representatives.[2] He spent many years in trying to persuade the North to adopt the remedy for the terrific evil of which such acts were the inevitable symptoms, that the Civil War at length forced upon it— the remedy of non-complicity. In a statement of the attendant circumstances of the case, he notes it as a significant fact, suggestive of the extent to which Southern sympathy had infected the wealthy and fashionable circles in the North, that the leading citizens of Boston itself refused to take part in the gatherings to rebuke the deed ; and he adds : " When Mr. Sumner returned to Boston, November 3d, 1856, though received by crowds in the streets and by the State authorities, the windows of every house in Beacon Street (the *élite* quarter), through which he passed, except those of Prescott and Samuel Apple-

---

[1] Phillips's Sketch of Sumner, in Johnson's *New Universal Cyclopædia, in loco.*

[2] *Vide* his various speeches of the period in the *Liberator.*

ton, had their blinds closed to show indifference or contempt."[1]

Treading close upon the heels of the assault upon Sumner, came that history-making Convention at Philadelphia which organized the Republican party. The Free Soil party was now only a name. The Whig party was nothing but a memory—

"Wicked but in will, of means bereft,"

its Pro-Slavery elements had been absorbed in the Democratic party, which the South had selected for its perfect service. Its Anti-Slavery constituents made overtures to the Free Soil chiefs and suggested a union. Recognizing the propriety of not requiring either to join the other, both suggested a new party with a new name. At the Quaker City, on June 17th, the fusion was consummated and the name was coined—the Republican party commenced its career. Amid unbounded enthusiasm the platform was adopted. It welcomed all, without regard to past differences, who were opposed to the repeal of the Missouri Compromise,—all who were against the extension of slavery into the Territories,—all who favored the admission of Kansas as a free State.[2] John C. Fremont was nominated for the Presidency, and Jessie, his wife, became the rallying cry of the new political crusade. The enthusiasm of the Convention soon communicated itself to the country. Who that witnessed it can ever forget the canvass that followed,—the "wide-awake" clubs,—the torch-light processions,—the frenzied meetings,—the hur-

---

[1] Johnson's *New Universal Cyclopædia*, Phillips's Notice of Sumner
[2] *Ib.*, Dana's article on the Republican party.

rying to and fro,—the bombarding press,—the passion of words,—the war of ballots? The recollection of those thrilling scenes lives side by side with the outbreak of the Rebellion itself, of which, indeed, they were the prelude.

James Buchanan was elected; but by a narrow majority. The South forecast the future. The slave-holders drew their heads closer together and multiplied their conferences and their plots.

Mr. Phillips welcomed the advent of the Republican party. He regarded its canvass as a public education. But he was too much of a seer to believe in its competency, with its avowed principles, to effect a cure of the national distemper. It afforded alleviation—nothing more. The Republican party clamored for the non-extension of slavery. He sought its death. The Republican party said, "Localize it." He knew that even though localized it would, in the very nature of things, continue to distract and convulse. The Republican party said, "Slavery must let go of Kansas." He retorted, "Slavery must set every bondman free." The Republican party said, "Bind the maniac." He advised, "Cast out the devil."

Presently God vindicated the wisdom of Mr. Phillips.

With such convictions, he signed the call for a Disunion Convention, to be held in Worcester, Mass., in January, 1857. The Convention met on the 15th inst. with a large attendance.[1] Charles Francis Adams, Joshua R. Giddings, Amasa Walker, Henry Wilson, and other prominent men, sent let-

---

[1] *Vide Liberator*, vol. xxvii, pp. 14, 27.

ters,—all in sympathy with the object of the Abolitionists, but in opposition to their methods.[1] Mr. Garrison spoke at length, and in advocacy of his familiar maxim of " No Union with slave-holders." Mr. Phillips made two speeches, in which he criticised the limitations of the Republican propaganda ; reaffirmed his unalterable purpose to contend, not for the non-extension of slavery, but for its destruction ; emphasized the fact that the Union of the free States with the slave States brought these into necessary complicity with those, by tying them together under a Pro-Slavery Constitution, by mortgaging the wealth and power of the North to the South, and by exposing liberty in one section to the demoralizing influences of slavery in the other ; recited the history of the past in proof of it ; asserted the ability of the free States to form an unstained Union that should be strong as well as free ; and ended by declaring his belief that the mere act of withdrawal would win the plaudits of civilization and go far to carry emancipation down to the Gulf.[2]

The tone of these speeches is calm, logical, philosophical. They are keen as the maxims of Rochefoucauld, racy as any pages of Dean Swift, suggestive as an essay by Emerson, and uncompromising as—Wendell Phillips. "The South," said he, "is eternally crying : 'Give us our way, or we will break up the Union !' Let us reply : 'Free your slaves, or *we* will dissolve it !' " This position had one supreme advantage : it met the slave-holders on their own ground, answered them in their own tone —everybody could understand it.

---

[1] *Vide Liberator*, vol. xxvii., p. 15.   [2] *Ib.*, pp. 18, 32.

The Disunion Convention had hardly adjourned, when the oligarchy, speaking this time through the Supreme Court of the United States, announced a decision which emphasized the declarations of Mr. Phillips touching the Pro-Slavery character of the Union. Dred Scott, a negro slave, had been carried by his master, an army officer, into a free State. Here he married the slave woman of another officer. Both were sold and returned to Missouri; where Scott sued for their freedom, alleging that their transportation into a free State had *ipso facto* worked their emancipation. The case was decided adversely in the State courts,—was appealed to the Supreme Court of the nation,—and now, Chief Justice Taney decided, in brief, that the Constitution recognized no distinction between slaves and other property; that slaves, therefore, might be taken wherever other property might be taken; that the Union was bound to protect property-owners against all assailants; and that the black race, as beings of an inferior order, "had no rights which white men were bound to respect."[1]

Thus did the South put back of the various laws of Congress on the questions at issue, and back of the Constitution, the authoritative interpretation of the tribunal of last appeal. Slavery was sustained. The free State laws discriminating slave property from other property were unconstitutional and void. Slavery was national—freedom was sectional.

"Well," commented Mr. Phillips, as he finished reading the dictum of Chief-Justice Taney, "on all the legal points involved, the Supreme Court sus-

---

[1] *Vide Liberator*, vol. xxvii., p. 45.

tains my claims for a dozen years. It is infamous. But it is the law of the United States. How now about the Pro-Slavery character of the Union? Am I not right in seeking to withdraw?"[1]

The Dred Scott decision opened the eyes of the Northern leaders. For the first time they saw, what the Abolitionists had seen since 1843—the everlasting impossibility of mixing oil and water, fire and snow, life and death. The South had recognized it, too; and had been striving with magnificent audacity for years and years to nationalize slavery, to supplant freedom, with only such resistance at the North as a little band of "fanatics" could make. Now, the Rip-Van-Winkle North awoke from its long sleep, rubbed its eyes, and realized that twice two are four! Thus, Abraham Lincoln, in a speech at Springfield, Ill., on June 17th, 1858, exclaimed: "'A house divided against itself cannot stand.' I believe this Union cannot endure permanently half-slave and half-free."[2] These words made the political fortune of Mr. Lincoln. Three years earlier, William Lloyd Garrison had uttered precisely the same words—and they fell on deaf ears.[3]

In the same strain spoke William H. Seward, on October 25th, 1858, at Rochester, N. Y.: "Shall I tell you what this collision means? They who think it is accidental, unnecessary, the work of interested and fanatical agitators, and therefore ephemeral, mistake the case altogether. It is an *irrepressible conflict* between opposing and enduring forces, and

---

[1] Letter to Theodore Parker (MS.).
[2] *Vide* Arnold's "Lincoln," p. 114.
[3] "William Lloyd Garrison," vol. iii., p. 420.

it means that the United States must and will, sooner or later, become either entirely a slave-holding nation or entirely a free-labor nation."[1]

This idea of an "irrepressible conflict" was as trite as the multiplication table to Mr. Phillips. He had been proclaiming it almost from the start, and had outlined the only adequate remedy—the destruction of slavery. Mr. Lincoln and Mr. Seward had now reached the proclamation. They were still several years on the other side of the remedy.

Hume, a Tory historian, thanks the Puritans for saving liberty in England. An American Hume will one day thank the Abolitionists for saving it here.

---

[1] Quoted in the *Liberator*, vol. xxviii., p. 177.

XXII.

IRREPRESSIBLE CONFLICT.

LIKE a calm morning which scowls by and by in cloud and storm, so broke the year 1859. A few of the weather-wise ones scanned the horizon and discerned the signs of the approaching tempest. Most listened incredulously, and trod on about their business. The disorders continued in Kansas. It was civil war in miniature. But the country had grown used to that. The South, complacent over the Dred Scott decision, and intrenched behind three lines of fortification,—the White House, Congress, and the Supreme Court, was resting on its arms. At the North, the Republicans were recruiting and drilling for the Presidential campaign of 1860.

The great anniversaries were held as usual,—the meetings crowded,—the speakers trenchant,—the discussions touching this and that phase of current affairs. On May 12th, Mr. Phillips spoke at a turbulent session of the National Women's Rights Convention, in New York City. One after the other, the orators of the occasion were driven off the platform by cat-calls and yells, until he took it and for two hours did as he would with the mocking crowd. In closing he said :

"I have neither the disposition nor the strength to trespass any longer upon your attention. The subject is so large, that it might well fill days instead of hours. It covers the whole surface of American society. It touches religion, purity, political economy, wages, the safety of cities, the growth of ideas, the very success of our experiment. If this experiment of self-government is to succeed, it is to succeed by some saving element introduced into the politics of the present day. You know this: your Websters, your Clays, your Calhouns, your Douglases, however intellectually able they may have been, have never dared or cared to touch that moral element of our national life. Either the shallow and heartless trade of politics had eaten out their own moral being, or they feared to enter the unknown land of lofty right and wrong.

"Neither of these great names has linked its fame with one great moral question of the day. They deal with money questions, with tariffs, with parties, with State law; and if, by chance, they touch the slave question, it is only like Jewish hucksters trading in the relics of saints. The reformers—the fanatics, as we are called—are the only ones who have launched social and moral questions. I risk nothing when I say, that the Anti-Slavery discussion of the last twenty years has been the salt of this nation: it has actually kept it alive and wholesome. Without it our politics would have sunk beyond even contempt. So with this question. It stirs the deepest sympathy; it appeals to the highest moral sense; it inwraps within itself the greatest moral issues. Judge it, then, candidly, carefully, as Americans; and let us show ourselves worthy of the high place to which God has called us in human affairs." [1]

Two weeks later, Mr. Phillips addressed the New England section of the same reform. We subjoin two paragraphs:

"Many a young girl, in her early married life, loses her husband, and thus is left a widow with two or three children. Now, who is to educate them and control them? We see, if left to her own resources, the intellect which she possesses, and which has remained in a comparatively dormant state, displayed in its full power. What a depth of heart lay hidden in that woman! She takes her husband's business, guides it as though it were a trifle; she takes her sons, and leads them; sets her daughters

---

[1] Austin's "Life and Times of Wendell Phillips," pp. 164, 165.

an example ; like a master-leader she governs the whole household. That is woman's influence. What made that woman? Responsibility. Call her out from weakness, lay upon her soul the burden of her children's education, and she is no longer a girl, but a woman.

"Horace Greeley once said to Margaret Fuller, 'If you should ask a woman to carry a ship around Cape Horn, how would she go to work to do it? Let her do this, and I will give up the question.' In the fall of 1856 a Boston girl, only twenty years of age, accompanied her husband to California. A brain fever laid him low. In the presence of mutiny and delirium, she took his vacant post, preserved order, and carried her cargo safe to its destined port. Looking in the face of Mr. Greeley, Miss Fuller said, 'Lo! my dear Horace, it is done. Now, say, what shall woman do next?'" (*Cheers.*)[1]

So passed the morning, so passed the noon of 1859. In the afternoon of the year Massachusetts did something that stirred Mr. Phillips to protest. The State permitted the statue of Webster to be placed in the State-House yard, with ostentatious ceremonies—Edward Everett eulogizing the recreant statesman who had gone over to the South in the "battle of the giants," and had bidden the commonwealth "smother its prejudices" and consent to hunt slaves.

A few weeks later, on October 4th, Mr. Phillips opened the "Fraternity" lecture course—the most popular Lyceum platform in Boston. The result was his lecture on "Idols," which, as a specimen of rhetoric and invective, is unexcelled. Referring to the statue, he said:

"No man criticises when private friendship moulds the loved form in
> 'Stone that breathes and struggles,
> Or brass that seems to speak.'

---

[1] Austin's "Life and Times of Wendell Phillips," p. 166.

Let Mr. Webster's friends crowd their own halls and grounds with his bust and statues. That is no concern of ours. But when they ask the State to join in doing him honor, then we claim the right to express an opinion. . . . We cannot but remember that the character of the commonwealth is shown by the character of those it crowns. A brave old Englishman tells us the Greeks had officers who did pluck down statues if they exceeded due symmetry and proportion. 'We need such now,' he adds, 'to order monuments according to men's merits.' Indeed we do! When I think of the long term and wide reach of his influence, and look at the subjects of his speeches,—the mere shells of history, drum-and-trumpet declamation, dry law, or selfish bickerings about trade,—when I think of his bartering the hopes of four millions of bondmen for the chances of his private ambition, I recall the criticism on Lord Eldon,—'No man ever did his race so much good as Eldon prevented.' Again, when I remember the close of his life spent in ridiculing the Anti-Slavery movement as useless abstraction, moonshine, 'mere rub-a-dub agitation,' because it did not minister to trade and gain, methinks I seem to see written all over his statue Tocqueville's conclusion from his survey of French and American democracy,—'The man who seeks freedom for anything but freedom's self, is made to be a slave!'"[1]

The echo of these sentences had hardly died away when others were heard, sharper, fiercer, more deadly—the echoes of John Brown's rifles among the hills of Virginia!

John Brown was a regular Cromwellian dug up from Naseby and Marston Moor. He was an Old Testament Christian, whose war-cry was, "The sword of the Lord and of Gideon." Going to Kansas, he had come in collision there with the "border ruffians" who swarmed across the boundaries of Missouri as the agents of slavery, and as a free-State

---

[1] "Speeches and Lectures," by Wendell Phillips, pp. 254, 259, 260.

chieftain had won fame as a Marion or Sumter. He was a devout guerilla of freedom. In person, tall, spare, farmer-like, he was built for roughing it.[1]

In order to understand this man, we must acquaint ourselves with his character and surroundings. Those marchings and countermarchings, yonder on the wild frontier, the skirmishes in Kansas, interspersed with occasional forays across the border into Missouri to snatch slaves into liberty, had taught him to feel that war already existed, and had suggested the invasion of the South at other and unsuspecting points. Accordingly, he came East in 1858, for the purpose of enlisting the co-operation of friends here in his plans. He saw Parker, Higginson, Sanborn, and secured their aid. Garrison was a non-resistant; hence an impossible confidant. Phillips was conducting a movement on the basis of moral suasion; therefore not likely to exchange ideas for rifles.[2] These two he met, but he shut them out from his confidence. Having secured men and material in modest measure, John Brown went into the neighborhood of Harper's Ferry, and on the night of October 16th, 1859, pounced upon the town, seized the United States Armory, and, with eighteen comrades, held the place for twenty-four hours. Then he was fought back into an engine-house, wounded, and finally captured by a file of United States marines sent from Washington, and commanded by Colonel Robert E. Lee, afterward general of the Confederate armies. Eight of his band were killed, six were captured, four escaped.[3]

---

[1] *Vide* "The Life of John Brown," by F. B. Sanborn.
[2] *Ib.* [3] *Ib.*, p. 552.

What followed? Everybody knows. John Brown was indicted for "murder and other crimes,"—tried, —convicted,—and, on December 2d, 1859, hung. Thus ended the Bunker Hill of the second Revolution.

Between the *émeute* and the execution many and stirring scenes were enacted. The slave-holders were naturally affrighted. Their thoughts by day, their dreams by night were haunted by spectres of insurrection. Northern sentiment was divided. The coolness and bravery of "old Ossawatomie," as he was called, after the town in Kansas where he dwelt, his self-sacrifice for a hated race, his tenderness, as shown in the caress of a negro child on the way to the scaffold, a dozen stories told of his prudence, skill, and courage on the border,—made him the hero of the hour. Nor did his scheme appear so insane at last as it did at first. For he entered Virginia—why? He told his captors in the wonderful address which he delivered to the court:

"I deny everything but what I have all along admitted—the design on my part to free the slaves. I intended, certainly, to have made a clean thing of the matter, as I did last winter, when I went into Missouri, and there took slaves without the snapping of a gun on either side, moved them through the country, and finally left them in Canada. I designed to have done the same thing again, on a larger scale. That was all I intended. I never did intend murder, treason, or the destruction of property, or to excite or incite slaves to rebellion, or to make insurrection." [1]

He had succeeded in Missouri; why not in Virginia? There he was sane enough; why crazy here?

---

[1] Sanborn's "Life of John Brown."

Comedy and tragedy are close akin. In the midst of the drama, it was laughable to hear the various comments. "What a pity he did not succeed!" "Why didn't he march off with his victory during the first twenty-four hours?" "What an outrage, to try a man while wounded and lying on a pallet!" Such were the utterances of all sorts of people in the streets, on the cars, at the fireside—indicative of widespread sympathy.[1]. The truth is, the South had been attacking the North on John Brown's principle, for years—in Kansas, for example, and in the blow at Sumner. This was only tit for tat. The North widely recognized it. Even conservatives felt a silent satisfaction, which was occasionally and grudgingly expressed as in the remark of a prominent Democrat in New York City : " I hope it will teach the South that playing with fire is dangerous."[2]

Although Mr. Phillips had not been in John Brown's secret, he was profoundly stirred by his heroism. The orator had spent his life in the endeavor to avoid the need of precisely such methods. He now realized that a new phase of the struggle was at hand. On November 1st, 1859, he lectured in Plymouth Church, Brooklyn, and took " Harper's Ferry" for a text. The lecture was as sensational as the occasion. It is sensational even as read to-day in the seclusion of the library. Turn over a leaf or two :

"Has the slave a right to resist his master ? I will not argue that question to a people hoarse with shouting ever since July

---

[1] "Speeches and Lectures," by Wendell Phillips, p. 286.

[2] So said the Hon. Daniel S. Dickinson to John F. Dix, afterward Governor of New York.

4th, 1776, that all men are created equal, that the right to liberty is inalienable, and that 'resistance to tyrants is obedience to God.' But may he resist to blood—with rifles? What need of proving that to a people who load down Bunker Hill with granite, and crowd their public squares with images of Washington; ay, worship the sword so blindly that, leaving their oldest statesmen idle, they go down to the bloodiest battle-field in Mexico to drag out a President? But may one help the slave resist, as Brown did? Ask Byron on his death-bed in the marshes of Missolonghi. Ask the Hudson as its waters kiss your shore, what answer they bring from the grave of Kosciusko. I hide the Connecticut Puritan behind Lafayette, bleeding at Brandywine, in behalf of a nation his rightful king forbade him to visit.

"But John Brown violated the law. Yes. On yonder desk lie the inspired words of men who died violent deaths for breaking the laws of Rome. Why do you listen to them so reverently? Huss and Wickliffe violated laws; why honor them? George Washington, had he been caught before 1783, would have died on the gibbet, for breaking the laws of his sovereign. Yet I have heard that man praised within six months. Yes, you say, but these men broke bad laws. Just so. It is honorable, then, to break bad laws, and such law-breaking history loves and God blesses! Who says, then, that slave laws are not ten thousand times worse than any those men resisted? Whatever argument excuses them, makes John Brown a saint."[1]

In the midst of this excitement, Mr. Phillips, who had been in Philadelphia a few days before, where a threatened mob did not act, wrote to Miss Grew:

"These are stirring times and hopeful for the cause. I am glad the mobocrat[2] liked me, though some radical might think his liking an equivocal compliment; but I accept it heartily. It comports with my philosophy. I have become so notorious

---

[1] "Speeches and Lectures," pp. 279 *sq.*

[2] The "mobocrat" was a highly distinguished leader of riots in Philadelphia, who was, on one occasion, so entirely captivated by Mr. Phillips's eloquence that he sat quietly through his lecture, and held in restraint the men whom he had led thither for the purpose of breaking up the meeting.

that at Albany, Kingston, and Hartford, the Lyceum could not obtain a church for me ; and the papers riddled me with pellets for a week ; but that saved advertising and got me larger houses gratis. At Troy they even thought of imitating Staten Island and getting up a Homœopathic mob, but couldn't." [1]

Mr. Phillips's marvellous power of rapid thought combined with peerless expression, is well known to those who frequently heard him in lectures or debate. It was illustrated on the occasion referred to in the letter just quoted, when he delivered in Philadelphia his lecture on "Toussaint L'Ouverture." The execution of the death-sentence of John Brown was near at hand. Mr. Phillips, on his arrival in the city, in the morning, was told that his evening audience would expect him to speak of that appalling fact. He replied that it had no connection with the lecture which he had been invited to deliver ; that an interpolated passage upon another subject was scarcely to be thought of. But he was assured that, whether it belonged to the lecture or not, the demand was imperative ; speak upon it he must.

From the time of his arrival in the city, in the morning, until his appearance upon the platform, in the evening, with the exception of some fifteen minutes, he was surrounded by his friends, and occupied with social converse. Yet he introduced into that lecture an eloquent and thrilling passage concerning John Brown, which so marvellously fitted into it that it might have been an original portion of it.

While John Brown lay in prison awaiting execution, a meeting was held in Boston to raise funds for the relief of his impoverished family. John A. An-

---

[1] Letter to Miss Grew (MS.). An attempt was made to mob him on Staten Island about this time, but failed.

drew presided. Emerson represented New England letters. Phillips stood for the negro race, on whose behalf the hero was condemned. The Rev. J. M. Manning, of the "Old South" Church, said: "I am here to represent the church of Sam Adams and Wendell Phillips; and I want all the world to know that I am not afraid to ride in the coach when Wendell Phillips sits on the box."[1]

When she had strangled the soul out of it, Virginia delivered the body of John Brown to his friends. They took it reverently and laid it in the grave at North Elba, his old home, with the Adirondacks for a monument. Mr. Phillips met the *cortége* in New York City, and journeyed thence to the final resting-place. Standing by the grave he pronounced the burial address, from which we give an extract:

"Marvellous old man! . . . He has abolished slavery in Virginia. You may say this is too much. Our neighbors are the last men we know. The hours that pass us are the ones we appreciate the least. Men walked Boston streets, when night fell on Bunker Hill, and pitied Warren, saying, 'Foolish man! Thrown away his life! Why didn't he measure his means better?' Now we see him standing colossal on that blood-stained sod, and severing that day the tie which bound Boston to Great Britain. That night George III. ceased to rule in New England. History will date Virginia emancipation from Harper's Ferry. True, the slave is still there. So, when the tempest uproots a pine on your hills, it looks green for months,—a year or two. Still, it is timber, not a tree. John Brown has loosened the roots of the slave system; it only breathes,—it does not live,—hereafter."[2]

This was a long look ahead. It was prophecy then and history at last. Philosophers love to trace

---

[1] Reminiscences by Charles W. Slack, of Boston.
[2] "Speeches and Lectures," p. 290.

the result to the cause,—to find the result in the cause. Phillips did this at North Elba. In the actual John Brown he saw a million possible ones; and in the possibility he beheld the end.

There was a Star-Chamber inquiry at Washington for the men who had aided and abetted John Brown. Theodore Parker, T. W. Higginson, F. B. Sanborn, and others, were suspected; but no papers could be found. They existed! Mr. Phillips brought a budget of them from North Elba, which he placed for safe keeping in the hands of Governor John A. Andrew, and which at a later day the Governor returned to the respective writers.[1] Had these been discovered, John Brown would not have hung alone.

---

[1] Recollections of F. B. Sanborn (MS.).

XXIII.

THE WINTER OF SECESSION.

In Macbeth, the witch stirs the pot and utters her incantation:
> "Black spirits and white,
> Red spirits and gray."

So now all kinds of spirits, good, bad, nondescript, materialized, each paramount in turn. Over all, however, was the Spirit of Providence!

The spirit of sorrow, an unbidden guest, sat at many hearthstones when, on May 10th, 1860, Theodore Parker died. Stricken with consumption, he had gone to Europe in search of health, and reaching Florence, expired within sight of the cathedral whose doors Michel Angelo said were fit to be the gates to paradise. Mr. Phillips went heavy-hearted and sober-faced for many a day. That home in the rear of his own residence would be broken up—was broken up. That light in the study over there was quenched at last, like the brighter light of intellect and goodness that had kindled and outshone it.

In their grief, the congregation of Theodore Parker turned to Mr. Phillips. They were not in theological sympathy, but they were in personal and moral accord; and through the fall and winter of 1860–61 the orator frequently occupied their platform, delivering from it several of his most celebrated orations, and having on it some of his most thrilling experiences—as we shall see. The society of Mr. Parker worshipped in the Music Hall. A tender commemorative service was held there when the sad news came from Italy, at which Mr. Phillips spoke with great sweetness and beauty.

On November 18th, he pronounced before the same society a notable discourse on " The Pulpit." The utterance is interesting and important, because it gives his conception of its functions and scope. At the outset, Phillips expressed his appreciation of the essential idea of the Church, viz., the stated expression of devotional feeling. Then he urged the pulpit to recognize its duty and preach to life. He believed the Gospel should be applied to daily affairs. He criticised the silence of the ministry on living questions, and declared this fatal to the permanent influence and usefulness of the sacred office. The function of the pulpit, he said, was to awake and instruct the moral nature. He then proceeded :

" Politics takes the vassal and lifts him into a voter. The press informs him concerning the happenings of the day. The school gives him elementary instruction. We need in addition a pulpit—moral initiative. I value the Sunday for this : it gives opportunity for such instruction. The devil invented work— forced it. When we clutched a day and gave it to the soul, we redeemed one seventh of the time from the devil and gave it to God. The pulpit should use the day and opportunity for the training of the community in the whole encyclopædia of morals —social questions, sanitary matters, slavery, temperance, labor, the condition of women, the nature of the Government, responsibility to law, the right of a majority, and how far a minority may yield, marriage, health,—the entire list. For all these are moral questions and they are living questions, not metaphysics, not dogmas. Hindostan settled these thousands of years ago. Christianity did not bury itself in the pit of Oriental metaphysics ; neither did it shroud itself in the hermitage of Italian doctrine.

The pulpit, as seen in the North of Europe and in this country, is not built up of mahogany and paint. It is the life of earnest men, the example of the community; a forum to unfold, broaden, and help mankind. That is the pulpit. If this were recognized and acted upon, people would not desert the Church, as they tend to do; or go, if at all, from a mere sense of duty; but would be drawn to the pulpit as they are to the press and the theatre, by a felt want."[1]

The spirit of discord rent the Democratic party in twain on the eve of the election, in 1860; one faction insisting upon a committal of the party to the doctrine of the equal right of slave property to enter all the Territories, while the other held out for a reference of the whole question to the Supreme Court —which had just decided it affirmatively in the Dred Scott case! The result was the nomination of Stephen A. Douglas by the Northern, and of John C. Breckenridge by the Southern, Democrats. This insured the election of the Republican candidate. The truth is that the slave-holders had matured and were now ready to precipitate secession. They deliberately engineered the disruption of the Democratic party in order to secure Republican success and thus gain a pretext for disunion. But this was God's way of providing a plentiful contingent of war Democrats presently, when they should be needed.

The spirit of wisdom guided the Republican Convention to the choice of Abraham Lincoln as President, instead of William H. Seward, whom every one expected to win the nomination. This was God's way of providing the man for the hour.

The spirit of fun called into being a "Union" party, which served to introduce an element of hu-

---

[1] *Vide* "The Pulpit," a pamphlet in the Boston Public Library

mor into the canvass, keeping the country in good temper before it went quite mad. This was God's way of easing up the nation before subjecting it to the impending strain.

Mr. Lincoln was elected. In the evening of the day after the election, while the streets were noisy with paraders, Mr. Phillips lectured in Boston.

"For the first time in our history," said he, "the slave has elected a President. In 1760 what rebels felt, James Otis spoke, George Washington achieved, and Everett praises to-day. The same routine will go on. What fanatics now feel, Garrison prints, Lincoln will achieve, and, at the safe distance of half a century, some courtly Everett will embalm in matchless panegyrics. You see exactly what my hopes rest upon. Growth! The Republican party have undertaken a problem the solution of which will force them to our position." [1]

Mingling with the spirits mentioned, yet solitary, was another, hot from below and sulphureous,—the mob spirit now abroad, and never fiercer. The Abolitionists were its special victims, and Boston, as being their headquarters, its prominent theatre. On December 2d, 1860, a meeting was announced in the Tremont Temple to discuss the abolition of slavery. It was the anniversary of John Brown's execution. The mayor turned mobocrat and thrust the discussionists out of doors. The Belknap Street colored church was their asylum; a roof that deserves to be held in honor by every lover of free speech; for here lips were ungagged when they were padlocked elsewhere for thirty years.[2]

"Mr. Phillips," writes a participant, "spoke that night with regal magnificence and dauntless courage; while the court-way beside the church, and the street in front, were filled with angry

---

[1] "Speeches and Lectures," pp. 294, 314.   [2] *Ante*, p. 70.

and yelling rioters. They thought Phillips could not emerge without passing through their ranks, and they were prepared for violence toward him. But there was a rear passage-way, very narrow, from the meeting-house through to South Russell Street; and out by that avenue, single file, walked Phillips and his friends, and thence up the hill to Myrtle, and so to Joy, Street, and across the Common to Mr. Phillips's Essex Street residence. When the mob heard that Mr. Phillips had escaped, they rushed up the hill, and overtook his escort just as it had descended the stone steps leading to the Beacon Street mall. They found a cordon of young men, forty or more in number, who, with locked arms and closely compacted bodies, had Phillips in the centre of their circle, and were safely bearing him home. Timidity, or a conviction that an assault would be fruitless, prompted them to take satisfaction at the discovery only in yells and execration." [1]

Two weeks later Theodore Parker's church invited the orator to fill their pulpit. The Pro-Slavery sentiment of the city registered an oath that he should not speak. He concluded that he would. And he selected for his theme the men who had attempted to muzzle free speech on December 2d:

"That morning," says one of the officers of the church, "saw a crowd within its walls never exceeded since. Mr. Phillips was on hand in due course, calm as nature on a spring morning. Whoever heard that discourse never will forget it. It was, from beginning to end, one terrible arraignment of the mob-spirit in America. He used no rose-water flavor in describing the rioters of the Tremont Temple gathering, but in the most scathing language made personal issue with the well-known social and political leaders on that occasion. As he poured out his blistering anathemas, I sat trembling lest I should hear the snap of a pistol that should send a ball into his glowing and pulsating form. But there was no violence attempted. His sympathizers fully equalled the malecontents; and the mayor, on the appeal of the directors of the hall, had the audience interspersed with police-

---

[1] "Reminiscences of Charles W. Slack."

men in plain clothes. When the services were over, and Mr. Phillips withdrew from the hall by the Winter Street entrance, court and street were found to be filled by the baffled rioters ready for assault. Just then two sections of young men, double file, took Mr. Phillips, with a friend on each side of him, between them, and escorted him up Washington Street to his residence in entire safety. This escort was fully armed, and it would have been a sad day for the mob had Mr. Phillips been assaulted. For nearly a week after, a portion of these young men remained on duty at Mr. Phillips's house for his protection." [1]

In a letter to Miss Mary Grew Mr. Phillips thus refers to these experiences:

"I hardly know what to say to you about our mob. It was not the murderous mob of 1835. Still there were dangerous elements in it. The police think, and so do many friends, that I should not have got home, Sunday, alive, without the protection of the police; but though there were some fists doubled, and pistols seen, still there were twenty stanch men around me, armed; and even without the police, I think, we should have made our own way. The Monday evening meeting, I regretted to hold where we were compelled to, as it left the colored people exposed all night to the remains of the mob. But we are all safe, and I suppose nothing more will trouble us till our annual meeting in January. They boast, in State Street, that we shall not hold any Anti-Slavery meetings this winter. We'll see.

"You know the owners of Music Hall refused us the hall. The Fraternity offered bonds for $50,000; then the trustees said they would consent if another speaker could be substituted. Had our mayor been here we should not have got the hall. But Heaven took him to Washington. So Mr. Clapp was acting mayor. He behaved nobly and secured, probably, the casting vote which, at half-past eleven P.M., obtained for us the hall.

"The Brothers Hallowell are on hand on all occasions. The eldest had my right arm as we came home from the Music Hall; his brother in front of me. The pleasantest item is, the

---

[1] "Reminiscences of Charles W. Slack."

German Turners held a meeting Sunday evening, and voted 'to protect free speech and free speakers;' and a squad of them has watched our house every night since, though I never heard of it till days after. That's worth being mobbed for. There's some good in the world, spite of original sin."[1]

On the day previous to the scene in Music Hall, South Carolina seceded. The other Gulf States soon followed—seven in all. The Border States lingered. Then the North went on its knees; offered the South *carte blanche;* would she only deign to name her terms and remain in the Union? Liberty bills were rescinded. Congress passed an amendment to the Constitution by the requisite two-thirds majority, forbidding the abolition of slavery and any interference with the return of "persons held to labor." A "Peace Congress" assembled in Washington and outran the Congress that sat in the Capitol in the race of subserviency—"anything, everything, only stay!" The Gulf States had gone. They looked on with amused disdain. The Border States still hesitated.

Mr. Phillips spent these three weeks trying to persuade the North to rise from its knees and let the South go. He thought, rightly, that the attitude of the free States was the most shameful in the long history of servility. He welcomed peaceable disunion, and said the North could afford to pay millions to be rid of such neighbors. On January 20th, 1861, he was announced to occupy Theodore Parker's pulpit again and his subject was published—"Disunion!" On the 19th inst. Garrison penned these lines to Oliver Johnson, in New York City:

---

[1] Letter to Miss Grew (MS.).

"It will be a fortnight, to-morrow, since I have been out-of-doors. It is on this account I have not replied to your letter giving me an extract of a plot in embryo for a murderous assault upon our dear and noble friend, Wendell Phillips. I thought it best, on the whole, to say nothing to him about it ; but that his precious life is in very great danger, in consequence of the malignity felt ånd expressed against him in this city since the John Brown meeting, there is no doubt among us. Hence, we are quite sure of a mobocratic outbreak at our annual meeting on Thursday and Friday next ; and, though some of us may be exposed to personal violence, Phillips will doubtless be the object of special vengeance. The new mayor, Wightman, is bitterly opposed to us, refuses to give us any protection, and says if there is any disturbance he will arrest our speakers, together with the trustees of Tremont Temple ! What a villain ! I should not wonder if blood should be shed on the occasion, for there will be a resolute body of men present, determined to maintain liberty of speech. Whether an attempt will be made to break up the Anti-Slavery Festival at Music Hall, on Wednesday evening, remains to be seen. But all will work well in the end.

"Phillips is to speak at the Music Hall to-morrow forenoon, before Mr. Parker's congregation, and another violent demonstration is anticipated. Mayor Wightman refuses to order the police to be present to preserve order. This makes the personal peril of Phillips greater than it was before." [1]

Mr. Phillips spoke, and never more calmly, never more powerfully. The mob, as before, occupied the hall, and the approaches to it.[2] And, as before, he was escorted to his home by a self-appointed bodyguard.[3]

On the 24th inst., the annual meeting of the Massachusetts Anti-Slavery Society (referred to as impending by Mr. Garrison in his letter to Mr. John-

---

[1] "William Lloyd Garrison," vol. iv., p. 3.
[2] "Speeches and Lectures," by Wendell Phillips, p. 343.   [3] *Ib.*

son) was held. At least *one* session was held. Of this Mrs. Lydia Maria Child has left a graphic pen-and-ink sketch. Addressing a friend, she writes :

"I would rather have given fifty dollars than attend the meeting, but conscience told me it was a duty. I was excited and anxious, not for myself, but for Wendell Phillips. Hour after hour of the night I heard the clock strike, while visions were passing through my mind of that noble head assailed by murderous hands, and I obliged to stand by without the power to save him.

"I went very early in the morning, and entered the Tremont Temple by a private labyrinthine passage. There I found a company of young men, a portion of the self-constituted bodyguard of Mr. Phillips. They looked calm, but resolute and stern. I knew they were all armed, as well as hundreds of others ; but their weapons were not visible. The women friends came in gradually by the same private passage. It was a solemn gathering, I assure you ; for though there was a pledge not to use weapons unless Mr. Phillips or some other Anti-Slavery speaker was personally in danger, still nobody could foresee what might happen. The meeting opened well. The Anti-Slavery sentiment was there in strong force, but soon the mob began to yell from the galleries. They came tumbling in by hundreds. The papers will tell you of their goings-on. Such yelling, screeching, stamping, and bellowing I never heard. It was a full realization of the old phrase, ' All hell broke loose.'

"Mr. Phillips stood on the front of the platform for a full hour, trying to be heard whenever the storm lulled a little. They cried, ' Throw him out ! ' ' Throw a brickbat at him ! ' ' Your house is afire ; don't you know your house is afire ? Go put out your house.' Then they'd sing, with various bellowing and shrieking accompaniments, ' Tell John Andrew, tell John Andrew, John Brown's dead ! ' I should think there were four or five hundred of them. At one time they all rose up, many of them clattered down-stairs, and there was a surging forward toward the platform. My heart beat so fast I could hear it ; for I did not then know how Mr. Phillips's armed friends were stationed at every door, and in the middle of every aisle. They formed a firm wall, which the mob could not pass. At last it was announced that the police were coming. I saw and heard nothing of them, but there was a lull. Mr. Phillips tried to speak, but his voice was again drowned. Then, by a clever stroke of management, he stooped forward, and addressed his speech to the reporters stationed directly below him. This tantalized the mob ; and they began to call out, ' Speak louder ! We want to hear what you're saying ;' whereupon he raised his voice, and for half an hour he seemed to hold them in the hollow of his hand. But as soon as he sat down, they began to yell and sing again, to prevent any more speaking." [1]

In the afternoon the mayor once more interfered, and by his command the hall was not opened at night.[2]

Was Mr. Phillips silenced ? Oh, no ! On February 17th, he re-entered Parker's pulpit and spoke on " Progress," still serenely, still uncompromisingly, still with the mob for an audience, and a phalanx of armed friends for a rampart. While he was speaking a string of fifty or more rioters pushed into the hall and surged toward the desk. They were soon stayed by the protecting cordon in front of the orator. Here they stood and listened, and listening were touched, so that at last they broke with the rest of the audience into wild applause ! Phillips was always proud of this proof of his persuasive powers—rioters transformed into sympathizers !

---

[1] " Letters of Lydia Maria Child," pp. 147, 149.

[2] *Vide Liberator*, vol. xxxi., p. 17. What Mr. Phillips said to the reporters was : " While I speak to these pencils, I speak to a million of men. What, then, are those boys ? We have got the press of the country in our hands. Whether they like us or not, they know that our speeches sell their papers. With five newspapers we may defy five hundred boys. . . . My voice is beaten by theirs, but they cannot beat types. All hail and glory to Faust, who invented printing, for he made mobs impossible !" *Ib*.

His family physician and firm ally, Dr. David Thayer, who was present, relates that as the band entered, one of them addressed a bystander, supposing him to be a malcontent, and pulling a noosed rope half out of his overcoat pocket, said in a whisper, "See! we are going to snake him out and hang him with this on the Common." The person addressed drew out a revolver, pushed it into the eyes of the ruffian, and cried: "God d—n you, if you don't get out of this hall, I'll blow your brains out!" He got out in a hurry. He had mistaken his man. Dr. Thayer said he thought it justifiable profanity.[1] When the address was ended, the brave doctor spirited Mr. Phillips into his waiting buggy, and drove him home at a two-forty pace—the city ordinance to the contrary, notwithstanding. For days, that house was an arsenal. Friends encamped within, well armed. The police stood without, while the mob transformed the vicinity into a pandemonium.

"If those fellows had broken in, would you have shot them, Mr. Phillips?" asked a lady friend.

"Yes," was the quiet answer,—"just as I would shoot a mad dog or a wild bull!"[2]

"During all this time," remarks Mr. T. W. Higginson, an eye-witness, "there was something peculiarly striking and characteristic in his demeanor. There was absolutely nothing of bull-dog combativeness; but a careless, buoyant, almost patrician air, as if nothing in the way of mob-violence were worth considering, and all the threats of opponents were simply beneath contempt. He seemed like some

---

[1] The writer had this from Dr. Thayer's own lips.
[2] Told by Mrs. Eleanor F. Crosby.

English Jacobite nobleman on the scaffold, carelessly taking snuff, and kissing his hand to the crowd, before laying his head upon the block."

So passed, for Mr. Phillips, the winter of secession. He ran a gauntlet of mobs three months long —unhurt. This was God's way of vindicating free speech by the freest speaker in the world.

XXIV.

UNDER THE FLAG.

During the months whose history has just been traced as it was localized in the experience of Mr. Phillips, the country was vexed and tormented, rent and crazed, like the demoniac in the Scriptures, by devils. The Gulf States gone; the Border States still balancing; party feeling so belligerent that men and women of opposite politics talked bullets when they met; the press voicing and increasing the prevalent perplexity and animosity; business demoralized; a horrible uncertainty, more appalling than the most dreadful assurance, populating the continent with rumors,—but how describe the indescribable?

Out of this chaos certain facts stalked into the consciousness of the North. It was known that the disgraceful administration of James Buchanan was about to end. It was the avowed intention of the lingering Catilines of secession to effect a *coup d'état* and take possession of the Capital. It was openly asserted that Abraham Lincoln should never be inaugurated. The South was united. The North— it was Ishmael multiplied into twenty million.

Time passed. The confusion deepened. The President-elect stole disguised into Washington. Buchanan left the White House. Lincoln entered 't and assumed the government. General Winfield

Scott, faithful among the faithless, held the Capital in the name of the nation. The new Executive delivered his inaugural—conciliatory in tone, yet self-possessed and courageous; offering to enforce the Fugitive Slave Law, and recommending the States to ratify the Constitutional amendment just passed by Congress, making the abolition of slavery impossible; but affirming the purpose to uphold and vindicate the supreme authority of the nation.

This was the South's opportunity. God intervened and made the slave-holders deaf. He meant to destroy the monster iniquity. The secessionists were convinced that the North would not fight—that it could not. For was it not hopelessly divided? Did not Jefferson Davis have in his pocket a letter from ex-President Franklin Pierce, in which the recreant New Englander declared that if there should be war the fighting would not be in the South but in the North?[1] Was there not every reason to believe that the Pro-Slavery sympathizers here would find occupation for Mr. Lincoln at home, should he move toward coercion? Moreover, the treasury—had not that been emptied by the pilferers who held office for this purpose under the late Administration? The navy—was not that artfully scattered in distant seas? The army—was not that reduced to a corporal's guard? Had not the arsenals been despoiled of arms, which the Confederates now handled? What could the President do, if he would? Why, he had been robbed of all means precisely with a view to this emergency.

The secessionists laughed at Lincoln's overtures.

---

[1] Greeley's "American Conflict," vol. i., p. 513.

Suppose they returned, how could legislation muzzle Northern sentiment? Had they not tried that for fifty years? It was the type of society in the North that they dreaded. It was from this that they wished to separate themselves. One thing, however, gave them anxiety. They desired the adherence of the Border States to the Confederacy. To secure this they decided to "fire the Southern heart"—never imagining the shot which did that would also fire the heart of the North. This was their supreme, but natural, blunder. Had the flag been left unassailed there would have been a peaceable dissolution of the Union. God again interfered.

On April 12th, 1861, Fort Sumter was bombarded!

The result was unimaginable. It did, indeed, have the expected effect in the Border States, most of which made haste to secede.

But at the North, instead of being a signal for a Pro-Slavery insurrection, it stirred a protest of indignant patriotism from the very graveyards. There was "such an uprising in every city, town, and hamlet, without distinction of sect or party, as to seem," wrote Mr. Garrison, "like a general resurrection of the dead."[1] In the first fierce moment of arousal, all talk of compromise ceased. The empty exchequer was filled by a national loan. A navy was extemporized, as if by magic. Canada and Europe were ransacked for arms. And in response to the President's call for volunteers to suppress the rebellion, every farm, every workshop, every counting-room, every fireside transformed citizens into soldiers and made Washington a camp.

---

[1] *Vide Liberator*, vol. xxxi. p 66.

In a moment the whole situation changed. With corresponding rapidity, the attitude of individuals altered. Senator Douglas ceased to be a dough-face and became a patriot. Benjamin F. Butler, up to this moment a Northern man with Southern principles, experienced a change of heart and was born again. Garrison "remembered to forget" that he was a non-resistant and made the *Liberator* over from a Quaker gun into a columbiad.

Mr. Phillips veered with the rest. He had been a Disunionist for freedom's sake since 1843. All winter he had been advising the North to let the South go in peace. Now he, too, favored war and wished to save the Union. Was he not inconsistent? No, he changed, not his *principles*, but his *methods*. He had been aiming at—what? The emancipation of the negro race and the liberation of the North from slave-holding domination. He now saw, with intuitive quickness, that the war for the Union was the Providential way of attaining both objects. As slavery lay at the bottom of the difference between the sections, it was clear that slavery must be abolished in order to final union. Two ideas, therefore, took possession of him now and shaped his course, viz., free the blacks as a war measure, and then enfranchise them. This policy he urged throughout the war and throughout the period of reconstruction, and finally harvested it in the Proclamation of Emancipation and in the three amendments to the Constitution. To those who criticised his present position and accused him of inconsistency his triumphant reply was:

"People may say this is strange language for me,—a Disunionist. Well, I was a Disunionist sincerely, for twenty years.

I did hate the Union, when union meant lies in the pulpit and mobs in the streets, when union meant making white men hypocrites and black men slaves. (*Cheers.*) I did prefer purity to peace,—I acknowledge it. The child of six generations of Puritans, knowing well the value of union, I did prefer disunion to being the accomplice of tyrants. But now—when I see what the Union must mean in order to last, when I see that you cannot have union without meaning justice, and when I see twenty millions of people, with a current as swift and as inevitable as Niagara, determined that this Union shall mean justice, why should I object to it? I endeavored honestly, and am not ashamed of it, to take nineteen States out of this Union, and consecrate them to liberty, and twenty millions of people answer me back, 'We like your motto, only we mean to keep thirty-four States under it.' Do you suppose that I am not Yankee enough to buy union when I can have it at a fair price?"[1]

Learning of Mr. Phillips's change of views, and on fire themselves with the enthusiasm of the hour, Theodore Parker's society invited the orator to occupy their desk on Sunday, April 21st, nine days after the firing of "the shot heard round the world."

"They dressed their pulpit," remarks one of their number, "in the national colors. Over the occupant's head was an arch of bunting, decked with laurel and evergreen. Thousands crowded into the hall. Mr. Phillips was promptly on hand, with —for the first time in his public career—an audience wholly in sympathy with his expected speech. The atmosphere was charged with patriotism. Men's faces, especially those of the old Abolitionists, were aglow with a confident hope. Again was Mr. Phillips equal to the occasion! He welcomed the national outbreak as the sure precursor of the death of human slavery in republican America. He built up his magnificent expectancy of the results of the war, sentence by sentence, thrilling the audience with grand and noble aspiration. He yielded, in the furnace of his patriotic and humane warmth, all his old-time predilections, and stood, disinthralled, for the Union and the flag,

---

[1] *Vide* "Speeches and Lectures," p. 440.

the Constitution of the fathers, and its future interpretation in the interest of liberty on this continent. How the audience applauded! How they cheered! The men who were there to mob him three months before, now were his strongest indorsers. They crowded the platform to congratulate him when he closed, and joy and satisfaction beamed on every countenance. It had been a Pentecostal season; and the divine outflow of humanity, justice, and the rights of man, had baptized every one of that immense throng! It required no phalanx of armed men to escort Mr. Phillips home that day; for he was almost, figuratively, borne in the arms of a grateful citizenship to his modest abode!"[1]

From this famous speech we extract a few sentences to indicate its trend:

"All winter long, I have acted with that party which cried for peace. The Anti-Slavery enterprise to which I belong started with peace written on its banners. We imagined that the age of bullets was over; that the age of ideas had come; that thirty millions of people were able to take a great question, and decide it by the conflict of opinions; that, without letting the ship of state founder, we could lift four millions of men into liberty and justice. We thought that if your statesmen would throw away personal ambition and party watchwords, and devote themselves to the great issue, this might be accomplished. To a certain extent it has been. The North has answered to the call. Year after year, event by event, had indicated the rising education of the people,—the readiness for a higher moral life, the calm, self-poised confidence in our own convictions that patiently waits—like the master for a pupil—for a neighbor's conversion. The North has responded to the call of that peaceful, moral, intellectual agitation which the Anti-Slavery idea has initiated. Our mistake, if any, has been that we counted too much on the intelligence of the masses, on the honesty and wisdom of statesmen as a class. Perhaps we did not give weight enough to the fact we saw, that this nation is made up of different ages; not homogeneous, but a mixed mass of different centuries. The North thinks,—can appreciate argument,—is the nineteenth century,

---

[1] Reminiscences of Charles W. Slack.

—hardly any struggle left in it but that between the working-class and the money-kings. The South dreams—it is the thirteenth and fourteenth century,—baron and serf,—noble and slave. Jack Cade and Wat Tyler loom over its horizon, and the serf, rising, calls for another Thierry to record his struggle. There the fagot still burns which the doctors of the Sorbonne called, ages ago, 'the best light to guide the erring.' There men are tortured for opinions, the only punishment the Jesuits were willing their pupils should look on. This is, perhaps, too flattering a picture of the South. Better call her, as Sumner does, 'the Barbarous States.' Our struggle, therefore, is between barbarism and civilization. Such can only be settled by arms. (*Prolonged cheering.*) The Government has waited until its best friends almost suspected its courage or its integrity; but the cannon shot against Fort Sumter has opened the only door out of this hour. There were but two. One was compromise; the other was battle. The integrity of the North closed the first; the generous forbearance of nineteen States closed the other. The South opened this with cannon-shot, and Lincoln shows himself at the door. (*Prolonged and enthusiastic cheering.*) The war, then, is not aggressive, but in self-defence, and Washington has become the Thermopylæ of liberty and justice. (*Applause.*) Rather than surrender that Capital, cover every square foot of it with a living body (*loud cheers*); crowd it with a million of men, and empty every bank vault at the North to pay the cost. (*Renewed cheering.*) Teach the world once for all, that North America belongs to the Stars and Stripes, and under them no man shall wear a chain. (*Enthusiastic cheering.*) In the whole of this conflict, I have looked only at liberty, —only at the slave. Perry entered the battle of the Lakes with 'Don't give up the ship!' floating from the masthead of the 'Lawrence.' When with his fighting flag he left her crippled, heading north, and, mounting the deck of the Niagara, turned her bows due west, he did all for one and the same purpose,— to rake the decks of his foe. Steer north or west, acknowledge secession or cannonade it, I care not which; but 'proclaim liberty throughout all the land unto all the inhabitants thereof.'" (*Loud cheers.*)[1]

---

[1] "Speeches and Lectures," p. 398.

In pursuance of his purpose to support the Administration and educate public opinion, Mr. Phillips entered heart and soul into a personal canvass of the country and made himself ubiquitous during the remainder of 1861. In December he visited New York and spoke to an audience that recalled the one in Music Hall on April 21st. His aim was to strike into the inmost conscience of the country the essential nature of the strife, and the hopelessness of compromise. Said he :

"It is the aristocratic element which survived the Constitution, which our fathers thought could be safely left under it, and the South to-day is forced into this war by the natural growth of the antagonistic principle. You may pledge whatever submission and patience of Southern institutions you please, it is not enough. South Carolina said to Massachusetts, in 1833, when Edward Everett was Governor, ' Abolish free speech,—it is a nuisance.' She is right,—from her standpoint it is. (*Laughter.*) That is, it is not possible to preserve the quiet of South Carolina consistently with free speech ; but you know the story Sir Walter Scott told of the Scotch laird, who said to his old butler, ' Jock, you and I can't live under this roof.' ' And where does your honor think of going ? ' So free speech says to South Carolina to-day. Now I say you may pledge, compromise, guarantee what you please. The South well knows that is not your purpose,—it is your character she dreads. It is the nature of Northern institutions, the perilous freedom of discussion, the flavor of our ideas, the sight of our growth, the very neighborhood of such States, that constitutes the danger. It is like two vases launched on the stormy sea. The iron said to the crockery, ' I won't come near you.' ' Thank you,' said the weaker vessel ; ' there is just as much danger in my coming near you.' This the South feels ; hence her determination ; hence, indeed, the imperious necessity that she should rule and shape our Government, or of sailing out of it.

"And the struggle is between these two ideas. Our fathers, as I said, thought they could safely be left, one to outgrow the other. They took gunpowder and a lighted match, forced them into a stalwart cannon, screwed down the muzzle, and thought they could secure peace. But it has resulted differently; their cannon has exploded, and we stand among the fragments.

"Now some Republicans and some Democrats—not Butler and Bryant and Cochrane and Cameron, not Boutwell and Bancroft and Dickinson, and others—but the old set—the old set say to the Republicans, 'Lay the pieces carefully together in their places; put the gunpowder and the match in again, say the Constitution backward instead of your prayers, and there will never be another rebellion!' I doubt it. It seems to me that like causes will produce like effects." [1]

In a letter which Mr. Garrison wrote to Oliver Johnson, the editor of the *Anti-Slavery Standard*, in New York City, there is an interesting reference to this speech, and an amusing account of Mr. Phillips's habits of revision:

"You will see in the *Liberator*, this week, the speech of Mr. Phillips, delivered in New York, as revised and corrected by himself. And such revision, correction, alteration, and addition you never saw, in the way of emendation! More than two columns of the *Tribune's* report were in type before Phillips came into our office; and the manipulation these required was a caution to all reporters and type-setters! I proposed to Phillips to send his altered 'slips' to Barnum as a remarkable curiosity, and Winchell suggested having them photographed! But Phillips desired to make his speech as complete and full as he could, and I am glad that you are to receive it without being put to any trouble about it. Doubtless, you will be requested to make some new alterations; for he is constantly criticising what he has spoken, and pays no regard to literal accuracy. This speech will be eagerly read, as it touches ably upon many interesting points." [2]

Mr. Phillips's mind was critical. His taste was exquisite. He never cared to see his speeches in

---

[1] "Speeches and Lectures," pp. 426, 428.
[2] Quoted in "William Lloyd Garrison," vol. iv., p. 39.

print. But if they were printed he wished them to appear in proper shape. Hence his painstaking revision. Nor did the amended copy ever quite satisfy him. Probably, like the after-dinner speaker who made a poor speech and then went home, lay awake all night and thought what a splendid speech he might have made,—he was perplexed by the very wealth of his resources. He never made a poor speech; but his temperament made him exacting and fastidious.

Simultaneously with the efforts above referred to, the Agitator now delivered far and wide his marvellous lecture on "Toussaint L'Ouverture," the negro creator of Hayti. The doubt in these days touched the capacity of the blacks,—their courage, their susceptibility to improvement, their humanity. With the San Domingo insurrection for an illustration, Mr. Phillips showed "that the negro blood, instead of standing at the bottom of the list, is entitled, if judged either by its great men or its masses,—by its courage, its purpose, or endurance, to a place as near the Anglo-Saxon as any other blood known in history."[1] He had a genius for this kind of portraiture; and he made Toussaint as familiar to the American Lyceum as John Brown or Washington. Thus he rendered to the nation an immense service, immediate and remote; immediate, because public opinion was thus fashioned to tolerate and soon to demand the arming of the blacks for the defence of the Union; remote, because prejudice was dispelled, a race was rehabilitated in its own respect and in the respect of others, and it was thus made easier for

---

[1] *Vide* "Speeches and Lectures," pp. 468–94.

whites and blacks to get on together in the new relations of freedom.

Considering the purpose for which it was prepared and the limitations incidental to the Lyceum, it is not too much to claim that the lecture on Toussaint stands at the head of this department of literature. Its delivery was an enchantment. Without this, however, the critic feels the subtle charm, and admires the wealth of historical reference, the keen analysis, the effective anecdote, the spicy satire, the nice portrayal of character, the epigrammatic point, the varied splendor of diction. But to those who can only read it, we may say, as Æschines did to his applauding scholars at Rhodes, when he had recited the oration of Demosthenes that resulted in his banishment: "You admire now: how would your admiration have been raised could you have heard him speak it?"

XXV.

THE STRUGGLE OF TWO CIVILIZATIONS.

War, like peace, requires adjustment. It cannot be waged successfully without accumulated material and practical skill. In the appeal to arms the South had every advantage of long preparation, the choice of time, military habits, and initiative. The North was unready, was without the martial spirit, and lacked dexterity. For fifty years, the South had been a camp, and the North had been a workshop. Hence, at the start, secession won victories and the Union learned by defeat.

Providence again! For had the Rebellion been quelled within a year or two, slavery would have survived. Strange to say, there was no general recognition of the fact in the free States that the death-grapple was between hostile systems. The very coiner of the phrase, "irrepressible conflict" was now in the Cabinet, exerting himself to patch up a peace on the impossible basis of the *status quo ante bellum*. And the author of the expression, "A house divided against itself cannot stand," was now in the White House making every effort to restore the Union with slavery intact. Under such tutelage, the word compromise, buried beneath the passionate resentment of the nation when the flag was insulted, was dug up and revived in the community. Thus, President Lincoln assured Horace Greeley that his intention was to save the Union without reference to slavery—which was as though a physician should say : "I mean to cure my patient without reference to the disease."

However much others, in and out of office, might doubt and hesitate, the Abolitionists did not. Mr. Phillips as their mouthpiece never tired of emphasizing the opportunity and the necessity of Abolition, and the means, in the war power of the Government. In furtherance of this object, he co-operated with a large number of prominent gentlemen of Massachusetts in the organization of an Emancipation League. Recognizing that slavery was the "origin and mainspring of the Rebellion," the leaguers pledged themselves to make and direct sentiment in that channel. On March 10th Mr. Phillips addressed his colleagues. The President had just taken his first Anti-Slavery step—trembling and uncertain as an infant's first step away from the mother's lap. It was a proposition to compensate the Border States for the gradual emancipation of their slaves —a proposition which the Border States promptly rejected. Mr. Phillips welcomed it as a sign of promise. "If the President has not entered Canaan, he has turned his face Zionward," he assured his associates ; and he interpreted the message as saying : "Gentlemen of the Border States, now is your time. If you want your money, take it, or if hereafter I should free your slaves without paying for them, don't say I did not offer to do it."[1] But God hardened Pharaoh's heart. He intended not gradual but immediate emancipation.

---

[1] *Vide Liberator*, vol. xxxii., p. 42.

In March, 1862, the orator went to Washington—his first visit. His reception was cordial. The ostensible object of his presence was the delivery of two lectures there, one literary, the other political. He spoke on successive evenings, to immense audiences which embraced the official life of the city. The curiosity to hear him was great, and he fully met all expectations. He brought himself on the platform. It was Wendell Phillips in his most incisive mood. In both Houses of Congress he was the recipient of marked attention. He also had an interview with Lincoln. "I told him," said he, "that if he started the experiment of emancipation, and honestly devoted his energies to making it a fact, he would deserve to hold the helm until the experiment was finished—that the people would not allow him to quit while it was trying."[1] At the same time he urged Lincoln to dismiss Seward from the Cabinet as a hopeless obstructive, but in vain.[2]

From the Capital, the lecturer went Westward, speaking here and there *en route*, always to crowds, and usually nowadays to sympathizers. Cincinnati, however, proved to be a disagreeable exception. Here a gang of murderous rioters, getting their inspiration, and perhaps their recruits, from the adjacent Kentucky, poured into the Opera House and fusilladed the "d—d Abolitionist" with various missiles, odorous and odious, as he stood in full exposure on the stage. Once he was struck; without noticing it, he proceeded, bland but satiric, every sentence a stab, and extorted the admiration of the

---

[1] *Vide Liberator*, vol. xxxiii., p. 110.
[2] *Ib.*, pp. 19, 26.

very assailants by his fearless bearing.[1] "I really imagined I was back in Boston," commented the orator, with a laugh. "The Cincinnati Opera House suggested Tremont Temple, and the rats of the West closely resembled those of the East. These and those alike nibble and gnaw—*and run.*"[2]

Mr. Phillips made himself more and more a whip and spur. He became censor-general. In season and out of season, he urged Congress, the Cabinet, the President to forge and hurl the only thunderbolt that could save the Union, or make it worth saving. From this standpoint, he criticised men and measures unsparingly. He loomed like the embodied spirit of justice. Mr. Lincoln was riding two hobbies—that of compensated emancipation in the Border States, secessionist at heart though in the Union by force and as wedded to slavery as the Carolinas; and that of colonization. The honest but ignorant rail-splitter was twenty years behind the times. We have heard Mr. Phillips's remarks regarding the first hobby. Touching the second, he said:

"Colonize the blacks! A man might as well colonize his hands; or when the robber enters his house, he might as well colonize his revolver. . . . We need the blacks even more than they need us. They know every inlet, the pathway of every wood, the whole country is mapped at night in their instinct. And they are inevitably on our side, ready as well as skilled to aid: the only element the South has which belongs to the nineteenth century. Aside from justice, the Union needs the blacks."[3]

---

[1] *Vide Liberator*, vol. xxxii., pp. 53, 54.

[2] Letter to Rev. John T. Sargent, from Cincinnati, March 25th, 1862 (MS.).

[3] *Vide* "Speeches and Lectures," pp. 545, 546.

He thought the hesitation of the Administration arose from its Whig antecedents. Listen to him:

"The Whig party, good as it was in many respects, virtuous in certain of its impulses, correct in some of its aspirations, had one defect: it had no confidence in the people, no trust in the masses; it did not believe in the conscience and intelligence of the million; it looked, indeed, upon the whole world as a probate court, in which education and wealth were the guardians. And so when our rulers entered on their work of defending the nation, they dared not trust the country to the hearts that loved it."[1]

With regard to the spirit of the great battle, he complimented the South upon its sincerity, and said:

"No man can fight Stonewall Jackson, an honest fanatic on the side of slavery, but John Brown, an equally honest fanatic on the side of freedom. They are the only chemical equals, and will neutralize each other. You cannot neutralize nitric acid with cologne water. William H. Seward is no match for Jefferson Davis. We must have what they have—positive convictions. Otherwise the elements of the struggle are unequal."[2]

Concerning the problem itself, he said:

"We have not only an army to conquer, but we have a state of mind to annihilate.... When England conquered the Highlands, she held them,—held them until she could educate them,—and it took a generation. That is just what we have to do with the South; annihilate the old South, and put a new one there. You do not annihilate a thing by abolishing it. You must supply the vacancy."[3]

He states and answers a constant taunt as follows:

"But men say, 'This is a mean thing; nineteen millions of people pitched against eight millions of Southerners, white men, and can't whip them, and now begin to call on the negroes.' Is

---

[1] *Vide* "Speeches and Lectures," p. 529.   [2] *Ib.*, p. 540.
[3] *Ib.*, p. 544.

that the right statement? Look at it. What is the South's strength? She has eight millions of whites. She has the sympathy of foreign powers. She has the labor of four millions of slaves. What strength has the North? Divided about equally—into Republicans and Democrats; the Republicans willing to go but half way, and the Democrats not willing to go at all. (*Laughter.*) It is like two men fighting. We will call them Jonathan and Charles. Jonathan is the North. His right hand, the Democratic party, he holds behind him. His left hand, his own tenderness of conscience uses to keep the slaves down. That is how he is to fight. No, that is not all. Upon his shoulders is strapped the West Point Academy like a stone of a hundred-weight. (*Laughter.*) The South stands with both hands, holding loaded revolvers, and, lest she should lose any time, John Bull is behind with additional pistols to hand the moment she needs them. These are the two powers which are fighting this battle." [1]

Some of these passages have been taken from a speech delivered by Mr. Phillips in New York during the anniversary week of 1863. In a letter to his wife, Mr. Garrison paints certain incidents which concern the orator:

"Phillips's meeting at the Institute, Monday evening, was a splendid one, and he acquitted himself in a way to gather fresh laurels for his brow. His speech was reported in full in the *Tribune* of Tuesday morning. At the conclusion of it, I was loudly called for, but held back. Then calls were made for Horace Greeley, who came forward and made a few remarks in his queer-toned voice and very awkward manner. The cries were renewed for me, and I said a few words, the applause being general and very marked. When I first entered the hall, and was conducted to a seat on the platform by the side of Mayor Opdyke, the audience broke out into repeated rounds of applause. What a change in popular sentiment and feeling from the old mobocratic, Pro-Slavery times! And, remember,

---

[1] *Vide* " Speeches and Lectures," p. 553.

this was a meeting called by the Sixteenth Republican Ward Association !"[1]

The utterances of Mr. Phillips in New York and elsewhere, expressed the feelings not only of the Abolitionists, but of a constantly-increasing multitude of Northern men and women. At last, the Administration heard and heeded. In September, 1862, President Lincoln issued his preliminary Proclamation of Emancipation—the proclamation of warning. It gave the rebellious States a hundred days of grace, and interjected the twin hobbies of Mr. Lincoln,—gradual and compensated emancipation in the Border States, and colonization. "It is a step in the right direction," said Mr. Garrison. "A step!" exclaimed Mr. Phillips, "it's a stride!"[2]

On January 1st, 1863, secession being unresponsive, came the second and final proclamation—the edict of freedom. The war power of the Union struck off the shackles of all slaves held in the revolted States. The North hailed it as the beginning of the end. Great public meetings confirmed and glorified the event.

As though God had been placated by this instalment of justice, success began from this hour to accompany the efforts of the nation. Grant at Vicksburg, Meade at Gettysburg, soon afterward dealt staggering blows to the Confederacy. Abroad, too, the effect was wholesome. The English aristocracy had all along openly sympathized with and covertly aided their fellow aristocrats in America. They had made a dozen attempts to recognize the independence of the Confederacy. Their ships, as Southern

---

[1] "William Lloyd Garrison" vol. iv., p. 78. [2] *Ib.*, p. 62, note.

privateers, had pirated upon our commerce, and driven it from the high seas. The American Anti-Slavery Society is entitled to praise, which it has never received, on account of its successful endeavors, through British agents, to enlighten England on American affairs. George Thompson, in the pay of this body, had been exerting himself from the outset in this good work and with the best results.[1] An influential "Emancipation Society" had been organized in London in the interest of the Union, with Thompson as its animating spirit, and his son-in-law, F. W. Chesson, as its executive. Among its members were John Stuart Mill, John Bright, Richard Cobden, Goldwin Smith, Justin McCarthy, Thomas Hughes, Professor Cairnes, Herbert Spencer, Baptist Noel, Newman Hall—the brainiest and worthiest leaders of British thought and life. Every one of these, and a host of others, led by the tireless and eloquent Thompson, gave weeks and months of work in behalf of the Union. If Lancashire suffered and made no sign, if the arrogant classes were checkmated by the alert masses, if England kept hands off in the struggle over here,—we owe it to these heroes. Are their names not

"On fame's eternal bead-roll worthy to be filed?"

George Thompson tried to persuade Gerrit Smith and Wendell Phillips to proceed to England and cooperate there in the creation and direction of public opinion. Mr. Phillips was inclined to go; but was held at home by his wife's infirmities.[2] Subse-

---

[1] "William Lloyd Garrison," vol. iv., p. 29, note; and pp. 65, 68, and 71-77.

[2] Letter to Gerrit Smith, in '63 (MS.).

quently Henry Ward Beecher, being abroad for *rest*, found what he sought in endless battles with unfriendly audiences, in which he won new fame for himself, and got ample compensation in the magnificent service rendered to his country. When the Emancipation Proclamation reached Great Britain, its reception there was only less enthusiastic than here. "It would have done you good," wrote Mr. Chesson to an American friend, "if you had heard Baptist Noel's speech, or attended the great meeting of the working-classes which we held on December 31st—the eve of freedom. Newman Hall's speech on this occasion was one of the best I ever listened to. He stated, in the fairest manner, every conceivable argument which had been urged in favor of the Slave Confederacy, or against the policy of the Federal Government, and then replied to them *seriatim*, demolishing every sophistry and gibbeting every falsehood, until the slavocracy had really not a rag left wherewith to conceal the revolting defects of their odious cause."[1]

The proclamation, followed as it was by the tremendous victories of Grant and Meade, gave the projected English intervention the *coup de grâce*.

Already triumphant in anticipation, but without relaxing the strain of unceasing exertion, Mr. Phillips now aided the formation of colored regiments in Massachusetts. Two of these were recruited in the spring of 1863, and were speedily supplied with the maximum number of men. These were the Fifty-fourth and the Fifty-fifth regiments. Robert G. Shaw was the colonel of one, and Edward N. Hal-

---

[1] *Vide* "William Lloyd Garrison," vol iv., pp. 72, 73.

lowell was the lieutenant-colonel of the other; both warm personal friends of the orator. The Fifty-fourth Massachusetts Regiment was the first body of colored soldiers despatched from the North. Mr. Phillips with Frederick Douglass and Garrison had often visited their camp and spoken words of cheer. When, on May 28th, 1863, the blacks marched proudly through the streets of Boston to embark for the front, his heart swelled, and as he stood in the mighty throng that lined the sidewalks to cheer their departure, startling memories significant of yet more stupendous changes made a tumult in his breast.[1] Others of the on-looking Abolitionists shared in his emotion. "You remember," wrote Lydia Maria Child, addressing another of the old guard, "Charles Sprague's description of scenes he witnessed from a window near State Street? First, Garrison dragged through the streets by a mob; second, Burns carried back to slavery by United States troops, through the same street; third, a black regiment, marching down the same street, to the tune of 'John Brown,' to join the United States Army for the emancipation of their race. What a thrilling historical poem might be made of that!"[2]

These men, and the whole contingent of colored troops did splendidly. Their friends had no occasion either to apologize for them or to regret their own efforts to enlist and despatch them.[3]

While these events were in progress, Mr. Phillips gave concurrent attention to another matter. He

---

[1] Letter to Lydia Maria Child (MS.).
[2] "Letters of Lydia Maria Child," p. 235.
[3] *Vide* George W. Williams's "History of the Colored Troops in the Rebellion."

had learned from bitter experience that Boston could not, that no great city could, decently govern itself. State laws, even city laws, were flouted when they ran counter to the prejudices or the interests of influential classes in the centres of population. Accordingly, he pleaded for and secured in Boston what is called a Metropolitan Police. Speaking from Theodore Parker's pulpit in the spring of 1863, he said :

"The capital of the civilized world, London, many years ago, found herself utterly unable to contend with the evils of accumulated population,—found municipal machinery utterly inadequate for the security of life or property in her streets ; and the national Government, by the hand of Sir Robert Peel, assumed the police regulation of that cluster of towns which we commonly call London, though the plan does not include the city proper. New York, on our continent, about six years ago, followed the example ; Baltimore and Cincinnati have done likewise to a greater or less extent, and so also have some of the other Western cities. The experience of all great accumulations of property and population reads us a lesson, that the execution of the laws therein demands extra consideration and peculiar machinery. The self-organized Safety Committees of San Francisco and other cities prove the same fact. Indeed, great cities are nests of great vices, and it has been the experience of republics that great cities are an exception to the common rule of self-governed communities. Neither New York, nor New Orleans, nor Baltimore—none of the great cities—has found the ballot-box of its individual voters a sufficient protection, through a police organization. Great cities cannot be protected on the theory of republican institutions. We may like it or not,—seventy years have tried the experiment, and, so far, it is a failure ; and if there is no resource outside of the city limits, then a self-governed great city is, so far as my experience goes, the most uncomfortable which any man who loves free speech can live in. It is no surprise, therefore, that we ask you no longer to let the police force represent the voters of Boston."

Having thus stated the case, he proceeded to recite the reasons for the change, in the non-execution of the temperance laws of the commonwealth, and in the denial of free speech. In reply to the objection that the proposed change was undemocratic, he said:

"Men say, to take the appointment of the police out of the hands of the peninsula is anti-democratic. Why, from 1620 down to within ten years, the State always acted on that plan. The State makes the law. Who executes it? The State. For two hundred years, the Governor appointed the sheriff of every county, and the sheriff appointed his deputies, and they executed the laws. The constables of the towns were allowed merely a subsidiary authority to execute by-laws, and help execute the State law. The democratic principle is, that the law shall be executed by an executive authority concurrent with that which makes it. That is democracy. The State law, naturally, democratically, is to be executed by the State. We have merely, in deference to convenience, changed that of late in some particulars, and we may reasonably go back to the old plan if we find that, in any particular locality, the new plan fails. Why not? In all other matters of State concern,—Board of Education, Board of Agriculture, and all the various boards,—the State has the control. You perceive this 'anti-democratic' argument can be carried out to an absurdity. Suppose the Five Points of New York should send word to the Fifth Avenue, 'We don't like your police; we mean to have one of our own, and it will be very anti-democratic for you to take the choice of our constables out of our hands.' Suppose North Street should send word to the City Hall, 'We have concluded to turn every other house into a grog-shop, or something almost as bad, and to appoint our own police; please instruct your police to keep out of our ward.' We should not say this was democratic. We should say, that as far as the interest of a community in a law extends, just so far that community has a right to a hand in the execution of it."[1]

It was in the autumn of 1863 that the edition of

---

[1] "Speeches and Lectures," p 516 *sq.*

Mr. Phillips's collected "Speeches and Lectures" was first published. The volume was eagerly caught up. It had not to wait until centuries should cobweb it, but was born a classic. From then until now the demand for it has been unceasing. In facetious mood, the orator took a copy to his wife, in which he had written on the title-page : "Speeches and Lectures. By Ann Phillips"—his way of recognizing her influence upon his career.

As the year 1863 waxed old two questions divided the country, in addition to the war, though in fact growing out of it—reconstruction and the re-election of Mr. Lincoln. Having overrun and subjugated large sections of the South, the nation was confronted by the problem as to the practical disposition to be made of them. The Administration favored the readmission of such portions of these sections as were conterminous with the old State boundaries, under the ancient State constitutions, altered only sufficiently to recognize the freedom of the blacks. Mr. Phillips set himself against this. He maintained that freedom, in the American conception, was only complete when it included the elective franchise and equal rights before the law.[1] On these vital points the State Constitution of Louisiana, which was the commonwealth then specially in question, remained precisely where it always had stood—with a *code noir* as black as Algiers. Because Mr. Lincoln refused to make such changes as should harmonize the conquered territories with the American conception of freedom, conditions precedent to readmission, the Agitator vigorously opposed his renomination. He

---
[1] *Vide Liberator*, vol. xxxiv., p. 22.

favored any one of half a dozen other names which were unobjectionable from an Abolitionist's point of view.[1] The issue was decided in the Republican Convention, and in the subsequent national election, adversely to Mr. Phillips, who submitted to the inevitable. He was wise in objecting to such shilly-shally reconstruction—mistaken in preferring Fremont to Lincoln; a man who, when he stumbled, always stumbled forward. The position he took at this moment brought him into collision with the majority of Unionists,—Garrison among the rest.[2] After events convinced him of his erroneous judgment.[3]

The war was now gasping ward the end. Grant, transferred from the West to the East, had struck unity and infused vigor into the hitherto unsystematic and sluggish military operations of the Union. Sherman marched through the Confederacy to the sea,—Lee was pushed back, stubbornly but vainly contesting every step,—Richmond was captured,—Appomattox was reached,—and, on April 9th, 1865, the Rebellion collapsed!

Side by side with these victories of war strode other victories of peace. The nation had been convinced at last that there could be no permanent reconciliation until slavery was buried in the grave which yawned to receive the Confederacy. This conviction, after the fashion of popular government, soon expressed itself in appropriate legislation.

---

[1] *Vide* various speeches and acts of Mr. Phillips at this period, as reported in the *Liberator*, vol. xxxiv., pp. 81, 83, 87, 94.

[2] *Vide* "William Lloyd Garrison," vol. iv.; pp. 107-12.

[3] "Lincoln was slow, but he got there. Let us thank God for him." Thus he wrote, in 1866, to the Rev. John T. Sargent (MS.).

Maryland and Missouri made haste to join the sisterhood of free States. Illinois repealed her "black laws," as infamous as the kindred codes of the South, and more inexcusable. Then came the Thirteenth Amendment to the Constitution of the United States, forever abolishing slavery. Coupled with the toppling military fortunes of the Confederacy, as they were, it is not surprising that these transcendent achievements should have produced a frenzy of joy from ocean to ocean. Men hugged one another in the streets. The churches sent the Amen of the nation into the ear of God—to whom a grateful continent ascribed the glory !

While all were happy, the colored people were exultant. They celebrated the jubilee from the Gulf to the Lakes. One memorable meeting of this kind specially concerns us—the Boston Celebration. For George Thompson (who had hurried across the Atlantic to be "in at the death") and Garrison and Phillips were with them to voice their feelings.[1] But the eloquence of the occasion itself out-thundered even such orators. Slavery was dead ! Immediate and unconditional emancipation was embalmed in the fundamental law of the Republic ! The prophetic vision of Wendell Phillips was realized :

"When the smoke of this conflict clears away, the world will see under our banner one brotherhood—and on the banks of the Potomac, the Genius of Liberty, robed in light, four-and-thirty stars for her diadem, broken chains under her feet, and an olive branch in her right hand."[2]

---

[1] *Vide Liberator*, vol. xxxv., p. 37.
[2] "Speeches and Lectures," p. 414.

XXVI.

SHADOW IN SUNSHINE.

On April 14th, 1865, exactly four years after the surrender of Fort Sumter, the vindicated and glorified flag was raised again over the very citadel whence it had been snatched by treason, and the Stars and Stripes waved above the cradle and the grave of the Rebellion. The company gathered to take part in the dramatic ceremonial was notable, and included Major Anderson (the hero of both dates), Judge Holt, Senator Henry Wilson, H. W. Beecher (the orator of the day), and by special invitation of the National Government, those twins of Abolition, George Thompson and William Lloyd Garrison.

Garrison in Charleston! And without the smell of tar upon his garments! One never-to-be-forgotten morning, he stood at the tomb of Calhoun. Laying his hand upon the monument, the Abolitionist said solemnly: "Down into a deeper grave than this slavery has gone, and for it there is no resurrection." Fit the hour, fit the man, and fit the place for the burial service of human bondage.[1] Devils shrieked, but angels chanted "Alleluia!"

Later, on the same day, the blacks gave their friend a delirious welcome. Surrounded by wildly applauding thousands he stood; when out from the

---

[1] *Vide Liberator*, vol. xxxv., p. 76.

press came the spokesman of the negroes, leading two little girls, neatly dressed, by the hand. Addressing Mr. Garrison, he said:

"Sir, it is with pleasure that is inexpressible that I welcome you here among us, the long, the steadfast friend of the poor, down-trodden slave. Sir, I have read of you. I have read of the mighty labors you have had for the consummation of this glorious object. Here you see stand before you your handiwork. These children were robbed from me, and I stood desolate. Many a night I pressed a sleepless pillow from the time I returned to my bed until the morning. I lost a dear wife, and after her death that little one, who is the counterpart of her mother's countenance, was taken from me. I appealed for her with all the love and reason of a father. The rejection came forth in these words: 'Annoy me not, or I will sell them off to another State.' I thank God that, through your instrumentality, under the folds of that glorious flag which treason tried to triumph over, you have restored them to me. And I tell you that it is not this heart alone, but there are mothers, there are fathers, there are sisters, and there are brothers, the pulsations of whose hearts are unimaginable. The greeting that they would give you, sir, is almost impossible for me to express; but, sir, we welcome and look upon you as our saviour. We thank you for what you have done for us. Take this wreath from these children; and when you go home, never mind how faded the flowers may be, preserve them, encase them, and keep them as a token of affection from one who has lived and loved." (*Cheers.*)[1]

And a man who could thus think, feel, express himself, a few months before had been an article of merchandise![2]

Toward evening of this day, to him, of pleasurable experiences, Mr. Garrison went out to the adjacent

---

[1] *Vide Liberator*, vol. xxxv., p. 72.

[2] His name was Samuel Dickerson. His speech was his own, and was conceived and spoken as given above.

camp of the Fifty-fifth Massachusetts (colored) Regiment. Crowded around were the plantation "hands," clothed in the rags and ignorance inherited from the dead iniquity. "Well," cried Mr. Garrison, "you are free at last. Let us give three cheers." He led off. To his amazement, there was no response. The poor creatures looked at him with a surprise equal to his own. He had to give the second and the third cheers also without them. *They did not know how to cheer !* [1]

If the scene at Charleston was dramatic, the scene at Washington was more so—tragedy outdone. While Garrison was being *fêted*, on the very day described, Lincoln lay dead. The creator of the Anti-Slavery movement in America was in Carolina, rejoicing with the freedmen. The President who was the instrument of the emancipation, was in heaven, presenting three millions of broken fetters before the throne of Justice and Love.

Amid the general consternation caused by the bullet of Wilkes Booth, Mr. Phillips was besought to express the sorrow and recite the lesson of the hour. This he did, on April 19th, in the Tremont Temple, in Boston :

"These are sober days. The judgments of God have found us out. Thirty years ago, none heeded the fire and gloom which slumbered below. It was nothing that a giant sin gagged our pulpits ; that its mobs ruled our cities, burned men at the stake for their opinions, and hunted them like wild beasts for their humanity. It was nothing that in the lonely quiet of the plantation the eye of lust and the whip of rage fell on the unpitied person of the slave. In vain did a thousand witnesses crowd our highways telling the world the horrors of the prison-

---

[1] *Vide* " William Lloyd Garrison," vol. iv., p. 149.

house. None stopped to consider. None believed. But what the world would not look at, God has set to-day in a light so ghastly that it dazzles us blind. What we would not believe, God has written all over the face of the continent with the sword's point, in the blood of our best beloved. We believe the agony of the slave's hovel when it takes its seat at our own board.

"And what of him in whose life fluid this lesson is writ? He sleeps in the blessings of the poor whose fetters God commissioned him to break. Who among living men may not envy him? Suppose that, when a boy, he floated on the slow current of the Mississippi, idly gazing at the slave upon its banks, some angel had lifted the curtain and shown him that in his prime he should see America rocked to its foundation in the effort to break these chains, and should himself marshal the hosts of the Almighty in the grandest and holiest war that Christendom ever knew, and hurl the thunderbolt of justice that should smite the proud system to the dust: then die, leaving a name immortal in the sturdy pride of one race and in the undying gratitude of another. Would any credulity, however sanguine, would any enthusiasm, however fervid, have enabled him to believe it? Fortunate man! He lived to do it!"[1]

As in a drama, subsidiary incidents, kindred and suggestive, lead up to the great tableaux, so the two scenes enacted at Charleston and at Washington were preceded or accompanied by other examples of retributive justice, undreamed-of contrast, and startling coincidence. Harper's Ferry had been burned by General Tyndale, who three years before went to Virginia to claim the body of John Brown and take it North,—then insulted and threatened, now putting the torch to the hotel where the mob raged on him, and only stopping the conflagration, when it reached the engine-house, "the Gibraltar,"

---

[1] *Vide* the Boston press of April 20th, 1865, for reports of this striking address, not otherwise in print.

as Wendell Phillips called it, "from which the brave old man fired the first gun at Virginia slavery."[1]

A daughter of John Brown had established a school for colored children in the very residence of Henry A. Wise, the governor who hung her father, and "old Ossawatomie's" portrait hung on the wall of the slave-holder and looked down approvingly upon the work. A son of Frederick Douglass was likewise teaching in Maryland, in the place where the negro orator had been a slave, and whence he had followed the North Star to freedom. The plantation of Jefferson Davis had been transformed into a "contraband" camp, and was finally bought and worked by the former slaves of the Confederate President. The estate of General Lee, at Arlington, became a freedmen's village, with a "Garrison Street" and a "Lovejoy Street," and at last a resting-place for the Union dead.[2] Mighty tragedy! whose four acts were four years, with a continent for a stage, with two races for the actors, and with episodes and *dénouements* unimaginable.

The first feeling of the Abolitionists was that now their work was done. On second thought, they perceived their mistake. The freedmen, without civil rights, ignorant, poor, needed sympathy and direction almost as desperately as they had needed emancipation. They were but half free, in a republic, until they were seated in self-ownership, not only, but clothed and in their right mind as citizens.

So far all were agreed. At the annual meeting of the American Anti-Slavery Society in New York

---

[1] *Vide Liberator*, vol. xxxiii., p. 37.
[2] *Vide* "William Lloyd Garrison," vol. iv., p. 133.

City, in May, 1865, the pioneers disagreed as to the continuation of the old agencies. Mr. Garrison contended that the national society should dissolve at this session, since slavery was abolished; that its existence isolated its members when isolation was no longer needful, as co-workers abounded, and that what remained to be done could be done better through other channels.[1] Mr. Phillips differed. He emphasized the fact that the Thirteenth Amendment, though passed by Congress, had not yet been ratified by the States, and that hence slavery was not legally abolished; that the historic position of the society outside of parties and churches gave it moral authority, vindicated by the past, and mightier in present circumstances; that its pledge bound it in spirit, if not verbally, to life and action until the freedom of the blacks should be signed and sealed not alone by emancipation but by citizenship; and that Abolitionists could labor for these ends most efficiently on their time-honored platform.[2]

The discussion was prolonged and warm, Messrs. Edmund Quincy, Oliver Johnson, and Samuel May, Jr., concurring with Mr. Garrison; while Anna E. Dickinson, Frederick Douglass, Robert Purvis, Charles Lennox Remond, and others supported Mr. Phillips. The society resolved to go on by a vote of 118 to 48. Mr. Phillips was elected President, and succeeded Mr. Garrison, who persisted in retiring. Aaron M. Powell took editorial charge of the society's organ, the *Anti-Slavery Standard*, replacing Messrs. Quincy and Johnson, who also with-

---

[1] *Vide* "William Lloyd Garrison," vol. iv., p. 157 *sqq*.
[2] *Vide Liberator*, vol. xxxv., pp. 81, 82.

drew. A new Executive Committee was chosen. Then an adjournment was carried amid great rejoicing.[1]

Two weeks later, the debate was transferred to the anniversary meeting of the Massachusetts Anti-Slavery Society, in Boston; and later still to the annual meeting of the New England Society, in the same city; when Mr. Phillips again triumphed by a majority of three to one;[2] and he thus held these three organizations together throughout the heated and perilous period of reconstruction.

This controversy divided the veterans into two camps, a larger and a smaller, at an hour when it would have been wiser for them to have remained united. It kept some at the front and sent others to the rear, when all were needed in the battle. It also caused bad feeling at the time—which eventually gave place to the old friendliness. Mr. Phillips, however, neither felt nor expressed himself toward the schismatics, otherwise than with the heartiness of former years. He realized that the difference was one of expediency rather than principle—of methods, not of objects. Hence, he went on loving and lauding Mr. Garrison as of yore.[3]

An evidence of the changed attitude of Boston toward its most illustrious son was given in the summer of 1865, by a pressing request which reached him from the School Committee, to address the children of the city at their annual Festival, on July 28th. Mr. Phillips complied, and showered down reminiscences, anecdotes, aphorisms, sage bits of advice,

---

[1] *Vide* " William Lloyd Garrison," vol. iv., p. 161. [2] *Ib.*, p. 175.
[3] *Vide Liberator*, vol. xxxv., p. 26.

exhortations to lofty duty, in a manner so genial and charming, that young and old were alike instructed and captivated. In a hasty note he described the scene to a friend detained by illness :

"I spoke at the Children's Festival. Such a sight ! twelve hundred lads and lasses ; twelve hundred more adults, dignitaries, etc., with Zerrahn's great orchestra. I was popular and bewildered. Hisses I understand, but cheers, and such cheers ! However, the sight of some old faces, Manley's black beard, and Stearns's long one, and George Thompson [1] in the audience taking snuff, reassured me. I followed Dana, upon a cricket, three feet square (where Zerrahn stands to lead the band). I spoke without gesture ; fearing if I moved a finger, I should topple over on one side and fall into Mayor Lincoln's arms." [2]

There was no evidence of these straitened circumstances in the orator's address, at any rate—neither in the matter nor in the manner of it. Which goes to show that the eye and the ear are not very trustworthy witnesses.

The closing event of the year 1865 was the formal proclamation of the ratification by the requisite number of States (twenty-seven out of thirty-six) of the Thirteenth Amendment forever prohibiting slavery in the Republic. What remained to be done ? The next and necessary step was the vitalizing the prohibition by securing for the freedmen equal rights before the law. Involuntary servitude was illegal. Now the black man must be lifted into his place beside the white man, with the ballot as his certificate of citizenship.

---

[1] Mr. Thompson soon after returned to England, where he died, October 7th, 1878.
[2] Letter to Rev. John T. Sargent (MS.).

BOOK III.

AFTERNOON.

1866-1879.

I.

FROM BATTLE-FIELD TO FORUM.

BROADLY grouped, two policies now divided the country. One was the "grasp-of-war" policy. It rested on the facts of the case,—the non-existence of local governments in the Southern States,—their military occupation,—the unprecedented condition of the population, with the whites self-despoiled of power and the blacks newly emancipated,—and the necessity of subordinating all else to the welfare of the Republic. The other was the "insurrection" policy. It assumed that the Southern States retained their autonomy; that the war power ended with the cessation of actual hostilities; that no authority remained with the National Government save such as it held over the States which had not seceded; and that the South should be permitted at once to reorganize on the former basis, subject only to the Thirteenth Amendment. The first was the policy of the Republican party,—the second that of the Democratic party. Between these theories, however, an infinite variety of views prevailed, founded on one or the other of them, but shading off into the extremes, with every imaginable intervening color— the rainbow outvied.

The martyr President was hardly cold in the grave before his successor revealed his purpose to desert his party and ".secede" to the Democracy. Andrew Johnson had posed as a radical, was steeped in pledges to bind the sheaves gleaned by the war-sickle, and was hailed by the radicals as a distinct advance upon Lincoln,—as the special representative of the extreme Union sentiment. Sprung from the lowest class at the South, he was without education, but possessed native vigor and a strong will. Thus dowered, he extemporized what he styled "my policy," which was essentially a Southern programme, and set himself to wrest from the nation the fruits of its hard-won success.

In common with the majority, Mr. Phillips had turned expectantly to President Johnson. "I believe in him," said he.[1] Bitter, therefore, was his chagrin, unspeakable his disgust, when the patriot of yesterday dropped the mask and disclosed the traitor of to-day. He instantly trained his guns and opened fire upon this new enemy. "Jefferson Davis Johnson," the orator dubbed him.[2] And he regarded the situation as more critical than it had been at any time since 1861. Everything was at stake, nothing was decided. The South was still a unit, angry from defeat, and enraged at the freedmen. The North was again divided. The battle was adjourned from Appomattox to Washington, and there seemed every reason to fear that the poisonous remnants of the slave system would linger and fester for half a century—like Jacobitism in England or Bourbonism in France.[3]

Late in the year 1865 he wrote to a relative:

---

[1] *Vide Liberator*, vol. xxxv., p. 86.
[2] *Vide Anti-Slavery Standard*, vol. xxviii., August 11th.
[3] *Vide Liberator*, vol. xxiv., p. 81.

"As for the cause, everything I hear, public and private, from Washington, increases my anxiety about this suffrage question. We shall get all we absolutely bully out of this Administration, and no more. Four of the Cabinet are right; but I fear the President is wrong. All this makes so much more important, not merely advocating the negro's right to the ballot, but letting the Government know that we oppose it if it does not grant this. As Charles Sumner said to Lincoln, 'Reconstruct on the basis of the Declaration of Independence, or count me among the opponents of your Administration.' That is the talk and action which governments hear and obey." [1]

The dangers of that nightmare hour were aggravated by the purpose of the Administration to huddle together any pretext of a government and railroad the seceded States back into the Union, in order to secure for Johnson the Southern vote in the election of 1868; the renegade being troubled by that peculiar American political distemper yclept the Presidential bee in the bonnet.

Mr. Seward was the Mephistopheles of the scene: "How many stars do we want on the flag?" he asked, "shall we not have them all?" To which James Russell Lowell replied: "As many *fixed* stars as you please, but no more *shooting* ones." [2]

Mr. Phillips never before or afterward experienced such anxious and laborious days and nights. He was drained in mind, body, and purse. The withdrawal of Mr. Garrison in this grave emergency thrust upon him the duty of sustaining the Anti-Slavery societies, formulating their platforms, and animating their gatherings. He became an editorial contributor to the *Anti-Slavery Standard*, and from this coigne of

---

[1] Letter to Miss Grew (MS.).
[2] *Vide Anti-Slavery Standard*, vol. xxvii., No. 29.

vantage discharged sharp arrows into the ranks of the opposition, as the Saracen in Scott's story manœuvred against the Knight of the Leopard. These contributions, continued during four years, covered the whole field of controversy, and frequently included outside topics, as the Indian question, and a succession of pleas for the enfranchisement of the Chinese.[1] As time passed, too, and one and another of the veterans exchanged earth for heaven, he published in the *Standard* obituaries marked by the exquisite taste and appreciative beauty characteristic of the man.[2]

Mr. Phillips was in touch with Sumner, Wilson, Wade, in the Senate, with Kelley, Stevens, Colfax, in the House, and with the formers and leaders of public opinion in the community. He was recognized as the most prominent figure in unofficial life. Every word he spoke or wrote had the weight of an oracle. His articles were regularly transferred from the columns of the *Standard* to the pages of the leading journals of both parties.[3] His speeches were caught up and echoed with similar eagerness across

---

[1] *Vide Anti-Slavery Standard*, vols. xxvii., xxviii., xxix., xxx., *passim*.

[2] *Ib.*

[3] An indication of this is found in the following editorial remarks, clipped from the Rochester, N. Y., *Morning Express*, and quoted in the *Standard*, vol. xxviii., April 20th : " We print to-day the latest of Mr. Phillips's articles, as we have for months printed his editorials. No other man in the country has been so gloriously and generally right during the last quarter of a century as Wendell Phillips. He is the soul of integrity, and is as chivalrous as Bayard. To this groundwork of manly and useful character, he adds a remarkable political sagacity which no partisan could possibly possess. His writings and speeches are certain to become classics and will be read and readable centuries hence."

the continent. "What does Phillips say?" was a first inquiry regarding each new phase of the struggle; and what he said shaped thought and made sentiment surprisingly. At no other period since their organization, had the American Anti-Slavery Society, the New England Anti-Slavery Society, and the Massachusetts Anti-Slavery Society possessed the influence they now wielded; and they were so many multiplications of Wendell Phillips, worked by his friends and vitalized by his spirit. The independence of these bodies, with no candidate to elect, no party to guard, no personal interests to jeopard, and contending alone for essential principles, disarmed suspicion and opened the public ear and mind. The statesmen at the Capital gratefully recognized the value of their service. "Hold the societies together," wrote Sumner to Phillips, "the crisis is grave. You and they are doing indispensable work; in this I express the conviction of every Senator and every Representative on our side of pending questions."[1] The crowds in attendance upon the meetings, and the reception of Mr. Phillips's utterances, show the feelings of the people.

In May, 1866, at the anniversary of the American Anti-Slavery Society, Mr. Phillips photographed the situation in the following antithetical resolution:

"The Rebellion has not ceased, it has only changed its weapons. Once it fought, now it intrigues; once it followed Lee in arms, now it follows President Johnson in guile and chicanery; once its headquarters were in Richmond, now it encamps in the White House."[2]

---

[1] Letter from Sumner, March 17th, 1866 (MS.).
[2] *Vide Anti-Slavery Standard*, vol. xxvii., May 19th.

In speaking on this resolution, he said:

"I have a great delight in taming animals. Rarey is a hero of mine. The other day I read of the taming of a lion in Paris. They took a stuffed hussar jacket, covered with a hundred brass buttons, and they put it in the den. He tore it to pieces and devoured it and had an awful fit of indigestion—lay a sick lion for a week. Afterward, whenever a man clad in a hussar jacket came into the cage, the lion lay silent and submissive before him. He would never touch a hussar jacket, whatever it had in it. Now America devoured one hussar jacket with 'John Tyler' written on it, and another with 'Fillmore' written on it, and now another in Andy Johnson. Not as wise as the brute, in spite of political indigestion, this nation goes on devouring hussar jackets."[1]

In the summer of 1866, Mr. Phillips was urged to accept a nomination for Congress from his district. It was felt that he might be there what John Bright was in Parliament. Journals like the *Commonwealth* and the *Voice*, in Boston, the *Daily Times* and the *Independent*, in New York, strongly favored the project. The Agitator, however, better understood his own mood and habit. He refused even to consider a nomination. His position now was unique; made so by his perfect independence. When the elder Pitt was made Earl of Chatham and passed out of the House of Commons and into the House of Lords, the great Commoner went into eclipse. Some one missing the familiar figure, asked Chesterfield what had become of Pitt. "He has had a fall upstairs," was the answer. Phillips did not wish to abdicate his present office and lose himself in the crowd of Congressional nobodies,—to fall upstairs. He preferred to remain untrammelled, as

---

[1] *Vide Anti-Slavery Standard*, vol. xxvii., May 19th.

a professor of ethics in the university of the American conscience.

Using, then, the old agencies, and continuing to serve the Lyceum, he went up and down instructing, warning, inspiring. From the close of the war onward, Mr. Phillips was in enormous demand. No lecture course was esteemed complete without him. His name was an unfailing magnet. Had he been twelve instead of one, and could he have given every night in the year to the Lyceum, the calls would not have been met. The lecture season began in the autumn and ended in the following spring. Months in advance his dates were filled. The season of 1866-67 he opened in Boston with a lecture on "The Swindling Congress," viz., the Thirty-ninth, which put juggles for justice. It was in this lecture that he said:

"There have never been any friends of the Southerner in the Northern States but the Abolitionists. The Democrats deluded him; the Whigs cheated him; the Abolitionists stood on his border and said: 'It is in vain for you to fight against the thick bosses of Jehovah's buckler. You are endeavoring to sustain a system that repudiates the laws of God and the spirit of the nineteenth century; put it away, or you will make blood and bankruptcy your guests.' But the maddened South closed its eyes and rushed on to destruction. Now we say, 'Come into line with the age, found your economy on righteousness, and then spindles will make vocal every stream and fill every valley.'"[1]

From Boston the lecturer proceeded Westward and was welcomed everywhere enthusiastically.[2] During the day and on Sundays he usually spoke on

---

[1] *Vide Anti-Slavery Standard*, vol. xxvii., No. 42.
[2] *Ib.*, vol. xxvii., March 9th.

"Temperance;" in the evenings, as often as possible, on the crisis.[1] His remedy for existing ills was simple—land, education, and the ballot for the negro; and the means he found in the war power under which the nation had the right to make itself safe.[2] At Keokuk, Ia., one of the dailies said of his lecture there:

"His arguments grow on you. You are pleased and interested while he speaks ; it is not until afterward that he becomes wonderful to you. You shouldn't commence to pass judgment on his speeches earlier than twelve hours after their delivery. The strict enforcement of this rule would damage the reputation of most orators ; this man it would enthrone and crown as king in the realm of suggestive thought."[3]

At St. Louis, the *Daily Despatch* printed his lecture on the "Times" in full and remarked editorially: "Wendell Phillips has exercised a greater influence on the destinies of the country as a private man than any public man, or men, of his age."[4]

From Alton, Ill., on April 14th, 1867, Mr. Phillips wrote to the *Standard*, describing the grave of Lovejoy, and added:

"The gun fired at him was like that at Sumter—it scattered a world of dreams. Looking back, how wise as well as noble his course was. Incredible, that we should have been compelled to defend his ' prudence.' What world-wide benefactors these ' imprudent ' men are! How ' prudently ' most men creep into nameless graves ; while now and then one or two forget themselves into immortality."[5]

The orator returned to Boston the third week in April well and in good spirits, after giving over sixty

---

[1] *Vide Anti-Slavery Standard*, vol. xxvii., March 9th. [2] *Ib.*, No. 10.
[3] Keokuk *Gate City*. [4] Cited in *Standard*, vol. xxviii., April 27th
[5] *Ib.*

lectures and travelling more than twelve thousand miles.[1]

In May we find him in New York City in attendance on the annual meeting of the American Anti-Slavery Society; the sessions being spicy and thronged. A week later, he was in Boston on the platform of the New England Anti-Slavery Society, where he said:

"Our effort should be to infect the South with the North,— the North of education and equality,—the North of toleration and self-respecting labor,—the North of books and brains. If the South had conquered us, she would have called the roll of her slaves on Bunker Hill and put her flag over Faneuil Hall. Our victory means, ought to mean, Bunker Hill in the Carolinas and Faneuil Hall in New Orleans." [2]

An event occurred in the summer of 1867 which gave Mr. Phillips pain and entailed upon him great expense. Francis Jackson, dying in Boston some years before, had left a will bequeathing $10,000 to the Anti-Slavery cause. Of this will Messrs. Phillips, Garrison, Bowditch, Quincy, May, Whipple, and Edmund Jackson, the testator's brother, were executors, with Mr. Phillips as chairman. The Thirteenth Amendment abolished slavery before the money became available. The question then arose among the executors as to the proper disposition of the fund. The majority agreed with Mr. Phillips that it ought to go toward the support of the *Anti-Slavery Standard* in the battle for negro enfranchisement. The minority, composed of seceders from the American Anti-Slavery Society, and not in sym-

---

[1] *Vide Anti Slavery Standard*, vol. xxviii., April 27th.
[2] *Ib.* Report of May Anniversary in Boston. First week in May.

pathy with its organ, wished to hand over the bequest to the Freedmen's Union for educational purposes. The court assured the executors that the money should follow their recommendation, if they were agreed. They could not agree, and it went by direction of the court to the use designated by the minority. "Thus," wrote Mr. Phillips, in an explanatory letter to the *Standard*, "the money of Mr. Jackson was diverted from the object to which he devoted it, because a minority of his trustees were not willing to accord to the majority that liberty which the majority granted them, and report a plan to which all could agree."[1] Such a plan had been agreed upon, by which the fund was to be divided between the *Standard* and the freedmen. Mr. Garrison, on the eve of departing for Europe, withdrew his assent to it, with the result narrated. He based his action on the recent passage of the Civil Rights Act, under which certain privileges were secured to the blacks.[2] But as it required two additional amendments to the Constitution to complete the enfranchisement of the negro race, and as these were not finally ratified until years later, it should seem that his excuse was flimsy. It is impossible to avoid the conclusion that the conduct of the minority of the trustees was dictated by pique and grudge. They discharged a Parthian arrow at the cause which persisted in living after they had pronounced the funeral oration. The immediate effect of it was to throw upon Mr. Phillips, personally, a load of

---

[1] *Vide Anti-Slavery Standard*, vol. xxviii., August 10th and 24th. The minority consisted of Messrs. Garrison, Quincy, and May.

[2] *Vide* "William Lloyd Garrison," vol. iv., p. 237 *sq*.

pecuniary responsibility which the fund would have helped him to carry. And all this was understood. He thought this conduct was unkind and unworthy, and felt it keenly ; in which thought and feeling his friends did and do concur.

An Anti-Slavery Conference was called to meet in Paris, in August, 1867, for a comparison of views on the part of distinguished Abolitionists from all quarters of the globe. From this gathering Mr. Phillips excused himself, on the ground that the battle was still raging in America. He held that absence at such a moment would be like a soldier's leaving the front for the rear, and exchanging wounds for honors in the midst of the fight.[1] There might be a time for junketing, but it had not yet come over here.

The Agitator gave the first week in November, 1867, to the Pennsylvania Anti-Slavery Society and held large and successful meetings in Philadelphia and the vicinity. At Wilmington, Del., he received a written welcome, signed by prominent citizens, and a Godspeed in his work.[2] Thence he proceeded on his lecture tour for the season of 1867-68. An interesting incidental visit was paid at Vassar College, where he addressed the Literary Societies on " Street Life in Europe." The young ladies were interested in the lecture and charmed with the lecturer.[3]

In the course of the season Mr. Phillips addressed the Lyceum at Gloucester, Mass., and, returning home by the cars the next morning, fell in with a lady who got upon the train at a way-station. She

---

[1] *Vide Anti-Slavery Standard*, vol. xxviii., September 21st.
[2] *Ib.*, November 16th.   [3] *Ib.*, December 17th.

was a Southern refugee, who had been suddenly reduced from affluence to poverty, and was supporting herself and her fatherless children by giving an occasional lecture before a country audience. It was a struggle; for the field was full, and she was almost unknown and friendless; but with a brave heart she worked on, never asking a dollar of aid from any society or individual. Mr. Phillips saw her get upon the car, and asked her to take a seat beside him. It was a winter day; and she was thinly clad, shivering from the exposure of a long ride in the open air of the cold morning. Observing this, Mr. Phillips asked:

"Where did you speak last night?"

She told him it was at a town about ten miles distant from the railway.

"And—I wouldn't be impertinent—how much did they pay you?"

"Five dollars, and the fare to and from Boston."

"Five dollars!" he exclaimed; "why, I always get one or two hundred; and your lecture must be worth more than mine,—you give facts, I only opinions."

"Small as it is, I am very glad to get it, Mr. Phillips," answered the lady. "I would talk at that rate every night during the winter."

He sat for a moment in silence; then he put his hand into his pocket, drew out a roll of bank-notes, and said, in a hesitating way:

"I don't want to give offence, but you know I preach that a woman is entitled to the same as a man if she does the same work. Now, my price is one or two hundred dollars; and, if you will let me divide it with you, I shall not have had any more than you, and the thing will be even."

The lady at first refused ; but, after a little gentle urging, she put the bank-notes into her purse. At the end of her journey, she counted the roll, and found it contained one hundred dollars. It may add a point to this incident to say (what is the truth) that the lady was a niece of Jefferson Davis.[1]

The most generous of men, Mr. Phillips was also the most tender. His friends, Mr. and Mrs. Aaron M. Powell, lost a rose-bud daughter in the winter of 1867. Here is his letter of condolence, valuable for the insight it gives, and for its disclosure of his faith :

"December 22.

" I know how weak words are to comfort you in such a loss. Be sure our hearts go out to you in loving and tenderest sympathy. God give you all consolation, and hold up your hearts.

" These little pets twine around our hearts so closely, it is such agony to part from them ! But such partings wean us, as we need to be, from these scenes. How near and dear that world becomes after such transfers ! After all, this dear blessing, lent for a little while, is not taken away, only lifted that you may more easily look up to it."[2]

President Johnson was now completely alienated from his party and in collision at all points with Congress. He stood as the great obstructionist, vetoing reconstruction legislation as fast as bills were passed. A clamor arose for his impeachment, which was undertaken. Mr. Phillips favored it in the *Standard* and on the platform. He laughed over and quoted far and wide the witticism of Petroleum

---

[1] Austin's " Life and Times of Wendell Phillips," pp. 243-45.
[2] Letter to Aaron M. Powell (MS.).

V. Nasby: "The President does not believe that power should be concentrated in three or four hundred men in Congress, but thinks it ought to be safely diffused throughout the hands of one man—A. Johnson."

The outcome of the Johnson muddle was that the President was not impeached out of office, but in the course of the struggle his power was extensively curtailed. Phillips, Lincoln-like, put it in a story: "Congress has deposed him without impeachment. 'Friend, I'll not shoot thee,' said the Quaker to the foot-pad, 'but I'll hold thy head in the water until thee drown thyself.' The Republican party has taken a leaf out of that scrupulous Christian's book."[1] He thought that the Executive power had unduly increased and needed to be diminished. The present condition of Johnson reminded him of the English monarchy: "Heaven forbid that the land of the Tudors and Stuarts should abolish royalty. Keep kings; but, like the Egyptian mummy-makers, draw out all blood and reduce them to forms. The function of an English monarch nowadays is, like that of the queen bee, to be fed and beget successors."[2]

The months of February and March, 1868, Mr. Phillips spent in the West.[3] In May he was again in attendance on the anniversary of the American Anti-Slavery Society in New York City. The uppermost question just now was as to who should succeed President Johnson. General Grant was apparently the coming man. The orator opposed his nomination

---

[1] *Standard*, vol. xxviii., July 27th. [2] *Ib*
[3] *Ib.*, months of February and March, *passim*.

for two reasons : First, because he lacked civil experience ; second, because he had not pronounced himself on the issues of the day. He contended that a civilian, not a soldier, was needed in the White House—that the standard-bearer should be a man of outspoken convictions, not a sphinx.[1] Through the summer and fall of 1868 this was his constant, his unpopular, and his unsuccessful plea,—this, and the reiterated demand for negro suffrage. " Having in the past," he cried, with reference to the latter topic, " done full justice to the countrymen of Emmet and O'Connell, of Goethe and Körner, even of Isaiah and the Maccabees, let us give to the negro a chance to show that Toussaint L'Ouverture was not a splendid monster, but a fair representative of the capacity of his race."[2]

Under Radical prodding, Congress had passed a fourteenth amendment to the Constitution ; which, despite the frantic opposition of President Johnson, the Southern whites, and the Northern Democracy, the requisite number of States at length adopted—public proclamation of the fact being made in July, 1868. This made the freedmen citizens of the United States and of the several States wherein they were domiciled, but it left each State to regulate the right to vote. It was another instalment of justice. Public opinion, however, demanded for the negro the ballot. On this point Phillips had educated the country, which now believed what he said : " The black man without the ballot, is the lamb given over to the wolf."[3] Hence, a fifteenth amendment was

---

[1] *Standard*, vols. xxvii. and xxviii.   [2] *Ib.*, vol. xxviii., July 27th.
[3] *Anti-Slavery Standard*, vol. xxx., No. 3.

mooted, to secure this essential safeguard of citizenship.

Wendell Phillips held himself in readiness to counsel and assist resistance to tyrants not only at home but abroad. The island of Crete, anchored in the Mediterranean and steeped in classic memories, the storehouse whence the ancient Egyptians and Phœnicians brought civilization into Europe,—had burst into rebellion against the "unspeakable Turk," and her people were engaged in an unequal struggle for liberty. Christian nations looked on in sympathy. A ladies' fair was held in Boston, in 1868, to raise money for the far-away heroes. Naturally, they turned to Mr. Phillips to plead their cause. Just as naturally he responded in a speech which sobbed with pathos while it thrilled. Perhaps the orator never spoke more beautifully; certainly he never spoke more ineffectually; for though the dollars called for were gotten, the crescent was soon set in triumph again above the cross.[1]

As he was now recognized as the foremost speaker of English in the world, Mr. Phillips was continually appealed to for oratorical "points." In response to such inquiries he was in the habit of recommending Holyoake's "Rudiments of Public Speaking" as holding the first place among all books on the subject. He kept a copy always at hand, which he had scribbled all over with his marginal notes. To a young collegian who had asked him questions concerning preparation for public speaking, he made the following reply, which is worthy of study as coming from a master:

---

[1] See the Boston dailies in May for an account of the fair.

"I think practice with all kinds of audiences the best of teachers. Think out your subject carefully. Read all you can relative to the themes you touch. Fill your mind ; and then talk simply and naturally. Forget altogether that you are to make a speech, or are making one. Absorb yourself into the idea that you are to strike a blow, carry out a purpose, effect an object, recommend a plan ; then, having forgotten yourself, you will be likelier to do your best. Study the class of books your mind likes. When you go outside this rule, study those which give you facts on your chosen topics and which you find most suggestive.

"Remember to talk up to an audience, not down to it. The commonest audience can relish the best thing you can say if you say it properly. Be simple : be earnest." [1]

This advice is stimulating. But after all, rules never made an orator ; any more than a knowledge of thorough-bass made Mozart, or skill in mixing colors made Raphael. It is as George William Curtis says : " The secret of the rose's sweetness, of the sunset's glory—that is the secret of genius and eloquence." [2]

---

[1] Quoted by Joseph Cook in his Monday lecture on Wendell Phillips, February 4th, 1884, and reported in New York *Independent*, February 14th, 1884.
[2] Curtis's "Oration on Wendell Phillips," p. 16.

II.

IO! TRIUMPHE!

LYCEUM engagements absorbed the time of Mr Phillips during the season of 1868-69. The theme he preferred was the ballot for the black man, and, as a rule, on this he was heard. The outlook was now bright. In February, 1869, Congress resolved to formulate the Fifteenth Amendment. This measure stirred the bitterness of race prejudice, awoke every Rip Van Winkle to protest, and provoked a last desperate outburst of profanity from the former slave-masters; but received the enthusiastic support of the wise and good. Charles Sumner, honorably conspicuous in all the legislation which harvested the results of the war, had charge of the amendment in the Senate. He blundered at a vital point—the Senate was about to reject it; the quick-sighted and sharp-witted Phillips detected and pointed out the mistake; Sumner rectified it; and the amendment was saved.[1]

On March 4th, 1869, "Jefferson Davis" Johnson vanished—U. S. Grant appeared. Thus time did what the politicians failed to do,—turned out a traitor and installed a patriot.

The next month, amid these hopeful signs for the

---

[1] Oliver Johnson says he had this from an ex-governor, a United States Senator, and a Cabinet officer. *Vide* "Garrison and his Times," p. 441.

negro, Mr. Phillips turned aside for a moment to advocate a kindred cause. With Julia Ward Howe, he went before the Legislature of Massachusetts to plead for female suffrage.[1] During the war the absorption of the country had been so utter that the women's movement could make no headway. "Never mind," said Mr. Phillips, "it is the negro's hour." The words lay and rankled in the memory of some of the ladies, who accused their champion of giving precedence to one reform over another— of preferring the negro to the ladies. Had the charge been true, it would have impeached both the justice and the gallantry of the alleged culprit. But he proved an alibi. In a communication to the *Woman's Advocate*, he defined the meaning of the unobjectionable phrase, and stated his position:

"I have always given, spoken, and printed for the cause, and am doing so now. When I said, in 1861, 'This is the negro's hour,' I meant in the sense of ripeness: as July is 'the grass's hour,' and as October is 'the apple's hour.'"[2]

In another article which appeared in the same journal, he defended his course in advocating the Fifteenth Amendment, even though it ignored female suffrage:

"Every change large enough to serve as a point on which to rally the nation, should have a separate discussion, and be decided by itself. Mixing up separate issues is like good Davie Deans's attachment to the Scottish Covenant. From his sick pillow he asked if the doctor had subscribed the Covenant. 'That's no matter now,' said his child. 'Indeed it is,' cried the old Covenanter; 'for if he has not, never a drop of his medicine shall go into the stomach of my father's son.'"[3]

---

[1] *Vide Anti-Slavery Standard*, vol. xxix., April 10th.
[2] *Woman's Advocate*, September, 1869. [3] *Ib.*, July, 1869.

He held, moreover, that woman suffrage would come, if at all, not by national action, but by State legislation—as would the abolition of slavery, had not the Rebellion armed the Union with the war power.[1]

In April, also, a week after the plea for female suffrage, the Agitator again addressed the Legislature of his native State in behalf of labor reform ; his special demand being for the appointment of a Labor commission to examine into the condition of the working classes of the Commonwealth. This speech was able and triumphant. The commission was appointed, and inaugurated the vast and far-reaching agitation of the Labor question.[2] Like the prophet he was, Mr. Phillips foresaw the speedy close of the Anti-Slavery epoch, and anticipated the next great issue. Close observers then forecast his future from his present course.

April was a busy month for Mr. Phillips. In addition to the legislative exertions above mentioned, he turned aside to address a Sunday gathering in Horticultural Hall, in Boston, on a religious theme. " Christianity is a battle—not a dream," he said, and then proceeded to vindicate it against those who would make it a mere matter of ecclesiasticism, on the one hand, and against those who represented it as the essence of posture and imposture, on the other hand. Christianity he regarded as the spirit of heaven at work on earth,—as a divine influence embodied in human life, and set to right wrongs and save the lost. Christ he regarded as the Author and

---

[1] *Woman's Advocate*, July, 1869.
[2] *Vide Standard*, vol. xxx., April 17th.

Finisher of redemption—His career as the model of every worthy and noble life. As he contended so should we contend, aiming to make God known to men. He considered this the best and most satisfactory of his utterances in this line, and gladly confessed his own indebtedness to the Nazarene for the knowledge of God and a disposition to serve his kind.[1]

In May, 1869, the American Anti-Slavery Society met in New York City. The Fifteenth Amendment was in process of ratification by the States. Victory was in the air. The veterans were jubilant—but vigilant. The topic was prejudice of race. Frederick Douglass and Senator Henry Wilson were among the speakers. Mr. Phillips acknowledged that he had been mistaken in his estimate of President Grant, whose course thus far had been praiseworthy, and added :

"I want a right hand stern as death, and a sword rough-ground, like those with which Wellington went into the battle of Waterloo, held over every Southern State to secure that peace which promotes industry."[2]

The lecture season of 1869-70 Mr. Phillips spent as usual, mostly in the cars, going to and from his Lyceum appointments. He thought he and Mr. John B. Gough could claim to be the great American travellers. "I know," said he, "every locomotive, every conductor, and the exact depth of the mud in every road in the country." In one of his lectures he referred to the Garrison mob of 1835.

---

[1] A synopsis of this important address may be found in the *Anti-Slavery Standard*, vol. xxx., April 17th.
[2] *Vide Anti-Slavery Standard*, vol. xxx., No. 3.

The reference provoked Colonel Theodore Lyman, the son of the mayor who figured discreditably in the riot, to rush into print in defence of his father. The orator respected Colonel Lyman's filial feeling, but nevertheless vindicated the truth of history. After a vivid statement of the facts,[1] he said in his rejoinder:

"Twenty years ago, I affirmed, 'The time will come when sons will deem it unkind to remind the world of acts their fathers now take pride in.' That hour has come. I refer to old shames, not to insult the dead, but to control the living. Evil-doers have one motive more to restrain them, if they can be made to feel that their children will blush for the names they inherit. I bring these things up to show that reformers have terrible memories; and that even if base acts win office and plaudits to-day, the ears of the actor's children will tingle at the report of them half a century hence."[2]

March 30th, 1870, is an ever-memorable date. It was then that President Grant proclaimed the adoption of the Fifteenth Amendment, which provided that neither the nation nor any of the States composing it should abridge the right of any citizen to vote on account of race, color, or previous condition of servitude. The struggle was ended. Freedom had crowned her work. Mr. Phillips read the proclamation in Leroy, N. Y. Sitting down, he dashed off a few jubilant lines to his *alter ego*, the Rev. John T. Sargent, of Boston:

"LEROY, N. Y., March 30, 1870.

'DEAR JOHN: Let me exchange congratulations with you.

---

[1] *Vide ante*, p. 51.
[2] *Vide* Boston *Commonwealth*, November 13th, 1869.

Our long work is sealed at last. The nation proclaims Equal Liberty. To-day is its real 'Birthday.'
'Io! Triumphe!'
Thank God.
"Affectionately,
"WENDELL PHILLIPS."[1]

Of course, he knew that legislation cannot bring in the millennium. Statutes never turn sinners into saints. Prejudice dies hard. It must be lived down and shamed out. A race, like an individual, has to earn respect. A student of history, he remembered how the adherents of the exiled Stuarts pledged the Pretender in secret bumpers in the Scotch Highlands and beyond the seas—how Jacobitism stained the pages of Sir Walter Scott a hundred years after the Revolution of 1688; and how the *ton* in the Faubourg St. Germain clung to the sentiment of royalty, and dreamed of the French lilies while living under the tricolor. No; Mr. Phillips was aware that the negroes would have to face prejudice perhaps for generations, and would be dwarfed in their own estimation and in the feeling of the community by the associations of their servitude. The remedy for this could be found only in time and achievement. Meanwhile it was much that the law was color-blind. The arena was now open. Manhood might attest itself.

The mission of the American Anti-Slavery Society was fulfilled. What remained save to meet once more, formally announce the consummation, and disband? On April 9th, 1870, the Abolitionists, with the smell of smoke on their garments, held their commemoration at Steinway Hall, in New York

---

[1] This letter is in MS.

City. The attendance was immense, the rejoicing ecstatic. Mr. Phillips, as President of the Society, was in the chair. Letters were read from a host of coworkers, including Sumner, Colfax, Boutwell, Whittier, and Lydia Maria Child.[1] Lucretia Mott, O. B. Frothingham, Robert Purvis, Julia Ward Howe, John T. Sargent, and many others of the "old guard," were grouped on the platform.[2] The streets were alive with colored people, marching in vociferous procession. As Mr. Phillips rose to say the last word, he received the ovation of his life. He referred to it ever after as ample compensation for all his toils, and bore the memory of the meeting to the grave as the chief pleasure of his career. In speaking of what he owed the cause, he said:

"It has taught me faith in human nature. When I read a sublime fact in Plutarch, of an unselfish deed in a line of poetry, or thrill beneath some heroic legend, it is no longer fairyland. I have seen it matched."[3]

In closing, he added:

"We will not say 'Farewell,' but 'all hail.' Welcome, new duties! We sheathe no sword. We only turn the front of the army upon a new foe."[4]

At the business meeting which followed, the Society refused to die—it adjourned *sine die*.[5]

Thus, with a befitting celebration, and at the proper time, the American Anti-Slavery Society passed into history. Had it dissolved earlier it would not have fulfilled its pledge. For what was its pledge? It was to free the slave. But freedom is a comprehensive word. It includes not merely the having

---

[1] *Vide Anti-Slavery Standard*, vol. xxx., April. [2] *Ib.* [3] *Ib.* [4] *Ib.* [5] *Ib.*

shackles struck from our wrists and ankles, but our possession of the rights and privileges enjoyed by freemen—not only emancipation, but enfranchisement. Complete liberty was only just now attained.

It was said by Mr. Garrison and the little band who withdrew with him, after the passage by Congress of the Thirteenth Amendment, that the rest could be gotten through other agencies. Perhaps so ; nevertheless what became of their pledge in that organization to contend for the freedom of the blacks? Besides, by parity of reasoning, they might likewise have excused their desertion at any other hour after the grand political rally for freedom. The peculiar excellence of the American Anti-Slavery Society was that it conducted a moral agitation,— that it stood outside of sects and parties as their critic and inspirer,—that it held up, amid compromises and compromisers, the ideal of absolute justice,—that it refused to be satisfied with anything else or less. This function was never more essential than during the four years from 1866 to 1870; and it was never more magnificently subserved. All honor to the faithful men and women who held together not only with Canaan in sight, but until they were mustered out in the peace and plenty of the promised land. "Wolfe died," wrote Sumner, "in the arms of victory ; and such is the fortune of your noble society."[1]

Of the personal services of Mr. Phillips during these years when the fruits of the war were to be secured, it is impossible to speak extravagantly.

---

[1] Letter to the American Anti-Slavery Society, at this commemorative meeting. *Vide Standard*, vol. xxx., April.

His position as President of the American Anti-Slavery Society gave him, what Mr. Garrison now lacked,—a distinctive platform. The former leader was lost in the crowd. The new chief stood out in clean-cut prominence. His speeches were events. He gave the country a succession of electric shocks. Injustice was stunned. Liberty was reanimated. He watched every move of the slippery gamesters at Washington with unflagging vigilance, criticising, suggesting, analyzing, insisting; and by directing universal attention to the game, made them play fair and square. "More than to any other, more than to all others," said Senator Henry Wilson, "the colored people owe it that they were not cheated out of their citizenship after emancipation, to Wendell Phillips."[1]

The successful Abolitionist found it difficult to realize his victory. It seemed too good to be true. On May 4th, 1870, a meeting was held in the Tremont Temple, in Boston, at which he expressed this feeling and announced his conviction that he was not dreaming. He was asked to introduce the new colored senator from Mississippi, Mr. Revels, who now occupied the seat of Jefferson Davis! In fulfilling the grateful duty, he said:

"You remember when we were children and read the 'Arabian Nights,' that after some gorgeous description of crests of light and cimeters of gold and crowns of gems, the Caliph clapped his hands and the dream burst—we were sitting on the cold ground. I felt, as I sat behind Senator Revels, like clapping my hands to see whether the scene would change—whether it was all a fairy mistake. I could hardly realize that fifteen hundred people had come to Tremont Temple to see a senator of

---

[1] Letter to Charles Sumner, April 19th, 1870 (MS.).

that race so long victimized. I was in Western New York when the proclamation of the ratified Fifteenth Amendment came at night. With the gray light of the morning I sprang to my feet to see if there was really a proclamation. I should like to feel the senator to assure myself that he is flesh and blood.

"At the Lovejoy Meeting, in 1837, the Attorney-General of Massachusetts said the idea of taking the chains off these negroes was like letting loose the hyenas. Gentlemen of Boston, I introduce to you a hyena! Well, then, later Senator Toombs told us that, if we ever dared to fire a gun, he would call the roll of his slaves on Bunker Hill. Behold the first one that has answered —a senator of the United States." [1]

It was in 1870, too, that Italy realized the dream of centuries and achieved her unity, with Rome as the head of the reanimated body-politic. The cosmopolitan soul of Wendell Phillips was almost as much gratified by the success of the Italian liberators as he was by the crowning of his own work. When a warm invitation reached him to celebrate the auspicious occurrence with the Italians in New York City, he made an effort to attend; but that failing, he wrote a jubilant letter which was read amid loud plaudits:

"BOSTON, October 27.

"At all times, the fate of Rome has been of utmost interest. Every scholar, every lover of art, every student of jurisprudence, every apostle of liberty, remembers that, after leading the old world, Rome guarded its treasures across the gulf of the middle and troubled ages. To every lover of the past and every servant of the future it seems natural to call Italy 'My Country.' Three centuries ago she inspired modern civilization. In this generation the battle for European liberty has centred on Rome. At last she opens her gates to the nineteenth century.

"Congratulations to Garibaldi and Mazzini. They behold the

---

[1] *Vide* Moncure D. Conway's article on Wendell Phillips, in the *Fortnightly Review*, London, vol. viii., p. 64 *sq.*

morning. What will the noon be? Nothing less than Europe a brotherhood of republics.

"Kings, like other spectres, will vanish at the cock-crowing.

"May the glory and service of Rome in this new epoch transcend her 'trebly hundred triumphs' and all the splendor of the age of Leo.

"Fraternally,

"WENDELL PHILLIPS." [1]

The friends of Mr. Phillips had long desired him to sit for a picture or bust. He disliked anything of the sort; but at last consented to permit Mr. Martin Milmore, a sculptor who had a genius for portraiture, to reproduce his features. The sculptor was over a year in getting the mouth in satisfactory shape. One cold winter night he saw in the Boston *Transcript* that Mr. Phillips was to speak that evening in Chelsea. He went over without taking time to go home for an overcoat. As he sat in the hall listening to the orator what was missing came to him in a flash. He returned to his studio at eleven o'clock, uncovered the plaster, and worked away until past midnight. When he met Mr. Phillips the next day and showed him the result, he said: "You may consider your work as done." This, also, was in 1870. Mr. Milmore's bust is a beautiful work, and his *chef d'œuvre*. "I put my soul in it," remarked the sculptor, "but, after all, how far short of the original it is!"

---

[1] *Vide The National Standard*, New York, November 12th, 1870.

III.

"NEW OCCASIONS TEACH NEW DUTIES."

At the date when the Fifteenth Amendment was adopted (the hammer which drove the last nail into the coffin of negro slavery), Wendell Phillips was in his sixtieth year. Thus, he was still in the prime of life. His correct habits had preserved his bodily and mental powers in full vigor. His eye was as bright and sharp, his endurance as great, his nerves as steady, his thinking as sinewy, his speech as classic as in early manhood. Time had only ripened and mellowed without impairing his faculties at any point.

It might be thought that his hand-to-hand grapple with slavery, thirty-three years long, now entitled him to a victor's repose. His old friend, Edmund Quincy, acting on this principle, had reverted to the life of elegant leisure from which the Anti-Slavery movement had wrenched him. Mr. Garrison, resting under the approaches of old age, appeared in public nowadays only as impulse stirred him, and while continuing to watch the interests of the freedmen, and to advocate the causes with which he had identified himself in the past, espoused no new reforms. Mr. Phillips disdained the conservatism which usually coats men with moss in the afternoon of life. This was partly temperamental,—the result of robust health, but came more from principle. He felt this life to be a battle-field, not a couch. He loved to repeat the words which Tocqueville uttered when Sumner left him in Europe on the eve of returning home, and which he exemplified : " Life is neither a pain nor a pleasure, but serious business, which it is our duty to carry through and conclude with honor." [1] Accordingly, he said gayly to a friend, " Now that the field is won, do you sit by the camp-fire, but I will put out into the underbrush." [2]

Mr. Phillips meant what he said. He " put out." Retaining all his former interest in the affairs of his old clients, the negro and woman, he took on new interests as fast as these disclosed themselves. Current issues had a fascination for him, —especially if they had any moral bearing. He delighted, too, in keeping ahead of the times, and in beckoning the age up and on. The temperance question had from the start a warm place in his heart and a large place in his speech. For many years he had been a total abstainer. His own practice in this regard he urged others to adopt. He also favored and never tired of publicly pleading for prohibition as the only adequate remedy for tipsy streets. Now that he was measurably free from the entanglements arising from slavery, he gave this question ever-increasing prominence on the platform.

Another issue which at once enlisted his enthusiastic co-operation was Labor Reform. This, slavery being abolished, was the next inevitable battle. While every workingman was degraded in the en-

---

[1] Phillips's article on Sumner in *Johnson's Cyclopædia*.
[2] Curtis's " Oration on Wendell Phillips," p. 31.

slavement of the colored laborers of the South, it was necessary to secure enfranchisement there before contending for enlarged opportunities everywhere. The law must acknowledge manhood before it could logically concede rights and privileges which presuppose manhood. With this accomplished, the demand for better wages, easier hours, more comforts, and the erection of legal barriers against the greed of employers in behalf of employés,—followed, as the day follows the night.

Many of the old Abolitionists broke down at this point. They saw plainly enough the enormity of negro slavery. They could not see the enormity of wage-slavery. That guilt was the wickedness of the slave owners. This guilt was their wickedness— would affect, if they acknowledged it, their dividends, impeach their business habits, invade their relations to their "hands." The wealthier among them realized the immeasurable difference between *meum* and *tuum*. When their former coadjutor began to apply the principles of the Anti-Slavery reform to this correlated movement, they balked, and accused him of " preaching crusades on difficult problems which he had never seriously studied."

The truth is, Mr. Phillips began to study the labor question at the moment when he took up Anti-Slavery. The one necessitated the other. Papers found in his library and bearing his notes, made certainly as far back as 1840, prove it. Among these is one entitled " The Slavery of Poverty," published fifty years ago—wonderfully keen and suggestive, and carried on in a dialogue between a converted slave-holder and an Abolitionist, which is covered with the orator's comments.[1] He followed his principles wherever they took him. A logical conclusion had no terrors for him. In England there is an inn called "The Six Alls." On the sign that hangs in front stands the Queen, in her robes of state, and she says: "I rule all." On her right hand is a priest, who says: "I pray for all." Below him is a soldier, who says: "I fight for all." On her left hand is a lawyer, who says: "I plead for all." Below him is a doctor, who says: "I cure all." At the very bottom stands a workingman in his shirt-sleeves, grimy, beaded with perspiration, and he says: "I pay for all!" Mr. Phillips's idea was that, since the workingman paid for all, he was entitled to consideration. What created capital? Labor. Very well; then give labor its fair proportion of profits. Make legislation guarantee this.

The workingmen received their renowned ally with enthusiasm. They made him their standard-bearer, and fell into rank under the banner he lifted. They were now organized in Massachusetts as a separate political party (the Labor party), and on September 8th, 1870, their State Convention nominated Mr. Phillips for Governor. Four days earlier, the Prohibition Convention conferred on him the same honor. He fully represented both ideas, and reluctantly consented to enter the canvass as the exponent of both. He knew there was no chance for his election. Had there been, he would not have accepted the joint nominations. The canvass would

---

[1] This curious pamphlet now rests in the Boston Public Library, among the books, etc., which Mr. Phillips gave that institution a year or two before his death.

be simply a protest and an education—agitation in the shape of politics.

At the Labor Convention the orator presided. He drew up and read the platform, which is subjoined as his "confession of faith."

"We affirm, as a fundamental principle, that labor, the creator of wealth, is entitled to all it creates.

"Affirming this, we avow ourselves willing to accept the final results of the operation of a principle so radical, such as the overthrow of the whole profit-making system, the extinction of all monopolies, the abolition of privileged classes, universal education and fraternity, perfect freedom of exchange, and, best and grandest of all, the final obliteration of that foul stigma upon our so-called Christian civilization, the poverty of the masses. Holding principles as radical as these, and having before our minds an ideal condition so noble, we are still aware that our goal cannot be reached at a single leap. We take into account the ignorance, selfishness, prejudice, corruption, and demoralization of the leaders of the people, and, to a large extent, of the people themselves ; but still, we demand that some steps be taken in this direction : therefore,—

"*Resolved*, That we declare war with the wages system, which demoralizes alike the hirer and the hired, cheats both, and enslaves the workingman ; war with the present system of finance, which robs labor, and gorges capital, makes the rich richer, and the poor poorer, and turns a republic into an aristocracy of capital ; war with these lavish grants of the public lands to speculating companies, and, whenever in power, we pledge ourselves to use every just and legal means to resume all such grants heretofore made ; war with the system of enriching capitalists by the creation and increase of public interest-bearing debts. We demand that every facility, and all encouragement, shall be given by law to co-operation in all branches of industry and trade, and that the same aid be given to co-operative efforts that has heretofore been given to railroads and other enterprises. We demand a ten-hour day for factory-work as a first step, and that eight hours be the working-day of all persons thus employed hereafter. We demand, that, whenever women are employed at public expense to do the same kind and amount of work as men perform, they shall receive the same wages. We demand that all public debts be paid at once in accordance with the terms of the contract, and that no more debts be created. Viewing the contract importation of coolies as only another form of the slave-trade, we demand that all contracts made relative thereto be void in this country, and that no public ship, and no steamship which receives public subsidy, shall aid in such importation." [1]

This platform he proceeded to explain and enforce in an able speech, from which we quote a single paragraph:

"If any man asks me, therefore, what value I place upon this movement, I should say it is, first, the movement of humanity to protect itself; and, secondly, it is the insurance of peace; and, thirdly, it is a guarantee against the destruction of capital. We all know that there is no war between labor and capital,—that they are partners, not enemies,—and their true interests on any just basis are identical. And this movement of ballot-bearing millions is to avoid the unnecessary waste of capital.

"Well, gentlemen, I say so much to justify myself in styling this the grandest and most comprehensive movement of the age." (*Applause.*) [2]

A few days later Mr. Phillips formally accepted the Labor and Prohibition nominations in letters which are worthy of attention. The first was addressed to the Labor Reformers:

"BOSTON, September 12, 1870.
Charles Cowley, Esq.

"DEAR SIR: You send me notice that the Labor Reform party of Massachusetts, which met at Worcester on the 8th inst., has done me the honor to nominate me for the office of Governor.

"I have no wish to be Governor of Massachusetts: and, flat-

---

[1] *Vide* "The Labor Question," by Wendell Phillips. Published by Lee & Shepard, Boston.
[2] *Ib.*

tering as is this confidence, I thoroughly dislike to have my name drawn into party politics; for I belong to no political party. But I see nothing in your platform from which I dissent, and the struggle which underlies your movement has my fullest and heartiest sympathy.

"You are kind enough to say that my life has been given to the cause of workingmen. The adoption of the Fifteenth Amendment sweeps in all races, and gives the cause a wider range. Capital and labor—partners, not enemies—stand face to face, in order to bring about a fair division of the common profits. I am fully convinced, that hitherto legislation has leaned too much—leaned most unfairly—to the side of capital. Hereafter it should be impartial. Law should do all it can to give the masses more leisure, a more complete education, better opportunities, and a fair share of profits. It is a shame to our Christianity and civilization, for our social system to provide and expect that one man at seventy years of age shall be lord of many thousands of dollars, while hundreds of other men, who have made as good use of their talents and opportunities, lean upon charity for their daily bread. Of course, there must be inequalities. But the best minds and hearts of the land should give themselves to the work of changing this gross injustice, this appalling inequality. I feel sure that the readiest way to turn public thought and effort into this channel, is for the workingmen to organize a political party. No social question ever gets fearlessly treated here till we make politics turn on it. The real American college is the ballot-box. On questions like these, a political party is the surest and readiest, if not the only, way to stir discussion, and secure improvement.

"If my name will strengthen your movement, you are welcome to it.

"Allow me to add, that, though we work for a large vote, we should not be discouraged by a small one.

"Yours truly,
"WENDELL PHILLIPS."[1]

The second letter was an acceptance of the Prohibition nomination, and was, in part, as follows:

---

[1] *Vide* Boston daily papers of September 13th, 1870.

"BOSTON, September 13, 1870.

"DEAR SIR: I have no wish to be Governor of Massachusetts. But, to rally a political party, disinterested men must give years to the work of enlightening the public mind, and organizing their ranks. In that work I am willing to be used. My inclinations would induce me to decline the nomination; but I dare not do so in view of the vast interests involved in your movement, which call on each one of us to make every sacrifice to insure its success.

"No one supposes that law can make men temperate. Occasionally some sot betrays the average level of liquor intelligence, by fancying that to be our belief and plan. Temperance men, on the contrary, have always known and argued that we must trust to argument, example, social influence, and religious principle, to make men temperate. But law can shut up those bars and dram-shops which facilitate and feed intemperance, which double our taxes, make our streets unsafe for men of feeble resolution, treble the peril to property and life, and make the masses tools in the hands of designing men to undermine and cripple law.

"The *use* of intoxicating liquors rests with each man's discretion. But the *trade* in them comes clearly within the control of law. Many considerations—and among them the safety and success of republican institutions—bid us put forth the full power of the law to shut up dram-shops. We have never yet ruled a great city on the principle of self-government. Republican institutions, undermined by intemperance, are obliged to confess that they have never governed a great city here, on the basis of universal suffrage, in such way as to preserve order, protect life, and secure free speech.

"New York, ruled by drunkards, is proof of the despotism of the dram-shop. Men whom murderers serve that they may escape, and because they have escaped the gallows, rule that city. The ribald crew which holds them up could neither stifle its own conscience, nor rally its retinue, but for the help of the grog-shop. A like testimony comes from the history of our other great cities. State laws are defied in their streets; and by means of the dram-shop, and the gilded saloons of fashionable hotels, their ballot-box is in the hands of the criminal classes,—

of men who avowedly and systematically defy the laws. Indeed, this is the case in Boston.

"Since your nomination was made, I have been honored with another by the workingmen of Massachusetts. Their cause is a powerful ally of yours. Whatever lifts the masses to better education and more self-control, and secures them their full rights, helps the temperance cause. Indeed, theirs is a radical movement, broad as the human race, and properly includes everything that elevates man, and subjects passion and temptation to reason and principle.

"But the only bulwark against the dangers of intemperance is prohibition. More than thirty years of experience have convinced me, and as wide an experience has taught you, that this can only be secured by means of a distinct political organization. Thoroughly as I dislike to have my name used in a political canvass, I do not feel that I have the right to refuse its use if you think it will strengthen your party.

"I am, very respectfully yours,
"WENDELL PHILLIPS."[1]

In the ensuing election, the Labor and Prohibition candidate received over twenty thousand votes. Thus both questions were launched and afloat in the Old Bay State.

---

[1] *Vide* Boston daily papers of September 14th, 1870.

IV.

LIVING ISSUES.

It is not enough to be ready to go where duty calls. A man should stay around where he can hear the call. In morals, practice is the test of conscience. There never lived one who put his conduct closer to his principles, whose ear was keener to hear, and whose hand was readier to do, than Wendell Phillips. This was his favorite text, when his friends expostulated with him, and urged him to tone down his absolute truth : "Whether it be right in the sight of God to hearken unto you rather than unto God, judge ye." He never scrupled to break a friendship, and he constantly did it when it would have dissuaded him from obeying a call to announce a right and denounce a wrong. It was both amusing and painful to observe how former adherents fell away from him because he believed in Benjamin F. Butler.

This gentleman was the *bête noir* of Massachusetts respectability. As the old Federalists were wont to frighten their children to sleep by crooning Thomas Jefferson, so Beacon Hill and State Street, in Boston, made a bugaboo of Butler, in the decade between 1870 and 1880. The man in the play said to his rival : "Sir, your conduct, past, present, and future, is excessively disagreeable !" so the kid-gloved and cologne-water magnates of the Bay State could see nothing to commend in what the noted attorney had done, was doing, or proposed to do.

Mr. Phillips had known Butler from a boy. His Pro-Slavery course before the war was hateful. His war record, especially in his civil acts, was grand. By coining the word "contraband," he had practically emancipated thousands of slaves before Lincoln dreamed of emancipation. By his administration in New Orleans he had taught the Crescent City both manners and morals. And now he had joined and was serving the Labor movement, which his unrivalled executive ability promised to organize, and his leadership of the bar gave him the means of legally intrenching. Himself a man of nerve, he admired the General's pluck, dash, vigor. The two went into partnership on purpose to rattle the dry bones in Massachusetts. They did it. Under their manipulation, very corpses were galvanized into the semblance of life.

Mr. Garrison frowned and drew away. Ralph Waldo Emerson, who had admired Mr. Phillips for thirty years, no longer wished to see him in Concord. Strange! Whether right or wrong regarding Butler, no one doubted the honesty of the orator's attachment to him. Yet these excellent men broke the friendship of a lifetime on a point of disagreement in judgment. The advocate of freedom, who had claimed and practised the largest liberty of expression and association for himself; and the advocate of toleration, who had impeached the intolerance of New England,—both of them not only discountenanced (which they might have done without inconsistency), but for awhile actually cut their old-time colleague. How little the great are! How narrow the broad ! Few of us ever discover bigots among those who agree with us. On his part, Phillips, grander than either, went on loving them—and held on in his course without swerving a hair's breadth.

He shocked and frightened upper-tendom by announcing[1] the gubernatorial candidature of General Butler six months in advance of the occurrence. And he foretold that he would run on a mixed Republican and Labor platform. The prediction was fulfilled. The campaign was one of the most exciting ever known. Phillips spoke often and powerfully, dwelling upon his favorite theme ("the twins," he called them), Labor and Temperance; his most notable utterance being at a vast assemblage "of all parties" on Salisbury Beach, with the Atlantic for a background, a September sky for a sounding-board, and 1871 for a punctuation mark. Touching on Labor, he said :

"The great question of the future is money against legislation. My friends, you and I shall be in our graves long before that battle is ended ; and, unless our children have more patience and courage than saved this country from slavery, republican institutions will go down before moneyed corporations. Rich men die ; but banks are immortal, and railroad corporations never have any diseases. In the long run with the legislatures, they are sure to win."[2]

Referring to Butler, he confessed that the General "had done many things he would have asked him to do differently," and added :

"But I will tell you a secret, friends. If I were Pope to-day, there is not a man among all the candidates, Butler included,

---

[1] To a *Tribune* "interviewer" in the summer of 1871.
[2] Boston daily papers of September 14th, 1871.

whom I would make a saint of,—not one. The difficulty is, saints do not come very often ; and, when they do come, it is the hardest thing in the world to get them into politics. I don't believe, that if you could import a saint, brand-new and spotless, from heaven, that he could get a majority in the State of Massachusetts for any office that has a salary."[1]

The contest was for the Republican nomination, which another candidate (Washburn) finally got ; but only after Phillips and Butler had shaken the State as the angels shook the sheet in the New Testament.

A month after the Republican Convention which threw Butler overboard (October 31st, 1871), Mr. Phillips delivered in the Music Hall, Boston, the most elaborate of all his Labor speeches. Let us read a few passages. In opening, he painted the danger as lying in incorporated wealth :

"Our fathers, when they forbade entail and provided for the distribution of estates, thought they had erected a barrier against the money power that ruled England. They forgot that money could combine ; that a moneyed corporation is like the papacy, a succession of persons with a unity of purpose. Now, as the land of England in the hands of thirty thousand land-owning families has ruled it for six hundred years, so the corporations of America mean to govern ; and unless some power more radical than ordinary politics is found, will govern inevitably. The survival of republican institutions here depends upon a successful resistance of this tendency. The only hope of any effectual grapple with the danger lies in rousing the masses, whose interests lie permanently in the opposite direction."[2]

Next the orator passed to answer certain criticisms :

---

[1] Boston daily papers of September 14th, 1871.
[2] "The Labor Question," by Wendell Phillips, published by Lee & Shepard, Boston, p. 13.

"We are asked, Why hurry into politics? We see the benefit of going into politics. If we had not rushed into politics, had not taken Massachusetts by the four corners and shaken her, you never would have written your criticisms. We rush into politics because politics is the safety-valve. We could discuss as well as you if you would only give us bread and houses, fair pay and leisure, and opportunities to travel: we could sit and discuss the question for the next fifty years. It's a very easy thing to discuss, for a gentleman in his study, with no anxiety about to-morrow. Why, the ladies and gentlemen of the reign of Louis XV. and Louis XVI., in France, seated in gilded saloons and on Persian carpets, surrounded with luxury, with the products of India and the curious manufactures of ingenious Lyons and Rheims, discussed the rights of man, and balanced them in dainty phrases, and expressed them in such quaint generalizations that Jefferson borrowed the Declaration of Independence from their hands. There they sat, balancing and discussing sweetly, making out new theories, and daily erecting a splendid architecture of debate, till the angry crowd broke open the doors, and ended the discussion in blood. They waited too long, discussed about half a century too long. You see, discussion is very good when a man has bread to eat, and his children all portioned off, and his daughters married, and his house furnished and paid for, and his will made; but discussion is very bad when

. . . "'Ye hear the children weeping, O my brothers!
Ere the sorrow comes with years;'

discussion is bad when a class bends under actual oppression. We want immediate action."[1]

Another criticism touched the use of the word labor.

"All men labor. Rufus Choate and Daniel Webster labor, say the critics. Every man who reads of the Labor question knows that it means the movement of the men that earn their living with their hands; that are employed, and paid wages;

---

[1] "The Labor Question," pp. 14, 15.

are gathered under roofs of factories, sent out on farms, sent out on ships, gathered on the walls. In popular acceptation, the working class means the men that work with their hands, for wages, so many hours a day, employed by great capitalists; that work for everybody else. Why do we move for this class? 'Why,' asks a critic, 'don't you move for all workingmen?' Because, while Daniel Webster gets forty thousand dollars for arguing the Mexican claims, there is no need of anybody's moving for him. While Rufus Choate gets five thousand dollars for making one argument to a jury, there is no need of moving for him, or for the men that work with their brains,—that do highly disciplined and skilled labor, invent, and write books. The reason why the Labor movement confines itself to a single class is because that class of work does not get paid, does not get protection. Mental labor is adequately paid, and more than adequately protected. It can shift its channels: it can vary according to the supply and demand. If a man fails as a minister, why, he becomes a railway conductor. If that doesn't suit him, he turns out, and becomes the agent of an insurance-office. If that doesn't suit, he goes West, and becomes governor of a Territory. And if he finds himself incapable of either of these positions, he comes home, and gets to be a city editor. He varies his occupation as he pleases, and doesn't need protection. But the great mass, chained to a trade, doomed to be ground up in the mill of supply and demand, that work so many hours a day, and must run in the great ruts of business,—they are the men whose inadequate protection, whose unfair share of the general product, claims a movement in their behalf." [1]

He thus describes his ideal:

"My ideal of civilization is a very high one; but the approach to it is a New England town of some two thousand inhabitants, with no rich man and no poor man in it, all mingling in the same society, every child at the same school, no poor-house, no beggar, opportunities equal, nobody so proud as to stand aloof, nobody so humble as to be shut out."

With reference to a remedy, he thought graded taxation would be helpful.

---

[1] "The Labor Question," pp. 16, 17.

"The labor of yesterday, capital, is protected sacredly. Not so the labor of to-day. The labor of yesterday gets twice the protection and twice the pay that the labor of to-day gets. Why is it not entitled to an equal share?

"Are you quite certain that capital—the child of artificial laws, the product of society, the mere growth of social life—has a right to only an equal burden with labor, the living spring? We doubt it so much that we think we have invented a way to defeat the Pennsylvania Central. We think we have devised a little plan—Abraham Lincoln used to have a little story—by which we will save the Congress of the nation from the moneyed corporations of the State. When we get into power, there is one thing we mean to do. If a man owns a single house, we will tax him one hundred dollars. If he owns ten houses of like value, we won't tax him one thousand dollars, but two thousand dollars. If he owns a hundred houses, we won't tax him ten thousand dollars, but sixty thousand dollars; and the richer a man grows, the bigger his tax, so that when he is worth forty million dollars he shall not have more than twenty thousand dollars a year to live on. We'll double and treble and quintuple and sextuple and increase tenfold the taxes, till Stewart out of his uncounted millions, and the Pennsylvania Central out of its measureless income, shall not have anything more than a moderate lodging and an honest table. The corporations we would have are those of associated labor and capital,—co-operation." [1]

Mr. Phillips repeated the substance of this speech in Steinway Hall, New York, on December 7th, 1871, and at various other places and times during that winter. Indeed, he intermingled Temperance and Labor in his Lyceum work now, as he had Anti-Slavery in former times. And outside of the Lyceum, on whatever platform, he gladly stood to plead for the relief of poverty. Thus, he addressed the International Grand Lodge of St. Crispin in April, 1872, in a speech only second in importance

---

[1] "The Labor Question," p. 23.

to the Music Hall speech above mentioned. From this, also, we extract a passage or two, important as showing his position and disclosing his methods of treatment :

"Let me tell you why I am interested in the Labor question. Not simply because of the long hours of labor ; not simply because of a specific oppression of a class. I sympathize with the sufferers ; I am ready to fight on their side. But I look out upon Christendom, with its three hundred millions of people ; and I see, that, out of this number of people, one hundred millions never had enough to eat. Physiologists tell us that this body of ours, unless it is properly fed, properly developed, and carefully nourished, does no justice to the brain. You cannot make a bright or good man in a starved body ; and so this one third of the inhabitants of Christendom, who have never had food enough, can never be what they should be. Now, I say that the social civilization which condemns every third man in it to be below the average in the nourishment God prepared for him, did not come from above : it came from below ; and, the sooner it goes down the better. Come on this side of the ocean. You will find forty millions of people, and I suppose they are in the highest state of civilization ; and yet it is not too much to say, that, out of that forty millions, there are ten millions, at least, who get up in the morning and go to bed at night, and spend all the day in the mere effort to get bread enough to live. They have not elasticity enough left to do anything in the way of intellectual or moral progress.

"I take, for instance, one of the manufacturing valleys of Connecticut. If you get into the cars there at 6.30 o'clock in the morning, as I have done, you will find, getting in at every little station, a score or more of laboring men and women, with their dinner in a pail ; and they get out at some factory that is already lighted up. Go down the same valley about 7.30 in the evening, and you will again see them going home. They must have got up about 5.30 ; they are at their work until nigh upon eight o'clock. There is a good, solid fourteen hours. Now, there will be a strong, substantial man, like Cobbett, who will sit up nights studying, and who will be a scholar at last among them, perhaps ; but he is an exception. The average man, when he gets home at night, does not care to read an article from the *North American*, nor a long speech from Charles Sumner. No ; if he can't have a good story, and a warm supper, and a glass of grog, perhaps, he goes off to bed. Now, I say that the civilization that has produced this state of things in nearly the hundredth year of the American Republic did not come from above.

"I believe in the temperance movement. I am a temperance man of nearly forty years' standing ; and I think it one of the grandest things in the world, because it holds the basis of self-control. Intemperance is the cause of poverty, I know ; but there is another side to that : poverty is the cause of intemperance. Crowd a man with fourteen hours' work a day, and you crowd him down to a mere animal life. You have eclipsed his aspirations, dulled his tastes, stunted his intellect, and made him a mere tool, to work fourteen hours, and catch a thought in the interval ; and, while a man in a hundred will rise to be a genius, ninety-nine will cower down under the circumstances. Now, I can tell you a fact. In London, the other day, it was found that one club of gentlemen, a thousand strong, spent twenty thousand dollars at the club-house during the year for drink. Well, I would allow them twenty thousand dollars more at home for liquor, making in all forty thousand dollars a year. These men were all men of education and leisure : they had books and paintings, opera, race-course, and regatta. A thousand men down in Portsmouth in a ship-yard, working under a boss, spent at the grog-shops of the place, in that year, eighty thousand dollars,—double that of their rich brethren. What is the explanation of such a fact as that ? Why, the club-man had a circle of pleasures and of company : the operative, after he had worked fourteen hours, had nothing to look forward to but his grog.

"That is why I say, lift a man, give him life, let him work eight hours a day, give him the school, develop his taste for music, give him a garden, give him beautiful things to see, and good books to read, and you will starve out those lower appetites. Give a man a chance to earn a good living, and you may save his life. So it is with women in prostitution. Poverty is the road to it : it is this that makes them the prey of the wealth and the leisure of another class. Give a hundred men in this country good wages and eight hours' work, and ninety-nine will disdain to steal. Give a hundred women a good chance to get a good living, and ninety-nine of them will disdain to barter their virtue for gold. You will find in our criminal institutions to-day a great many men with big brains, who ought to have risen in the world,—perhaps gone to Congress. You may laugh, but I tell you the biggest brains don't go to Congress. Now, take a hundred criminals: ten of them will be smart men; but take the remainder, and eighty of them are below the average, body and mind: they were, as Charles Lamb said, 'Never brought up; they were dragged up.' They never had any fair chance: they were starved in body and mind. Now, just so long as you hold two thirds of this nation on such a narrow, superficial line, you feed the criminal classes."[1]

He urged upon workingmen the vital importance of organization and said:

"Now, let me tell you where the great weakness of an association of workingmen is. It is that it cannot wait. It does not know where to get its food for next week. If it is kept idle for ten days, the funds of the society are exhausted. Capital can fold its arms, and wait six months; it can wait a year. It will be poorer, but it does not get to the bottom of the purse. It can afford to wait; it can tire you out, and starve you out. And what is there against that immense preponderance of power on the part of capital? Simply organization. *That makes the wealth of all the wealth of every one.* So I welcome organization. I do not care whether it calls itself trades-union, Crispin, international, or commune: anything that masses up a unit in order that they may put in a united force to face the organization of capital, anything that does that, I say Amen to it. One hundred thousand men! It is an immense army. I do not care whether it considers chiefly the industrial or the political questions; it can control the nation if it is in earnest. The reason why the Abolitionists brought the nation down to fighting their battle is that they were really in earnest, knew what they wanted, and were determined to have it. Therefore they got it. The leading statesmen and orators of the day said they would never

---

[1] "Labor Question," pp. 29-32.

urge Abolition ; but a determined man in a printing-office said that they should, and—they did it.

"And so it is with this question exactly. Brains govern this country ; and I hope to God the time will never come when brains won't govern it, for they ought to. And the way in which you can compel the brains to listen and to attend to you on the question of labor, actually to concentrate the intellectual power of the nation upon it, is by gathering together by hundreds of thousands, no matter whether it be on an industrial basis or a political basis, and say to the nation, ' We are the numbers, and we will be heard,' and you may be sure that you will."[1]

While thus occupied on the platform the indefatigable reformer was equally busy with his pen. As a sample of his work for temperance, take this striking double picture, which he sent to one of the journals of the day, and called " Two Sides of One Canvas" :

"One beautiful afternoon in August, there came to me the heart-broken wife of a State-prison convict. We tried to plan for his pardon and restoration to home and the world. It was a very sad case. He was the only surviving son of a very noble man—one who lived only to serve the poor, the tempted, and the criminal. All he had, all he was, he gave unreservedly to help thieves and drunkards. His house was their home. His name their bail to save them from prison. His reward their reformation. It was a happy hour to hear him tell of the hundreds he had shielded from the contamination and evil example of prisons, and of the large proportion he had good reason to believe permanently saved. Out of hundreds, he once told me, only two left him to pay their bail, forfeited by neglect to show themselves in court according to agreement—only two !

" Bred under such a roof, the son started in life with a generous heart, noble dreams, and high purpose. Ten years of prosperity, fairly earned by energy, industry, and character, ended in bankruptcy, as is so often the case in our risky and

---

[1] " The Labor Question," pp. 26, 27.

changing trade ; then came a struggle for business, for bread—temptation—despair—intemperance. He could not safely pass the open doors that tempted him to indulgence, forgetfulness, and crime. How hard his wife wrought and struggled to save him from indulgence, and then to shield him from exposure ! How long wife, sister, and friends labored to avert conviction and the State prison ! 'I would spare him gladly,' wrote the prosecuting attorney, 'if he would stop drinking. He shall never go to prison if he will be a sober man. But all this wretchedness and crime comes from rum.'

" Manfully did the young fellow struggle to resist the appetite. Again and again did he promise, and keep his promise perhaps a month, then fall. He could not walk the streets and earn his bread soberly while so many open doors—opened by men who sought to coin gold out of their neighbors' vices—lured him to indulgence. So, rightfully, the State pressed on, and he went to prison. An honored name disgraced, a loving home broken up, a wide circle of kindred sorely pained, a worthy, well-meaning man wrecked. Sorrow and crime ' all comes from rum,' says the keen-sighted lawyer.

" As I parted from the sad wife on my door-step, I looked beyond, and close by the laughing sea stood a handsome cottage. The grounds were laid out expensively and with great taste. Over the broad piazza hung lazily an Eastern hammock, while all around were richly painted chairs and lounges of every easy and tempting form. Overhead were quaint vases of beautiful flowers, and the delicious lawn was bordered with them. On the lawn itself gayly dressed women laughed merrily over croquet, and noisy children played near. A span of superb horses pawed the earth impatiently at the gate, while gay salutations passed between the croquet-players and the fashionable equipages that rolled by. It was a scene of beauty, comfort, taste, luxury, and wealth. *All came from rum.* Silks and diamonds, flowers and equipage, stately roof and costly attendance, *all came from rum.* The owner was one who, in a great city, coined his gold out of the vices of his fellow-men.

" To me it was a *dissolving view*. I lost sight of the gay women, the frolicsome children, the impatient horses, and the ocean rolling up to the lawn. I saw instead the pale convict in his cell twelve feet by nine ; the sad wife going from judge to attorney, from court to Governor's Council, begging mercy for her *overtempted* husband. I heard above the children's noise, the croquet, laugh, and the surf waves, that lawyer's stern reason for exacting the full penalty of the law—*all this comes from rum.*

" ' Woe unto him that giveth his neighbor drink. Woe unto him that buildeth his house by unrighteousness and his chambers by wrong, for the stone shall cry out of the wall, and the beam out of the timber shall answer it.' "

V.

GRANT—GREELEY—FROUDE.

THE Presidential campaign of 1872 was one of the most curious on record. Grant was the Republican nominee. The Democrats in their despair selected Horace Greeley, always their bitter foe, but now considered available because he had quarrelled with Grant and kicked over the party traces. Stranger yet, Senator Sumner, also at odds with the President, had gone over to the support of Greeley, and was appealing widely to the colored voters to support the "Copperhead" candidate, on the ground that he was an Abolitionist. Mr. Sumner and Mr. Motley had been ill-used by the Administration. Sumner had been deprived of his Chairmanship of the Foreign Affairs Senatorial Committee, because of his opposition to Grant's proposed acquisition of San Domingo; and Motley had been recalled from England, where he had been the American Minister, on account of his friendship with Sumner and as a stab at the Massachusetts senator. Both Sumner and Motley were old and close friends of Mr. Phillips, who keenly felt and resented their ill-treatment. Later he defended both, and set their wrongs right before the public. At present, while smarting under the injustice done them, he nevertheless supported Grant's candidature and opposed Greeley's, on account of the policies and parties in competition.

In the summer of 1872, in response to an invitation from the colored people of Massachusetts to address them on the question of the hour, and help them resolve their doubts caused by their inclination to vote the Republican ticket and their respect for Mr Sumner, who urged them toward Greeley,—Mr. Phillips wrote a letter analyzing the situation and giving the asked-for advice. It was in his happiest vein, and is subjoined as a vivid portrayal of that anomalous canvass:

" My judgment is the exact opposite of Mr. Sumner's. I think every loyal man, and especially every colored man, should vote for General Grant, and that the nation and your race are only safe in the hands of the old, regular Republican party.

"Some may ask how I come to think thus, when I was one of the few loyal men who protested, in 1868, against Grant's nomination, and seeing that I have so often affirmed that the Republican party has outlived its usefulness,

"Gentlemen, the reasons which lead me to my present opinion, in spite of my former views, ought to give my judgment more weight with you. I am forced by late developments to my present position.

"You remember, that, in 1868, I emphatically denied General Grant's fitness for the Presidency. Derided by the Republican press, I went from city to city protesting against his election. In private, with Mr. Sumner and others, I argued long and earnestly against the risk of putting such a man into such an office. At that time they saw only his great merits, and supported him heartily. The defects of his Administration are no surprise to me. I may say, without boasting, that I prophesied those defects. I do not wish to hide them to-day. I entirely agree with Mr. Sumner as to the grave fault and intolerable insolence of the Administration in the San Domingo matter. I think the frequent putting of relatives into office highly objectionable, and the sad career of Webster is warning enough against any man in public life venturing to accept gifts from living men. These and other defects are no surprise to me. The eminent merits of General Grant's Administration are, I confess, a surprise to me.

"His original and Christian policy toward the Indians is admirable, and, standing alone, is enough to mark him a statesman. His patience amid innumerable difficulties in our foreign relations is wonderful in one bred a soldier. The aid the Administration has given to the industrial and financial prosperity of the country is a great merit. General Grant's prompt interference for justice to workingmen in defiance of those about him, relative to the execution of the eight-hour law, I shall always remember. The crime of the Republican party in tolerating the Ku-Klux is flagrant. But the President and his immediate friends deserve our gratitude for their efforts and success in that matter. His services to the Fifteenth Amendment, I shall never forget. When some, even of the foremost Abolitionists, doubted, and were lukewarm, I wrote to Senator Wilson, asking him to urge General Grant to put three lines into his first message commending that measure to Congress and the country. The answer came back, 'You are too late. General Grant's message was finished before your note arrived, and the recommendation you wish is in it.' It still remains lamentably true, that the colored man has no full recognition at the North, and no adequate protection in the South—shame to the Administration and to the Republican party! But his friends may fairly claim that, during the last three years, the negro has steadily gained in the safe exercise and quiet enjoyment of his rights.

"If General Grant is set aside, who is offered us in his place? Horace Greeley. I need not tell you, my friends, what Horace Greeley is: we Abolitionists knew him only too well in the weary years of our struggle. He had enough of clear, moral vision to see the justice of our cause; but he never had courage to confess his faith. If events had ever given him the courage, he never would have had principle enough to risk anything for an idea. A trimmer by nature and purpose, he has abused even an American politician's privilege of trading principles for success. As for his honesty—for twenty years it has been a byword with us that it would be safe to leave your open purse in the same room with him; but, as for any other honesty, no one was ever witless enough to connect the idea with his name.

"Gentlemen, I have another interest in Grant's re-election.

The Anti-Slavery cause was only a portion of the great struggle between Capital and Labor. Capital undertook to own the laborer. We have broken that up. If Grant is elected, that dispute, and all questions connected with it, sink out of sight. All the issues of the war are put beyond debate, and a clear field is left for the discussion of the Labor movement. I do not count much on the recognition of that movement by the Republican Convention, though I gratefully appreciate it. But I see in the bare success itself, of General Grant, the retiring of old issues, and the securing of a place for new ones.

"If Greeley is elected, we shall spend the next four years in fighting over the war-quarrels, constitutional amendments, negroes' rights, State rights, repudiation, and Southern debts. And we shall have besides a contemptuous ignoring of the Labor question. Its friends were at Cincinnati. The Convention scorned their appeals, and Mr. Schurz himself affirmed that Labor was 'not a live issue.' President Grant means peace, and opportunity to agitate the great industrial questions of the day. President Greeley means the scandal and wrangle of Andy Johnson's years over again, with secession encamped in Washington.

"We have forgiven. But duty to the dead, and to the negro, forbids us to *trust* power to any hands, without undoubted, indubitable certainty that such hands are *trustworthy*. If we fail in this caution, we shall only have decoyed the negro into danger, and left him doubly defenceless. I wish my voice could be heard by every colored man down to the Gulf,—not because they need my advice. No: they understand and see the danger. But I should like to rally them to help us, a second time, to save the nation. I should say to them, 'Vote, every one of you, for Grant, as you value property, life, wife, or child. If Greeley is elected, arm, concentrate, conceal your property, but organize for defence. You will need it soon, and sadly.'

"Workingmen, rally now, to save your great question from being crowded out, and postponed another four years.

"Soldiers, at the roll-call in November, let no loyal man fail to answer to his name." [1]

This advice was heard and heeded. Greeley was

---

[1] *Vide* Boston *Daily Advertiser*, August 10th, 1872.

buried under an adverse vote, and Grant remained for a second term in the White House.

From the commencement of his public career, Mr. Phillips had been in profound sympathy with Ireland in her sorrows and sufferings under English misrule. He had visited the Emerald Isle,—had seen the misery,—had marked the prejudice,—had imbibed the spirit of Emmet, of Grattan, of Moore,—had been intimate with O'Connell, whose eulogist he made himself. Probably no other American, certainly no other American of prominence, was so familiar with the story of Ireland's woes as he was, both from personal observation and from study. For thirty years he never omitted an opportunity to plead her cause before the grand jury of the American people. As that cause came up more and more frequently for consideration over here, he correspondingly increased the number and pungency of his speeches on that topic.

In 1873 James Anthony Froude, who masqueraded as an historian, and who was a brilliant pamphleteer, landed in Boston and delivered a series of lectures on England and Ireland (which he subsequently repeated in the large cities),—ingenious, able, and misleading. The one man fitted by genius, knowledge of the subject, and the possession of the public ear, to challenge his statements, explode his falsehoods, elevate Ireland in American esteem,—was Wendell Phillips. And self-prompted, he assumed the congenial task. In a lecture entitled "Inferences from Froude," careful in statement, judicious and judicial in tone, and in a style that coruscated, before the culture of Boston, amid a tumult of applause, the deed was done. Mr. Phillips traversed the entire field of controversy. We can give no more than a specimen page or two :

"When during the Franco-Prussian War, Bismarck smote England contemptuously in the face, in the presence of all Europe, why did she not draw the sword ? She never had been reluctant to draw the sword. She had been the great intermeddler for the last three centuries. There could not be a crisis in the remotest corner of the globe, about the most insignificant motive in the world, that England did not put in her mailed hand. Palmerston's laurels were all won from meddling in other people's messes. If China wished to give up opium, England wished it to be there. If Portugal and Spain differed, Canning must send his fleet to watch over the safety of Lisbon. She never knew a war that she could leave alone. Why did she break the great historic precedent of two hundred years in this single instance ?

"I believe, that instead of England's having conquered Ireland, in the true, essential statement of the case, as it stands to-day, Ireland has conquered England ! She has summoned her before the bar of the civilized world, to answer and plead for the justice of her legislation ; she has checkmated her as a power on the chess-board of Europe ; she has monopolized the attention of her statesmen ; she has made her own island the pivot upon which the destiny of England turns ; and her last great statesman, Mr. Gladstone, owes whatever fame he has, to the supposition that at last he has devised a way by which he can conciliate Ireland, and *save* his own country.

"I thank Mr. Froude that he has painted the Irishman as a chronic rebel. It shows that at least the race knew that they were oppressed, and gathered together all the strength that God had given them to resist. They never rested contented. It is by no means, therefore, a surprise that a patriotic Englishman, looking back on the last three centuries, should long to justify his nation and his own race, after having conceived that it has all the brains, and two thirds of the heart of the world. It volunteered to be the guardian of this obstinate Ireland. It volunteered to furnish a government to the distracted, ignorant, poverty-stricken, demoralized millions of Ireland. It has been three hundred years at the experiment ; and Mr. Froude told us the other evening, that, rather than let Ireland go,—weary of their long failure,—rather than let Ireland go, they would exterminate the Irish race! What a confession of statesmanship! ' We have tried for three hundred years to manufacture a government, and at the end of it our alternative is extermination!'

"Well, you see, the world asks, whence comes this result? Was the English race incapable? Did it lack courage? Did it lack brains? Did it lack care? Did it lack common sense? Did it lack that discriminating sagacity which knows time and place? What is the meaning of this failure? And, of course, the only answer of an Englishman who is unwilling to tear down the great splendor of his flag, is, to find the cause in the dogged incapacity of Ireland, and not in any lack of his own country. Mr. Froude is obliged to prove that the Irish were left by God *unfinished*, and that you cannot, by any wit of man, manufacture a citizen out of an Irishman. He is shut up to this argument: for, unless he proves the Irishman a knave, he is obliged, from the facts of the case, to confess England a fool; that is the grand alternative.

"He comes, therefore, to us with that purpose. He comes to excuse England on the ground of Irish incapacity. Well, it was a marvellously bad choice of a jury: for there were a number of logical, middle-aged gentlemen, who met in Philadelphia, on the fourth day of July, 1776, and asserted that God created every man fit to be a citizen; that he did not leave any race so half made up and half finished, that they were to travel through the cycle of three hundred years under the guardianship of any power. And, on that fourth day of July, they established the corner-stone of American political faith, that all men are capable of self-government; while the whole substratum of this course of lectures, by this eloquent British scholar, was the claim that God left Ireland so unfinished that a merciful despotism was necessary." [1]

The fact that he was thus confronted on the threshold of his American tour by the most formidable orator in the world, by whom his facts were denied

---

[1] *Vide* the pamphlet containing the lecture in various public libraries.

his theories refuted, his object disclosed,—naturally discouraged Mr. Froude, and he soon retired from the unequal contest ; while Mr. Phillips received the grateful thanks of Erin.

Mrs. Phillips had taken a fancy to Swampscott, down by the sea, as a summer residence. Her husband, always desirous of carrying out her wishes, had secured an abode there ; and there they passed the summer of 1873, as they had that of 1872. He enjoyed this breathing spell, before active life again caught him up and whirled him away.

The cold weather soon did this, and the "vagabond lecturer" (as he nicknamed himself) set out once more upon his travels. In December, 1873, he looked in upon a fine gathering of the Woman Suffragists at Faneuil Hall, and spoke with his accustomed vim and finish, with the Rev. James Freeman Clarke, Mrs. Mary A. Livermore, Frederick Douglass, Mrs. Lucy Stone, and Mr. Garrison as fellow-orators. Mr. Phillips regarded the restricted sphere of woman as due to her own indifference and to masculine selfishness. It never occurred to him to attribute it, as Miss Frances E. Willard did, not long ago, to the *dress* of the gentler sex:

"Catch Edison and constrict him inside a wasp waistcoat, and be sure you'll get no more inventions ; bind a bustle upon Bismarck, and farewell to German unity ; coerce Robert Browning into corsets, and you'll have no more epics ; put Parnell into petticoats, and Home Rule is a lost cause."

On the whole, we freely admit that we should be sorry to see these gentlemen in any such rig.

VI

OLLA PODRIDA.

THE year 1874 was not specially notable in the life of Mr. Phillips. He did not vegetate by any means, but occupied the hours largely with routine duties,—lecturing in the winter and spring, and resuming the platform in the fall, after the summer interruption.

In July he received some pamphlets from the English reformer, George J. Holyoake, which he acknowledged in a letter from which we extract a few paragraphs touching upon current topics:

"I wish I could have an hour's talk with you on this Labor and Capital question,—one, perhaps, to have as angry an agitation as slavery caused. Wealth, with you, governs; but its power is, I suppose, somewhat masked, sometimes counterveiled or checked by other forces. With us it rules, bare, naked, shameless, undisguised. Our *incorporated* wealth, often wielded by a single hand, is fearful with direct, and still more with indirect, power. We have single men who wield four hundred million dollars, so shaped that towns, counties, States, are its vassals. Two or three united railways (*one* president) will subject a State to their will. Vanderbilt is reported to say, "It is cheaper and surer to buy legislatures than voters." This is the peril of universal suffrage. Then, rum rules our great cities whenever it chooses to exert its power. The sadness of the whole thing is, one hardly sees whence the cure is to come. I *believe*, I don't *see*. Truly our movements demand a most patient faith. I never expected to see any success of our Anti-Slavery struggle. Fortified in Church, State, and capital, the system would have outlived this generation, and perhaps the next, with ordinary shrewdness on the part of its friends. The gods made them mad on their way to destruction, and so hastened it.

"Neither shall I live long enough to see any marked result of our Labor movement here, though it is true that our masses ripen marvellously quick ; but, as you've said, the cliques, jealousies, distrust, and ignorance of workingmen are our chief obstacles. Indeed, we sometimes get better help from open-hearted capitalists. Your ranks are infinitely better trained than ours to stand together on some one demand just long enough to be counted, and so insure that respect which numbers always command in politics where universal suffrage obtains. Then we'd have all the *brains* of the land, our servants, and soon gain that *attention* which is *here* half of success. But I suppose all this is familiar to you, as well as the strength we expect from related questions,—finances, mode of taxation, land tenure, etc. There'll never be, I believe and trust, a class-party here, Labor against Capital, the lines are so indefinite, like dove's-neck colors. Three fourths of our population are to some extent capitalists ; and, again, all see that there is really, and ought always to be, alliance, not struggle, between them. So we lean chiefly on related questions for growth : limitation of hours is almost the only special measure. But enough." [1]

At this time a sorry state of things prevailed in the South. The Secession States had been reconstructed, and a struggle was going on between the loyal and the disloyal elements down there for the control. Louisiana, particularly, heaved with insurrection. She, too, had resumed her Statehood and used it to oppress the negroes. The Governor had been placed in power by their votes, and made himself their champion. The Legislature was filled with their foes, and became an engine of oppression.

---

[1] *Vide* Austin's "Life and Times of Wendell Phillips," pp. 304, 305.

With the Governor on one side and the Legislature on the other, Louisiana was as stormy as the Bay of Biscay. Finally the Governor appealed to the Administration to assist him in maintaining law and order. President Grant straightway ordered General Sheridan, who was in command of the Department, with his headquarters at New Orleans, to support the State executive. Instantly there arose throughout the Union a clamor against Grant and Sheridan from the Democrats and the Greeley Republicans. The National Government was accused of trampling upon State rights—quite the old rebel yell. Public meetings were held to denounce the "outrage;" among the rest, one in Boston, on January 15th, 1875, in Faneuil Hall. The call for this last had been largely signed by Greeley Republicans, who, however, were mostly absent when the meeting was held, the old hall being crowded by Democrats, with a contingent of regular Republicans who had come in to watch the proceedings. Mr. Phillips, greatly interested in the Louisiana plot, sat quietly in the gallery. Resolutions were read denouncing Grant and Sheridan. The speakers one after another had their say, loud cries for Phillips ringing through the hall as each concluded and the next was introduced. Neither the chairman nor the orator paid any attention to these calls, until the programme was ended, when the demand was so loud and persistent that it could not be ignored. At last, the chairman said: "This is Faneuil Hall—sacred to free speech. If any gentleman desires to speak, he shall be heard."

Mr. Phillips rose in the gallery, but was called to the platform. Amid the din he soon made himself heard and commanded attention. The meeting claimed to speak for Boston, although all the speakers were outsiders. The orator dwelt on this fact with great effect :

"Here are Adams, from Quincy, Saltonstall, from New York, and this, that, and the other gentleman, from Salem, Cambridge, Worcester—everywhere but Boston. In the absence of Dana, Bigelow, Bartlett, the bar is not here. In the absence of the merchants of the city, commerce is not here. This meeting represents individuals—nothing else. Boston is not here."

He then proceeded to make a lucid constitutional argument in the vindication of Grant and Sheridan, and ended thus :

"I wanted to record my protest against these resolutions condemning President Grant and General Sheridan for doing their duty. Other men have done this by their absence. I choose to do it by my presence,—in this very hall, and under this roof, where I have so often labored for the liberty which Louisiana now threatens."

The speech was boisterously applauded, and hissed, too—an old-time scene. But the presence and speech of Mr. Phillips killed the purpose for which the meeting had been called. An amendment to the resolutions was offered, praising Grant and Sheridan, and carried, though the chairman declared it lost. And so the denunciation exploded in a laugh at the denouncers. Boston had spoken—but not in the expected way.[1]

A question of wider interest than the Louisiana muddle, related in these days to the currency.

Worcester defines currency to be "that which passes for money in a country ; the aggregate of

---

[1] *Vide* Boston dailies of January 16th, 1875, and New York *Tribune*, January 16th, 1875.

coin, bills, notes, etc., in circulation." Of course, the first care of a country is to establish a currency —has been since the dawn of history. When the precious metals were scarce, other standards of value were used. Iron was the coin of the Spartans, copper that of the Romans. Next silver came in. Finally, St. Louis adopted a gold currency for France. Since then gold and silver have formed the double standard, until recently, when England substituted gold alone. But as there is neither gold nor silver enough in existence to carry on the business of these modern commercial times, each country has supplemented the metals by a bank-note currency, convertible into gold or silver on demand.

When the Rebellion broke out, the Government, in order to conduct its stupendous operations, issued bonds to raise money, and notes, called greenbacks from their color, as a circulating medium. The situation was desperate. Money-lenders would not buy the bonds save at a heavy discount; and though the greenbacks were a legal tender, it took two or three dollars in currency to make a gold dollar. With the success of the Union, the greenbacks appreciated, but gold continued to command a fluctuating premium. The constant endeavor of the Government from 1865 onward to 1878, when it succeeded, was to resume specie payments—that is, to make the greenbacks worth their face value. Meanwhile, through these years trade was disturbed, financial panics were frequent and gold remained in Europe.

The plans for remedying these evils were as numerous as the individuals who proposed them. Mr. Phillips had his plan. He first stated it in public at a meeting of the American Social Science Association, in Boston, on March 3d, 1875. Briefly, his points were these :

1. Take away from the banks the right to issue bills, and call in those now in circulation.

2. Let the Government supply a national currency ample to meet the demands of business—its issue being secured by the wealth of the country.

3. Reduce the heavy rates of interest by calling in outstanding interest-bearing bonds.

The results of such a policy, he contended, would be fourfold, viz., to redeem and destroy the present greenbacks, and thus silence the complaint that Government had not kept faith in their redemption ; to put the currency on a basis as stable as the national resources, and thus avoid the danger of interference by the gold rings here and abroad ; to make the bonds a good permanent investment for capitalists ; and to develop the country by making it possible for individual borrowers to get money at a low rate from the Government by placing collateral in its hands.

This would make the new greenbacks as good as gold. It would bring about practical resumption of specie payments. Before long the Government bonds would command a premium.[1]

"Three times within a dozen years," said he "capitalists with their knives on the throat of the Government, have compelled it to cheat its largest creditor, the people ; whose claim, Burke said, was the most sacred. First, the pledge that greenbacks should be exchangeable with bonds was broken. Secondly, debts originally payable in paper, as Sherman confessed in the Senate, were made payable in gold. Thirdly, silver was

---

[1] *Vide* New York *Tribune*, March 4th, 1875.

demonetized, and gold made the only tender. A thousand millions were thus stolen from the people."[1]

These views Mr. Phillips embodied in a lecture on "Finance," which he delivered widely for several years. In the fall of 1875 he exchanged shots with Carl Schurz on this question, his pistol being the New York *Herald*,[2] while Schurz's revolver was the New York *Tribune*. It was like a French duel—neither was hurt. The Agitator never claimed originality for his financial theories. He held them in common with a host of others, many of whom were among the shrewdest and most successful of American financiers. But his way of stating and defending them was all his own, and was characterized by his usual ingenuity and brilliancy of style.

While a heretic in finance, Phillips was orthodox in another branch of political economy—he was a Protectionist. On a certain occasion the Hon. David A. Wells, the eminent free-trader, read a paper in a circle of savants, enforcing his views. Mr. Phillips, who was among the listeners, expressed his dissent, when the essayist was through:

"Fifteen years ago I advocated free trade. I was misled by theoretical arguments, but was set right by Mr. Henry Cary, the patriarch of political economy. I heard Cary say: 'I had just finished a crushing reply to the New England tariff men,—one that I thought demolished their whole structure of argument. I went to bed delighted with my success in stating my case. Somehow I could not help seeing that, though the logic seemed perfect, it did not cover the facts. On paper it was all right; out in the world the facts were the other way. I lay awake all night, chewing on the contradiction, and arose the next morning a tariff man.' Any one who listened from Cary's lips to the

---

[1] "Reminiscences of the Radical Club," p. 165.
[2] New York *Herald*, October 6th, 1875, and *Tribune*, October 9th.

stern facts which converted him in that night of anxious, honest thought would never again be duped by free trade.

"Nations are large enough to be considered separately from each other. Internal industry should be diversified. Under free-trade rule our country would be wholly agricultural. Other elements must be considered besides the mere question of wealth. Should we lose our diversified occupations, we would suffer a great loss, though there might be a pecuniary gain. Nations might gain the whole world—that is, half the material wealth of the world—and yet lose their own souls and most of their bodies, too. Theories are pleasing things, and seem to get rid of all difficulties so very easily. One must begin to abstract principles and study them. But wisdom consists in perceiving when human nature and this perverse world necessitate making exceptions to abstract truths. Any boy can see an abstract principle. Only threescore years and ten can discern precisely when and where it is well, necessary, and right to make an exception to it. That faculty is wisdom, all the rest is playing with counters. And this explains how the influx into politics of a shoal of college-boys, slenderly furnished with Greek and Latin, but steeped in marvellous and delightful ignorance of life and public affairs, is filling the country with free-trade din.

"National lines—artificial lines—trip up fine theories sadly. If all the world were under one law, and every man raised to the level of the Sermon on the Mount, free trade would be so easy and so charming! But while nations study only how to cripple their enemies,—that is, their neighbors,—and while each trader strives to cheat his customer and strangle the firm on the other side of the street, we must not expect the millennium." [1]

The centennial of the birth of Daniel O'Connell occurred on August 6th, 1875. The Irish race celebrated it around the globe. In Boston, the observance was most remarkable. Wendell Phillips was the orator of the occasion, the vast Music Hall the place, and applauding thousands the participators.

---

[1] "Reminiscences of the Radical Club," pp. 162, 163.

The oration was a masterpiece—the apotheosis of one agitator by another. It ranks among the half dozen supreme efforts of the kind in the English language, and displays the marvellous powers of Mr. Phillips at their best.[1]

Later in the year he threw into a single presentation the three questions nearest his heart, and under the caption of "Temperance, Labor, and Woman"[2] pleaded these causes simultaneously. This, too, was a remarkable achievement; not on account of any novelty of views, for these were more or less familiar to his audiences, but because of the felicitous manner in which he fitted such seemingly diverse themes together, and made them seem related parts of one great whole.

For years the Indians had been numbered among Mr. Phillips's principal clients. In 1875 he prepared a lecture on this subject, and gave it frequently. His solution of the Indian problem was like his solution of all such questions—love and justice. He thought the redman had been shamefully abused,— held on the frontier,—surrounded by soldiers, not laws,—robbed of his lands as often as white greed coveted them,—sent for redress to a colonel, not to a court,—and dealt with under a policy of extermination rather than civilization, our weapons a musket and a whiskey-bottle. This he contrasted with the English method in Canada, where a white man could vault into the saddle and ride from Montreal to the Pacific without a pistol,—where civilization had adopted the Indians as fast as they were reached,—

---

[1] *Vide* Appendix for the oration in full.

[2] This lecture was widely reported at the time, but no complete report is now at hand.

and where the Crown had spent nothing for a hundred years for blood and spoliation; while the United States had lavished hundreds of millions only to place our Government on a level with the barbarism it condemned. He hailed the Indian policy of General Grant as the first suggestion, since William Penn, of a Christian heart and a sane mind touching the aborigines on the part of the Republic.[1]

Chronic outbreaks on the frontier, such as the Modoc war and the episode of Sitting Bull and General Custer, gave timeliness and point to these utterances. Indeed, Mr. Phillips seldom wasted his ammunition on dead issues; his aim being, like Pope's, to

"Shoot folly as it flies."

On his birthday, this year, he received a lovely basket of flowers from some thoughtful friends, which he thus noticed:

"November 29, 1875.

"DEAR FRIENDS: It is pleasant to have some one remember our birthdays. It carries us back to times of childhood,— mother, brothers, and sisters. How laughingly and joyously we counted them up then, as they came only too slowly along, keeping back the presents we longed for. Now they hurry-scurry on, coming round so quickly.

"Well, we all walk along together. We shall keep abreast.

"Ann will cosset and enjoy your beautiful basket for many a week, and I shall enjoy her joy in it.

"Yours faithfully,
"WENDELL PHILLIPS."

Mr. and Mrs. Sargent.

---

[1] The lecture on the Indians was never fully reported—only outlined. But in 1866 and the succeeding years Mr. Phillips frequently dealt with the question in the columns of the *Anti-Slavery Standard*, to which those interested are referred.

At another time, in this same year, he wrote in a different vein, to Mrs. John T. Sargent:

"DEAR MADAM: You know my benevolence. Well, it is therefore that I hasten to inform you of your good fortune.

"Most people leave legacies when they die.

"But you know Tom Appleton says that ' when good Yankees die they go to Paris.' Well, one of your friends, starting for Paris, seems to have imagined that she was dying. At any rate, she acted as if dying and left you a legacy. This is it: 'When you come to Boston go down with a strong porter to the *Commonwealth* rooms and you'll find there the bust of Colonel Shaw.'

"Edmonia Lewis, starting for Europe, said to me: 'That dear, good woman, I do love her. I want her to have it. Give it to her as my legacy.'

"There, be happy and proud. And if you can't go *on* a bust, go *after* one."[1]

---

[1] Letter in the possession of Mrs. J. T. Sargent (MS.).

VII.

USEFULNESS.

The philanthropy of Wendell Phillips was local as well as cosmopolitan. That he pleaded for the negro in the South and the Indian in the West, for the Irishmen under the tyranny of England and the Cretan beneath the Sultan's cimeter, is known. He also saw, felt for, and relieved the want that sobbed, and sometimes stole and stabbed, just 'round the corner. For years, he spent a large part of each morning in court, at the jail, or in some wretched home, looking up needy cases, helping indigent women to honest work, or defending some poor fellow who was hurt or hunted.

One night, in crossing Boston Common, on his return from a late meeting, he was accosted by a street-walker. She looked into his face, instinctively felt her mistake, and said : " You are not one of my sort, but, for the love of God, give me money !" He glanced kindly in her face, saw there the wreck of comeliness, took her arm, and pacing back and forth, drew out her story. It was the old one,—misplaced affection, —betrayal,—desertion,—a child left on her hands,— no means of virtuous livelihood,—the street. Now she wanted money for the child. He investigated, found she had not lied, and helped her to a new life.[1]

---

[1] The writer had this story from several friends of Mr. Phillips who were acquainted with the facts.

Mr. Phillips haunted the streets of Boston. "They are a good place for the study of human nature," said he; "better than the theatre, for here both tragedy and comedy are real—and so are the actors." His friend, William I. Bowditch, discovered him one morning, when the pavement was thronged with business men, leaning against the granite wall of a bank on State Street, like a mendicant. "Wendell," said he, "if you want these people to give you money you must take off your hat and hold it in your hand."[1]

All Bostonians have a local pride; Phillips loved the very stones of his native city. "No one who heard it," remarks Mr. Higginson, "can ever forget the thrilling modulation of his voice when he said at some special crisis of the Anti-Slavery agitation: 'I love inexpressibly these streets of Boston, over whose pavements my mother held up tenderly my baby feet; and if God grants me time enough, I will make them too pure to bear the footsteps of a slave.'"[2] The historic landmarks of the city were his delight. He regarded them as the noblest instructors. Therefore, when the "Old South" Church was threatened with destruction, he exerted himself for salvation. This was peculiarly dear to him as the oldest of Boston's public edifices, older than the Old State House, older than Faneuil Hall, dating from 1729. The religious society which owned it had sold the building, and business was about to raze it and occupy the site. To save it $400,000 were required. The people of the Commonwealth shared

---

[1] Mr. Bowditch is authority for this story.
[2] Higginson's "Wendell Phillips," p. 14.

in the orator's feeling, and $200,000 were obtained by popular subscription.

On June 14th, 1876, Mr. Phillips spoke in the "Old South" Church in the interest of this movement.

"Except the Holy City," he asked, "is there any more memorable place on the face of the earth than this? Athens has her Acropolis, but the Greek can point to no such immediate results. Her influence passes into the web and woof of history, mixed with a score of other elements; and it needs a keen eye to follow it. London has her Palace and Tower, and her St. Stephen's Chapel; but the human race owes her no such memories. France has spots marked by the sublimest devotions; but the pilgrimage and the Mecca of the man who believes in and hopes for the human race is not to Paris. It is to the seaboard cities of the great republic. And when the flag was assailed, when the merchant waked up from his gain, the scholar from his studies, and the regiments marched one by one through the streets, which were the pavements that thrilled under their footsteps? What walls did they salute as the regimental flags floated by to Gettysburg and Antietam? These! Our boys carried down to the battle-fields the memory of State Street, and Faneuil Hall, and the 'Old South' Church. . . .

"Go ask the Londoner, crowded into small space, what number of pounds laid down on a square foot, what necessities of business, would induce him to pull down the Tower, and build a counting-house on its site! Go ask Paris what they will take from some business corporation for the spot where Mirabeau and Danton, or, later down, Lamartine saved the great flag of the tri-color from being drenched in the blood of their fellow-citizens! What makes Boston a history? Not so many men, not so much commerce. It is ideas. You might as well plough it with salt, and remove bodily into the more healthy elevation of Brookline or Dorchester, but for State Street, Faneuil Hall, and the 'Old South' Church!

"What does *Boston* mean? Since 1630, the living fibre, running through history, which owns that name, means jealousy of power, unfettered speech, keen sense of justice, readiness to champion any good cause. That is the *Boston* Laud suspected, North hated, and the negro loved. If you destroy the scenes which perpetuate *that* Boston, then rebaptize her Cottonville or Shoetown."[1]

An interesting incident in connection with this oration was the presence of Dom Pedro, the Brazilian Emperor, in the audience. Mr. Phillips had met him in the afternoon at a delightful séance in the Chestnut Street parlors of his friends, Mr. and Mrs. Sargent,—arranged specially to enable Dom Pedro to meet Whittier, with whom he had corresponded many years concerning poetry and slavery. Phillips found the Emperor to be a thorough Abolitionist; and not long afterward he abolished slavery in Brazil; Whittier being, as he affirmed, his enlightener, and therefore the Brazilian liberator.

When the venerable poet entered and interrupted the conversation with Mr. Phillips, Dom Pedro rose, caught him in his arms and kissed him, after the fashion of the Latin race. The blushing Friend, diffident as a girl, was quite abashed, but with a cordial grasp of the hand drew his royal admirer to a sofa, where they sat and chatted for half an hour. Then the conversation became general. The Emperor, who spoke English perfectly, told of his driving over to see Bunker Hill Monument at six o'clock in the morning. He found the keeper abed. When he was at last aroused, his Majesty, having forgotten his purse, was obliged to borrow half a dollar of his hackman to pay the entrance fee. There was a laugh at this, and Mr. Phillips told him the rest of the story; how, two hours later, a well-known leader

---

[1] This oration, revised by Mr. Phillips, is on sale at the "Old South" Church, in Boston.

of the Boston *ton* came in, looked over the book, saw and recognized Dom Pedro's signature, and asked how the Emperor looked. Putting on his glasses to examine the handwriting, the fretful guardian muttered: "Emperor! that's a dodge; that fellow was only a scapegrace without a cent in his pocket."

Mr. Phillips was pleased with Dom Pedro. He found him intelligent, keenly interested in scientific, educational, and reformatory matters, and altogether the most remarkable specimen of democratic royalty imaginable. With the blood of the Bourbons, the Hapsburgs, and the Braganzas in his veins—the haughtiest and most despotic of houses—he was the unpretentious crony of radicals. He made himself a father to his people, and assured Phillips and Whittier that his ultimate purpose was to educate Brazil into republicanism.[1]

It was for its educational influence that the orator valued the "Old South" Church. Indeed, in one phase or another, he regarded education as the most essential interest of the State. Yet it is significant of the practical cast of his mind, that at the very time

---

[1] "Reminiscences of the Radical Club," pp. 301, 302. The recent revolution in that country we may be sure cost Dom Pedro no pangs. He only thought Brazil not yet ripe for self-government. He had held it a lifetime without disturbance, promoted peace and progress, and aggrandized the Empire. He dreaded to see Brazil imitate the other republics of South America, which, because unready for republicanism, are always disturbed, and change governments so fast that no president sits long enough to get a photograph. But what has occurred there he had prepared the way for. He was a crowned emancipationist and republican. The manner in which the revolutionists treated him is significant of their respect for his character and purposes. Dom Pedro is the only dethroned Emperor in history who was dismissed with regret, with presents, and with a pension.

when he was pleading for a sentiment as embodied in the "Old South," he should make in another place and relation a criticism upon the training of the young in the public and private schools as lacking in practical purpose.

"Our schools," he remarked, "ignore the fact that seven tenths of their scholars must earn their daily bread. They teach without reference to that. And the boys and girls after graduating have to unlearn what they have learned, and begin again in order to get a livelihood. They should be trained with constant reference to affairs—toward and not away from the farm, the shop, the counting-room. The instruction ought to be technical." [1]

The committee having in charge the preservation of the "Old South" Church had organized a lecture course in aid of their fund, and, remembering the oration in 1876, honored the orator by securing his services to open the series. The result was the production and delivery by him on May 17th, 1877, of a new biographical lecture on "Sir Harry Vane." From the "Old South" he carried it out to the Lyceum audiences of the country, and its success was instantaneous. Unfortunately, there is no phonographic report in existence, so that it cannot survive. But Sir Harry Vane was one of the heroes of Wendell Phillips. He placed the young English republican, who had been Governor of Massachusetts at the age of twenty-four, in advance of Winthrop, Adams, and Franklin; declared that he projected his ideas far into the future; and when a boy boldly announced the faith of the nineteenth century in the middle of the seventeenth.[2]

---

[1] *Vide* New York *Tribune*, December 7th, 1876.

[2] The daily press of Boston briefly reported the lecture on May 18th, 1877.

Mr. Phillips knew how to wait. But he had a retentive memory. We have mentioned the keenness with which he felt the injustice of the administration in recalling Motley from London in 1870, and in dropping Sumner from the Committee of Foreign Relations in 1871. The great senator died in 1874.[1] And now Motley, in 1877,[2] followed him to the grave. Prompted by the double bereavement, their survivor prepared and began to deliver, in November, 1877, a eulogy on " Charles Sumner," in which he vindicated these old friends. After a brief but affectionate portrayal of Sumner's career, he passed to the consideration of the historic difficulty between Grant and Secretary Fish on one side, and the senator and Motley on the other :

"General Grant has thrown the weight of his name against Mr. Sumner. I have a great respect for General Grant. I have been a Grant man when Faneuil Hall hissed me for it. I acknowledge his merits. I have no doubt of his sincere patriotism. But General Grant must remember that, when he impeaches history and the loftiest patriotism, there are blows to take as well as to give, and it is himself that provoked the quarrel. I have always known Mr. Sumner as the most methodical, laborious, painstaking, and business-like member of the Senate. The only members of Congress, in my day, who have had a regular ledger, or docket, of public employment and engagements, were General B. F. Butler and Mr. Charles Sumner. They were the only two members of Congress that I ever knew to do business on business principles, and I felt great surprise and indignation when the charge of negligence of public business was made by General Grant against Mr. Sumner. It was only outdone by the intimation that Charles Sumner had told a falsehood. As Schurz says in his eulogy, he was so direct, he could not carry anything by a flank movement. His nature was incapable of concealment. He had none of the usual tact of men who push

---

[1] On March 11th.   [2] On May 30th.

their plans in the world. He made up for it by superhuman energy, with which he bore down all opposition.

"The case to which General Grant refers is the removal of Mr. Sumner from the chairmanship of the Committee on Foreign Relations, which he says was proper and justifiable, because Mr. Sumner was negligent of public duty, and the confirmation of the act is found in the charge that Mr. Sumner had been detected in a falsehood. You remember Mr. Sumner's singular fitness for that chairmanship. Carl Schurz says no chairman ever came to the office so eminently fitted for it. This is the man removed for negligence, for leaving his pigeon-holes full of treaties. You remember the position of Mr. Fish when Sumner was deposed. You remember that the whole North surged with hot indignation. When did General Grant first find this out against Sumner? Why did they not think of this before? Why never utter it till now? If the opposition papers had known that Mr. Sumner was negligent, would they not have told of it? No; this charge is an after-thought. If it had been true, we should have heard of it from every chamber of types in the country. Go to the Republican papers and the anti-Grant papers; they never heard of these charges.

"But General Grant says that Mr. Sumner lied. I remember the occasion. Pardon me if I recite it. Mr. Sumner received from the hands of General Grant the treaty of San Domingo,— from General Grant, who drove up to his door while he was sitting with some friends at dinner-table. He said to the President, 'I will look at the bill. I trust I shall have the pleasure of supporting the administration.' They were words of politeness, of courtesy merely, without having examined the instrument. When he went home, and examined it, he found the dark treachery to the black race. The next day he found General Grant, and took back even the courteous words. He pointed out the objections to the treaty, laid before him the impossibility of his supporting it, and urged a reconsideration of the action of the administration. General Grant listened in silence,—perhaps I might say sullen silence. There was present a gentleman who has been in Washington for forty years, and he came away with Mr. Sumner. As they came down the stairs of the Executive Mansion, the gentleman remarked, 'What is the matter with the President? Do you think he understands you?' 'I should think he might,' replied Sumner. 'No, he doesn't,' was the response; 'he is in no state to understand anything.' If Grant never heard that Sumner took back that courteous pledge in the chamber of the White House, it was because his brain refused to perform its office. He is no judge of the veracity of the senator from Massachusetts.

"General Grant also refers to the action of Mr. Sumner in vindication of his friend, Mr. Motley. The case is a grave one. It concerns one of the noblest Americans who upheld our fame abroad. General Grant intimates that he was no American. I knew Lothrop Motley from boyhood. It is very true that, in his earlier European life, he drank too deep of the foreign spirit. In 1838 and 1840, he was largely European. But on his return to this country, ten years before the war, he told me, 'This is the greatest country in the world. This is a noble nation to work for. It is the noblest people. I have come back from Europe, and have relearned the value of America; have come home one of the humblest laborers, to make justice and liberty prosper.' It came from his heart. He was made over into a most enthusiastic American. I was not surprised when he sprang to the helm in the columns of the London *Times*. It was an echo of the old talks on the sidewalks. When Grant appointed him to England, he appointed the warmest American heart that ever beat.

"Now, when the senator has been in Mount Auburn for three years, when his pen cannot write a denial nor his lips utter a rebuke, now, bearing a lie on its lips, comes this accusation, that this senator, who never was absent from the Senate one hour (Mr. Sumner told me, in the last year of his life, 'I never was absent one hour till the last twelvemonth'), was removed for negligence. Find me one other man who has not lost weeks, or even months, by absence. Mr. Sumner refused opportunities to make hundreds of dollars by lecturing, because he was bound by his duties in the Senate.

"In the quarrel with Motley, the records in the State Department, in black and white, prove that the administration stooped to a falsehood. Mr. Fish exhorted Mr. Sumner to take the British mission,—told him he ought to go to London. Six months later the Minister was recalled, on the ground that he had leaned too much upon the opinion of a great Northern senator.

Mr. Sumner's indignant exclamation to Mr. Fish was, 'If Mr. Motley's leaning was an unpardonable sin, by what right did you sit in my study six months ago, and urge me to go to England, and press my views on the Alabama claims?' He said then and there, 'Sir, you are a tool of the President for base purposes; and this removal is out of spite.' And it is true. The testimony is on the files of the diplomatic service itself." [1]

While Mr. Phillips was thus occupied, an effort was made to persuade him to accept a Gubernatorial nomination,[2] which he refused to do; as he did also, in 1878, the offer of a nomination for Congress.[3]

There was one subject, delicate and painful, upon which Wendell Phillips had felt strongly for half a century,—the right treatment and care of the insane. Indeed, there had been a time when his own family had discussed the expediency of shutting him up in a madhouse as an Abolitionist![4] Without doubt, scores of sane men and women whom relatives for one reason or another desired to get out of the way have been (shall we say still are?) thrust into straitjackets. Mercenary physicians and loose laws conduce to such rascalities. Feeling all this, persuaded of the crying need of vigilance, and taking advantage of a local stir caused by a flagrant case in the neighborhood (his usual cue), Mr. Phillips suggested a public meeting to ventilate the theme. It was held on February 3d, 1879. He made a thrilling speech, demanding the lifting of the veil of secrecy which covered the mismanagement of insane retreats. As the outcome, the Legislature of Massachusetts was

---

[1] *Vide* Dr. Holmes's "Memoir of Motley" for an impartial *exposé* of the subject as it concerns Motley.

[2] *Vide* Boston *Commonwealth* in the fall of 1877.

[3] *Vide* New York *Tribune*, November 4th, 1878.

[4] So Mr. Phillips told the writer in 1880.

memorialized to pass stringent laws concerning the committal of persons alleged to be insane, and to secure for them freedom of access, and the right of frequent and impartial examinations.[1]

Not many months after this action, the tireless friend of human kind was called to mourn the death of Garrison.[2] The cordial relations between these two had been largely resumed. Mr. Phillips felt the loss beyond expression. A part of his own being went into the coffin. On Wednesday, May 28th, 1879, in the presence of a churchful of the surviving colaborers of the father of American Emancipation, and after tender remarks from a number of old comrades, he took the stand to utter the last word. It was comprehensive,—the acknowledgment of personal indebtedness, analysis, characterization, pathos, inspiration; all in that word.[3] His neighbor and admirer, Dr. Samuel A. Green, who had heard him a hundred times, and in all moods, testifies that it was the most exquisite utterance and the most effective he ever heard even from Mr. Phillips's lips. "Yet," he adds, "it was extempore. After the address I chatted with him in his study and asked him about his preparation. He pointed to a piece of paper on the table. I took it up. There were four lines of points on a slip the size of a small envelope. 'How could you do it?' I asked. 'Ah!' was the reply, 'I was at work on that address for forty years!'"[4]

---

[1] *Vide* Boston *Daily Advertiser* of February 4th, 1879, for a report of the meeting.

[2] He died in New York City, May 23d.

[3] *Vide* tributes to William Lloyd Garrison at the funeral services, May 28th, 1879.

[4] Repeated to the writer by Dr. Green in September, 1889.

It was a happy coincidence that the next public call that reached the orator, after the funeral of his beloved comrade, should have come from their old protégés. An ominous exodus of the blacks from the South was in progress. Despised and skinned by the whites, thousands had started they knew not whither—anywhere to escape from the perdition they were in. The Southerners, unwilling to have them remain, yet frightened at the thought of losing their workmen, had combined to resist the stampede, and were more oppressive in their repressive than they had been in their expulsive methods.

A meeting was held in the Tremont Temple, in June, 1879, in Boston, to raise money for the assistance of those who wished to emigrate, and to protest against any denial of their right to travel. Mr. Phillips thundered and lightened in the style of a quarter of a century before. To illustrate the condition of the colored people, he told this story of a conversation some one had with one of the escaping band, black as night and ignorant as black,—yet knowing enough to want to get away:

" Where are you going?"

" Dunno."

" What are you going for?"

" Dunno."

" What are you going to do when you get there?"

" Dunno."

" Do you expect to improve your condition?"

" Couldn't wuss it nohow."[1]

A committee was appointed, of which Mr. Phillips was one; a sum of money was raised; a protest was

---

[1] *Vide* New York *Tribune*, June 25th, 1879.

sent to Washington ; the Government moved ; but the exodus continues, now increasing, now diminishing, but always proceeding, to the present day. Pharaoh finds it hard to believe in the omnipotence of Justice and Love.

Mr. and Mrs. Phillips passed the summer of 1879 at Beverly. On July 18th he writes thence to a friend :

"Here we are. Tuesday we drove down, seventeen miles, in two hours, an east wind favoring the horses. Ann bore it better than we feared she would. She enjoys the change of scene and folks—and the stillness. . . . I shall move 'round and keep active. I have already begun pistol practice, and amuse myself seeing how many times in twenty I can plant a ball within the size of the palm of my hand at twenty paces. I am not ashamed of my success. . . . The woods here are fine ; many prefer it to Nahant,—which I do not." [1]

---

[1] To Mrs. E. F. C. (MS.).

VIII.

THE RADICAL CLUB.

IN an aristocratic quarter of Boston, in an old, fashioned, roomy mansion resided the Rev. John T. Sargent, small in frame, large in soul. More than once we have had occasion to refer to his intimacy with Mr. Phillips. His wife was a kindred soul, and together they made their home the resort of the most gifted and progressive people in America. They were Unitarians in faith, and had domesticated under their roof an institution called "The Radical Club," which met statedly to discuss theological and other questions,—for the most part, it must be confessed, from an ultra-liberal standpoint. In attendance on the club one might find, almost any day, Emerson, Longfellow, Frothingham, John Weiss, Higginson, Holmes, Julia Ward Howe, Henry James,—a galaxy of celebrities.

Mr. Phillips, though not in theological accord with them, was a frequent guest of the club, and always welcome. It was curious to observe how the radical of radicals instantly assumed, when religion was upon the tapis, a position of exemplary conservatism. Many and doughty were the lances he broke in these tournaments of mind as the champion of orthodoxy.

On one occasion Mr. Emerson read an essay on "Religion," in which he claimed that Christianity was only one faith more, a modification of Judaism or Buddhism,—not ultimate truth, but a well-meant approximation, borrowing its ideas from the Greeks, from the Chinese, from every quarter.

Wendell Phillips said, in reply:

"He had never met a man of the old faith,—one worthy to be taken as a type of anything,—who denied that the religious sentiment had found meet and valuable and admirable expression in the mythologies; and he thought that three quarters of all the investigations which had been made into Oriental religions, translations of their books, inquiries into their history, and analyses of their faiths, had been by so-called orthodox men. Yale College was as learned in all that matter as Harvard. He did not think, therefore, they could claim that the truth, as it appeared in those books and in those religions, had not been recognized by orthodox men. The point where they separated was not there, by any means. Of course, the old religions and mythologies grew out of an inspired religious consciousness, to a certain extent. He never knew a man who denied it. Every intelligent man that he ever met, of any sect, acknowledged the contributions to the literature of the West that had been made by many of the older faiths; they had not neglected, they had not depreciated, that development. On all this we agree. There is a great deal of astronomical speculation in the world, yet that does not interfere with the fact that there is a true astronomical method. Because a great many scholars had speculated about the stars, did that show that Copernicus and Sir Isaac Newton are not upon the right track? The question was, 'Is there any indication anywhere that we have touched, even slightly, on absolute truth in any of the mythologies?' When it was claimed that some parts of the New Testament could be found in Æschylus and Sophocles and Epictetus, he admitted it; but, when any man said that the New Testament could be found in Confucius and Buddha, he stopped, and demanded the proof. He did not *know* that any Jew by the name of Jesus Christ had said, 'Do unto others as ye would that others should do to you;' but he knew that the best scholarship of Europe had scrutinized every line of the record in the most exhaustive manner, until we know, if we know anything, that, three hundred years after his death, he was supposed to have said it. So far they were on solid ground. It was said that Confucius, five hundred years before Christ, said, ' Do not do unto another as you would not have another do to you.' There was a remarkable similarity in these sentences, and very little probability that a Jew, in that narrow valley, ever heard of a Chinese. How did they know Confucius said it ? All they knew about the Chinese was not older than three hundred and fifty years. If they could prove to him that, three hundred years after the death of Confucius, he was supposed to have uttered those words, he would believe it, but not now ; and he did not give any more weight to the legends about Buddha. No story forty years old could be relied upon without scrutiny.

" But suppose it was admitted that Confucius and Buddha did say just what Christ did ? Steam and water were the same elements ; but water would not move a locomotive ; steam would. The Sermon on the Mount might be paralleled in Sophocles ; they might find a great deal in Confucius : but one was water, the other steam ; one had moved the world, the other had not. The proof that there was something unusual there was seen in the results. India had all the intellectual brilliancy that Greece had ; she touched all the problems, exhausted all the intellectual debate, thousands of years ago ; and there she lies to-day. On the other hand, here was Europe. She had made marvellous progress ; and, with the single exception of race, there was no element mixed in the European caldron to distinguish it from the Asiatic. Unless they were going to lay on this distinction of race the whole difference between European and Asiatic development, they had nothing but Christianity to account for it. It seemed to him that it was wiser to claim for Christianity the largest share in the merit of European civilization.

" Everybody knew that the Chinese had hospitals before Christ, if we are to trust history ; everybody knew all about their progress in civilization ; but they make no progress to-day. The bee could make an eight-sided cell better than Brunel could make it, but the bee can make nothing else. The Chinese had not advanced for a thousand years. They had every spring-board and fulcrum and motive-power to go ahead, and had not. Europe had constantly gone ahead. We had saved all we had got, and gained more. We had taken the classic and the Roman civilization,—taken their law, their ethics, their religious ideas, their idea of popular rights,—and we had carried them on. Europe was the hand and brain of the world to-day ; the pioneer, the constructor, the administrator of the world to-day ; and there was nothing underlying her to make her so, except race and Christianity. Other portions of the world had had the same intellect. Tocqueville had told us, in his report to the French Institute, that there was no theory or dream of social science ever debated in Europe that could not be found in the Hindoo discussions. The difference was not caused by a lack of intellect. Here was a fact to be explained, and it could not be brushed away by saying this man and the other made a very near approach. No doubt that was so : nobody ever denied it. God never left any race, nor any man, nor any time, without Himself ; and these twilights, and approaches to noon, were seen everywhere in history. But they had got, at last, the Copernican theory ; and no fact appeared that it did not explain. They had got, at last, the true chemical analysis ; and that went down, and weighed the atoms. They explained all new discoveries. The reason why he believed in Sir Isaac Newton was, that he gave the key to every fact, discovered no matter where. Sir Thomas Browne could tell a great many beautiful dreams about astronomy, but they did not explain the facts. Christianity had faced the facts and explained them. He claimed, therefore, that there was something essentially different in it from the religious experience of other races." [1]

At another sitting, the Rev. W. H. Channing read a paper on " The Christian Name." When the discussion began Mr. Phillips remarked :

" Christianity is a great moral power, the determining force of our present civilization, as of past steps in the same direction. Jesus is the divine type who has given His peculiar form to the modern world. Speculations as to why and how may differ, but we see the fact. We cannot rub out history. Europe shows a type of human character not paralleled anywhere else.

---

[1] " Reminiscences of the Radical Club," pp. 9-13, 15, 18, 19.

The intellect of Greece centred around power and beauty; that of Rome around legal justice. The civilization of modern Europe was inspired by a great moral purpose. Imperfect as it was, and limited in many ways, the religious element there had steadily carried those nations forward. The battle for human rights was finally fought on a Christian plane. Unbelief has written books, but it never lifted a million men into a united struggle. The power that urged the world forward came from Christianity. Mr. Channing has explained to us its origin. I look at its results, and they lead to the same conclusion. He claims to be Christian. So do I. The best part of the life of Europe may be traced to Christianity.

"The religious literature of Asia has been compared with the Christian Scriptures. The comparison is not just. That literature has many merits, and contains scattered sayings and precepts of great excellence; but there are heaps of chaff in that, and in the writings of the early Christian Fathers; none in the Gospels and Epistles. Of the mediæval writings, one half was useless. Of the boasted works of Confucius, seven tenths must be winnowed out, to find what the average reason of mankind would respect."[1]

One day, John Weiss spoke on "Heart in Religion," and contended that Jesus was effeminate. Whereupon Mr. Phillips said:

"You speculate as to whether Jesus was a masculine character. Look at the men who have learned of Him most closely, —at Paul and Luther and Wesley. Were they effeminate? yet the disciple is but a faint reflection of his Master. The character from which came the force which has been doing battle ever since with wrong and falsehood and error was nothing less than masculine; but sentiment is the toughest thing in the world,—nothing else is iron."[2]

The Rev. Dr. Hedge punctuated a session with an essay on "Spinoza," "who," he said, "supposes a single and a whole substance, comprising all

---

[1] "Reminiscences of the Radical Club," pp. 76, 77.
[2] *Ib.*, pp. 147, 148.

that is, and of which all phenomena, all finite substances, are modes. Therefore he is said to have turned the devil out of the world."

Wendell Phillips hereupon "protested against our judgment of men by their theories. Theoretically Calvinism dispenses with works; but where do we find a higher standard of morals or better works than among the Calvinists? While human nature is capable of a feeling of remorse—as if, having a will, one might have done right and had done wrong —we shall not be able to put aside a sense of personal responsibility, or to turn the devil out of doors. Spinoza gives no theory which explains away the fact of suffering, and he had seen suffering which he felt sure was unmitigated evil."[1]

Once "Quakerism" was under consideration. Mr. Phillips said:

"Quakerism showed the limitations of human nature. A religious genius arises, and bears the precise testimony needed by the world at that time; but if he tries to organize or perpetuate himself, he fails. George Fox was a great religious genius. William Penn was a trimmer, who, if he had lived in New England in our time, would have been a dough-face.

"The decline of Quakerism began early. Josiah Foster in that denomination was a pope. Elizabeth Fry was a noble woman; but in religion was a narrow-minded bigot, who would not stay in the house with Lucretia Mott because the latter did not believe in the Trinity. George Fox was motion. When he ceased to move Quakerism, it fell back. It has not continued the aggressive attitude which he took. Quakerism has taken care of its own poor, but has never combated pauperism in the community at large.

"Fox shows us how little we owe to colleges. The great religious ideas of modern Europe all came from the people. In-

---

[1] "Reminiscences of the Radical Club," p. 160.

tellect led by scholars opposes progress. If Fox were here among us, he would be as radical now as he was then, and would be again imprisoned as a disturber of society." [1]

Oliver Wendell Holmes, on a certain morning, read an essay on "Jonathan Edwards," dwelling with emphasis upon that theologian's tenet of "infant damnation" as the key to his system.

The Rev. Dr. Bartol, who was in the chair, called on Mr. Phillips, who remarked :

"The picture drawn by Dr. Holmes, though truthful and accurate so far as it goes, cannot be full or complete. As a whole, it cannot be just to Edwards : there must be other sides, which would soften and redeem it ; other doctrines, that explain and fill out the full religious life and character, and justify the profound and loving respect our fathers had for him. Else how can we account for the great fact of New England, which is the outcome of his and similar pulpits ?

"No one doubts that a large majority of the New England pulpits, one hundred years ago, sympathized with, and sustained, Edwards. These horrible doctrines, which Dr. Holmes shocked us with, were not Edwards's individual and singular views, but the common faith of New England. Now, religion and theological doctrines are great factors in forming character. If the pulpit of New England taught only, or mainly, these hateful, narrow, inhuman, and degrading doctrines,—if such was the *character* of its teaching,—whence came this generous, public-spirited, energetic, hopeful, broad, humane, self-respectful, independent, and free-thought New England, ready for every good work, and willing for every necessary sacrifice ?

"We must have a theory broad enough to cover all the facts. It used to be said, that 'He who makes religion twelve, and the world thirteen, is no true New Englander.' His religion was three quarters of a Yankee. What you gentlemen here call 'free religion' and 'liberal Christianity' is of very recent growth, and of still very narrow influence. But character is of slow growth. Any theory which narrows and degrades the New

---

[1] " Reminiscences of the Radical Club," pp. 178, 179.

England pulpit of the eighteenth century fails to account for the community which grew up under it."

To one who suggested as an explanation that our fathers never really believed such doctrines, Mr. Phillips replied :

"It will hardly do to maintain that the hard-headed and practical Yankee, so keen and ready witted in affairs, so free and bold in civil life, the world's intellectual pioneer, did not know or understand what he believed, in—to him—the most important matter of all, his religion. Four generations passed over the stage, and left us this Commonwealth, their creation,—sober, painstaking, serious, earnest men. We cannot accept the theory which represents their religion as carelessly taken up, loosely held, and only half understood. Great jurists, practical statesmen, profound scholars, liberal founders of academy, college, and hospital, boldly searching the world over for means to perfect institutions on which the world now models itself,—were these minds crippled by absurd dogmas, worldlings without faith, or hypocrites afraid to avow their real belief? True philosophy never accepts such theories to explain history. It is more natural and philosophical to suppose that the sketch we have listened to, admirable as it is, has not given all the sides of the picture."

Dr. Bartol suggested that Edwards's parish repudiated him : after twenty years listening to him, they voted against him ten to one.

"Mr. Phillips replied, 'That argument proves too much. We have just exhausted language in praising the eminent Christian spirit and untold influence of Dr. W. E. Channing. But we all know that, after Channing had preached twenty years to men who idolized him, they mobbed him for his Anti-Slavery ideas, and refused him the use of his own church for the funeral services of the Abolitionist Follen, Channing's most intimate and valued friend. Channing failed as thoroughly, forty years ago, in teaching his church justice and humanity, as Edwards did, a hundred years ago, in bringing his hearers to relish the idea of infant damnation. It will not do for Unitarians in

Boston to throw that Northampton vote in Edwards's face. Northampton never mobbed Edwards for his infant damnation, as Boston did Channing for his Anti-Slavery, in Faneuil Hall.'"[1]

These are, of course, disjointed utterances, the *disjecta membra* of running discussion. But they indicate Mr. Phillips's views. It was well understood, among his friends, that he believed in the orthodox creed, in the orthodox sense.

---

[1] "Reminiscences of the Radical Club," pp. 371-73.

IX.

LYCEUM EXPERIENCES.

The life of one who makes a business of lecturing is not easy. The popular conception is to the contrary. We see a brilliantly lighted hall, a well-dressed audience, an orator, who, as he steps to the desk in faultless attire, is received with applause; and we think, "What a charming career!" The separation from home, the weary travel, the broken sleep, the annoying delays or interruptions, the discomfort of different and indifferent hotels, the exposure to dyspepsia from the mixed diet, the dealing with all kinds of men, the being out in all sorts of weather,—these are prosaic facts which are hardly offset by an hour's experience in that more or less attractive hall.

Mr. Phillips was a (peripatetic) philosopher, and extracted what of comfort and fun he might from it all, though conscious enough of the hardships of the life. Moving about as he did, he adapted and adjusted himself to it. He was a great tea-drinker—a *tea*-totaler; English breakfast tea being his favorite beverage. This he carried in his travelling-bag, and made or had made always and everywhere. He also made an inseparable companion of a large gray shawl, which he habitually spread between the sheets of the bed and wrapped himself in—thus avoiding the colds and rheumatism that come from northeast chambers and damp bed-clothes. Always abstemious, he was specially so before speaking, his usual supper at such times consisting of three raw eggs and as many cups of tea.

The orator's repertoire was encyclopædic. It embraced a vast list: Travel, like "Street Life in Europe;" science, like "The Lost Arts;" current politics, like "The Times," or "The Lesson of the Hour;" reform, like "Temperance," "Labor," "Woman," "The Indians," or, in earlier days, "Anti-Slavery;" controversy, like "Inferences from Froude;" political economy, like "Finance;" political philosophy, like "Agitation," which was for many years his favorite college commencement address; education, like "Training;" legal topics, like "Law and Lawyers," and "Courts and Jails;" foreign matters, like "The Irish Question;" lectures of polite interest, like "The Press;" biography, like "Toussaint," "O'Connell," "Sir Harry Vane," and "Sumner;" religion, like "Christianity a Battle, not a Dream." Perhaps no speaker of his day, or any day, treated a greater variety of topics, or with more even excellence, than Wendell Phillips; so that it was difficult to say in which department he was most at home. Such was his magnetism of manner and witchery of style that he could talk entertainingly about a broom-handle. The *speaker* was always interesting, whether the *subject* was or not. Men and women went to hear him without interest in the theme, often predetermined to dislike him, and sat breathless through the hour, and were amazed when he stopped to find that sixty or ninety minutes had elapsed.

Another peculiarity of his lectures was that he

never spoke merely to amuse. However light and
airy the music, there was always a sub-bass of moral
purpose. He was even more instructive than entertaining. No one ever had a higher conception of
obligation. In his view, influence was a trust, to be
exerted, in Lord Bacon's phrase, "for the glory of
God and the relief of man's estate."

As illustrative of his experiences, we open a budget of his letters, written on the road, at various
times, and to different friends.

To a young lady who was a kind of protégé, of
whom Mrs. Phillips was fond, and who, in his absence, ministered to his wife, thus making it possible
for him to be away,—he writes from Illinois, "in
the cars," and with a lead pencil:

"What can I do for you, in return for all your kindness to
Ann, my dear child? Thanks seem to me very poor pay. Ann
has spoken of how much you have been to her, in her letters.
It is a great comfort to me to have you able to be so much to
her. . . . The weather is dull—only two days since I left that I
have seen the sun. Rain, clouds, damp, mud, and grim heavens.
Still the audiences are large.

"Since my letter from Chicago, I have been shaken in omnibuses and hacks to a terrible degree. The mud has been fearful. And then the sudden quick freeze, and it is iron in deep
ruts—horrible to ride on. I rejoice that dear old Boston (how
I love those streets!) has no such inflictions."

To the same friend he gives a description of one
of the oil towns in Pennsylvania:

"Here I am in an oil town—mud over the hubs of the wheels;
literally, one horse was smothered in it: the queerest crowd of
men, with trousers tucked in their boots; no privacy—hotels all
one crowd—chambers mere thoroughfares,—everybody passing
through at will. And here I must be all Sunday, unless some
train will carry me on in the direction I wish,

"I find some of the Boston people. Everybody here is making money: the first place I have found where this is the case. Explanation—they have just struck oil!"

Again, the next month, he writes:

"It has been intensely cold out here. I have been in the smaller towns, and have had poor hotels and a generally hard time—rushed from one train to another, and puffed from station to station. . . . In eleven days of travel I have slept in a regular bed but four nights. Still I have been fortunate in filling every engagement, and 'Sumner' has been the favorite subject.

"In Milwaukee I was at the 'Plunkington,' where I had a fine suite of rooms,—bath, chamber, parlor with pier-glass ten feet high and five feet broad; all the rooms opening into a central hall. Nothing showy, but just comfortable."

From Philadelphia, in the midst of absorbing social and professional duties, he is thoughtful of a friend in Boston who has artistic tastes, and writes:

"DEAR ELEANOR: Don't fail to go and see the pictures Williams and Everett are exhibiting. They are eminently worth studying.

"Opposite, as you mount the stairs, is one of three gems. It is a weird, lonesome desert. Joseph and Mary are travelling across it. He has fallen asleep on the sand. Mary and the baby Christ are lying in the arms of the Sphinx, also asleep. It is very original. Above it is another by the same artist (*Merson*, I think: there is a scrap lying on the table telling you about him and it); a tall Egyptian girl—handsome; but the value of the canvas lies in the wonderful cloth. You can hardly believe her dress, Indian cotton, is not real. And her girdle, a Roman scarf, is so true; not too highly colored, but the thing itself. Then as you stand looking on your right is a picture of a dozen sailors, taking their 'nooning' sleep—wonderfully lifelike and happily grouped, and telling the story of labor and rest —admirable! It is worth an hour's study. Be sure and carry your glasses."

From Davenport, Ia., he writes the Rev. Mr. Sargent:

"DEAR JOHN : I wish I had your sunbeam pen and a dainty sheet of scented paper to write this letter with and on. Its import demands both.

"I, the traveller, the 'elderly gentleman,' have been—kissed! in Illinois! Put that in your pipe and smoke it, if you can without its choking your envious soul! Yes, kissed!! on a public platform, in front of a depot, the whole world envying me. Don't you wish you could be invited out to such a glorious land? 'Who did it?' do you ask. I am not sure your jealous heart deserves to know. . . . But I will be merciful. It was an old man of seventy-three years—a veteran Abolitionist, a lovely old saint. In the early days of the cause we used to kiss each other like the early Christians; and when he saw me he resumed the habit.

"Dare I, after such a communication, ask to be remembered to your wife and household?"

On January 1st, 1879, he writes to Mr. and Mrs. Sargent :

'The happiest of New Years to you both. May the sunniest blue sky overarch all your course. Health, peace, comfort and troops of friends be with you and 'round you! This is written on a snowy night, before a soft coal fire in Erie, Pa.

"Ask Ann to show you my description :—Six feet in my socks—sixty-eight years old—and with 'squirrel tails' for whiskers."

He writes to a gentleman in Boston who was thought to resemble him, with mock solemnity, as follows, from Cleveland, O. :

"DEAR SIR : You know how I once admired your modesty when you seemed pleased with being taken for me. Allow me to minister to your still further growth in that Christian grace.

"The other evening, before my lecture, a wild, frowzy, haggard, uncombed Yankee came to me and said : ' Often, sir, when I am sitting in a tavern, men will walk 'round me three or four times and then swoop down and say, "*Mr. Phillips, I believe!*" '

"Now, you remember enough of the mathematics they pounded into you at college to know that 'things that are equal to a third are equal to each other.' So you may comfort yourself with the reflection that you resemble my gaunt Yankee double!

"With sympathy,
"Your ' DOUBLE.''

Mr. Phillips was once invited to attend a large meeting in a country town, where several church choirs were to give a musical entertainment; and they wanted him to deliver an appropriate address. He declined, saying that he knew nothing of music, could not sing, and did not know one note from another. The Committee of Arrangements implored and insisted, again and again. At last, overborne by their entreaties, he amiably (he would have said weakly) consented; relying, probably, on some unforeseen inspiration. His faith was justified. As he sat in the pulpit, surrounded by clergymen whose choirs were discoursing sacred music, and wondering what he should say, he spied, among the singers, a colored man. Instantly the inspiration came. The moral influence of music, its power to bring into harmony human souls, was his theme.

The county papers praised his address, and his wife laughingly told him that he had obtained applause on false pretences.

An invitation to go to Vermont, to lecture upon *trees*, he could not be induced to accept. He said that he knew an oak from an elm; but that was about the extent of his knowledge upon that subject.

Mr. Phillips went one night to lecture in a country town. His subject had not been announced. The Committee asked him how many lectures he had brought. "All of them," was the answer, "here;" tapping his forehead. The Committee could not agree which they would have, and referred the decision to the audience. They, too, were divided, some preferring "Toussaint L'Ouverture," while others voted for the "Lost Arts." Finally an old man arose and said : " S'pose we have both." Then addressing the orator, who sat an amused listener, he continued, "Couldn't you give us both?" The humor of the situation, and the Yankee sharpness which prompted a request for two lectures for one fee, amused Mr. Phillips. He consented and gave both, winding from one to the other, though the subjects were totally unrelated, with such deftness that it was impossible to detect where they were joined, and they seemed parts of a connected whole. The audience retired greatly pleased, and feeling that they had got their money's worth !

Wherever he went autograph-hunters, album in hand, lay in wait for him. Mr. Phillips good-naturedly responded and (as he said) "made his mark" in a thousand places. His favorite autographs were ;

" Count that day lost
Whose slow descending sun
Sees from thy hand
No worthy action done."

To this he usually added :

"John Brown taught these lines to each of his children :

" ' Peace, if possible.
Justice at any rate.' "

Or this by Mrs. Ellen Sturgis Hooper :

" I slept and dreamed that life was beauty.
I waked—to find that life was duty.
Was then thy dream a shadowy lie?

> Toil on, sad heart, courageously,
> And thou shalt find that dream to be
> A noonday light, and truth to thee."

And these lines by Lowell, his favorite of all:

> " Truth forever on the scaffold,
> Wrong forever on the throne;
> But that scaffold sways the future,
> And behind the dim unknown
> Standeth God within the shadow,
> Keeping watch above his own."

With the possible exception of Mr. John B. Gough, Mr. Phillips travelled longer and more constantly than any other public speaker in America. Yet though always on the cars, in the steamboat, or, in earlier days, in the stage-coach, he never met with a serious accident—striking proof of the comparative safety of travel.

But—easy work? Ask those who know!

BOOK IV.

EVENING.

1880-1884.

I.

STILL CONTENDING.

IN the nature of the case, a self-governed community can permanently exist only on the basis of virtue and intelligence. Intemperance is the negation of both. Hence, like every thoughtful observer, Mr. Phillips, as we know, hated grog and grog-shops. Always active for temperance, as his life proceeded he redoubled his exertions. He was never too busy to come up to its help against the mighty. Thus, in February, 1880, he spoke in the State House, in Boston, against license:

"We don't care what a man does in his own parlor. He may drink his champagne or whiskey, and we don't care. But the moment a man opens his shop, and sells, we will interfere. The moment he undertakes to sell liquor, the State has an absolute and unlimited right to step in. The question demands the extreme use of this power. Every man familiar with the execution of the law knows that three fourths of crime is due to rum, which fills your prisons and almshouses, and burdens your gallows. In every case in Great Britain and this country where the rum-shops have been closed, freedom from crime, freedom from taxation, follows. The law is unchanging: no liquor, no crime; no liquor, no tax. Wherever the English blood flows, it would seem that the stimulus of the stomach had supreme power. There are over two hundred laws of this Legislature endeavoring to curb this devil, but every one knows that we have never succeeded in curbing it for a moment. All over the State you will find whole towns that have been sold for a rum-debt. There was no law in the city on that sunny afternoon in October when Garrison was trampled underfoot. So it is to-day. There has not been a mayor for forty years who would enforce a liquor law, and there won't be for forty years to come. There is not a Republican to-day who can look into another Republican's face, and think of the license law, without laughing. It is but the tub thrown to the whale. Prohibition means something. License has been tried in every shape. As long ago as 1837 the fifteen-gallon law was tried, and numerous other devices have been tried since; but we have never gained a point. Every man who walks the street, knows that, whenever we have had a prohibitory law, there has been an immediate change in the amount of drinking. Under the license law, sometimes less arrests are reported; but there is nothing so easy to make lie as figures. If a poor man get his wheel caught in a rut, there will seven policemen rush to his rescue; but let there be a drunken row, you won't find a policeman within forty rods. There are four thousand rum-shops in Boston; and taking these four thousand, and their four thousand best customers, you will have eight thousand votes,—a larger number than decides any election. You can't execute a license law."[1]

The Rev. Dr. Bartol, in the pulpit of the "West (Unitarian) Church," had preached a series of sermons in the spring of 1880, in which he advocated moderate drinking, declared it "untrue that total abstinence is requisite either for self-protection or for example's sake," and branded prohibition as "fanaticism." In a pointed letter, which was widely published, Mr. Phillips contrasted the teachings of Dr. Bartol with those of his predecessor, the Rev. Dr. Charles Lowell, father of the poet, James Russell Lowell, who had recommended total abstinence. He adds:

"I wonder if the present generation of West Church sheep are intelligent enough to perceive the difference between these

---

[1] *Vide* Boston *Commonwealth*, spring of 1880.

two pulpits. And, if so, which do they look up to with the better satisfaction?

"Some temperance-men are surprised and indignant at what they consider Dr. Bartol's prostitution of the Liberal pulpit. Such men forget the history of the temperance movement in Boston. When Rev. John Pierpont, forty years ago, returned from the East, he stated, in his pulpit in Hollis Street, that the first thing he saw there (in Smyrna, I believe) was a barrel of New England rum,—N. E. RUM burned into its head in large capitals. He made this the text for an earnest and eloquent agitation of the temperance question. The richest parishioners were rum-makers and rum-sellers : their rum was then stored, I think, in the very cellar of his church. I will not mention their names : their children continue the manufacture and the traffic. They set to work, by reducing his salary, refusing to pay one dollar of it, mortgaging the church for heavy debt, and by every means, to drive Pierpont from the pulpit. Finding this ineffectual, they announced their determination to buy up every pew that could be had, and thus, securing a majority of votes, dismiss him from his charge. *Francis Jackson*, a name always to be written by Bostonians in letters of gold, and the late venerable Samuel May, led the temperance-men in resisting this plot. They succeeded *in form ;* they vindicated Mr. Pierpont on every trial, leaving no smell of fire on his garments ; but they could not 'hold the fort.' *In fact*, rum triumphed. The wealthy rum-sellers of the city, whether attending in Hollis Street or not, bought pews there,—pews they never used, —and finally obliged Mr. Pierpont to agree to vacate his pulpit. During the seven years of this hard-fought battle between the penniless, eloquent, and devoted apostle in the pulpit and the wealthy rum-sellers in the pews, the Unitarian clergy of Suffolk County gave the public to understand that they renounced all ministerial fellowship with Mr. Pierpont, never exchanged with him, or extended to him professional recognition or courtesy. With two or three exceptions (Rev. J. T. Sargent, Dr. Gannett, and one or two others—Mr. Theodore Parker was not then preaching in Boston), all the Liberal clergy shut him from their pulpits. In their last letter to Mr. Pierpont, the rum-sellers taunted him with the fact that hardly one of his clerical brethren in Boston would exchange with him. And, in his letter of farewell to the Unitarian Association, Mr. Pierpont refers to this desertion, and affirms that this repudiation of him by his brother clergymen was *the special thing* which made it impossible for him to remain in the Hollis Street pulpit; and, further, his certain knowledge that this course of conduct toward him was adopted, on their part, *on purpose, and with the intention*, to drive him from that pulpit.

"Mr. Bartol, therefore, does not prostitute the Liberal pulpit; although one might sigh for the purer Gospel Lowell preached in the West Church. Judged by the example and conduct of the vast majority of the Liberal clergy of Boston for the last forty years, such sermons as Dr. Bartol has of late delivered are just the preaching for which the Liberal pulpit was created and is sustained.

"WENDELL PHILLIPS." [1]

The summer of 1880 Mr. and Mrs. Phillips spent in Princeton, Mass., whence he writes under date of June 23d:

"We are in comfortable quarters—view everywhere and over everything. . . . I laze and ride on horseback, exploring the drives. In one ride I can see Monadnock, twenty-five miles north, and the blue hills of Milton, forty-five east. The rest of the time I sleep. I weigh one hundred and seventy-five pounds, and don't feel as old as I am. . . . The town is full of famous men and fashionable women." [2]

To another correspondent, he gives, July 21st, an amusing description of affairs:

"Up in the clouds here, only coming down to the lower world once a week, a letter from you would be cheerful at any time. But now it is rain, rain, rain, rain—Wachusett has hardly taken off its night-cap for a week. In such dampness a dry letter from you (if that were possible) would be a blessing. Fancy, then, when on one of the most drenching of all afternoons, I sailed

---

[1] Quoted in Austin's "Life and Times of Wendell Phillips," pp. 326 *sqq.*

[2] Letter to Mrs. E. F. C. (MS.).

down to the village and swam back bringing your pleasant note in my teeth, as the Spanish fellow (Camoens, was it?) did his poems. . . . Did you or your wife put that good story in the journals of a fellow who offered to a young lady, and she said: 'You scare me!' Modestly sitting quiet the beau forbore to disturb her for ten minutes, when she cried out—'*Scare me again!*'

"I have kept awake thus far, but it is an effort, as the quiet is so profound. A passer-by is an event. The only noise ever made is by the hens. The only thing that ever happens is when we miss the cat.

"But we always keep awake at the sunsets—they are splendid!"[1]

These restful days and nights put the orator's body and mind in training for the fall and winter. And the work he did made it clear that his vigor was unimpaired. In fact, two of the most effective blows he ever dealt were struck straight from the shoulder in 1881.

The first was at the Rev. Dr. Howard Crosby, of New York City, the Goliath of moderate drinking, who in January went to Boston and gave a lecture which he called "A Calm View of Temperance," but which was "calm" only by that figure of speech which names a thing by its opposite—like the Abbé Huc's account of a pestiferous hole in China, sacred to dirt and tenanted by vermin, but called by Chinese pride, "The hotel of the Beatitudes." Dr. Crosby was then Chancellor of the New York University. He had long been a foremost authority in Greek grammar. He claimed that he had patented a system (high license) which would prove more effective for temperance in a twelvemonth than prohibition

---

[1] Letter to Rev. J. T. Sargent (MS.).

would or could in a lifetime. The doctor certainly created a sensation; and, aside from the reckless manner in which he flung about the roughest words in the dictionary, made as able a showing as his side allowed.

The clergy of Boston invited Mr. Phillips to reply; which he did on January 24th, in the Tremont Temple, before a vast assembly, with annihilating effect. The subject in controversy is, and promises to be, of living interest. Hence, a somewhat full synopsis of Mr. Phillips's remarks should seem important. *Imprimis*, the orator gave a careful and honest analysis of the New Yorker's arguments, which he answered *seriatim*. The points are indicated in the following extracts:

"Dr. Crosby says 'total abstinence is contrary to revealed religion.' What is total abstinence? It is abstaining from the use of intoxicating liquors as a beverage ourselves and agreeing with others to do so. How is this contrary to revealed religion? Can any one cite a text in the Bible or a principle laid down there which forbids it? Of course not; no one pretends that he can. But Dr. Crosby's argument is that Jesus drank intoxicating wine and allowed it to others. There is no proof that He ever did drink intoxicating wine. But let that pass, and suppose, for the sake of the argument, that He did. What then? To do what Jesus never did, or to refuse to do what He did—are such acts *necessarily* 'contrary to revealed religion'? Let us see.

"Jesus rode upon an 'ass and a colt, the foal of an ass.' We find it convenient to use railways. Are they 'contrary to revealed religion'? Jesus never married, neither did most of His apostles. Is marriage, therefore, 'contrary to revealed religion'? Jesus allowed a husband to put away his wife if she had committed adultery, he himself being judge and executioner. We forbid him to do it, and make him submit to jury trial and a judge's decision. Are such divorce laws, therefore, 'contrary to revealed religion'? Jesus said to the person guilty of adultery : 'Go and sin no more.' We send such sinners to the State prison. Are our laws punishing adultery, therefore, 'contrary to revealed religion'? There were no women at the Last Supper. We admit them to it. Is this 'contrary to revealed religion'? We see therefore that Christians may, in altered circumstances, do some things Jesus never actually did, and that their so doing does not necessarily contravene His example; nor, unless it violates the *principles* He taught, does it tend to undermine Christianity.

"Now, there is a class of biblical scholars and interpreters who do assert that, wherever wine is referred to in the Bible with approbation, it is unfermented wine. Of this class of men Dr. Crosby says, 'Their learned ignorance is splendid;' they are 'inventors of a theory of magnificent daring;' they 'use false texts' and 'deceptive arguments;' 'deal dishonestly with the Scriptures;' 'beg the question, and build on air;' their theory is a 'fable' born of 'falsehoods,' supported by 'Scripture twisting and riggling;' their arguments are 'cobwebs,' their zeal outstrips their judgment, and they plan to 'undermine the Bible.' Who are these daring, ridiculous, and illogical sinners? As I call them up in my memory, the first one who comes to me is Moses Stuart, of Andover, whose lifelong study of the Bible, and profound critical knowledge of both its languages, place him easily at the head of all American commentators. 'Moses Stuart's Scripture View of the Wine Question' was the ablest contribution, thirty years ago, to this claim about unfermented wine, and still holds its place unanswered and unanswerable. By his side stands Dr. Nott, the head of Union College, with the snows of ninety winters on his brow. Around them gather scores of scholars and divines, on both sides of the Atlantic. In our day Taylor Lewis gives to the American public, with his scholarly indorsement, the exhaustive commentary by Dr. Lees on every text in the Bible which speaks of wine,—a work of sound learning, widest research, and fairest argument. The ripe scholarship, long study of the Bible, and critical ability of these men, entitle them to be considered experts on this question. In a matter of Scripture interpretation, it would be empty compliment to say that Dr. Crosby is worthy to loose the latchet of their shoes. Now, the truth is, the only 'castle built in the air' in this matter, is the baseless idea that the temperance movement uses dishonest arguments, or wrests the Scripture, because it maintains, that, where the drinking of wine as an article of diet is mentioned in the Bible with approbation, *unfermented* wine is meant. The fact is, there are scholars of repute on both sides of the question. But we do not claim too much when we say that the weight of scholarly authority is on our side.

"It is, indeed, mournful to look back and notice how uniformly narrow-minded men, hide-bound in the bark of tradition, conventionalism, and prejudice, have thrown the Bible in the way of every forward step the race has ever made. When the Reformation claimed that every Christian man was his own priest and entitled to read the Bible for himself the cry was: 'You are resisting and undermining the Bible.'

"One of the best proofs that the Bible is indeed a divine book is, that it has outlived the misrepresentations of its narrow and bigoted friends.

"But look at it a moment. The New Testament is a small book, and may be read in an hour or two. It is not a code of laws, but the example of a life and a suggestion of principles. It would be idle to suppose that it could describe in detail, specifically meet every possible question, and solve every difficulty that the changing and broadening life of two or three thousand years might bring forth. The progressive spirit of each age has found in it just the inspiration and help it sought. But when timid, narrow, and short-sighted men claimed such exclusive ownership in it that they refused to their growing fellows the use of its broad, underlying principles, and thus demanded to have new wine put into old bottles, of course the bottles burst and their narrow-surface Bible became discredited; but the real Bible soared upward, and led the world onward still, as the soul rises to broader and higher life when the burden of a narrow and mortal body falls away.

"From the Bible Dr. Crosby passes to the great weapon of the temperance movement—the pledge. This he calls 'unmanly,' 'a strait-jacket;' says it kills self-respect and undermines all character.

"Hannah More said: 'We cannot expect perfection in any one; but we may demand consistency of every one.'

"It does not tend to show the sincerity of these critics of our cause when we find them objecting in us to what they themselves uniformly practice on all other occasions. If we continue to believe in their sincerity, it can only be at the expense of their intelligence. Dr. Crosby is, undoubtedly, a member of a church. Does he mean to say that, when his church demanded his signature to its creed and his pledge to obey its discipline, it asked what it was 'unmanly' in him to grant and what destroys an individual's character—that his submission to this is 'foregoing his reasoning,' 'sinking back to his nonage,' etc. ? Of course he assents to none of these things. He only objects to a temperance pledge, not to a church one.

"The husband pledges himself to his wife, and she to him, for life. Is the marriage ceremony, then, a curse, a hindrance to virtue and progress ?

"Society rests in all its transactions on the idea that a solemn promise, pledge, assertion strengthens and assures the act. The witness on the stand gives solemn promise to tell the truth ; the officer about to assume place for one year or ten, or for life, pledges his word and oath ; the grantor in a deed binds himself for all time by record ; churches, societies, universities accept funds on pledge to appropriate them to certain purposes and to no other—these and a score more of instances can be cited. In any final analysis all these rest on the same principle as the temperance pledge. No man ever denounced them as unmanly. I sent this month a legacy to a literary institution, on certain conditions, and received in return its pledge that the money should ever be sacredly used as directed. The doctor's principle would unsettle society ; and, if one proposed to apply it to any cause but temperance, practical men would quietly put him aside as out of his head. These cobweb theories, born of isolated cloister-life, do not bear exposure to the mid-day sun, or the rude winds of practical life. This is not a matter of theory. Thousands and tens of thousands attest the value of the pledge. It never degraded, it only lifted them to a higher life. We who never lost our clear eyesight or level balance over books, but who stand mixed up and jostled in daily life, hardly deem any man's sentimental and fastidious criticism of the pledge worth answering. Every active worker in the temperance cause can recall hundreds of instances where it has been a man's salvation.

"But our agitation of the drink question is 'bulldozing' and 'intimidation.' This is only an unmanly whine.

"What is the pulpit? Does it not take admitted truths and press them home on conscience? Or does it not seek to prove principles the listener does not admit, and then urge him to their practice? Does it not criticise, and affirm, and denounce, seeking to waken the indifferent, convince the doubting, and claim consistent action of all? Does it wait until the sinner acknowledges its principles before it denounces his action as a sin? By no means. Is church discipline visited only on those who see and confess their sins? Is it not used to rouse them to a sense of the principle they will not acknowledge, and hold them up to the rebuke and take from them the respect of their fellows? If our temperance agitation is 'intimidation,' then nine tenths of the land's pulpits are bulldozers and the other tenth is useless. What does the Bible say of those who prophesy smooth things, and whose order was Nathan obeying when he said, 'Thou art the man?'

"Dr. Crosby says it is false, our constant assertion that moderate drinking makes drunkards. Will he please tell us where, then, the drunkards come from? Certainly teetotalers do not recruit these swelling ranks. Will he please account for the million-times repeated story of the broken-hearted and despairing sot, or the reformed man, that 'moderate drinking lulled them to a false security until the chain was too strong for them to break?' Will he please explain that confession forced from old Sam Johnson, and repeated hundreds of times since by men of seemingly strong resolve, 'I can abstain: I can't be moderate?' Do not the Bible, the writers of fiction, the master dramatists of ancient and modern times, the philosopher, the moralist, the man of affairs,—do not all these bear witness how insidiously the habits of sensual indulgence creep on their victim until he wakes to find himself in chains of iron, his very will destroyed?

"But our movement is the delight of rum-sellers and the great manufacturer of drunkards. How is it, then, that anxious and terror-stricken rum-sellers assemble in conventions to denounce us and plan methods of resisting us? No such conventions were ever heard of or needed until the last twenty years. How is it that they mob our lecturers and break up our meetings? Was Dr. Crosby or any of his class ever mobbed by rum-sellers? How is it that, the moment we get one of the prohibitory laws, 'which delight rum-sellers,' passed, these delighted men form parties to defeat every man who voted for it, crowd the lobbies to repeal it, and never rest until, by threat or bribes, they have repealed it? If rum-sellers long and pray for the coming of the millennium of prohibition, why don't they all move down to Maine, and get as near to the desired heaven as they can? If rum-sellers delight in our total-abstinence labors, how ungrateful in them to allow their organs all over the world to misrepresent and deny what little success even Dr. Crosby allows we have had in Maine! They ought to chuckle over it and scatter the news far and wide. When Dr. Crosby has answered half these questions, we have some more difficulties to propound which trouble us, about the unaccountable freaks of these delighted rum-sellers, who, delighted as they are with our work, yet never can bear or praise the very men who, Dr. Crosby says, are constantly employed spending time and money in 'delighting' these unreasonable fellows.

"Dr. Crosby says that *we* are the cause of all the drunkenness, that the temperance movement is a failure, must be, and ought to be.

"I will prove that Christianity is a failure in the same way. The famous unbelievers, down from Voltaire, through Mill, to the last infidel critic, prove Christianity, by the same sort of argument, to be a failure and the cause of most of the evils that burden us. Exaggerate all the evil that exists, especially those vices that will never wholly die while human nature remains what it is; belittle and cast into shade all the progress that has been made; dwell with zest on the new forms of sin that each age contributes to the infamy of the race; keep your eyes firmly in the back of your head, and insist that there's nothing equal to what we had in old times—not even the snow-storms or the St. Michael pears—and the thing is done.

Before our movement began three-quarters of the farms of Massachusetts were sold under the hammer for rum-debts. You could not enter a public house in country or city, of the first-class or the smaller ones, except through a grog-shop. Their guests felt mean if they did not at dinner order some kind of wine, and often ordered it when they did not wish it. Now the grog-room is hidden from sight; men slink into it; and not more than one man in ten at the most fashionable hotels, and not one in fifty in common inns, orders wine at dinner. Then the sideboard of every well-to-do house was covered with liquors, and every guest was urged to drink; the omission to do which would have been held a gross neglect, if not an insult. No man was buried without a lavish use of liquor; no stage stopped without the traveller being thought mean if he did not help the house by taking a drink. Now one may travel hundreds of miles on rails which allow no liquor in their stations. Every farmer furnished drink to his men; famous doctors went drunk to their patients; the first lawyer in the Middle States was not singular when he held on by the rail in order to stand and argue, half-drunk, to the Supreme Court of the United States; rich men saw to it that every clergyman who attended a convention was plied with wine; and the preacher of the *concio ad clerum* was fed on brandy punch to place him on a more exhilarated level than his hearers. If a man caught sight of a grog-shop, he was as sure he had arrived in a Christian land as the shipwrecked sailor was when he caught sight of a gibbet. Dr. Crosby then had everybody, lay and clerical, on his side in construing the Bible; whereas now we are in a healthy majority.

"Even if the statistics showed that the amount of liquor consumed increased as fast as our population and wealth do—which they do not show, but just the contrary—that would not be sufficient evidence to prove that our movement has failed. The proper comparison is between what we were in 1820 and what *we should have been now* had not some beneficent agency arrested our downward progress. These evils, left to themselves, increase by no simple addition, but in cubic ratio.

"Does Dr. Crosby fancy this active movement and vast mass of fact, opinion, and testimony can exist without beneficial influence in an age ruled by brains? He does not, then, understand moral forces or his own times. When, twenty-five years ago, Frederick Douglass was painting the Anti-Slavery movement as a failure unless we would load our guns, Sojourner Truth asked: 'Frederick, is God dead?' When I see the doctor's unbelief in the efficacy of the moral power and the weight of this mass of conviction, I am tempted to ask him: 'Is your God dead?'

"Dr. Crosby closes by stating his plan and panacea. It is a regulated license. I will not delay you by criticising his or any other license plan. The statute books in forty States are filled with the abortions of thousands of license laws that were never executed, and most of them were never intended to be. We have as good a license-law in this State as was ever devised; and yet it leaves such an amount of defiant, unblushing grog-selling as discourages Dr. Crosby, and leads him to think nothing has been done at all. His own city, with license laws, is yet so ruled and plundered by rum, that timid statesmen advise giving up republicanism, and borrowing a leaf from Bismarck to help us. License has been tried under the most favorable circumstances, and with the best backing for centuries,—ten or twelve, at least. Yet Dr. Crosby stands confounded before the result. We have never been allowed to try prohibition except in one State, and in some small circuits. Wherever it has been tried, it has succeeded. Friends who know, claim this: enemies who have been for a dozen years ruining teeth by biting files, confess it by their lack of argument, and lack of facts except when they invent them." [1]

The second tremendous blow of our athlete of reform was dealt at Harvard College,—a blow between the eyes. He received an invitation to deliver the centennial Phi Beta Kappa oration in the summer of 1881. He accepted, and on June 30th spoke on "The Scholar in a Republic," with the official, professional, and mercantile culture of thirty States for an audience. "It was," remarks Mr. Higginson, who was present, "the tardy recognition of him by his own college and his own literary society, and proved to be, in some respects, the most remarkable effort of his life. He never seemed more at his ease, more colloquial, and more extemporaneous; and he

---

[1] *Vide* Phillips's "Review of Dr. Crosby's 'Calm View of Temperance.'" Published by National Temperance Society. New York, 1881, *passim*.

held an unwilling audience spellbound, while bating absolutely nothing of his radicalism. Many a respectable lawyer and divine felt his blood run cold, the next day, when he found that the fascinating orator whom he had applauded to the echo had really made the assassination of an emperor seem as trivial as the doom of a mosquito."[1]

The Rev. James Freeman Clarke, an alumnus of Harvard, and an auditor, has also left an account of the event, which we transcribe:

"When I knew that Wendell Phillips was to give the Phi Beta Kappa oration at Cambridge, I was very curious to know what course he would take. I said, 'He has two opportunities, neither of which he has ever had before. He has always spoken to the people. Now he is invited to address scholars. He has an opportunity to deliver a grand academic discourse, and to show, that, when he chooses to do it, he can be the peer of Everett or Sumner on their own platform of high culture. He can leave behind personalities, forget for the hour his hatreds and enmities, and meet all his old opponents peacefully, in the still air of delightful studies. This is an opportunity he has never had before, and probably will never have again.'

"'But there is another and different opportunity now offered him. Now, for the first and only time, he will have face to face before him the representatives of that Cambridge culture which has had little sympathy with his past labors. He can tell them how backward they were in the old Anti-Slavery contest, and how reluctant to take part in any later reforms. If he has been bitter before, he can be ten times as bitter now. He can make this the day of judgment for the sins of half a century. This opportunity, also, is unique. It will never come again. Can he resist this temptation, or not?'

"It never occurred to me that he would accept and use both opportunities, but he did so. He gave an oration of great power and beauty, full of strong thoughts and happy illustrations, not

---

[1] Higginson's obituary notice, pp. 14, 15.

unworthy of any university platform or academic scholar. It was nearly, though not wholly, free from personalities ; but it was also one long rebuke for the recreant scholarship of Cambridge. It arraigned and condemned all scholarship as essentially timid, selfish, and unheroic. It gave a list of the leading reforms of the last forty years, in none of which Cambridge scholarship had taken any share,—Anti-Slavery, Woman's Rights, the wrongs of Ireland, reform in criminal legislation, — and wound up the catalogue by denouncing as disgusting cant all condemnation of Russian Nihilism and its methods. He admitted, that, in a land where speech and the press are free, recourse to assassination is criminal, but defended 'dynamite and the dagger' as the only methods of reform open in Russia."[1]

There had been two previous Phi Beta Kappa orations at Cambridge which were epoch-making— Everett's, in 1824, when he apostrophized Lafayette, who was on the platform ; and Emerson's, in 1837, which turned out to be an unlooked-for excursion into untrodden domains of thought. Phillips's was the highest water-mark in style and expression— " the ocean-wave kissing the Alps."[2]

"Well," was his comment, "I suppose they wanted me to bring *myself.*"

In the course of his Phi Beta Kappa address, Mr. Phillips made a reference to Civil Service Reform which called forth criticism, and which impelled him to a further statement of his views. Said he :

"For George William Curtis, the leader of the Civil Service Reform, I have the most sincere respect. His place as statesman, scholar, and reformer is such, and so universally recog-

---

[1] Quoted in Austin's "Life," pp. 342, 343.
[2] *Vide* the full text of the address in the Appendix.

nized, that praise from me would be almost impertinence. But a large proportion of the party in New York, and a still larger proportion of its adherents in Massachusetts, justify all I have said of it and them.

"My plan of Civil Service Reform would be the opposite of what they propose. I should seek a remedy for the evils they describe in a wholly different direction from theirs,—in fearless recourse to a further extension of the democratic principles of our institutions.

"Let each district choose its own postmaster and Custom-House officials. This course would appeal to the best sense and sober second thought of each district. Responsibility would purify and elevate the masses, while Government would be relieved from that mass of patronage which debauches it.

"Their plan is impracticable, and ought to be; for it contravenes the fundamental idea of our institutions, and contemplates a coterie of men kept long in office,—largely independent of the people,—a miniature aristocracy, filled with a dangerous *esprit de corps*. The Liberal party in England has long felt the dead-weight and obstructive influence of such a class. The worst element at Washington in 1861, the one that hated Lincoln most bitterly, and gave him the most trouble,—the one that resisted the new order of things most angrily and obstinately, and put the safety of the city into most serious peril,—was the body of old office-holders, poisoned with length of official life, scoffing at the people as intrusive intermeddlers; men in whom something like a fixed tenure of office had killed all sympathy with the democratic tendency of our system.

"Some might fear that our Government could not be carried on without this patronage.

"Hamilton is quoted as saying, 'Purge the British Government of its corruption, and give to its popular branch equality of representation, and it would become an *impracticable* government.'

"The British Government has been pretty well purged, and its popular branch comes now very near to equality of representation. Yet, spite of Hamilton's prophecy, the machine still works, and works better and better for every successive measure of such purification and reform.

"So our Government, relieved of the weight of this debasing

patronage, would disappoint the sullen forebodings of Tory misgiving, and rise to nobler action." [1]

There was another part of the world, tumultuous as America had been in the Anti-Slavery days, where the orator was desired to "bring himself." In grateful recognition of his services to Ireland, which were marked through the Land League campaign, when he took the stump and uttered words that echoed across the ocean and inspired Erin,— Mr. Phillips, a few months after the Cambridge triumph, received the following call:

OFFICE OF THE "IRISH WORLD,"
NEW YORK, Oct. 31, 1881.

"*Wendell Phillips, Boston.*

"I have just received the following cable from Mr. Egan, Land League Treasurer, Paris:

"'Will Wendell Phillips come to Ireland, to advocate No Rent during the suspension of Constitutional liberties? The League will pay all expenses. Reply.

'PATRICK EGAN.'

"I beg you, Mr. Phillips, to hearken to this as an inspiration and a call from God Himself. You are the one man in America fitted for the glorious mission. All Ireland will rise to its feet to bless and cheer you. Never did Cæsar receive such an ovation. Civilization will look on in admiring wonder. The good which your heroic act will effect is incalculable; and your name, consecrated in the memory of a grateful people, will live while time endures.

"PATRICK FORD." [2]

Appreciating the compliment, but unable to go, he penned a declination:

---

[1] "Scholar in a Republic." Notes: Note 2.
[2] *Vide* the *Irish World*, November, 1881.

"BOSTON, Nov. 2, 1881.

Mr. Patrick Ford:

"SIR : I receive with humility the summons you send me, well knowing, that, in any circumstances, I could not do a tenth part of what your partiality makes you think I could.

"But, in this case, humanity, constitutional government, and civilization itself claim his best service of every man.

"Ireland to-day leads the van in the struggle for right, justice, and freedom.

"England has forfeited her right to rule, if she ever had any, by a three hundred years' exhibition of her unfitness and inability to do so. The failure is confessed by all her statesmen of both parties for the last hundred years.

"Discontent, poverty, famine, and death are her accusers.

"Her rulers cannot plead ignorance. Their own shameless confessions, repeated over and over again, admit that England's rule has been unjust, selfish, and cruel. She has planned that Ireland should starve, hoping she would then be too weak to resist.

"To-day, while her Government tramples under foot every principle in English history that makes men honor it, the world waits in sure and glad expectation of her defeat, confident that her overthrow will be the triumph of right, justice, and civilization.

"The three thousand miles of ocean that separate us from her shores, enable us to judge her course as dispassionately as posterity will judge it a hundred years hence ; and we see the mad blunders of her Government as posterity will see them.

"Let Ireland only persevere, and her victory is certain.

"With unbroken front, let her assault despotism in its central point, RENT. Ireland owes none to-day,—certainly not to a class whose government is the prison and the bayonet.

"How cheerfully would I do my part ! How gladly would I share in the honors of such a struggle ! But the state of my health obliges me to give up public speaking. I can only bid you God-speed, and pray for your speedy and complete success.

"Yours very respectfully,

"WENDELL PHILLIPS."

The orator was the most modest of men. A

"fuss" with himself in the middle of it he specially disliked. Learning that his admirers proposed to celebrate his approaching seventieth birthday, he hastened to nip the project in the bud. Writing on the day following the date of his letter to Mr. Ford, to one who was at the headquarters of the movement, he said :

"Please understand that any such thing would be *very disagreeable* to me. I particularly request that you have no hand in it. And should you hear of any one intending such a notice of the day, please let him understand my wishes." [1]

His feeling was evidently like that of Washington, when, as he stood before the surrendering army of Cornwallis, some of the Continental troops began to cheer as that officer came forward to yield his sword. The noble Virginian turned and said : "Let posterity cheer for us." [2] Posterity may be confidently relied upon to do it in both cases.

---

[1] Letter to Mrs. E. F. C. (MS.). [2] Phillips's "Speeches," p. 68 *sy*.

II.

LENGTHENING SHADOWS.

THE perennial popularity of Wendell Phillips and his surprising mental and physical strength in the evening of his life, may be measured by three tests: the continuous demand for his services; the undiminished size of his audiences; and his activity. He neither looked nor acted like an old man. That he sometimes wearied of his peripatetic routine is true, as witness these lines written from Albany, N. Y., in December, 1881: " I work hard, and battle with snow-storms and drifts as I used to do ten years ago, and hoped I shouldn't now. But must be what must." [1]

When the spring of 1882 opened, he found himself, to his unutterable grief, forced to leave the house in which he had resided since 1841—the only home he had known since he left his mother's roof, the scene of his whole married life, a spot steeped in the memories and associations of more than forty years. The city had long projected the widening of the adjacent Harrison Avenue, an improvement which would necessitate the demolition of No. 26 Essex Street. He and his wife (for Mrs. Phillips was as reluctant to move as her husband) had postponed the evil day by influence with the authorities. Both desired to die where they had lived. He predicted his own

---

[1] Letter to Mrs. E. F. C. (MS.).

demise in the near future, and announced that he would not reach the age of seventy-four.[1] Nevertheless, in 1882 the city decided that the contemplated change could no longer wait.

With a heavy heart, the apostle of progress, now made, by the irony of fate, himself a victim of improvement, set out to find a new house. In the neighborhood he discovered a house much like the old one. It was in Common Street,—No. 37. Hither he moved. No easy task. For there in Essex Street was the accumulation of a lifetime. With many a sigh, the exiled couple collected, assorted, and carted away their *lares et penates*. Their effort was to reproduce the Essex Street interior here in Common Street. The wife's apartment bore a singularly close resemblance to the former chamber. To make it more homelike, the thoughtful husband transferred thither the old mantel and open grate, and the furniture was similarly arranged. But they never felt quite at home again. Their friends noted their homesickness with sorrow. It was widely thought that Boston might have let one more of her streets stay crooked and narrow a little longer as a graceful compliment to her most illustrious son. But the Puritan capital did not awake until after he was gone to recognize the value of the Puritan orator.

Mr. Phillips walked one day with a friend to the familiar corner and stood looking at the spot—the old house gone. "It was hard," said he, "that the city would not let me stay till the end in my home for forty years!" Then, after a pause, he turned

---

[1] So he told ex-Mayor Samuel A. Green and others.

with the remark: "It is no matter. I am almost through with it all."[1]

In a letter addressed to his friend Aaron M. Powell, of New York City, and dated August 16th, 1882, he writes:

"You ought to know what I did with my Anti-Slavery library. Did I tell you? I sent a complete file of the *Standard*, from 1840 to 1872, to Mr. Spofford, for the Congressional Library; also three volumes of the *Liberator* to fill up his gaps, which are now not many. I sent the Astor Library a complete file of the *Liberator*. It had all the *Standards*. I gave the Boston Public Library a complete file of the *Standard* (it had almost perfect *Liberator*); and all my reports, pamphlets, and surplus numbers of newspapers, bound and unbound, *Emancipators* and *Heralds of Freedom*, they agreeing to distribute. So you see I have acted as my own executor, to get rid of twenty-five hundred volumes."

The fall and winter of 1882–83 were devoted by Mr. Phillips to lecturing, as usual—his last Lyceum round. He prepared and delivered in Boston, New York, Philadelphia, and elsewhere, a new lecture, "The Yardstick," in which he argued the question of Capital and Labor, arraigned the existing parties as representing dead issues, and called Christians and patriots to organize on a platform of to-day.

At the end of the season he went with Mrs. Phillips to Belmont, near by, for the summer. From this village he wrote, on August 17th, 1883, a description of his environment:

"Nothing is changed here. We plod on as usual. . . . I go in town twice a week and sometimes thrice; reading and dozing the other days. Boston is crowded notwithstanding our ab-

---

[1] Recollections of Mrs. E. F. C. (MS.).

sence! I don't think I could live all the time in the country. It would make me a Rip Van Winkle in ten months."

On the last day of August he informs the same friend of his sudden return to town :

"We are at 37 Common Street. Ann was so uncomfortable that we were obliged to run in ; and here we are—dust, noise, heat!

"Ann says, and I repeat with emphasis, don't bring back an owl. Cruel, as he must be caged, and for an Abolitionist it is a gross violation of principle.

"Then, only silly women, with no brains, have animal pets like that. There's enough to do and care for in this world without saddling ourselves with such fooleries. Forgive plain speech. I only care for you, and am
"Affectionately,
"WENDELL PHILLIPS." [2]

Toward the end of 1883, the surviving founders of the American Anti-Slavery Society, together with later members, arranged to hold a meeting in Philadelphia to commemorate the fiftieth anniversary of its organization. The Agitator was urgently invited. Circumstances were such that he could not leave home, and he sent a letter to Mr. Robert Purvis, Chairman of the Committee of Arrangements. It is important as outlining his position in these late moments of his life, and containing his advice (final, as it proved) to his ancient co-workers :

"BOSTON, December 3, 1883.

"MY DEAR PURVIS : I am very sorry that I cannot be with you to-morrow.

"You know I was not one of the founders of the American Anti-Slavery Society. But I should be glad to meet the few who survive of that devoted band, congratulate them on the marvel-

---

[1] Written to Mrs. E. F. C. (MS.).   [2] *Ib.*

lous work they began, and join them in rejoicing that so many of their comrades lived to see the completion and triumph of their movement. I think that agitation did more to reveal the workings of republican institutions, and awaken men to their dangers and duties as citizens, than any previous event in our history.

"As the Latin proverb says in Carlyle's translation, 'Every road leads to the end of the world,' so this movement touched in its progress all the great questions of the age,—right of private judgment, place of the Bible, questions of race and sex, the tenure of property, the relations of citizens and law, and of capitalist to labor, with many others. With all these we were brought face to face, and many of them we were forced to discuss at full length. Now that the first great purpose of the movement is accomplished, it seems wasteful that the skill and experience got from thirty years of such labor and agitation should be lost.

"The freedmen still need the protection of a vigilant public opinion, and will need it for the rest of this generation. Labor and its kindred question, Finance, claim our aid in the name of that same humanity and justice which originally stirred us. We always proclaimed that it was not only the protection of the negro we aimed at, but that we sought to establish a principle, the rights of human nature.

"In that view it seems to me we are narrow and wanting if we do not contribute the energy and skill which so many years have aroused and created, to those questions which flow so naturally out of ours and belong to the same great brotherhood. Let it not be said that the old Abolitionist stopped with the negro, and was never able to see that the same principles he had advocated at such cost claimed his utmost effort to protect all labor, white and black, and to further the discussion of every claim of down-trodden humanity. Let it be seen that our experience made us not merely Abolitionists, but philanthropists.

"Yours faithfully,

"WENDELL PHILLIPS." [1]

Mr. R. Purvis.

---

[1] *Vide* Commemorative Pamphlet of the Proceedings. Philadelphia, 1884.

It will be observed that the letter to Philadelphia bears the date of December 3d. On the 26th of the month, the orator went to the "Old South" Church, in Boston, to take part in the exercises at the unveiling of Anne Whitney's statue of Harriet Martineau—his personal friend. Mrs. Mary A. Livermore presided. William Lloyd Garrison, Jr., spoke, and was followed by Mr. Phillips. As the well-known and honored face and form appeared, the assembly, largely composed of ladies, broke into hearty applause:

"Webster once said, that 'In war there are no Sundays.' So in moral questions there are no nations. Intellect and morals transcend all limits. When a moral issue is stirred, then there is no American, no German. We are all men and women. And that is the reason why I think we should indorse this memorial of the city to Harriet Martineau, because her service transcends nationality. There would be nothing inappropriate if we raised a memorial to Wickliffe, or if the common-school system of New England raised a memorial to Calvin; for they rendered the greatest of services. So with Harriet Martineau, we might fairly render a monument to the grandest woman of her day, we, the heirs of the same language, and one in the same civilization; for steam and the telegraph have made, not many nations, but one, in perfect unity in the world of thought, purpose, and intellect. And there could be no fault found with thus recognizing this counsellor of princes, and adviser of ministers, this woman who has done more for beneficial changes in the English world than any ten men in Great Britain. In an epoch fertile of great genius among women, it may be said of Miss Martineau, that she was the peer of the noblest, and that her influence on the progress of the age was more than equal to that of all the others combined. She has the great honor of having always seen the truth one generation ahead; and so consistent was she, so keen of insight, that there is no need of going back to explain by circumstances in order to justify the actions of her life. This can hardly be said of any great Englishman, even by his admirers. We place the statue here in Boston because she has made herself an American. She passed through this city on the very day when Mr. Garrison was mobbed on State Street. Her friends feared to tell her the truth when she asked what the immense crowd were doing, and dissimulated by saying it was post-time, and the throng were hurrying to the office for mail. Afterward, when she heard of the mob and its action, horror-struck, she turned to her host, the honored president of a neighboring university; and even he was American enough to assure her that no harm could come from such a scene; said it was not a mob, it was a collection or gathering. Harriet Martineau had been welcomed all over America. She had been received by Calhoun in South Carolina, the Chief Justice of Virginia had welcomed her at his mansion. But she went through the South concealing no repugnance, making her obeisance to no idol. She never bowed anywhere to the aristocracy of accident. This brave head and heart held its own throughout that journey. She came here to gain a personal knowledge of the Abolitionists, and her first experience was with the mob on State Street. Of course she expressed all the horror which a gallant soul would feel. You may speak of the magnanimity and courage of Harriet Martineau; but the first element is her rectitude of purpose, by which was born that true instinct which saw through all things. We have had Englishmen come here, who were clear-sighted enough to say true words after they returned home; but this was a woman who was welcomed by crowds in the South, and about whom a glamor was thrown to prevent her from seeing the truth. It is easy to be independent when all behind you agree with you, but the difficulty comes when nine hundred and ninety-nine of your friends think you wrong. Then it is the brave soul who stands up, one among a thousand, but remembering that one with God makes a majority. This was Harriet Martineau. She was surrounded by doctors of divinity, who were hedging her about with their theories and beliefs. What do some of these later travellers who have been here know of the real New England, when they have been seated in sealed houses, and gorged with the glittering banquets of social societies? Harriet Martineau, instead of lingering in the camps of the Philistines, could, with courage, declare, 'I'll go among the Abolitionists, and see for myself.' Shortly after the time of the State Street mob, she came to Cambridge ; and her hosts there begged her not to put her hand into their quarrels. The Abolitionists held a meeting there. The only hall of that day open to them was owned by infidels. Think of that, ye friends of Christianity. And yet the infidelity of that day is the Christianity of to-day. To this meeting in this hall Miss Martineau went to express her entire sympathy with the occasion. As a result of her words and deeds, such was the lawlessness of that time, she had to turn back from her intended journey to the West, and was assured that she would be lynched if she dared set foot in Ohio. She gave up her journey, but not her principles.

"Harriet Martineau saw, not merely the question of free speech, but the grandeur of the great movement just then opened. This great movement is second only to the Reformation in the history of the English and the German race. In time to come, when the grandeur of this movement is set forth in history, you will see its proportions and beneficial results. Harriet Martineau saw it fifty years ago, and after that she was one of us. She was always the friend of the poor. Prisoner, slave, wage-serf, worn-out by toil in the mill, no matter who the sufferer, there was always one person who could influence Tory and Liberal to listen. Americans, I ask you to welcome to Boston this statue of Harriet Martineau, because she was the greatest American Abolitionist. We want our children to see the woman who came to observe, and remained to work, and, having once put her hand to the plough, persevered until she was allowed to live where the pæan of the emancipated four millions went up to heaven, showing the attainment of her great desire." [1]

On this occasion it was universally remarked that Mr. Phillips seemed well and strong. The graceful dignity of posture, the finished elocution, the silvery music of the voice, the sparing yet significant gesture, the keen eye, the noble expression of countenance—not one of the familiar features of his oratory

---

[1] Boston *Daily Advertiser*, December 4th, 1883.

was missed. And the audience retired in the hope and with the expectation of hearing him for years to come. No one imagined it to be the last public appearance of Wendell Phillips.

It was.

III.

SUNDOWN.

ON New Year's morning of 1884, the Rev. Dr. Sheldon Jackson, who was interested in the establishment of education in Alaska, called at the house in Common Street to solicit the aid of the people's Tribune in bringing his project to the attention of Congress. Mr. Phillips expressed his sympathy, and at once sat down and wrote as follows to the Hon. Patrick Collins, a representative from Massachusetts at Washington—the last words of public concern traced by his pen :

"MY DEAR SIR : Is it wholly in order to write a Congressman a Happy New Year?

"Well, if it is not, excuse my ignorance of parliamentary customs.

"I want to ask a favor. There will come before Congress some measure toward the creation of a territorial government in Alaska, which, you will hardly believe, is without government, court, or schools, though we have possessed it since 1867, and we found all those there when Russia surrendered it to us ; and though Alaska yields some three hundred thousand dollars annually—a fifth part of which sum would pay all the cost of schools, court, governor, etc.

"The Rev. Dr. Sheldon Jackson, who is a missionary there, will introduce himself to you ; and I ask for him and his cause your favorable consideration.

"Yours cordially,
"WENDELL PHILLIPS." [1]

---

[1] *Vide* Boston *Herald*. Phillips memorial edition, February 4th, 1884.

The serious illness of Mrs. Phillips imprisoned her husband through January. He hardly left her room. On the 26th inst. Mr. Phillips was suddenly seized with agony of the chest. Ominous symptom! His father and three of his brothers had died after similar warning. The family physician, Dr. David Thayer, was instantly summoned. He made a thorough examination and confirmed the worst fears of the household. It was a case of angina pectoris. The remedies administered brought temporary relief. Mr. Phillips lay on a lounge, self-possessed and smiling. This occurred in the forenoon.

In the afternoon an intimate friend called and conversed with him at length. "I found him," she says, "as serene as ever he was, although Dr. Thayer had just informed him that the morning's pain was a death-warrant. I asked him about his faith. He said it was absolute. We then spoke of Christ, in whom he believed as divine. Quoting the words which Riehm, in his biography of Hupfeld, puts into the mouth of that eminent Semitic scholar and critic, he said: 'I find the whole history of humanity before Him and after Him points to Him, and finds in Him its centre and its solution. His whole conduct, His deeds, His words have a supernatural character, being altogether inexplicable from human relations and human means. I feel that here there is something more than man.' When I raised objections, he told me, in substance, that nothing but the Spirit of Christ had enabled him to suffer and endure what he had. 'Then you have no doubt about a future life?' I asked. His answer was in these words: 'I am as sure of it as I am that there will be a to-morrow.'"[1]

---
[1] Recollections of Mrs. E. F. Crosby (MS.).

On Sunday the pain returned. He suffered terribly. The physician reappeared, and the ailment seemed to yield to his treatment. The patient brightened on Monday. On Tuesday he was quite himself. All felt hopeful. When Wednesday dawned there was a relapse. Through that day and the next he lay in agony. The doctor, surrounded by medical assistants, remained in constant attendance. On Friday relief came, but only for a space. The paroxysms returned with redoubled terror. Mr. Phillips fainted, and was revived with difficulty. As the pain continued anæsthetics were administered. On Saturday he was again relieved. When Dr. Thayer, at his request, told him the probable result, he smiled and said :

"I have no fear of death. I have long foreseen it. My only regret is for poor Ann. I had hoped to close her eyes before mine were shut."

He lay quietly through the day in the full possession of his faculties. His chief anxiety was for "Ann"—his care for half a century; for her, and lest he should give unnecessary trouble to the willing watchers at the bedside. At fifteen minutes past six o'clock on Saturday evening, February 2d, he sighed gently, closed his eyes, and "passed away as calmly as though going to sleep."[1]

Serene, self-forgetful, thoughtful of others, and most of all with *her* in his mind and heart, he died as he had lived—WENDELL PHILLIPS to the end.[2]

---

[1] The author had these particulars from the lips of Dr. Thayer.

[2] Mrs. Phillips survived her husband a little more than a year. She was tenderly cared for by relatives and friends, and died, April

23d, 1885, in the Common Street home. "The few lifelong friends who were privileged to look upon her face the following Easter morning, were startled by its expression. She lay as if asleep, with all the purity and guilelessness of her youthful face ripened into maturity. It seemed transfiguration." "Memorial of Ann Phillips," by Mrs. Anna G. Alford, p. 20.

IV.

"AT EVENTIME IT SHALL BE LIGHT."

The announcement of Mr. Phillips's death was followed by a wonderful outburst of feeling, in which surprise, grief, admiration, love, were strongly mingled. Nor was there heard in the chorus of remark one discordant note. As the death-tidings sped from ocean to ocean, cities, towns, hamlets uprose and uncovered; while, with choked utterance, negroes with whom he had been bound, women whom he loved with the purity of an anchorite, Irishmen whose aspirations for the green flag over Castle Green he shared and uttered, Labor Reformers whose fellow he had made himself, the poor and miserable now doubly impoverished and unhappy, —whispered brokenly the name they loved.

As the Amphion-lips were hushed yonder in the plain house on Common Street, the music of his life was repeated by the pulpit, platform, and press,— music, solemn as a psalm, inspiring as a battle hymn. The South joined the North, saw the real friend in the seeming foe; and in New Orleans, Charleston, and Richmond tender words were spoken as the bulletins announced, "Wendell Phillips is dead."

The shock in Boston, and the sorrow, were peculiarly marked. On Sunday, February 3d, the bereavement was the topic of subdued conversation in every home, and the text in all the churches. On

Monday, the Legislature, then in session, appointed a committee to formulate the feeling of the commonwealth; and the Common Council held a special meeting to mature appropriate action on the part of Boston. At the same time the Labor Reformers were in session at the Tremont House, arranging for a public memorial meeting on Tuesday night in Faneuil Hall; while opposite in Tremont Temple Joseph Cook in his Monday lecture was discoursing of the dead orator, and declaring that " fifty years hence it would not be asked, 'What did Boston think of Wendell Phillips?' but 'What did Wendell Phillips think of Boston?'"

Meantime, telegrams, letters of condolence, personal inquiries came pouring in from everywhither, giving evidence that this loss was not local but national; and that, as some one said, the apostle of humanity deserved a monument in Dublin, in St. Petersburg, and in Charleston, as well as in Boston.

The Legislature adopted a report which was at once discriminating and eulogistic, saying:

"The Orator's fellow-citizens have always respected him for every domestic virtue and for a grandly stoical simplicity of life. Full of the generous spirit of self-sacrifice, seeking no public honor, devoting his life and great powers to the cause of the oppressed even to his own heavy loss, standing firm against any and every injustice like the hills of his native State, volcanic in his outbursts of wrath against oppression, Wendell Phillips stands as the strongest type of the fearless, uncompromising reformer." [1]

The City Council spoke in a similar strain, and provided for the delivery of a eulogy under the

---

[1] *Vide* Report of Committee of Massachusetts Legislature, accepted February 6th, 1884.

auspices of Boston—which was pronounced a little later by the one man in America best fitted for the task by kindred culture, sympathetic feeling, and graceful eloquence, Mr. George William Curtis, who said :

"As we recall the story of that life, the spectacle of to-day is one of the most significant in our history. This memorial rite is not a tribute to official service, to literary genius, to scientific distinction ; it is a homage to personal character. It is the solemn public declaration that a life of transcendent purity of purpose, blended with commanding powers, devoted with absolute unselfishness, and with amazing results, to the welfare of the country and of humanity, is, in the American Republic, an example so inspiring, a patriotism so lofty, and a public service so beneficent, that, in contemplating them, discordant opinions, differing judgments, and the sharp sting of controversial speech, vanish like frost in a flood of sunshine." [1]

The gathering in Faneuil Hall on Tuesday evening was strikingly and suggestively comprehensive. Labor, Woman Suffrage, Irish Nationality, Temperance, Anti-Slavery,—all were represented by prominent exponents, and each in turn twined a wreath of laurel on the brow of him who had been the consummate embodiment of all.

The next day, Wednesday, at eleven o'clock, the funeral took place. The dear dust was borne to the adjacent Hollis Street church,[2] where, in the presence of a vast and cosmopolitan congregation, services were held of touching simplicity,—a few verses of Scripture and a brief prayer by the Rev. Samuel

---

[1] Curtis's "Eulogy," pp. 4, 5.
[2] The pall-bearers were Judge S. E. Sewall, Dr. Oliver Wendell Holmes, Theodore D. Weld, John M. Forbes, Wendell Phillips Garrison, Lewis Hayden (colored), Charles K. Whipple, William I. Bowditch, Richard Hallowell, and Edward M. Davis.

Longfellow (the brother and biographer of the poet), and a faltering word by the Rev. Samuel May,[1] both comrades of Mr. Phillips.

From the church, in compliance with a request so general that it assumed the tone of a command, the body was borne by a guard of honor composed of two colored companies of the State Guard and preceded by muffled drums through crowded streets, the windows filled, the sidewalks lined with sympathetic spectators, to Faneuil Hall, where he had made history,—a final, and on his part who lay there in the coffin an unresponsive visit.

Here, from one o'clock until four, the body lay in state. Beautiful floral tributes abounded. But the hall was otherwise unadorned. The scene out on the streets and along the approaches to the entrance was unprecedented. Thousands and thousands of people struggled for a place in the line, eager for a last look at the noble countenance. These thousands were of both sexes, all colors, every race, and every social grade : here, an old colored woman, the tears streaming down her cheeks, and crying as she passed the casket, " He was de bes' fren' we ever had !" there, an Irishman, the brogue and the wit silenced now beside the still tongue which had pleaded so often for Erin ; here, a lad whom he had befriended and secured employment for ; there, a gray-haired merchant who " knew Wendell at school ;" here, a group of boys and girls who had a filial pride in this father of the commonwealth ; there,—yes, Frederick Douglass, who in passing exclaimed, " I loved him,

---

[1] Mr. May conducted the services at the funeral of Mrs. Phillips, also, the next year.

and I wanted to see this throng, to feel the grip he had on the community; 'tis wonderful!" So it went on for hours, the crowd increasing instead of diminishing, becoming more instead of less diversified; all here to pay an honest tribute to him of whom, as of the Master, it might be said, "the common people heard him gladly."

At last twilight began to shake down her curtains. In the face of the struggling thousands the doors were clanged to; the casket was removed; the line of march was retaken through massive lines of uncovered lookers-on; the Old Granery Burial Ground, on Boston Common, was reached; here, beside his father and mother in the family vault, all that was mortal of Wendell Phillips was laid away;[1] and the multitude dispersed.

Such was Boston's homage to her uncrowned king of thought and speech.

All this was thrown at the time by Nora Perry, who knew and loved Mr. Phillips, into thrilling verse:

> Along the streets one day with that swift tread
> He walked a living king—then "He is dead"
> The whisper flew from lip to lip, while still
> Sounding within our ears, the echoing thrill
> Of his magician's voice we seemed to hear
> In notes of melody ring near and clear.

---

[1] As early as 1877 Mr. Phillips had planned to be buried in the beautiful suburb of Milton, where he and his wife often passed their summers. Here he had purchased a lot; and hither on the death of Mrs. Phillips both were borne and finally interred. A plain slab now marks the spot, on which is chiselled, "Ann and Wendell Phillips." In referring to this, Theodore D. Weld said to the writer: "Wendell did not care to lie amid the beat of hurrying feet, but wished to be out where the birds sing and the flowers bloom."

So near, so clear, men cried, "It cannot be!
It was but yesterday he spoke to me;
But yesterday we saw him move along,
His head above the crowd, swift-paced and strong,
But yesterday his plan and purpose sped;
It cannot be to day that he is dead."

A moment thus, half dazed, men met and spoke,
When first the sudden news upon them broke;
A moment more, with sad acceptance turned
To face the bitter truth that they had spurned.
Friends said through tears, "How empty seems the town!"
And warring critics laid their weapons down.

How at the last this great heart conquered all
We know who watched above his sacred pall—
One day a living king he faced a crowd
Of critic foes; over the dead king bowed
A throng of friends who yesterday were those
Who thought themselves, and whom the world thought, foes.

V.

THE ORATOR.

THE great Agitator has now been long enough withdrawn from the arena which was the scene of his tumultuous career to make an estimate of his oratory both interesting and important. Interesting ; because his unique reputation provokes inquiry. Important ; because no fame, save that of a *prima donna*, is so intoxicating, while none, with the same exception, is so ephemeral as that of an orator. When the voice is hushed reputation becomes a memory. Like a bird on the wing, it must be bagged, if at all, as it flies and before it vanishes. The living presence embarrasses criticism ; which, however, is free when the man is gone, while many who knew and measured him survive. In such circumstances judgment observes the *juste milieu ;* being disentangled alike from the personal feeling, pro and con, inevitable in life, and from the ignorance which grows rank over his grave when he has been long dead.

But, after all, nothing is so difficult as portraiture ; for description is not life. A distinguished painter once said, referring to a tantalizingly elusive sitter : " I can do no more than just make a *memorandum* of such a face, and let fancy do the rest."

In his outward man Wendell Phillips was cast in classic mould. His oratorical mother was Maia, the

Eloquent, and his father was Jupiter, the Thunderer. Above the middle height, his form was patterned after the best models of manhood, and closely resembled, by actual measurements, the Greek Apollo. He was neither stout nor thin, but retained from youth to age his suppleness and grace of proportion. Of nervous, sanguine temperament, his complexion was ruddy, and gave him the appearance of one whose soul looked through and glorified the body. Hence that singular radiance which was often startling.

The head was finely set upon broad shoulders and a deep chest. The chin was full and strong, the lips red and somewhat compressed, the nose aquiline, the eyes blue, small but piercing, the brow both broad and high, the hair of that tawny hue artists love,—

> "The golden treasure nature showers down
> On those foredoomed to wear Fame's golden crown."

In middle life he lost a large part of his hair; but this only served the more clearly to reveal the superb contour of the skull. His profile was fine cut as a cameo. In expression, the face was at once intellectual and serene—wore a look of resolute goodness. His pose was easy and natural, every change of attitude being a new revelation of manly grace. No nobler physique ever confronted an audience. A patrician air accompanied him as inevitably as the *nimbus* does a saint on the canvas of Murillo or Titian. It is rare that an orator receives from nature such gifts of person. Thus his appearance was conciliatory and ingratiating. It filled and satisfied the eye ere the ear was addressed. On rising, he slowly buttoned his black frock-coat and advanced to his position on the platform with the easy deliberation of a gentleman stepping across his drawing-room. His attitude was a study for the sculptor—yet unconscious and natural. The weight of the body was usually supported upon the left foot, with the right slightly advanced at an easy angle. It was an attitude of combined firmness and repose—perfect economy of muscular effort. Critics felt the force of the orator's own remark: "In a public speaker physical advantages are half the battle."

How describe the voice? It was of no great range. In the higher register it was thin. But in the middle and lower notes, where he usually held it, it resembled the tones of Paganini's violin. It was smooth. It was sweet. It was penetrating. And it was so exquisitely modulated that every finest shade of thought, each most delicate distinction of expression, was discriminated as he spoke. He had a faculty of pouring a world of meaning into those quiet utterances,—indignation, wit, sarcasm, suggestion, moral appeal, legal argument, what he would; and all without once raising his voice. It was like Ole Bull's inspired playing on one string—that being more expressive, under his bow, than the whole instrument in any other hands. Connoisseurs have testified that no other speaker here or in Europe put such intense feeling into so small a compass of voice, scaling the heights and sounding the depths of oratory in a colloquial tone. In one of his lectures, speaking of a certain locality in Florence, he said: "As I walked the pavement I suddenly came upon this inscription, under my very feet, 'On this spot, three hundred years ago, sat Dante!'"

It was uttered simply, yet with such an entire change of voice and manner, that you saw what he saw—the image of the Tuscan poet who went down into hell. Dante was conjured into being and stood revealed in the solemn hush of that rhetorical pause.

His enunciation was an added charm. Each word was as distinctly uttered as though it were a newly coined gold piece. Yet he never elocutionized. There was nothing pedantic in his utterance. Like every thing else about his oratory, it was natural— or seemed so. But as the words dropped in rhythmic succession from his lips, always without hesitation, each one the best that could possibly be chosen to express his thought, it was a revelation of the strength and beauty of our mother tongue. What you listened to seemed a cross between a strain of music and a poem. This rhythmic quality is difficult to manage. It easily becomes sing-song. Edward Everett, with all his cunning, carried it to excess—was immeasurably measured. A close observer could frequently detect his hand covertly beating time to his words, like the baton of a leader of the orchestra. In Mr. Phillips the rhythm was felt rather than perceived. The cadence was lulling and beguiling, never obtrusive. In rate of utterance he was neither fast nor slow—slow enough to be distinctly heard, yet fast enough to give the impression of animation.

The orator's action comported with his style. Its effectiveness resided in its significance. He made many more gestures than he got credit for; but they were so subordinated to the thought and so illustrative of it, that they eluded attention and seemed only parts of one whole. Hence their pro-

priety and ease deceived all but sharp observers into
a belief in their infrequency. There they were,
nevertheless. He freely used the open palm, now
with one hand, now with both. In the more moderate emphasis of feeling he placed the index finger in
the open palm. In the expression of ideas that were
repugnant he employed the averted palm. Imagination influenced the gestures and led to the temperate use of highly symbolic action—always, however,
as a help to the language.[1] Thus the arms, the
hands, the fingers became co-ordinate features with
the countenance, the lips, the eyes, and were moulded
into a consummate, poetic *tout ensemble*. Indeed, he
impressed you as being unable to twist his form or
use his limbs ungracefully. All the while there was
no study, no attitudinizing. It seemed Phillips's
"way."

"The keynote to the oratory of Wendell Phillips," remarks a
competent critic, "lay in this: that it was essentially conversational,—the conversational raised to its highest power. Perhaps
no orator ever spoke with so little apparent effort or began so
entirely on the plane of his average hearers. It was as if he
simply repeated, in a little louder tone, what he had just been
saying to some familiar friend at his elbow. The effect was
absolutely disarming. Those accustomed to spread-eagle eloquence felt, perhaps, a slight sense of disappointment. Could
this easy, effortless man be Wendell Phillips? But he held them
by his very quietness: it did not seem to have occurred to him
to doubt his power to hold them. The poise of his manly figure,
the easy grace of his attitude, the thrilling modulation of his
perfectly trained voice, the dignity of his gesture, the keen pene-
tration of his eye, all aided to keep his hearers in hand. The
colloquialism was never relaxed; but it was familiarity without
loss of keeping. When he said isn't and wasn't, or even, like

---

[1] *Vide* an interesting article on Mr. Phillips in the *Andover Review*,
vol. i., pp. 309 *sqq.*, 1884.

an Englishman, dropped his g's, it did not seem inelegant; he might almost have been ungrammatical, and it would not have impaired the fine air of the man. Then, as the argument went on, the voice grew deeper, the action more animated, and the sentences came in a long, sonorous swell, still easy and graceful, but powerful as the soft stretching of a tiger's paw. He could be terse as Carlyle, or his periods could be as prolonged and cumulative as those of Choate or Evarts: no matter; they carried in either case the same charm." [1]

In tone and manner, although thus conversational, Mr. Phillips was at the same time elevated. It has been said that speaking which is merely conversational has no lift to it; the mind may be held by it, but is not impressed. On the other hand, speaking which has no every-day manner as its basis is stilted and fatiguing. The orator should frame his style on the level of plain, common-sense talk. Then this ought to lead out and up toward vistas of cloud-land and the music of the spheres.[2] In this regard Wendell Phillips is a model. He had many surprises of thought and diction; but made most frequent use of short, terse sentences whose sense was felt the instant they struck the ear, and whose epigrammatic point made them stick (and sometimes tingle) in the memory.

It was this colloquial quality, infinitely varied yet without interruption, which made him the least tedious of speakers. You heard him an hour, two hours, three hours—and were unconscious of the lapse of time. Indeed, he never seemed to be making a speech. It was no oration for the crown, with drum

---

[1] Thomas Wentworth Higginson, in his obituary notice.
[2] "Golden Age of American Oratory," by Edward G. Parker. Notice of Wendell Phillips.

and trumpet declamation,—only a gentleman talking! He had exactly the manner for an agitator, it was so entirely without agitation. This repose, fire under snow, enabled him to husband all his electricity and flash it out to magnetize the audience.

But the matter of his speech was in sharp contrast with his manner. This was in constant movement, and sparkled with epigram, laughed with anecdote, vibrated with argument, thrilled with appeal, glowed with vivid description, abounded in apt quotation gleaned from the whole field of history, biography, and ethics,—a splendid panorama, brilliant as the essays of Macaulay, aglow with diffused fire. He was a great coiner of striking phrases; as when he said, "Liberty, even in defeat, knows nothing but victory." He was master of epithets, which, when he affixed them, clung and stung; as when he styled Rufus Choate a "political mountebank," and characterized Daniel Webster, after his famous (and infamous) 7th of March speech in the Senate, as "Sir Pertinax McSycophant," and referred to the "cuckoo lips of Edward Everett," and spoke of one of the mayors of the Boston of mob days as, "not a mayor, but a lackey in the mayor's chair." It was this astonishing contrast between the matter of his speech that resembled Vesuvius in full eruption, and the manner, as halcyon as a summer landscape, —it was this that bewildered while it riveted those who heard him for the first time. His foes were at the same moment angered by the matter and fascinated by the manner. The *Richmond Inquirer*, speaking of him before the Rebellion, said: "Wendell Phillips is an infernal machine set to music."

Seldom moving, never outside of a small circle,

and speaking in this self-contained way, of course he never lost his head. Addressing, as he did, audiences bitterly hostile through a great part of his career,—audiences not seldom assembled expressly to put him down, his serene self-possession placed at his service his whole battery of unparalleled resources; and in these battles with the mob he never failed to conquer a hearing. He would tell a story; he would make some prominent interrupter a target for his wit; he would shame the rioters into silence; he would appeal to their better instincts; he would demand fair play; if the disturbance became too boisterous, he would turn to the reporter's table and say: "Howl on: through these fingers I address an audience of 30,000,000!" and thus pique the rioters into silence by curiosity: in one way or another, and without descending from his lofty pedestal of self-respect, he was sure to have his say, and in the most uncompromising style.

Take as an illustration of his adroitness in managing an unruly crowd a passage from his speech at the Lovejoy meeting in Faneuil Hall, which made him famous, away back at the outset of his career— that marvellous extempore reply to Attorney-General Austin. He had asserted that Lovejoy died for defending the freedom of the press. Then he added:

"The disputed right which provoked the Revolution—taxation without representation—is far beneath that for which he died. [Here there was a strong and general expression of disapprobation, as though he were belittling the heroes of 1776. With a commanding gesture, Mr. Phillips cried:] One word, gentlemen. As much as *thought* is better than *money*, so much is the cause in which Lovejoy died nobler than a mere question of taxes. James Otis thundered in this hall when the King did but touch his pocket. Imagine, if you can, his indignant eloquence, had England offered to put a gag upon his lips." (*Tremendous cheering.*)

Such instances might be multiplied *ad infinitum*. How well he could tell a story let this passage show—taken from one of his earlier addresses :

"That most eloquent of all Southerners, as I think Mr. Sargent S. Prentiss, of Mississippi, was addressing a crowd of four thousand people in his State, defending the tariff, and in the course of an eloquent period which rose to a beautiful climax, he painted the thrift, the energy, the comfort, the wealth, the civilization of the North, in glowing colors,—when there rose on the vision of the assembly, in the open air, a horseman of magnificent proportions ; and just at the moment of hushed attention, when the voice of Prentiss had ceased and the applause was about to break forth, the horseman exclaimed, ' D— the North !' The curse was so much in unison with the habitual feeling of a Mississippi audience that it quenched their enthusiasm, and nothing but respect for the speaker kept them from cheering the horseman. Prentiss turned upon his lame foot, and said :

"' Major Moody, will you rein in that horse a moment ?'

"He assented. The orator went on :

"' Major, the horse on which you ride came from Upper Missouri ; the saddle that surmounts him came from Trenton, N. J. ; the hat on your head came from Danbury, Conn. ; the boots you wear came from Lynn, Mass. ; the linen on your shirt is Irish, and Boston made it up ; your broadcloth coat is of Lowell manufacture, and was cut in New York ; and if to-day you surrender what you owe the " d— North" you would sit stark naked.' "

Frederick Douglass (himself one of the most effective of orators) has well said :

"Eloquent as Mr. Phillips was as a lecturer, he was far more effective as a debater. Debate was to him the flint and steel which brought out all his fire. His memory was wonderful. He would listen to an elaborate speech for hours, and, without a single note of what had been said, in writing, reply to every part of it as fully and completely as if the speech were written out before him. Those who heard him when not confronted by an opponent have a very limited comprehension of his amazing resources as a speaker." [1]

In power of invective, Mr. Phillips, by common acknowledgment, stands at the head of all orators, ancient or modern. He gave new meaning to the word *Philippic*. Certain it is that as it regards popular effect, immediate effect, nothing equals this quality on the platform—nothing can compensate the lack of it in an orator. As the immortality of Junius lies in his personalities, as Patrick Henry is best remembered by his characterization of the dishonest contractor with whose name he made the colonies ring, so Wendell Phillips will ever be remembered because of those thunderbolts which he hurled so serenely ; and which, because of his calmness, enchanted while they appalled. It was like witnessing a fire or a battle.

As an instance of this, and also of the classic style of which he was master, study his lecture on "Idols," in which occurs the following celebrated passage referring to Rufus Choate :

"Yet this is the model which Massachusetts offers to the Pantheon of the great jurists of the world !

"Suppose we stood in that lofty temple of jurisprudence,—on either side of us the statues of the great lawyers of every age and clime,—and let us see what part New England—Puritan, educated, free New England—would bear in the pageant. Rome points to a colossal figure, and says, ' That is Papinian, who, when the Emperor Caracalla murdered his own brother, and ordered the lawyer to defend the deed, went cheerfully to death,

---

[1] Address in Washington, D. C., before the colored people, on Wendell Phillips, after his funeral in 1884.

rather than sully his lips with the atrocious plea; and that is Ulpian, who, aiding his prince to put the army below the law, was massacred at the foot of a weak, but virtuous throne.'

"And France stretches forth her grateful hands, crying, 'That is D'Aguesseau, worthy, when he went to face an enraged king, of the farewell his wife addressed him—"Go! forget that you have a wife and children to ruin, and remember only that you have France to save."'

"England says, 'That is Coke, who flung the laurels of eighty years in the face of the first Stuart, in defence of the people. This is Selden, on every book of whose library you saw written the motto of which he lived worthy, "Before everything, Liberty!" That is Mansfield, silver-tongued, who proclaimed,

> '"Slaves cannot breathe in England; if their lungs
> Receive our air, that moment they are free."

This is Romilly, who spent life trying to make law synonymous with justice, and succeeded in making life and property safer in every city of the empire. And that is Erskine, whose eloquence, spite of Lord Eldon and George III., made it safe to speak and to print.'

"Then New England shouts, 'This is Choate, who made it safe to murder; and of whose health thieves asked before they began to steal.'"[1]

These words are sufficiently sensational as they lie under the eye in cold type. Imagine, then, the effect as they fell from the lips of the orator. There is no more tremendous climax on record.

No doubt Mr. Phillips, like all supreme speakers, was a born fighter. He had the *certaminis gaudia*—the joy of disputation—common to intellectual gladiators. Occasionally, this got the better of his judgment, and he fought to win, as well as for the glory of God. But when it did, like a skilful rider, he soon recovered the reins of his conscience and made

---

[1] "Speeches and Lectures," p. 253.

glad amends. It must be conceded that rarely are such magnificent abilities so conscientiously directed.

The orator almost always spoke without notes. On the few occasions when he used them they were an evident embarrassment : it was like an eagle walking. At the start he was accustomed to prepare his speeches with care ; but as we have seen, his first great success was won off-hand, and "afterward," as one of his intimates tells us, "during that period of incessant practice which Emerson makes the secret of his power, he relied generally upon his vast accumulated store of facts and illustrations, and his tried habit of thinking on his legs." Of course, his lectures ("The Lost Arts," "Street Life in Europe," "Daniel O'Connell," "Sir Harry Vane," and the rest) were all carefully prepared—though never written out. So also were some of his elaborate speeches, like those on "Disunion," and "Progress," and the "Phi Beta Kappa" oration at Cambridge, in the summer of 1881. But he was never so felicitous, never so thrilling, never so commanding as when most extemporaneous,—and especially if hissed or mobbed. Then his port and utterance afforded a spectacle of the moral sublime.

The truth is, he was *always* preparing. He read, studied, thought, with one eye on the platform. Whatever could "point a moral or adorn a tale" he carefully appropriated and thrust into some mental pigeon-hole, where he could lay hands on it and bring it out on occasion. In speaking of his habit of preparation, he said : "The chief thing I aim at is to master my subject. Then I earnestly try to get the audience to think as I do."

Mr. Phillips had a theory that speaking and writing

require such different habits of mind that success in one arena makes failure quite sure in the other. In proof of this he used to cite Patrick Henry, Fisher Ames, Sargent S. Prentiss, Tom Corwin, and Henry Clay, monarchs of the platform, but who seldom wrote ; and whose speeches are dry reading—probably because their reputation dwarfs the text, which seems doubly lifeless without the speaker's personality, like a body when the spirit is departed. Accordingly, he took little interest in his speeches after they were delivered. Each had a purpose at the moment, performed its errand, and was left to die. Even his lectures he did not care to see in print. He thought they would not read as he made them sound—nor do they. Yet Wendell Phillips refutes his own theory. For though, of course, we miss the living presence, spite of this drawback, the published speeches are wonderfully stirring, and seem, in Milton's phrase, "The precious life-blood of a master spirit treasured up on purpose to a life beyond life." They afford, beyond all comparison, whether in America or in England, the best specimens in literature of extemporaneous eloquence. Some of them suggest Burke in the Senate and Plato in the groves of the Academy. Read, for example, the "Philosophy of the Abolition Movement,"[1] in which he vindicates the justice and shows the reason of the Anti-Slavery crusade in a diction brocaded with splendor. Or turn to the speech on "Woman's Rights,"[2] delivered at Worcester, in Massachusetts, in 1851,—a presentation which, affirms George William Curtis, "more than any other single im-

---

[1] "Speeches and Lectures," p. 98.   [2] *Ib.*, p. 11.

pulse, launched that question upon the sea of popular controversy." [1] Yes; the printed speeches are a precious legacy—a memento and an inspiration. Would that we had more of them!

In commenting upon his characteristics as a speaker, Clarence Cook observes that they "were a logical, lawyer-like setting out of his subject and great closeness in his argument, so that if he went off a little to meet an interruption, or to answer a question, or to parry the thrust of an insult or threat interjected, he quickly returned and beat out the iron on his anvil." [2]

The oratory of Wendell Phillips illustrated the truth that, after all, character is the secret of the highest speech. As the Sage of Concord puts it: "There is no eloquence without a man behind it." Academic rhetoric may charm; the arts of the trained advocate, the hired argument of an Ogden Hoffman or a Rufus Choate may astonish; the selfish appeals of the political orator may win noisy applause from those who hope to devour the loaves and fishes of party; but the oratory that holds the present and moulds the future must have for a basis the moral element. Eloquent utterance *plus* character—what can equal that?

Here Mr. Phillips was supreme. Everybody knew, he made those who heard him feel that he was not posing for popular effect. He stood the embodiment of a cause. Every sentence was surcharged with moral conviction. It was perceived

---

[1] "Wendell Phillips," a eulogy delivered before the municipal authorities of Boston, Mass., April 18th, 1884.
[2] In Johnson's *New Universal Cyclopædia, in loco.*

that he suppressed rather than expressed all he felt. From opening to close his words, distinct and softly rounded as though stamped on satin, were warm with the composed passion of an honest nature face to face with heaven-defying wickedness. Such speech has the force of dynamite. It convicts while it convinces. It compels respect by deserving it.

The period in which Mr. Phillips lived was prolific of great speakers—like all eras of revolution. They march in battalions, on both sides of Mason and Dixon's line. In a broad characterization, those of the South were more declamatory; those of the North were more argumentative. The Southerners excelled in outburst power; the Northerners were, as a rule, less volcanic. Those talked bullets; these believed in ideas. It was the difference between rain in summer and rain in winter—the same element; but in one case liquid, and in the other case snow At the same time it must be confessed that the North did not lack for tongues of fire.

If we compare Wendell Phillips with others of his contemporaries, we shall find that he was excelled by one and another in special qualities. At the South, Calhoun was more logical in his general style, Clay was more thrilling, Prentiss was more picturesque. At the North, Webster had a more sustained splendor of diction and greater majesty. Everett surpassed him in elaboration, and indulged in more frequent bursts of beauty. Choate was more electric. Corwin better pleased the crowd—was half clown and the other half genius. Sumner was more pretentiously the scholar, and excelled in copious illustration that exhausted a subject to the bottom. Chapin oftener soared. Beecher abounded more in the bravuras of oratory—was an embodied thunderstorm. Lincoln was superior in the Eastern art of story-telling—the ability to pack the entire meaning of the hour in a pat anecdote. Douglass had more pathos. Curtis might be better depended upon as a speaker for set occasions. Ingersoll exceeded him in the art *ad captandum vulgus*. Nevertheless, in the perfect moulding of an orator he surpassed each of these. On the whole he was a more interesting and instructive speaker than any of his contemporaries in their palmiest days. This is superlative praise; but the record is true. Let it be written while living witnesses can attest it and before his eloquence, like the song of Orpheus, fades into a doubtful tradition.

Yes; as an orator Wendell Phillips was peerless. He possessed that quality which Emerson thought the highest of all,—of being "something that cannot be skipped or undermined." Those who were privileged to hear him often, and who were familiar as well with the best eloquence on both sides of the Atlantic, will agree with Professor Bryce, the philosophic Englishman whose recent delineation of our institution is the only rival of D'Tocqueville's "Democracy in America,"—that "he was in the opinion of competent critics one of the first orators of the present century, and not more remarkable for the finish than for the transparent simplicity of his style, which attained its highest effects by the most direct and natural methods."[1]

The greatest of compliments is imitation. The whole school of Anti-Slavery speakers echoed the

---

[1] "The American Commonwealth," vol. ii., p. 659.

manner and especially the intonations of Wendell
Phillips. More important than this, his style set a
fashion. It taught the bar, the pulpit, the platform
the value of high-bred conversationalism as the most
effective vehicle of thought and emotion. With his
advent roar and rant went out of date. The era of
trained naturalism opened. Thus he made every
speaker and every audience his debtor.

VI.

THE MAN.

TURNING now from the orator, we pass to a critical estimate of the man.

Genius is of three kinds. Some men are great in a single faculty, which overshadows the rest and rules in the realm of mind ; others, in kindred faculties with mutual affinities ; others still in the general range and elevation of all the higher powers. The genius of Wendell Phillips, as Theodore D. Weld points out, in a passage of wise discrimination, was of this latter type. "It was no king among his other powers, but a ruler among rulers, each co-ordinate with each in a balanced equality. Strong in each of its elements, ethic, æsthetic, logical, philosophical, critical, emotional, imaginative, all these with conscience and indomitable will were the rounded man himself. The large stature of his powers, their exalted level, each a vital constituent of his genius, made him in their combination what he was—an aggregation of great mental and moral forces crystallized into character."

He had feminine intuition with masculine reason. The whole ground of rights and wrongs, not only in gross but in detail, not more in the coarser than in the most refined features of both, he instantly saw, grasped, and discriminated.

When he had chosen, there he stood, serene, self-poised, never lonely though alone, untroubled by doubt with everybody else in a quandary,—

" The star that looked on tempests and was still unshaken."

He had both kinds of courage ; that highest, the moral, which held him firm, true, unmoved by scoff of foe or kiss of friend ; and that lowest, the physical, which led him to confront a mob or brave assassination with the nonchalance of a veteran campaigner stooping to tie his shoe in a rain of bullets.

The genius of Mr. Phillips was highly cultivated. All that early training, later culture, and foreign travel could do to polish and refine had been done. When, therefore, such a man so dowered left the Palace of Pharaoh for the brick-yard, the companionship of princes for the society of slaves, the force of his conviction and the fibre of his manhood may be measured.

He retained through life the taste and habits of scholarship. The classics were often in his hands and on his lips. Mediæval Latin, too (the language of the learned world for a thousand years), was an open book to him. We might change a little and apply to him that which Macaulay quotes Denham as felicitously saying of Cowley : " He spoke the tongue, but did not wear the clothes of the ancients." Of modern languages, French was his favorite, and he had the accent of a Parisian ; but he also read German, Italian, and Spanish.

While in college Mr. Phillips formed a habit, which he never lost, of making special historic periods subjects of microscopic investigation. Thus he spent a twelvemonth in studying the English Revolution of 1640—the seed-time of modern political ethics and religious opinion. He ransacked every speech, memoir, novel, play, from Clarendon to Godwin, and made himself the best authority of his time upon that epoch. In the same way he devoted a year to the reign of George III.—the birth-time of American liberty. The history of the Colonial and Revolutionary period he knew by heart. The story which his friend Motley retold with such graphic power, that wonderful romance of Holland, he had at the end of his tongue. And Lamartine was hardly more familiar than Phillips with the French Revolution—in which, as Carlyle said, the eighteenth century committed suicide by blowing its own brains out.

He studied chemistry as other men read novels, for amusement. He was fond of those authors who (like the late Charles Reade) freshen things. He kept himself thoroughly acquainted with modern governmental action; and General Butler, a competent witness on such a point, affirms that after he quitted the law he by no means laid aside its study: "Whoever in his later years had an opportunity to converse with him on legal topics was surprised to find how thoroughly he kept pace with the modifications of legal principles as shown in current decisions of the courts."

With reference to his scholarly preferences an intimate friend writes:

"The character of a man is revealed by a knowledge of his heroes. Those of Mr. Phillips in English history were Sir Walter Raleigh, Andrew Marvel, Pym, Sir Harry Vane, Cromwell, Chesterfield, De Foe, Lady Mary Wortley Montagu, John Hunter, James Watt, and Brindley. In American history they were Jay, Franklin, Hamilton, Sam Adams, and Eli Whitney.

Among novelists. Richardson was a favorite ; Scott he knew by heart. In French literature he preferred Sully, Rochefoucauld, De Retz, Pascal, Tocqueville, Guizot, and Victor Hugo. In English, his pets were Swift, Ben Jonson, Jeremy Taylor, Massenger, Milton, Southey, Lamb, the elder D'Israeli, and ' all of Horace Walpole.' He was late in opening Shakespeare. Elizabeth Barrett Browning he regarded as the first of modern poets. And he thought that George Eliot and Charlotte Brontë saw life deeper and truer than either Dickens or Thackeray, though they lacked the artistic skill of their more celebrated contemporaries."

At the same time Mr. Phillips was an omnivorous reader of newspapers. These have been called the American Bible. We may be sure, however, that he scanned them, not with idolatrous eyes, but for the light they threw upon contemporaneous affairs —for this, and for their inevitable forecast of what lay ahead. He knew, none better, the charm of anecdote, the value of illustrations fetched from history and biography. His speeches abound in apt cullings from these sources. This wide range and varied taste stored his mind with effective stories and telling facts. When once on his legs and in full career he laid the hand of a master upon the entire encyclopædia of knowledge, and seemed " crowned with the spoil of every science and decked with the wreath of every muse."

Mr. Phillips has been termed the latest and the largest of the Puritans. The elixir of conscience diffused through his clerical ancestors was concentrated and potted in him. This gave him an unparalleled moral ascendency. His career was a splendid exhibition of conscientiousness. Born in the purple, equipped with intellectual gifts and culture, and dowered with personal charms and accomplishments admirably fitted to secure him any place to which he might aspire in society, in the Senate, or at the bar, had he consented to file down his truth and turn but a little aside from the narrow path of conviction; he left his decorated world, sacrificed his brilliant prospects, threw up his early friendships and scorned the allurements which fascinate mankind,—all for a principle. Such self-denial is sublime. Since Christ, life for others has been the highest kind of life. Hence Mr. Phillips takes an undisputed place among heroes and saints.

Of his benevolence what was his whole life but the expression? There are some who, while lavish of words and even of personal efforts, are stingy when the coin demanded is coin current. Not so Mr. Phillips. His liberality was unbounded. Literally, he gave away a fortune. Among his effects after his death was found an old memorandum book, covering the years from 1845 to 1875. In this he credits himself with personal gifts aggregating over $65,000. And this was but a fraction of what he bestowed— only what he handed out at home and with the memorandum book within reach. Some of the entries are curious. They show that he supported many families in whole or in part; and not a few well-known names figure among his beneficiaries. Page after page reads like this,—John Brown figuring conspicuously:

John Brown	$10.00
A poor Italian	2.00
Mrs. Garnaut	10.00
Poor man	1.00
Refugee	5.00

The orator's wealth has been exaggerated. He inherited something from his parents. His wife also added to the common stock. But it is certain that their joint fortunes never exceeded $100,000. During many years Mr. Phillips made large sums by his lectures. His income from this source ranged from $10,000 to $15,000 a year. He might have lived in luxurious ease. No one would have criticised. Instead of that, he dwarfed his wants to the minimum. His house was in a quarter of Boston never fashionable, and at last given over to shops. It was almost bare : partly, no doubt, because the lifelong invalidism of Mrs. Phillips and the lack of children deprived him of an incentive to dwell under a lordlier rooftree ; but chiefly in order that he might be free to spend in unselfishness. That plain house—was it not a Mecca ? The panting fugitive knew it, and tested its hospitality and strong protection. The unfortunate of whatever color, sex, age, social condition, wore the threshold thin with their needy feet. Who ever heard of anybody's being turned away unpitied, unaided ? Aside from this unstinted private charity, he gave like a prince and through decades to the great causes that were near and dear to him. Many were the students, black and white, whom he supported. He would frequently travel long distances to deliver a lecture for the benefit of some deserving scholar, to whom he would make over the whole proceeds.

During the Anti-Slavery period, when invited to lecture here, there, and yonder, and asked to name his price, his habitual response was :

" If you want a literary lecture, the price is so and so [a high one]. But if you will let me speak on slavery I will come for nothing and pay my own expenses!"

This was a sly way he had of bribing unfriendly lyceums—and it usually succeeded. Even when he spoke on a literary theme, conservative committees were always fearful lest this dealer in forensic firebrands should smuggle into his sentences gunpowder enough to blow up the hall. They listened between fear and admiration, half expecting an explosion, and felt as Burns did when he wrote his "Epistle to a Young Friend:"

> ' Perhaps it may turn out a sang,
> Perhaps turn out a sermon."

When Mr. Phillips died he left almost nothing. He said to a friend only two or three days before his death that he had no wish to leave a fortune to anybody or anything; that his idea of living was to walk with open heart and open hand from day to day; and that he had done all he could in this way—he had been his own executor.

His general benevolence assumed a special and tender form where "Ann" was concerned. His devotion to her was idyllic. He gave her an amount and quality of attention quite unprecedented. Once when her sickness deepened into immediate danger, he waited on her for sixty days without leaving the house. He found in that invalid's chamber opportunity for the exercise of every domestic virtue. Denied the experience of fatherhood, he made "Ann" both wife and child. Was she secluded? He shut himself in. Was she lonely? He became her sufficient companion. Was she in pain? He medicined her with sympathy. Did she want this, would she have that? It was laid at her feet.

When in town, he went to market and ordered the dinner, because he "knew Ann's tastes." Indifferent about the table for himself, he became a very epicure for her. He would buy two boxes of strawberries, so that she might have the best of each. He would go over a bushel of potatoes to get a peck of one size to bake for her breakfast. In purchasing peas, he would handle every pod to see that they were soft and tender, "as Ann wanted them." Winter or summer, pleasant or stormy, he might frequently be seen at night foraging for "Ann," who had a sudden invalid's whim for chicken or ice cream. There were times, of course, when the peculiar ailment of Mrs. Phillips made her fretful and exacting. He never lost his temper or his patience on such occasions, was never hurried or flurried, but went about low-voiced and composed, uncomplaining and attentive. Womanhood owes Wendell Phillips a heavy debt. But no other item in the indebtedness is so heavy as the gratitude due him for that knight-errantry of half a century.

Under his own roof Mr. Phillips was quiet,— almost taciturn. He was the most unexacting and gentle of men—grateful for any attention. He read to Mrs. Phillips and entertained her with outside news daily, but this was usually at or about tea-time. The evenings at home he passed in his own study, reading, writing, meditating, as the demands upon him or his mood might dictate. Callers were always welcome, and were sure, whatever their errand, of a patient hearing and a gracious dismission.

In Mr. Phillips there was no guile. His nature, like his life, was open and without concealment.

Neither was there a trace of self-display, nor hardly of self-consciousness. He thought of himself last and least, spent almost nothing upon himself, and made no provision for posthumous fame. Never were equally great powers wedded to such modesty nor enshrined in a form so gracious and urbane.

He had no personal enemies. In private life all said of him :

> " None knew thee but to love thee,
> Nor named thee but to praise."

In his personal habits Mr. Phillips was as conservative as he was radical in his thought and speech. We have mentioned his attachment to his home for forty years. In the same way he frequented one tailoring establishment for half a century. He had his hair trimmed by one barber for nearly two generations. He loved Washington Street, in Boston, as Dr. Johnson did Fleet Street, in London, and strolled along its pavements with serene enjoyment, indifferent to newer thoroughfares. He always shaved himself. He always blacked his own boots. On these points he was extremely particular—and on one other, viz., the quality of his linen ; which he insisted should be absolutely free from cotton and cobweb fine.

Thus loving the old, while preaching the new ; rooted after the flesh in the past, while soaring in spirit into the future ; moving like a moss-back along the grooves of custom, while pleading for a reconstruction of the whole social order : Wendell Phillips was an embodied contradiction ;—an animated antithesis, himself more epigrammatic than the most striking phrase he ever coined.

In fact, there are traces of this personal conservatism even in his radicalism : as when in denouncing a *bad* government he was careful not to denounce *all* government ; or when in condemning Pro-Slavery churches, he upheld Christianity ; or when in demanding women's rights, he defended marriage as Christ taught it and as Christians have practised it. Radical though he was, he was not an anarchist, nor an atheist, nor a free-lover.

Moreover, as he combined radicalism and conservatism in himself, so he was a singular compound of strength and gentleness, impetuosity and calmness, stoicism and feeling. It was like fire under snow. The same contrast marked his manners, which were at once patrician and democratic , not arrogant, still less obtrusively affable ; but tinctured by a dignified yet kindly reserve which commanded some measure of deference from all who came in contact with him.

There was a marked resemblance between his public and private bearing—the same easy grace, the same unaffected simplicity, the same honeyed cadence of tone. One got a just idea of his oratory from his carriage and utterance on the sidewalk or at the hearthstone. This charm of manner, together with his wealth of knowledge, made him the most instructive and delightful of companions—when he would talk. Because, as a rule, he preferred to listen ; which he explained by saying :

"I learn something from every one."

In his dress the orator was simple but neat, and near enough to the mode not to appear singular. He had the enviable faculty, often commented upon, of never having his garments appear either shabby or new. Indeed, he showed his exquisite refinement in his clothing as in everything else. It was all-pervading. As no one ever heard him say a coarse thing or tell an indelicate story, so he was never seen in a " loud " cravat or an ultra coat.

From first to last Mr. Phillips was an unshaken believer in the people. His republicanism was based on an indestructible faith in the average capacity and trustworthiness of the race. He held, with John Bright, that the first five hundred men who pass in the Strand would make as good a parliament as that which sits at St. Stephen's. He believed with his favorite Rochefoucauld that all are wiser than any. He had the feeling, which in his case was a passion, that responsibility will educate the lowest into self-control, and thorough self-control into fitness for popular government. Hence his pleas for the negroes, for the Irishmen, for the laborer, and for woman. He loved to quote those words which the younger D'Israeli puts into the mouth of one of his heroes in " Vivian Grey :" " The people, Mr. Grey, are not often wrong." Not that Mr. Phillips esteemed the sentiment of a given community at a given time to be correct. His life of ceaseless opposition to the popular opinion proves this. He believed in men not in *esse*, but in *posse*—in the divine possibilities wrapped up in human nature. His whole career is a magnificent commentary on this faith.

Yet if others doubt this truth, he of all men might have doubted—he, whose life was lived under the frown of public opinion ; he, whose chosen function was battle with an ignorant majority ; he, whose most sacred ideals were crucified amid the execrations of the mob. Just the same he went serenely on, and appealed from Philip drunk to Philip sober —from the people ill-informed to the people better informed ; and was sure that to-morrow would rectify to-day.

"But," remarks Mr. George William Curtis, "while he cherished this profound faith in the people, and because he cherished it, he never flattered the mob, nor hung upon its neck, nor pandered to its passion, nor suffered its foaming hate or its exultant enthusiasm to touch the calm poise of his regnant soul." Whether the crowd hissed or applauded, he stood their friend and teacher. His confidence in their ultimate position did not intermit. How else could he have been their Tribune?

Here his example is beyond praise. At a time when educated men too often borrow their tone from London and Berlin ; when it is fashionable to hem and haw over universal suffrage ; when *quid nuncs* suggest, if they do not assert that the Fathers were wrong when they built the Republic upon the rock of popular sovereignty ;—it is refreshing, it is inspiring to come face to face with his unqualified faith in the wisdom and durability of the American idea.

As he believed in the American idea, so he believed in the American method of reform. "I know," said he, "what reform needs and all it needs in a land where discussion is free, the press untrammelled, and where public halls protect debate. Submit to risk your daily bread, expect social ostracism, count on a mob now and then, ' be in earnest, don't equivocate, don't excuse, don't retreat a single inch,' and you will be finally heard." In this country thought is more explosive than dynamite, unfettered lips are better than secret societies, the ballot is surer than the bayonet—such was his political creed. Thus his career is a grand object-lesson, teaching the efficacy of constitutional agitation.

It is not easy to estimate his influence. The difficulty is due to his exceptional position. In weighing the character of a statesman, for instance, we might refer to the public measures he introduced or advocated, the treaties he negotiated, the party he led. In measuring a great lawyer it would be easy to catalogue the famous cases he argued, to paint the juries he mesmerized into submission, to indicate the laws he wrote or expounded. Or in characterizing an inventor, the service he rendered could be distinctly named and traced in all its helpful ramifications. But this man stood alone. He had no party. He belonged to no church.

In an important sense, however, this very isolation increased his influence. Belonging nowhere, he belonged everywhere. He won early recognition as a continental censor. He was the public prosecutor for humanity. Standing for half a century the most prominent figure on the platform; speaking incessantly, and always to large audiences, he certainly did more than any other individual to create the public sentiment which by and by seized the hand of Abraham Lincoln and wrote the proclamation of emancipation. In those years, and since, he was a tireless seed-planter. Through the afternoon and evening of his life he was in close touch with clergymen, editors, teachers, statesmen—the creators of public opinion : a leader of the leaders.

He was such a consummate master of the art of putting things that his mere statement was argument. He gave to the causes he espoused a standing in the court of intellect and scholarship—which they usually sadly needed. Thus he made first Abolition, and then Woman's Rights, and then Total Abstinence, and then Labor Reform, each in its turn a hated and outcast name, respectable and respected in a social and mental and learned sense by identifying himself with them and flinging over their discussion the graces of his genius. The large result of his labors is triumphantly avouched and everywhere acknowledged in so far as his Anti-Slavery record is concerned.

"Let no one despise the negro any more," exclaimed a distinguished man of letters after hearing the orator, "he has given us Wendell Phillips!"

Naturally, he is the hero of the colored people. He stands first, and there is no second, in the affection of the educated among the race he did so much to lift. "He knew this class better," remarks Robert Purvis (a magnificent specimen of it), "than any one else, and sympathized more keenly with its aspirations. With us his name is sainted and his words are law."

Critics allege in disparagement of Mr. Phillips's influence that he made no disciples and left no followers. This is only apparently true. He never aimed at personal aggrandizement. He was a reformer—not a politician; a propounder of truth—not a stereotyper of it into statutes. Such a function was inconsistent with immediate popularity. On principle, he kept a quarter of a century ahead. Hence, the times had and have to grow up to him. But while his views have seldom been adopted in their length and breadth, they have infected and increasingly dominated the mind of the country. He had and has the secret intellectual support of the educated classes. In life he won the hearts of young men,—especially in seats of learning, who, when he was announced to speak, crowded the hall, and could not be kept away by any device of old-fogyism. This ascendency he is likely to keep.

Another criticism touches the Agitator's use of invective. But if he wore the thunder-robe, it was a stern sense of duty that impelled him to put it on. In an age when the public conscience was asleep, it was his function to startle and alarm. His denunciation in such circumstances was true kindness—the kindness of the surgeon who cuts to cure. There was never any malice in the blow he struck, any envy in the shaft he sped.

The personalities of Mr. Phillips were born of moral indignation, in part ; and in part they were the result of circumstances. When he began to discuss slavery there was a conspiracy of silence. Men said : "You shall not talk on this subject." When he insisted upon speaking, the conspiracy of silence became a conspiracy of deafness. Men said : "Very well, talk on ; but our ears are our own. We will not hear you." Slavery hid itself behind lawyers, and said : "I am legal !" behind merchants, and said : "I am respectable !" behind statesmen, and said : "I am patriotic !" behind clergymen, and said : "I am religious !" It could only be assailed through these men. Nor would the community listen to a mere ethical discussion. Hence Phillips struck at slavery through its defenders. The howl of some wounded popular idol forced attention. Himself the calmest and sweetest of men, the Agitator used invective as a weapon. It used to be said that he never slew an antagonist but with a sunbeam. And it has been conceded that most of his criticisms of public men history justifies.

Complaint is made that after the abolition of slavery Mr. Phillips continued to use the same terrible weapon,—that sunstroke is as fatal as knife or pistol. The answer is easy. Are not the lords of the loom as objectionable as were the lords of the lash? Ought not the makers of drunkards to be pilloried in the contempt of the community? Legree on the plantation is not more hateful than Legree in the counting-room. A doctor of divinity screening slavery is no more monstrous than a doctor of divinity defending grog-sellers. If men do not want to be stigmatized they must not act basely. Decorous rascals can be frightened into decency even when they are bad at heart. Exposure has terrors that deter from evil. Thus invective is a whip and a spur. It was necessary yesterday, and is useful to-day. Welcome the man who is an embodied Day of Judgment.

It has been charged that Mr. Phillips showed a failure of judgment in his later years. The same charge was brought against his earlier judgment until success crowned it. Perhaps it is only because he is still ahead that his judgment is again impeached. When the agitation of Temperance, Home Rule, Labor and Capital, the Treatment of the Insane, Woman's Rights, Finance, Municipal Misgovernment, the Indian Question, Oppressed Nationalities, the Corruption of Parties, Chinese Enfranchisement (eleven reforms which he discussed for years) shall be finally closed, it is more than probable that, like "Abou Ben Adhem's name," in Leigh Hunt's poem, Wendell Phillips will again head the list of benefactors. "Let those who say he did not understand Labor and Capital," cries Joseph Cook, "wait fifty years, until Macaulay's Huns and Vandals appear on this continent, and then ask whether Wendell Phillips understood the necessities of the case."

In certain features, Phillips strikingly resembled Milton. This which the brilliant essayist wrote of the poet would equally fit the orator:

"He pressed into the forlorn hope. When his opinion seemed likely to prevail he passed on to other subjects. There is no more hazardous enterprise than that of bearing the torch of truth into those dark and infected recesses in which no light has ever shone. But it was his choice and pleasure to penetrate the noisome vapors and to brave the terrible explosion. Those who most disapprove of his opinions must respect the hardihood with which he maintained them. He, in general, left to others the credit of expounding and defending the popular parts of his creed. He took his stand upon those which the great body of his countrymen reprobated as criminal or derided as paradoxical. His radiant and beneficent career resembled that of the god of light and fertility."

No; we have no apologies to make for Wendell Phillips. What, did he never err? He did: he was human. But his mistakes, as in his estimate of Lincoln, of Johnson, of Grant, were in judgment, never in conduct. His errors concerned men and measures, not ethics. His life was governed by a divine polarity. His twin maxims were justice and love. They held him true,—and will any man, until God abdicates. Hence,

" —— nothing is here for tears,
No weakness, no contempt, dispraise, nor blame;
Nothing but well and fair."

WENDELL PHILLIPS.

In the life of St. Bernard by Gregory the Great (historian worthy of his hero), it is related that at the hour when holy hymns exhale from the cloister in the midst of silence and darkness, the man of God was gazing heavenward through the grated window of his cell. Suddenly there shone round about him a dazzling light in which every form of beauty that could bewitch the senses, every subtle temptation that could fascinate the mind, every allurement that could damn the soul, floated before his eyes as though gathered to a focus in one ray of sunshine. " He saw it," says the inscription, which may still be read in the tower upon Monte Casino where he dwelt, "and scorned it." Wendell Phillips had two similar visions and made two similar answers. The first was in his youth, when the sirens came and sang their seductions to him, offering him the world and the glory of it, if he would forswear philanthropy. The second came in his prime. The war was ended. Slavery was dead. His name was on all lips. His reputation as the orator of the successful cause was cosmopolitan. He might have been the most popular and courted of Americans. The Governorship of his native State, a seat in the lower House of Congress, the Senatorship—any honor was within his easy reach. In such circumstances, his continued choice of hated causes, his rigid application of his principles to the reforms that were still unwon, his dedication of his powers and his ripe experience to the service not of one race alone, but of humanity, his deliberate rejection of the crown and acceptance of the cross,—was the grandest reach of his career ; grander than that early self-surrender, because this was made at an age when he had full knowledge of the meaning and value of all he forfeited. From that hour, instead of falling off, his character and influence took on new grandeur.

The record is made,—so far, at least, as to fix his name and fame "'twixt Orion and the Pleiades." We may say of him as Grattan said of Fox: "You must measure such a mind by parallels of latitude." Nay, we may apply to him his own words spoken over Garrison's coffin: "Serene, fearless, marvellous man! mortal, with so few shortcomings!"

He will not be replaced. When Dr. Johnson died, Gerard Hamilton exclaimed: "Johnson is dead. Let us go to the next best; nobody can be said to put you in mind of Johnson." So we cry: Phillips is dead. We go to the next best; THERE IS NO OTHER WENDELL PHILLIPS.

VII.

PHILLIPSIANA.

WE throw together in this chapter a few sayings, stories, and epigrams of Mr. Phillips. He was a great utterer of such sentences, and the collection might easily be swelled into a volume. But the lack of space enforces brevity.

Men cry out against sentiment as though it were weakness. But what is Bunker Hill Monument? Sentiment! Why did Massachusetts send the bust of Sam Adams to stand in the Rotunda at Washington? Sentiment! This is the strongest element in the strongest character. A package was found among the papers of Dean Swift—that old, fierce hater, his soul full of gall, who faced England in her maddest hour and defeated her with his pen charged with lightning hotter than Junius's. Wrapped up among his choicest treasures was found a lock of hair. "Only a woman's hair," was the motto. Deep down in that heart full of strength and fury, there lay this fountain of sentiment, calming and shaping all that character. Nelson on the broad sea, a thousand miles off, signalled, "England expects every man to do his duty." What was that? Sentiment. It made a hero of every sailor. Yes, it made every sailor a Nelson. Cæsar, crossing the Alps, drew his whole army aside to spare a tree.

We circumnavigate the globe to find men to teach us. We tempt Agassiz from his birthplace to question nature for her secrets. Save the teachers God has put in our streets—teachers of law, order, justice, freedom, brotherhood, self-sacrifice, the nobleness of that life which serves men, and the happiness of his death who leaves the world better for his having lived.

Genius can mould no marble so speaking as the spot where a brave man stood or the scene where he labored.

Some men say the Old South Church is ugly. I should be ashamed to know whether it is ugly or handsome. Does a man love his mother because she is handsome? Could any man say whether his mother was ugly? Must we remodel Sam Adams on a Chesterfield pattern? Would you scuttle the Mayflower if you found her Dutch in build?

Knowledge does not fortify a man against crime. It does not create character. You can educate the brain so as to make it despise violence—only to fall more in love with cheating. What is called civilization drives away the tiger, but breeds the fox.

A certain man spent all his money on a house. Some one asked him to contribute to build an insane asylum. "Gracious!" cried he, "I *have* built one already."

I lectured one night in a New England town on "The Lost Arts." When I finished a lady said:

"I was interested in the lecture, but it didn't seem to have much relation to the origin of law."

"What do you mean, madam?" I asked.

"Why," said she, "weren't you to lecture on '*The Law Starts*'?"

Here are four lines from an old song which workingmen ought to commit to memory and ponder:

> " My lord rides out at the castle gate,
> My lady is grand in bower and hall,
> With men and maidens to cringe and wait:
> *But John o' the smithy pays for all.*"

A politician is a man who lives by whispering at Washington what he wouldn't for all the world have known at home, and whispering at home what he wouldn't for all the world have known in Washington, and who is politically dead the moment he is equally well known in both places.

I once spent the night with a clergyman, an old friend, who had the habit of reading his sermons. I asked him why he did so. He went on to give me the reasons, and became animated. "Well," said I, "I am tired to-night, but I have been very much interested in what you said. Nevertheless, if you had *read* your remarks I should have gone to sleep."

Would any young enthusiast on fire for a new reform be crazy enough to go to State Street, Beacon Street, or Harvard College for countenance ? If so, he must be *very* young, and will soon learn better.

I passed the other day one of our city churches which has *on* it authentic likenesses of the apostles not *in* it.

Luther, Calvin, Wesley, show that no man can be faithful to the truth in his pulpit or on the platform and be popular in his own generation.

The English Constitution comes down to us through the ages not by the steps of logical deduction, but by transmigration, like that of Eastern mythology, through martyrs and patriots.

Some people's idea of agitation is like the clown in the classic play, two thousand years ago, who seeing a man bring down with an arrow an eagle floating in the blue ether above, said : "You needn't have wasted that arrow—the fall would have killed him !"

Keep your prejudices in favor of justice and liberty. "Get rid of this prejudice," said David Hume to his Christian mother. "My son," was her reply, "can you show me anything better ?"

When I was asked, the other day, how it happened there was so much learning at Cambridge, I answered : "Because nobody carries any away."

A number of years ago a poor man, whose case, for some reason or for no reason skilfully presented, had excited a good deal of sympathy among Boston philanthropists, conceived the

idea of having an entertainment given for his benefit, and prevailed upon the Rev. William R. Alger and myself to give him what would be known in theatrical circles as a benefit. The affair was very well advertised, men being even employed to carry placards about town, a means of advertising more novel then than now, and it was expected that Music Hall, the place chosen for the exercises, would be crowded. But from some cause or other, the weather, rival attractions, or what not, the patronage was so light that the amount received for the tickets was not sufficient to pay the expenses. On the day following the lecture I received a call from the beneficiary, who informed me that the expenses were $20 more than the receipts, and, just as I opened my lips to express regrets, the visitor added coolly :
" I suppose that, of course, you and Mr. Alger will be responsible for the balance."

Opinion is not truth, but only truth filtered through the standpoint, the disposition, or the mood of the spectator.

In the old Anti-Slavery days I lectured in Cincinnati. At the same time there was a convention of ministers in session. The next morning I took the cars, seating myself quite near the door. The car was full of white cravats, so that it looked like an adjourned session of the convention. Presently, a sleek, well-fed man bustled on to the platform, and addressing the brakeman, asked :

" Is Mr. Phillips on board ?"

" Yes," was the reply " there he sits back of the door."

The man came into the car—he was evidently a clergyman. In a loud voice he cried, pointing his finger at me :

" Are you Mr. Phillips ?"

" I am, sir."

" Are you trying to free the niggers ?"

" Yes, sir, I am an Abolitionist."

" Well, why do you preach your doctrines up here ? Why don't you go there ?" pointing toward Kentucky, just across the Ohio River.

" Excuse me," said I, " are you a preacher ?"

" I am, sir."

" Are you trying to save souls from hell ?"

"Yes, sir, that is my business."

"*Well, why don't you go there?*"

There was a roar, and my critic vanished in the next car.

Men marvel at the uprising which hurled slavery to the dust. It was young men who dreamed dreams over patriot graves— enthusiasts wrapped in memories! Marble, gold, and granite are not real: the only reality is an idea.

My advice to workingmen is this:

If you want power in this country; if you want to make yourselves felt; if you do not want your children to wait long years before they have the bread on the table they ought to have, the leisure in their lives they ought to have, the opportunities in life they ought to have; if you don't want to wait yourselves,— write on your banner, so that every political trimmer can read it, so that every politician, no matter how short-sighted he may be can read it, "We never forget! If you launch the arrow of sarcasm at labor, we never forget; if there is a division in Congress, and you throw your vote in the wrong scale, we never forget! You may go down on your knees, and say, 'I am sorry I did the act;' and we will say, 'It will avail you in heaven, but on this side of the grave, never.'" So that a man, in taking up the labor question, will know he is dealing with a hair-trigger pistol, and will say, "I am to be true to justice and to man: otherwise I am a dead duck."

Hung Fung was a Chinese philosopher well-nigh a hundred years old. The Emperor once said to him:

"Hung, ninety years of study and observation must have made you wise. Tell me, what is the great danger of a government?"

"Well," quoth Hung, "it's the rat in the statue."

"The rat in the statue!" repeated the Emperor. "What do you mean?"

"Why," retorted Hung, "you know we build statues to the memory of our ancestors. They are made of wood, and are hollow and painted. Now, if a rat gets into one you can't smoke it out—it's the image of your father. You can't plunge it into the water—that would wash off the paint. So the rat is safe because the image is sacred."

May 23, 1879.

MY DEAR FRIEND: I read your remarks on cremation with hearty interest. They were very happily put, and struck me as fresh and original to a remarkable degree, for when every one is talking it is hard to put the topic in a new light.

It is years since I've read Sir Thomas Browne's "Urn Burial," but I fancy there might be some flowers culled thence for use in this new discussion. Did you quote him?

Thank you for a sight of your utterances. Make my kindest compliments to your wife, to whom I send the best and latest photograph of Sumner, as a sly means of getting mine in along with and under cover of it.

Yours cordially,
WENDELL PHILLIPS.[1]

Rev. Carlos Martyn.

---

[1] See opposite page for fac-simile of Mr. Phillips's penmanship.

Send the best &
latest photograph
of Sumner, or a
sly means of getting
mine in along with
Sumner cover of it —

  Yours cordially
  Wendell Phillips.

Rev Carlos Martyn

APPENDIX.

THE LOST ARTS.[1]

LADIES AND GENTLEMEN:

I am to talk to you to-night about "The Lost Arts,"—a lecture which has grown under my hand year after year, and which belongs to that first phase of the lyceum system, before it undertook to meddle with political duties or dangerous and angry questions of ethics; when it was merely an academic institution, trying to win busy men back to books, teaching a little science, or repeating some tale of foreign travel, or painting some great representative character, the symbol of his age. I think I can claim a purpose beyond a moment's amusement in this glance at early civilization.

I, perhaps, might venture to claim that it was a medicine for what is the most objectionable feature of our national character; and that is self-conceit,—an undue appreciation of ourselves, an exaggerated estimate of our achievements, of our inventions, of our contributions to popular comfort, and of our place, in fact, in the great procession of the ages. We seem to imagine, that whether knowledge will die with us, or not, it certainly began with us. We have a pitying estimate, a tender compassion, for the narrowness, ignorance, and darkness of the bygone ages. We seem to ourselves not only to monopolize, but to have begun, the era of light. In other words, we are all running over with a fourth-day-of-July spirit of self-content. I am often reminded of the German whom the English poet Cole-

---

[1] This lecture was never revised by Mr. Phillips, and is imperfect in form and expression. But it is the best report in existence.

ridge met at Frankfort. He always took off his hat with profound respect when he ventured to speak of himself. It seems to me, the American people might be painted in the chronic attitude of taking off its hat to itself ; and therefore it can be no waste of time, with an audience in such a mood, to take their eyes for a moment from the present civilization, and guide them back to that earliest possible era that history describes for us, if it were only for the purpose of asking whether we boast on the right line. I might despair of curing the habit of boasting, but I might direct it better !

Well, I have been somewhat criticised, year after year, for this endeavor to open up the claims of old times. I have been charged with repeating useless fables with no foundation. Take the subject of glass. This material, Pliny says, was discovered by accident. Some sailors, landing on the eastern coast of Spain, took their cooking utensils, and supported them on the sand by the stones that they found in the neighborhood : they kindled their fire, cooked the fish, finished the meal, and removed the apparatus ; and glass was found to have resulted from the nitre and sea-sand, vitrified by the heat. Well, I have been a dozen times criticised by a number of wise men, in newspapers, who have said that this was a very idle tale, that there never was sufficient heat in a few bundles of sticks to produce vitrification,—glass-making. I happened, two years ago, to meet, on the prairies of Missouri, Professor Shepherd, of Yale College. I mentioned this criticism to him. "Well," said he, "a little practical life would have freed men from that doubt." He went on : "We stopped last year in Mexico, to cook some venison. We got down from our saddles, and put the cooking apparatus on stones we found there ; made our fire with the wood we got there, resembling ebony ; and when we removed the apparatus there was pure silver gotten out of the embers by the intense heat of that almost iron wood. Now," said he, "that heat was greater than any necessary to vitrify the materials of glass." Why not suppose that Pliny's sailors had lighted on some exceedingly hard wood ? May it not be as possible as in this case ?

So, ladies and gentlemen, with a growing habit of distrust of a large share of this modern and exceedingly scientific criticism of ancient records, I think we have been betraying our own ignorance, and that frequently, when the statement does not look, on the face of it, to be exactly accurate, a little investigation below the surface will show that it rests on a real truth. Take, for instance, the English proverb, which was often quoted in my college days. We used to think how little logic the common people had; and when we wanted to illustrate this in the school-room,—it was what was called a *non sequitur:* the effect did not come from the cause named,—we always quoted the English proverb, "Tenterden steeple is the cause of Goodwin Sands." We said, "How ignorant a population!" But, when we went deeper into the history, we found that the proverb was not meant for logic, but was meant for sarcasm. One of the bishops had fifty thousand pounds given to him, to build a breakwater to save the Goodwin Sands from the advancing sea; but the good bishop, instead of building the breakwater to keep out the sea, simply built a steeple; and this proverb was sarcastic, and not logical, that "Tenterden steeple was the cause of the Goodwin Sands." When you contemplate the motive, there was the closest and best-welded logic in the proverb. So I think a large share of our criticism of old legends and old statements will be found in the end to be the ignorance that overleaps its own saddle, and falls on the other side.

Before I proceed to talk of these lost arts, I ought in fairness to make an exception. Over a very large section of literature, there is a singular contradiction to this swelling conceit. There are certain lines in which the moderns are ill satisfied with themselves, and contented to acknowledge that they ought fairly to sit down at the feet of their predecessors. Take poetry, painting, sculpture, architecture, the drama, and almost everything in works of any form that relates to beauty,—with regard to that whole sweep, the modern world gilds it with its admiration. Take the very phrases that we use. The artist says he wishes to go to Rome. "For what?" "To study the masters." Well, all the masters have been in their graves several hundred years. We are all pupils. You tell the poet, "Sir, that line of yours would remind one of Homer," and he is delighted. Stand in front of a painting, in the hearing of the artist, and compare its coloring to that of Titian or Raphael, and he remembers you forever. I recollect once standing in front of a bit of marble carved by Powers, a Vermonter, who had a matchless, instinctive love of art, and perception of beauty. I said to an Italian standing with me, "Well, now, that seems to me to be perfection." The answer was, "To be perfection,"—shrugging his shoulders,—"why, sir, that reminds you of Phidias!" as if to remind you of that Greek was a greater compliment than to be perfection.

Well, now, the very choice of phrases betrays a confession of inferiority; and you see it again crops out in the amount we borrow. Take the whole range of imaginative literature, and we are all wholesale borrowers. In every matter that relates to invention, to use, or beauty, or form, we are borrowers.

You may glance around the furniture of the palaces in Europe, and you may gather all these utensils of art or use; and, when you have fixed the shape and forms in your mind, I will take you into the museum of Naples, which holds the remains of the domestic life of the Romans, and you shall not find a single one of these modern forms of art or beauty or use, that was not anticipated there. We have hardly added one single line of beauty to the antique.

Take the stories of Shakespeare, who has, perhaps, written his forty-odd plays. Some are historical. The rest, two thirds of them, he did not stop to invent, but he found them. These he clutched, ready made to his hand, from the Italian novelists, who had taken them before from the East. Cinderella and her slipper is older than all history, like half a dozen other baby legends. The annals of the world do not go back far enough to tell us their origin.

All the boys' plays, like everything that amuses the child in the open air, are Asiatic. Rawlinson will show you that they came somewhere from the banks of the Ganges or the suburbs of Damascus. Bulwer borrowed the incidents of his Roman stories from legends of a thousand years before. Indeed, Dunlop, who has grouped the history of the novels of all Europe into one essay, says that in the nations of modern Europe there have been two hundred and fifty or three hundred distinct stories. He says at least two hundred of these may be traced, before Christianity, to the other side of the Black Sea. If this were my topic, I might tell you that even our newspaper-jokes are enjoying a very respectable old age. Take Maria Edgeworth's essay on Irish bulls and the laughable mistakes of the

Irish. The tale which either Maria Edgeworth or her father thought the best is that famous story of a man writing a letter as follows: "My dear friend, I would write you in detail, more minutely, if there was not an impudent fellow looking over my shoulder, reading every word." ("No, you lie: I've not read a word you have written!") This is an Irish bull, still it is a very old one. It is only two hundred and fifty years older than the New Testament. Horace Walpole dissented from Richard Lovell Edgeworth, and thought the other Irish bull was the best, —of the man who said, "I would have been a very handsome man, but they changed me in the cradle." That comes from Don Quixote, and is Spanish; but Cervantes borrowed it from the Greek in the fourth century, and the Greek stole it from the Egyptian hundreds of years back.

There is one story which it is said Washington has related, of a man who went into an inn, and asked for a glass of drink from the landlord, who pushed forward a wineglass about half the usual size (the teacups also in that day were not more than half the present size). The landlord said, "That glass out of which you are drinking is forty years old."—"Well," said the thirsty traveller, contemplating its diminutive proportions, "I think it is the smallest thing of its age I ever saw." That story as told is given as a story of Athens three hundred and seventy-five years before Christ was born. Why! all these Irish bulls are Greek,—every one of them. Take the Irishman who carried around a brick as a specimen of the house he had to sell; take the Irishman who shut his eyes, and looked into the glass to see how he would look when he was dead; take the Irishman that bought a crow, alleging that crows were reported to live two hundred years, and he meant to set out and try it; take the Irishman who met a friend who said to him, "Why, sir, I heard you were dead."—"Well," says the man, "I suppose you see I'm not."—"Oh, no!" says he, "I would believe the man who told me a good deal quicker than I would you." Well, those are all Greek. A score or more of them, of the parallel character, come from Athens.

Our old Boston patriots felt that tarring and feathering a Tory was a genuine patent Yankee firebrand,—Yankeeism. They little imagined that when Richard Cœur de Lion set out on one of his crusades, among the orders he issued to his camp of soldiers was, that any one who robbed a hen-roost should be tarred and feathered. Many a man who lived in Connecticut has repeated the story of taking children to the limits of the town, and giving them a sound thrashing to enforce their memory of the spot. But the Burgundians in France, in a statute now eleven hundred years old, attributed valor to the East of France because it had a law that the children should be taken to the limits of the district, and there soundly whipped, in order that they might forever remember the boundary-line.

So we have very few new things in that line. But I said I would take the subject of glass. It is the very best expression of man's self-conceit.

I had heard that nothing had been observed in ancient times which could be called by the name of glass,—that there had been merely attempts to imitate it. I thought they had proved the proposition : they certainly had elaborated it. In Pompeii, a dozen miles south of Naples, which was covered with ashes by Vesuvius eighteen hundred years ago, they broke into a room full of glass : there was ground glass, window-glass, cut-glass, and colored glass of every variety. It was undoubtedly a glass-maker's factory. So the lie and the refutation came face to face. It was like a pamphlet printed in London, in 1836, by Dr. Lardner, which proved that a steamboat could not cross the ocean ; and the book came to this country in the first steamboat that came across the Atlantic.

The chemistry of the most ancient period had reached a point which we have never even approached, and which we in vain struggle to reach to-day. Indeed, the whole management of the effect of light on glass is still a matter of profound study. The first two stories which I have to offer you are simply stories from history.

The first is from the letters of the Catholic priests who broke into China, which were published in France some two hundred years ago. They were shown a glass, transparent and colorless, which was filled with a liquor made by the Chinese, that was shown to the observers, and appeared to be colorless like water. This liquor was poured into the glass, and then, looking through it, it seemed to be filled with fishes. They turned this out, and repeated the experiment, and again it was filled with fishes. The Chinese confessed that they did not make them; that they were the plunder of some foreign conquest. This is not a singular thing in Chinese history; for in some of their scientific discoveries we have found evidence that they did not make them, but stole them.

The second story, of half a dozen, relates to the age of Tiberius, the time of St. Paul; and tells of a Roman who had been banished, and who returned to Rome, bringing a wonderful cup. This cup he dashed upon the marble pavement, and it was crushed, not broken, by the fall. It was dented some, and with a hammer he easily brought it into shape again. It was brilliant, transparent, but not brittle. I once made this statement in New Haven; and among the audience was Professor Silliman. He was kind enough to come to the platform when I had ended, and say that he was familiar with most of my facts, but, speaking of malleable glass, he had this to say,—that it was nearly a natural impossibility, and that no amount of evidence which could be brought would make him credit it. Well, the Romans got their chemistry from the Arabians; they brought it into Spain eight centuries ago, and in their books of that age they claim that they got from the Arabians malleable glass. There is a kind of glass spoken of there, that, if supported by one end, by its own weight in twenty hours would dwindle down to a fine line, and that you could curve around your wrist. Von Beust, the Chancellor of Austria, has ordered secrecy in Hungary in regard to a recently discovered process by which glass can be used exactly like wool, and manufactured into cloth.

These are a few records. When you go to Rome, they will show you a bit of glass like the solid rim of this tumbler,—transparent glass, a solid thing, which they lift up so as to show you that there is nothing concealed; but in the centre of the glass is a drop of colored glass, perhaps as large as a pea, mottled like a duck, finely mottled, with the shifting colored hues of the neck, and which even a miniature pencil could not do more perfectly. It is manifest that this drop of liquid glass must have been poured, because there is no joint. This must have been done by a greater heat than the annealing process, because that process shows breaks.

The imitation of gems has deceived not only the lay people, but the connoisseurs. Some of these imitations in later years have been discovered. The celebrated vase of the Genoa Cathedral was considered a solid emerald. The Roman Catholic legend of it was, that it was one of the treasures that the Queen of Sheba gave to Solomon, and that it was the identical cup out of which the Saviour drank at the Last Supper. Columbus must have admired it. It was venerable in his day; it was death for anybody to touch it but a Catholic priest. And when Napoleon besieged Genoa, the Jews offered to loan the Senate three million dollars on that single article as security. Napoleon took it, and carried it to France, and gave it to the Institute. Somewhat reluctantly the scholars said, "It is not a stone : we hardly know what it is."

Cicero said that he had seen the entire "Iliad," which is a poem as large as the New Testament, written on a skin so thin that it could be rolled up in the compass of a nut-shell. Now, this is imperceptible to the ordinary eye. You have seen the Declaration of Independence in the compass of a quarter of a dollar, written with glasses. I have to-day a paper at home, as long as half my hand, on which was photographed the whole contents of a London newspaper. It was put under a dove's wing, and sent into Paris, where they enlarged it, and read the news. This copy of the "Iliad" must have been made by some such process.

In the Roman theatre,—the Coliseum, which could seat a hundred thousand people,—the emperor's box, raised to the highest tier, bore about the same proportion to the space as this stand does to this hall ; and to look down to the centre of a six-acre lot, was to look a considerable distance. ("Considerable," by the way, is not a Yankee word. Lord Chesterfield uses it in his letters to his son, so it has a good English origin.) Pliny says that Nero the tyrant had a ring with a gem in it, which he looked through, and watched the sword-play of the gladiators,—men who killed each other to amuse the people,— more clearly than with the naked eye. So Nero had an opera-glass.

Mauritius the Sicilian stood on the promontory of his island, and could sweep over the entire sea to the coast of Africa with his *nauscopite*, which is a word derived from two Greek words, meaning "to see a ship." Evidently Mauritius, who was a pirate, had a marine telescope.

You may visit Dr. Abbot's museum, where you will see the

ring of Cheops. Bunsen puts him five hundred years before Christ. The signet of the ring is about the size of a quarter of a dollar, and the engraving is invisible without the aid of glasses. No man was ever shown into the cabinets of gems in Italy without being furnished with a microscope to look at them. It would be idle for him to look at them without one. He couldn't appreciate the delicate lines and the expression of the faces. If you go to Parma, they will show you a gem once worn on the finger of Michael Angelo, of which the engraving is two thousand years old, on which there are the figures of seven women. You must have the aid of a glass in order to distinguish the forms at all. I have a friend who has a ring, perhaps three-quarters of an inch in diameter, and on it is the naked figure of the god Hercules. By the aid of glasses you can distinguish the interlacing muscles, and count every separate hair on the eyebrows. Layard says he would be unable to read the engravings at Nineveh without strong spectacles, they are so extremely small. Rawlinson brought home a stone about twenty inches long and ten wide, containing an entire treatise on mathematics. It would be perfectly illegible without glasses. Now, if we are unable to read it without the aid of glasses, you may suppose the man who engraved it had pretty strong spectacles. So the microscope, instead of dating from our time, finds its brothers in the books of Moses,—and these are infant brothers.

So if you take colors. Color is, we say, an embellishment. We dye our dresses, and ornament our furniture. It is a luxury to gratify the eye. But the Egyptians impressed it into a new service. For them, it was a method of recording history. Some parts of their history were written; but when they wanted to elaborate history they painted it. Their colors are immortal, else we could not know of it. We find upon the stucco of their walls their kings holding court, their armies marching out, their craftsmen in the ship-yard, with the ships floating in the dock; and, in fact, we trace all their rites and customs painted in undying colors. The French who went to Egypt with Napoleon said that all the colors were perfect except the greenish-white, which is the hardest for us. They had no difficulty with the Tyrian purple. The buried city of Pompeii was a city of stucco. All the houses are stucco outside, and it is stained with Tyrian purple,—the royal color of antiquity.

But you cannot rely on the name of a color after a thousand years. So the Tyrian purple is almost a red,—about the color of these curtains. This is a city of all red. It had been buried seventeen hundred years; and if you take a shovel now, and clear away the ashes, this color flames up upon you, a great deal richer than anything we can produce. You can go down into the narrow vault which Nero built as a retreat from the great heat, and you will find the walls painted all over with fanciful designs in arabesque, which have been buried beneath the earth fifteen hundred years; but when the peasants light it up with their torches, the colors flash out before you as fresh as they were in the days of St. Paul. Our fellow-citizen Mr. Page spent twelve years in Venice, studying Titian's method of mixing his colors, and he thinks he has got it. Yet come down from Titian, whose colors are wonderfully and perfectly fresh, to Sir Joshua Reynolds, and although his colors are not yet a hundred years old, they are fading: the colors on his lips are dying out, and the cheeks are losing their tints. He did not know how to mix well. All this mastery of color is as yet unequalled. If you should go with that most delightful of all lecturers, Professor Tyndall, he would show you in the spectrum the vanishing rays of violet, and prove to you that beyond their limit there are rays still more delicate, and to you invisible, but which he, by chemical paper, will make visible; and he will tell you that probably, though you see three or four inches more than three hundred years ago your predecessors did, yet three hundred years after our successors will surpass our limit. The French have a theory that there is a certain delicate shade of blue that Europeans cannot see. In one of his lectures to his students, Ruskin opened his Catholic mass-book, and said, "Gentlemen, we are the best chemists in the world. No Englishman ever could doubt that. But we cannot make such a scarlet as that; and even if we could, it would not last for twenty years. Yet this is five hundred years old!" The Frenchman says, "I am the best dyer in Europe: nobody can equal me, and nobody can surpass Lyons." Yet in Cashmere, where the girls make shawls worth thirty thousand dollars, they will show him three hundred distinct colors, which he not only cannot make, but cannot even distinguish. When I was in Rome, if a lady wished to wear a half dozen colors at a masquerade, and have them all in harmony, she would go to the Jews; for the Oriental eye is better than even those of France or Italy, of which we think so highly.

Taking the metals. The Bible in its first chapters shows that man first conquered metals there in Asia; and on that spot to-day he can work more wonders with those metals than we can.

One of the surprises that the European artists received, when the English plundered the summer palace of the King of China, was the curiously wrought metal vessels of every kind, far exceeding all the boasted skill of the workmen of Europe.

Mr. Colton of the *Boston Journal*, the first week he landed in Asia, found that his chronometer was out of order, from the steel of the works having become rusted. The London *Medical and Surgical Journal* advises surgeons not to venture to carry any lancets to Calcutta,—to have them gilded, because English steel could not bear the atmosphere of India. Yet the Damascus blades of the Crusades were not gilded, and they are as perfect as they were eight centuries ago. There was one at the London Exhibition, the point of which could be made to touch the hilt, and which could be put into a scabbard like a corkscrew, and bent every way without breaking, like an American politician. Now, the wonder of this is, that perfect steel is a marvel of science. If a London chronometer-maker wants the best steel to use in his chronometer, he does not send to Sheffield, the centre of all science, but to the Punjaub, the empire of the seven rivers, where there is no science at all. The first needle ever made in England was made in the time of Henry the Eighth, and made by a negro; and when he died, the art died with him. Some of the first travellers in Africa stated that they found a tribe in the interior who gave them better razors than they had; the irrepressible negro coming up in science as in politics. The best steel is the greatest triumph of metallurgy, and metallurgy is the glory of chemistry.

The poets have celebrated the perfection of the Oriental steel; and it is recognized as the finest by Moore, Byron, Scott, Southey, and many others. I have even heard a young advocate of the lost arts find an argument in Byron's "Sennacherib," from the fact that the mail of the warriors in that one short night had rusted before the trembling Jews stole out in the morning to behold the terrible work of the Lord. Scott, in his "Tales of the Crusaders,"—for Sir Walter was curious in his love of the lost arts,—describes a meeting between Richard Cœur de Lion and Saladin. Saladin asks Richard to show him the wonderful strength for which he is famous, and the Norman monarch responds by severing a bar of iron which lies on the floor of his tent. Saladin say, "I cannot do that;" but he takes an eider-down pillow from the sofa, and, drawing his keen blade across it, it falls in two pieces. Richard says, "This is the black art; it is magic; it is the devil: you cannot cut that which has no resistance;" and Saladin, to show him that such is not the case, takes a scarf from his shoulders, which is so light that it almost floats in the air, and, tossing it up, severs it before it can descend. George Thompson told me he saw a man in Calcutta throw a handful of floss-silk into the air, and a Hindoo sever it into pieces with his sabre. We can produce nothing like this.

Considering their employment of the mechanical forces, and their movement of large masses from the earth, we know that the Egyptians had the five, seven, or three mechanical powers; but we cannot account for the multiplication and increase necessary to perform the wonders they accomplished.

In Boston, lately, we have moved the Pelham Hotel, weighing fifty thousand tons, fourteen feet, and are very proud of it; and since then we have moved a whole block of houses twenty-three feet, and I have no doubt we will write a book about it: but there is a book telling how Domenico Fontana of the sixteenth century set up the Egyptian obelisk at Rome on end, in the Papacy of Sixtus V. Wonderful! Yet the Egyptians quarried that stone, and carried it a hundred and fifty miles, and the Romans brought it seven hundred and fifty miles, and never said a word about it. Mr. Batterson of Hartford, walking with Brunel, the architect of the Thames tunnel, in Egypt, asked him what he thought of the mechanical power of the Egyptians; and he said, "There is Pompey's Pillar: it is an hundred feet high, and the capital weighs two thousand pounds. It is something of a feat to hang two thousand pounds at that height in the air, and the few men that can do it would better discuss Egyptian mechanics."

Take canals. The Suez canal absorbs half its receipts in cleaning out the sand which fills it continually, and it is not yet known whether it is a pecuniary success. The ancients built a canal at right angles to ours ; because they knew it would not fill up if built in that direction, and they knew such an one as ours would. There were magnificent canals in the land of the Jews, with perfectly arranged gates and sluices. We have only just begun to understand ventilation properly for our houses ; yet late experiments at the Pyramids in Egypt show that those Egyptian tombs were ventilated in the most perfect and scientific manner.

Again, cement is modern, for the ancients dressed and joined their stones so closely, that, in buildings thousands of years old, the thin blade of a penknife cannot be forced between them. The railroad dates back to Egypt. Arago has claimed that they had a knowledge of steam. A painting has been discovered of a ship full of machinery, and a French engineer said that the arrangement of this machinery could only be accounted for by supposing the motive power to have been steam. Bramah acknowledges that he took the idea of his celebrated lock from an ancient Egyptian pattern. De Tocqueville says there was no social question that was not discussed to rags in Egypt.

"Well," say you, "Franklin invented the lightning-rod." I have no doubt he did ; but years before his invention, and before muskets were invented, the old soldiers on guard on the towers used Franklin's invention to keep guard with ; and if a spark passed between them and the spear-head, they ran and bore the warning of the state and condition of affairs. After that you will admit that Benjamin Franklin was not the only one that knew of the presence of electricity, and the advantages derived from its use. Solomon's Temple, you will find, was situated on an exposed point of the hill : the temple was so lofty that it was often in peril, and was guarded by a system exactly like that of Benjamin Franklin.

Well, I may tell you a little of ancient manufactures. The Duchess of Burgundy took a necklace from the neck of a mummy, and wore it to a ball given at the Tuileries ; and everybody said they thought it was the newest thing there. A Hindoo princess came into court ; and her father, seeing her, said, "Go home, you are not decently covered,—go home ;" and she said, "Father, I have seven suits on ;" but the suits were of muslin, so thin that the king could see through them. A Roman poet says, "The girl was in the poetic dress of the country." I fancy the French would be rather astonished at this. Four hundred and fifty years ago the first spinning machine was introduced into Europe. I have evidence to show that it made its appearance two thousand years before.

Why have I groped among these ashes? I have told you these facts to show you that we have not invented everything— that we do not monopolize the encyclopædia. The past had knowledge. But it was the knowledge of the classes, not of the masses. "The beauty that was Greece and the grandeur that was Rome" were exclusive, the possession of the few. The science of Egypt was amazing: but it meant privilege—the privilege of the king and the priest. It separated royalty and priesthood from the people, and was the engine of oppression. When Cambyses came down from Persia and thundered across Egypt treading out royalty and priesthood, he trampled out at the same time civilization itself.

Four thousand years passed before the people came into existence. To-day learning no longer hides in the convent or slumbers in the palace. No! she comes out into every-day life, joins hands with the multitude and cushions the peasant. Our astronomy looks at but does not dwell in the stars. It serves navigation and helps us run boundaries. Our chemistry is not the secret of the alchemist striving to change base metals into gold. It is Liebig with his hands full of blessings for every farmer, and digging gold out of the earth with the miner's pickaxe. Of all we know I can show you ninety-nine items out of every hundred which the past anticipated and which the world forgot. Our distinction lies in the liberty of intellect and the diffusion of knowledge.

When Gibbon finished his history of Rome, he said: "We have iron and fire: the hand can never go back on the dial of time." He made this boast as he stood, at night, amid the ruins of the Corsani palace, looking out on the churches where the monks were chanting.

But what is to prevent history from repeating itself? Why should our arts not be lost,—our temples of Jupiter not fall,— our Rome not decline? Will our possession of iron and fire preserve them? Before Rome was peopled nations rose and fell with iron in one hand and fire in the other. Any civilization that is exclusive, any arts that are secret and individual must perish.

The distinctive glory of the nineteenth century is that it distributes knowledge; that it recognizes the divine will, which is that every man has a right to know whatever may be serviceable to himself or to his fellows; that it makes the Church, the schoolhouse, and the town hall its symbols, and humanity its care. This democratic spirit will animate our arts with immortality, if God means that they shall last.

DANIEL O'CONNELL.[1]

A HUNDRED years ago to-day Daniel O'Connell was born. The Irish race, wherever scattered over the globe, assembles to-night to pay fitting tribute to his memory,—one of the most eloquent men, one of the most devoted patriots, and the most successful statesman, which that race has given to history. We of other races may well join you in that tribute, since the cause of constitutional government owes more to O'Connell than to any other political leader of the last two centuries. The English-speaking race, to find his equal among its statesmen, must pass by Chatham and Walpole, and go back to Oliver Cromwell, or the able men who held up the throne of Queen Elizabeth. If to put the civil and social elements of your day into successful action, and plant the seeds of continued strength and progress for coming times,—if this is to be a statesman, then most emphatically was O'Connell one. To exert this control, and secure this progress, while and because ample means lie ready for use under your hand, does not rob Walpole and Colbert, Chatham and Richelieu, of their title to be considered statesmen. To do it, as Martin Luther did, when one must ingeniously discover or invent his tools, and while the mightiest forces that influence human affairs are arrayed against him, that is what ranks O'Connell with the few masterly statesmen the English-speaking race has ever had. When Napoleon's soldiers bore the negro chief Toussaint L'Ouverture into exile, he said, pointing back to San Domingo, "You think you have rooted up the tree of liberty, but I am only a branch. I have planted the tree itself so deep that ages will never root it up." And whatever may be said of the social or industrial condition

---

[1] Oration delivered at the O'Connell Celebration in Boston, August 6th, 1870.

of Hayti during the last seventy years, its *nationality* has never been successfully assailed.

O'Connell is the only Irishman who can say as much of Ireland. From the peace of Utrecht, 1713, till the fall of Napoleon, Great Britain was the leading State in Europe ; while Ireland, a comparatively insignificant island, lay at its feet. She weighed next to nothing in the scale of British politics. The Continent pitied, and England despised her. O'Connell found her a mass of quarrelling races and sects, divided, dispirited, brokenhearted, and servile. He made her a *nation*, whose first word broke in pieces the iron obstinacy of Wellington, tossed Peel from the Cabinet, and gave the government to the Whigs : whose colossal figure, like the helmet in Walpole's romance, has filled the political sky ever since ; whose generous aid thrown into the scale of the three great British reforms,—the ballot, the corn laws, and slavery,—secured their success ; a nation whose continual discontent has dragged Great Britain down to be a second-rate power on the chess-board of Europe. I know other causes have helped in producing this result, but the nationality which O'Connell created has been the main cause of this change in England's importance. Dean Swift, Molyneux, and Henry Flood thrust Ireland for a moment into the arena of British politics, a sturdy suppliant clamoring for justice ; and Grattan held her there an equal, and, as he thought, a nation, for a few years. But the unscrupulous hand of William Pitt brushed away in an hour all Grattan's work. Well might he say of the Irish Parliament which he brought to life, "I sat by its cradle, I followed its hearse ;" since after that infamous union, which Byron called a "union of the shark with its prey," Ireland sank back, plundered and helpless. O'Connell lifted her to a fixed and permanent place in English affairs,—no suppliant, but a conqueror dictating her terms.

This is the proper standpoint from which to look at O'Connell's work. This is the consideration that ranks him, not with founders of states, like Alexander, Cæsar, Bismarck, Napoleon, and William the Silent, but with men who, without arms, by force of reason, have revolutionized their times,—with Luther, Jefferson, Mazzini, Samuel Adams, Garrison, and Franklin. I know some men will sneer at this claim,—those who have never looked at him except through the spectacles of English critics, who despised him as an Irishman and a Catholic, until they came to hate him as a conqueror. As Grattan said of Kirwan, "The curse of Swift was upon him, to have been born an Irishman and a man of genius, and to have used his gifts for his country's good." Mark what measure of success attended the able men who preceded him, in circumstances as favorable as his, perhaps even better; then measure him by comparison.

An island soaked with the blood of countless rebellions, oppression such as would turn cowards into heroes, a race whose disciplined valor had been proved on almost every battle-field in Europe, and whose reckless daring lifted it, any time, in arms against England, with hope or without—what inspired them? Devotion, eloquence, and patriotism seldom paralleled in history. Who led them? *Dean Swift*, according to Addison "the greatest genius of his age," called by Pope "the incomparable," a man fertile in resources, of stubborn courage, and tireless energy, master of an English style unequalled, perhaps, for its purpose then or since, a man who had twice faced England in her angriest mood, and by that masterly pen subdued her to his will; *Henry Flood*, eloquent even for an Irishman, and sagacious as he was eloquent, the eclipse of that brilliant life one of the saddest pictures in Irish biography; *Grattan*, with all the courage, and more than the eloquence, of his race, a statesman's eye quick to see every advantage, boundless devotion, unspotted integrity, recognized as an equal by the world's leaders, and welcomed by Fox to the House of Commons as the "Demosthenes of Ireland;" *Emmet* in the field, *Sheridan* in the senate, *Curran* at the bar; and, above all, *Edmund Burke*, whose name makes eulogy superfluous, more than Cicero in the senate, almost Plato in the academy. All these gave their lives to Ireland; and when the present century opened, where was she? Sold like a slave in the market-place by her perjured master, William Pitt. It was then that O'Connell flung himself into the struggle, gave fifty years to the service of his country; and where is she to-day? Not only redeemed, but her independence put beyond doubt or peril. Grattan and his predecessors could get no guarantees for what rights they gained. In that sagacious, watchful, and almost omnipotent *public opinion*, which O'Connell created, is an all-sufficient guarantee of Ireland's future. Look at her! almost every shackle has fallen from her limbs : all that human wisdom has as yet devised to remedy the evils of bigotry and misrule has been done. O'Connell found Ireland a "hissing and a byword" in Edinburgh and London. He made her the pivot of British politics : she rules them, directly or indirectly, with as absolute a sway as the slave question did the United States from 1850 to 1865. Look into Earl Russell's book, and the history of the Reform Bill of 1832, and see with how much truth it may be claimed that O'Connell and his fellows gave Englishmen the ballot under that act. It is by no means certain that the corn laws could have been abolished without their aid. In the Anti-Slavery struggle O'Connell stands, in influence and ability, equal with the best. I know the credit all those measures do to English leaders ; but, in my opinion, the next generation will test the statesmanship of Peel, Palmerston, Russell, and Gladstone, almost entirely by their conduct of the Irish question. All the laurels they have hitherto won in that field are rooted in ideas which Grattan and O'Connell urged on reluctant hearers for half a century. Why do Bismarck and Alexander look with such contemptuous indifference on every attempt of England to mingle in European affairs ? Because they know they have but to lift a finger, and Ireland stabs her in the back. Where was the statesmanship of English leaders when they allowed such an evil to grow so formidable ? This is Ireland to-day. What was she when O'Connell undertook her cause ? The saddest of Irish poets has described her :

" O Ireland ! my country, the hour of thy pride and thy splendor hath passed ;
And the chain that was spurned in thy moments of power hangs heavy around thee at last.
There are marks in the fate of each clime, there are turns in the fortunes of men ;
But the changes of realms, or the chances of time, shall never restore thee again.

" Thou art chained to the wheel of the foe by links which a world cannot sever :
With thy tyrant through storm and through calm thou shalt go, and thy sentence is bondage forever.

Thou art doomed for the thankless to toil, thou art left for the proud
   to disdain ;
And the blood of thy sons and the wealth of thy soil shall be lavished
   and lavished in vain.

"Thy riches with taunts shall be taken, thy valor with coldness be
   paid ;
And of millions who see thee thus sunk and forsaken, not one shall
   stand forth in thine aid.
In the nations thy place is left void ; thou art lost in the list of the
   free ;
Even realms by the plague and the earthquake destroyed may revive,
   but no hope is for thee."

It was a community impoverished by five centuries of oppression,—four millions of Catholics robbed of every acre of their native land : it was an island torn by race-hatred and religious bigotry, her priests indifferent, and her nobles hopeless or traitors. The wiliest of her enemies, a Protestant Irishman, ruled the British senate ; the sternest of her tyrants, a Protestant Irishman, led the armies of Europe. Puritan hate, which had grown blinder and more bitter since the days of Cromwell, gave them weapons. Ireland herself lay bound in the iron links of a code which Montesquieu said could have been "made only by devils, and should be registered only in hell." Her millions were beyond the reach of the great reform engine of modern times, since they could neither read nor write.

In this mass of ignorance, weakness, and quarrel, one keen eye saw hidden the elements of union and strength. With rarest skill he called them forth, and marshalled them into rank. Then this one man, without birth, wealth, or office, in a land ruled by birth, wealth, and office, moulded from those unsuspected elements a power, which, overawing king, senate, and people, wrote his single will on the statute-book of the most obstinate nation in Europe. Safely to emancipate the Irish Catholics, and, in spite of Saxon, Protestant hate, to lift all Ireland to the level of British citizenship,—this was the problem which statesmanship and patriotism had been seeking for two centuries to solve. For this, blood had been poured out like water. On this, the genius of Swift, the learning of Molyneux, and the eloquence of Bushe, Grattan, and Burke, had been wasted. English leaders ever since Fox had studied this problem anxiously. They saw that the safety of the empire was compromised. At one or two critical moments in the reign of George III., one signal from an Irish leader would have snapped the chain that bound Ireland to his throne. His ministers recognized it ; and they tried every expedient, exhausted every device, dared every peril, kept oaths or broke them, in order to succeed. All failed ; and not only failed, but acknowledged they could see no way in which success could ever be achieved.

O'Connell achieved it. Out of this darkness he called forth light. Out of this most abject, weak, and pitiable of kingdoms he made a *power ;* and, dying, he left in Parliament a spectre, which, unless appeased, pushes Whig and Tory ministers alike from their stools.

But Brougham says he was a demagogue. Fie on Wellington, Derby, Peel, Palmerston, Liverpool, Russell, and Brougham, to be fooled and ruled by a demagogue ! What must they, the subjects, be, if O'Connell, their king, be only a bigot and a demagogue ? A demagogue rides the storm : he has never really the ability to create one. He uses it narrowly, ignorantly, and for selfish ends. If not crushed by the force, which, without his will, has flung him into power, he leads it with ridiculous miscalculation against some insurmountable obstacle that scatters it forever. Dying, he leaves no mark on the elements with which he has been mixed. Robespierre will serve for an illustration. It took O'Connell thirty years of patient and sagacious labor to mould elements whose existence no man, however wise, had ever discerned before. He used them unselfishly, only to break the yoke of his race. Nearly fifty years have passed since his triumph, but his impress still stands forth clear and sharp on the empire's policy. Ireland is wholly indebted to him for her political education. Responsibility educates : he lifted her to broader responsibilities. Her possession of power makes it the keen interest of other classes to see she is well informed. He associated her with all the reform movements of Great Britain. This is the education of affairs, broader, deeper, and more real than any school or college can give. This and power, his gifts, are the lever which lifts her to every other right and privilege. How much England owes him we can never know ; since how great a danger and curse Ireland would have been to the empire had she continued the cancer Pitt and Castlereagh left her is a chapter of history which, fortunately, can never be written. No demagogue ever walked through the streets of Dublin as O'Connell and Grattan did more than once, hooted and mobbed because they opposed themselves to the mad purpose of the people, and crushed it by a stern resistance. No demagogue would have offered himself to a race like the Irish as the apostle of peace, pledging himself to the British Government, that, in the long agitation before him, with brave millions behind him spoiling for a fight, he would never draw a sword.

I have purposely dwelt long on this view, because the extent and the far-reaching effects of O'Connell's work, without regard to the motives which inspired him, or the methods he used, have never been fully recognized.

Briefly stated, he *did* what the ablest and bravest of his forerunners had tried to do, and failed. He created a public opinion and unity of purpose (no matter what be now the dispute about methods), which make Ireland a *nation;* he gave her British citizenship, and a place in the imperial Parliament; he gave her a *press* and a *public:* with these tools her destiny is in her own hands. When the Abolitionists got for the negro schools and the vote, they settled the slave question; for they planted the sure seeds of civil equality. O'Connell did this for Ireland,—this which no Irishman before had ever dreamed of attempting. Swift and Molyneux were able. Grattan, Bushe, Saurin, Burrowes, Plunket, Curran, Burke, were eloquent. Throughout the island courage was a drug: they gained now one point, and now another; but, after all, they left the helm of Ireland's destiny in foreign and hostile hands. O'Connell was brave, sagacious, eloquent: but, more than all, he was a statesman; for he gave to Ireland's own keeping the key of her future. As Lord Bacon marches down the centuries, he may lay one hand on the telegraph, and the other on the steam-engine, and say, "These are mine, for I taught you how to study nature." In a similar sense, as shackle after shackle falls from Irish limbs, O'Connell may say, "This victory is mine; for I taught you the method, and I gave you the arms."

I have hitherto been speaking of his ability and success: by and by we will look at his character, motives, and methods. This unique ability, even his enemies have been forced to confess. Harriet Martineau, in her incomparable history of the "Thirty Years' Peace," has, with Tory hate, misconstrued every action of O'Connell, and invented a bad motive for each one. But even she confesses that "he rose in power, influence, and notoriety to an eminence such as no other individual citizen has attained in modern times" in Great Britain. And one of his by no means partial biographers has well said,—

"Any man who turns over the magazines and newspapers of that period will easily perceive how grandly O'Connell's figure dominated in politics, how completely he had dispelled the indifference that had so long prevailed on Irish questions, how clearly his agitation stands forth as the great fact of the time. . . . The truth is, his position, so far from being a common one, is absolutely unique in history. We may search in vain through the records of the past for any man, who, without the effusion of a drop of blood, or the advantages of office or rank, succeeded in governing a people so absolutely and so long, and in creating so entirely the elements of his power. . . . There was no rival to his supremacy, there was no restriction to his authority. He played with the enthusiasm he had aroused, with the negligent ease of a master ; he governed the complicated organization he had created, with a sagacity that never failed. He made himself the focus of the attention of other lands, and the centre around which the rising intellect of his own revolved. He transformed the whole social system of Ireland ; almost reversed the relative positions of Protestants and Catholics ; remodelled by his influence the representative, ecclesiastical, and educational institutions, and created a public opinion that surpassed the wildest dreams of his predecessors. Can we wonder at the proud exultation with which he exclaimed, 'Grattan sat by the cradle of his country and followed her hearse : it was left for me to sound the resurrection trumpet, and to show she was not dead, but sleeping?'"

But the method by which he achieved this success is perhaps more remarkable than even the success itself. An Irish poet, one of his bitterest assailants thirty years ago, has laid a chaplet of atonement on his altar, and one verse runs,—

> "O great world-leader of a mighty age !
> Praise unto thee let all the people give.
> By thy great name of LIBERATOR live
> In golden letters upon history's page ;
> And this thy epitaph while time shall be,—
> *He found his country chained, but left her free.*"

It is natural that Ireland should remember him as her *liberator*. But, strange as it may seem to you, I think Europe and America will remember him by a higher title. I said in opening, that the cause of constitutional government is more indebted to O'Connell than to any other political leader of the last two centuries. What I mean is, that he invented the great method of constitutional agitation. *Agitator* is a title which will last longer, which suggests a broader and more permanent influence, and entitles him to the gratitude of far more millions, than the name Ireland loves to give him. The "first great *agitator*," is his proudest title to gratitude and fame. Agitation is the method that puts the school by the side of the ballot-box. The Fremont canvass was the nation's best school. Agitation prevents rebellion, keeps the peace, and secures progress. Every steps she gains is gained forever. Muskets are the weapons of animals : agitation is the atmosphere of brains. The old Hindoo saw, in his dream, the human race led out to its various fortunes. First, men were in chains which went back to an iron hand ; then he saw them led by threads from the brain, which went upward to an unseen hand. The first was despotism, iron, and ruling by force. The last was civilization, ruling by ideas.

Agitation is an old word with a new meaning. Sir Robert Peel, the first English leader who felt he was its tool, defined it to be "the marshalling of the conscience of a nation to mould its laws." O'Connell was the first to show and use its power, to lay down its principles, to analyze its elements, and mark out its metes and bounds. It is voluntary, public, and above-board, —no oath-bound secret societies like those of old time in Ireland, and of the Continent to-day. Its means are reason and argument,—no appeal to arms. Wait patiently for the slow growth of public opinion. The Frenchman is angry with his Government : he throws up barricades and shots his guns to the lips. A week's fury drags the nation ahead a hand-breadth : reaction lets it settle half-way back again. As Lord Chesterfield said, a hundred years ago, "You Frenchmen erect barricades, but never any barriers." An Englishman is dissatisfied with public affairs. He brings his charges, offers his proof, waits for prejudice to relax, for public opinion to inform itself. Then every step taken is taken forever : an abuse once removed never reappears in history. Where did he learn this method ? Practically speaking, from O'Connell. It was he who planted its corner-stone,—argument, no violence ; *no political change is worth a drop of human blood.* His other motto was, " Tell the whole truth ;" no concealing half of one's convictions to make the other half more acceptable ; no denial of one truth to gain hearing for another ; no compromise ; or, as he phrased it, " nothing is politically right which is morally wrong."

Above all, plant yourself on the millions. The sympathy of every human being, no matter how ignorant or how humble, adds weight to public opinion. At the outset of his career the clergy turned a deaf ear to his appeal. They had seen their flocks led up to useless slaughter for centuries, and counselled submission. The nobility repudiated him : they were either traitors or hopeless. Protestants had touched their *Ultima Thule* with Grattan, and seemed settling down in despair. English Catholics advised waiting till the tyrant grew merciful. O'Connell, left alone, said, " I will forge these four millions of Irish hearts into a thunderbolt, which shall suffice to dash this despotism to pieces." And he did it. Living under an aristocratic government, himself of the higher class, he anticipated Lincoln's wisdom, and framed his movement " for the people, of the people, and by the people." It is a singular fact, that, the freer a nation becomes, the more utterly democratic the form of its institutions, this outside agitation, this pressure of public opinion to direct political action, becomes more and more necessary. The general judgment is, that the freest possible government produces the freest possible men and women,—the most individual, the least servile to the judgment of others. But a moment's reflection will show any man that this is an unreasonable expectation, and that, on the contrary, entire equality and freedom in political forms almost inevitably tend to make the individual subside into the mass, and lose his identity in the general whole. Suppose we stood in England to-night. There is the nobility, and here is the Church. There is the trading-class and here is the literary. A broad gulf separates the four ; and provided a member of either can conciliate his own section, he can afford, in a very large measure, to despise the judgment of the other three. He has, to some extent, a refuge and a breakwater against the tyranny of what we call public opinion. But in a country like ours, of absolute democratic equality, public opinion is not only omnipotent, it is omnipresent. There is no refuge from its tyranny; there is no hiding from its reach: and the result is, that if you take the old Greek lantern, and go about to seek among a hundred, you will find not one single American who really has not, or who does not fancy at least that he has, something to gain or lose in his ambition, his social life, or his business, from the good opinion and the votes of those about him. And the consequence is, that, instead of being a mass of individuals, each one fearlessly blurting out his own convictions, as a nation, compared with other nations, we are a mass of cowards. More than all other people, we are afraid of each other.

If you were a caucus to-night, and I were your orator, none of you could get beyond the necessary and timid limitations of party. You not only would not demand, you would not allow me to utter, one word of what you really thought, and what I thought. You would demand of me—and my value as a caucus speaker would depend entirely on the adroitness and the vigilance with which I met the demand—that I should not utter one single word which would compromise the vote of next week. That is politics; so with the press. Seemingly independent, and sometimes really so, the press can afford only to mount the cresting wave, not go beyond it. The editor might as well shoot his reader with a bullet as with a new idea. He must hit the exact line of the opinion of the day. I am not finding fault with him: I am only describing him. Some three years ago I took to one of the freest of the Boston journals a letter, and by appropriate consideration induced its editor to print it. And as we glanced along its contents, and came to the concluding statement, he said, "Couldn't you omit that?" I said, "No: I wrote it for that; it is the gist of the statement."—"Well," said he, "it is true: there is not a boy in the streets that does not know it is true; but I wish you could omit it."

I insisted; and the next morning, fairly and justly, he printed the whole. Side by side he put an article of his own, in which he said, "We copy in the next column an article from Mr. Phillips, and we only regret the absurd and unfounded statement with which he concludes it." He had kept his promise by printing the article: he saved his reputation by printing the comment. And that, again, is the inevitable, the essential limitation of the press in a republican community. Our institutions, floating unanchored on the shifting surface of popular opinion, cannot afford to hold back, or to draw forward, a hated question, and compel a reluctant public to look at it and to consider it. Hence, as you see at once, the moment a large issue, twenty years ahead of its age, presents itself to the consideration of an empire or of a republic, just in proportion to the freedom of its institutions is the necessity of a platform outside of the press, of politics, and of its church, whereon stand men with no candidate to elect, with no plan to carry, with no reputation to stake, with no object but the truth, no purpose but to tear the question open and let the light through it. So much in explanation of a word infinitely hated,—agitation and agitators, —but an element which the progress of modern government has developed more and more every day.

The great invention we trace in its twilight and seed to the days of the Long Parliament. Defoe and L'Estrange, later down, were the first prominent Englishmen to fling pamphlets at the House of Commons. Swift ruled England by pamphlets. Wilberforce summoned the Church, and sought the alliance of influential classes. But O'Connell first showed a profound faith in the human tongue. He descried afar off the coming omnipotence of the press. He called the millions to his side, appreciated the infinite weight of the simple human heart and conscience, and grafted democracy into the British Empire. The later Abolitionists, Buxton, Sturge, and Thompson, borrowed his method. Cobden flung it in the face of the almost omnipotent landholders of England, and broke the Tory party forever. They only haunt upper air now in the stolen garments of the Whigs. The English administration recognizes this new partner in the Government, and waits to be moved on. Garrison brought the new weapon to our shores. The only wholly useful and thoroughly defensible war Christendom has seen in this century, the greatest civil and social change the English race ever saw, are the result.

This great servant and weapon, peace and constitutional government owe to O'Connell. Who has given progress a greater boon ? What single agent has done as much to bless and improve the world for the last fifty years ?

O'Connell has been charged with coarse, violent, and intemperate language. The criticism is of little importance. Stupor and palsy never understand life. White-livered indifference is always disgusted and annoyed by earnest conviction. Protestants criticised Luther in the same way. It took three centuries to carry us far off enough to appreciate his colossal proportions. It is a hundred years to-day since O'Connell was born. It will take another hundred to put us at such an angle as will enable us correctly to measure his stature. Premising that it would be folly to find fault with a man struggling for life because his attitudes were ungraceful, remembering the Scythian king's answer to Alexander, criticising his strange weapon,—"If you knew how precious freedom was, you would defend it even with axes," —we must see that O'Connell's own explanation is evidently sincere and true. He found the Irish heart so cowed, and Englishmen so arrogant, that he saw it needed an independence verging on insolence, a defiance that touched extremest limits, to breathe self-respect into his own race, teach the aggressor manners, and sober him into respectful attention. It was the same with us Abolitionists. Webster had taught the North the 'bated breath and crouching of a slave. It needed with us an attitude of independence that was almost insolent, it needed that we should exhaust even the Saxon vocabulary of scorn, to fitly utter the righteous and haughty contempt that honest men had for man-stealers. Only in that way could we wake the North to self-respect, or teach the South that at length she had met her equal, if not her master. On a broad canvas, meant for the public square, the tiny lines of a Dutch interior would be invisible. In no other circumstances was the French maxim, "You can never make a revolution with rose-water," more profoundly true. The world has hardly yet learned how deep a philosophy lies hid in Hamlet's,—

> "Nay, and thou'lt mouth,
> I'll rant as well as thou."

O'Connell has been charged with insincerity in urging repeal, and those who defended his sincerity have leaned toward allowing that it proved his lack of common sense. I think both critics mistaken. His earliest speeches point to repeal as his ultimate object: indeed, he valued emancipation largely as a means to that end. No fair view of his whole life will leave the slightest ground to doubt his sincerity. As for the reasonableness and necessity of the measure, I think every year proves them. Considering O'Connell's position, I wholly sympathize in his profound and unshaken loyalty to the empire. Its share in the British Empire makes Ireland's strength and importance. Standing alone among the vast and massive sovereignties of Europe, she would be weak, insignificant, and helpless. Were I an Irishman I should cling to the empire.

Fifty or sixty years hence, when scorn of race has vanished, and bigotry is lessened, it may be possible for Ireland to be safe and free while holding the position to England that Scotland does. But during this generation and the next, O'Connell was wise in claiming that Ireland's rights would never be safe without "Home Rule." A substantial repeal of the union should be every Irishman's earnest aim. Were I their adviser, I should constantly repeat what Grattan said in 1810, "The best advice, gentlemen, I can give on all occasions is, ' Keep knocking at the union.' "

We imagine an Irishman to be only a zealot on fire. We fancy Irish spirit and eloquence to be only blind, reckless, headlong enthusiasm. But, in truth, Grattan was the soberest leader of his day ; holding scrupulously back the disorderly elements which fretted under his curb. There was one hour, at least, when a word from him would have lighted a democratic revolt throughout the empire. And the most remarkable of O'Connell's gifts was neither his eloquence nor his sagacity : it was his patience,—" patience, all the passion of great souls ;" the tireless patience, which, from 1800 to 1820, went from town to town, little aided by the press, to plant the seeds of an intelligent and united, as well as hot patriotism. Then, after many years and long toil, waiting for rivals to be just, for prejudice to wear out, and for narrowness to grow wise, using British folly and oppression as his wand, he moulded the enthusiasm of the most excitable of races, the just and inevitable indignation of four millions of Catholics, the hate of plundered poverty, priest, noble, and peasant, into one fierce, though harmonious mass. He held it in careful check, with sober moderation, watching every opportunity, attracting ally after ally, never forfeiting any possible friendship, allowing no provocation to stir him to anything that would not help his cause, compelling each hottest and most ignorant of his followers to remember that "he who commits a crime helps the enemy." At last, when the hour struck, this power was made to achieve justice for itself, and put him in London,—him, this despised Irishman, this hated Catholic, this mere demagogue and man of words, *him*,—to hold the Tory party in one hand, and the Whig party in the other; all this without shedding a drop of blood, or disturbing for a moment the peace of the empire. While O'Connell held Ireland in his hand, her people were more orderly, law-abiding, and peaceful than for a century before, or during any year since. The strength of this marvellous control passes comprehension. Out West I met an Irishman whose father held him up to *see* O'Connell address the two hundred thousand men at Tara,—literally to *see*, not to hear him. I said, "But you could not all hear even his voice."—"Oh, no, sir! Only about thirty thousand could hear him, but we all kept as still and silent *as if we did.*" With magnanimous frankness O'Connell once said, "I never could have held those monster meetings without a crime, without disorder, tumult, or quarrel, except for Father Mathew's aid." Any man can build a furnace, and turn water into steam,—yes, if careless, make it rend his dwelling in pieces. Genius builds the locomotive, harnesses this terrible power in iron traces, holds it with master-hand in useful limits, and gives it to the peaceable service of man. The Irish people were O'Connell's locomotive, sagacious patience and moderation the genius that built it, Parliament and justice the station he reached.

Every one who has studied O'Connell's life sees his marked likeness to Luther,—the unity of both their lives; their wit; the same massive strength, even if coarse-grained; the ease with which each reached the masses, the power with which they wielded them; the same unrivalled eloquence, fit for any audience; the same instinct of genius that led them constantly to acts, which, as Voltaire said, "Foolish men call rash, but wisdom sees to be brave;" the same broad success. But O'Connell had one great element which Luther lacked,—the universality of his sympathy; the far-reaching sagacity which discerned truth afar off, just struggling above the horizon; the loyal, brave, and frank spirit which acknowledged and served it; the profound and rare faith which believed that "the whole of truth can never do harm to the whole of virtue." From the serene height of intellect and judgment to which God's gifts had lifted him, he saw clearly that no one right was ever in the way of another, that injustice harms the wrong-doer even more than the victim, that whoever puts a chain on another fastens it also on himself. Serenely confident that the truth is always safe, and justice always expedient, he saw that intolerance is only want of faith. He who stifles free discussion, secretly doubts whether what he professes to believe is really true. Coleridge says, " See how triumphant in debate and motion O'Connell is! Why? Because he asserts a broad principle, acts up to it, rests his body on it, and has faith in it."

Co-worker with Father Mathew; champion of the Dissenters; advocating the substantial principles of the Charter, though not a Chartist; foe of the corn laws; battling against slavery, whether in India or the Carolinas; the great democrat who in Europe seventy years ago called the people to his side; starting a movement of the people, for the people, by the people,—show me another record as broad and brave as this in the European history of our century. Where is the English statesman, where the Irish leader, who can claim one? No wonder every Englishman hated and feared him! He wounded their prejudices at every point. Whig and Tory, timid Liberal, narrow Dissenter, bitter Radical—all feared and hated this broad, brave soul, who dared to follow Truth wherever he saw her, whose toleration was as broad as human nature, and his sympathy as boundless as the sea.

To show you that he never took a leaf from our American gospel of compromise; that he never filed his tongue to silence on one truth, fancying so to help another; that he never sacrificed any race to save even Ireland,—let me compare him with Kossuth, whose only merits were his eloquence and his patriotism. When Kossuth was in Faneuil Hall, he exclaimed, "Here is a flag without a stain, a nation without a crime!" We Abolitionists appealed to him, " O eloquent son of the Magyar, come to break chains! have you no word, no pulse-beat, for four millions of negroes bending under a yoke ten times heavier than that of Hungary?" He answered, " I would forget anybody, I would praise anything to help Hungary."

O'Connell never said anything like that. When I was in

Naples, I asked Sir Thomas Fowell Buxton, a Tory, "Is O'Connell an honest man?"—"As honest a man as ever breathed," said he, and then told me this story. "When, in 1830, O'Connell entered Parliament, the Anti-Slavery cause was so weak that it had only Lushington and myself to speak for it; and we agreed, that when he spoke I should cheer him, and when I spoke he should cheer me; and these were the only cheers we ever got. O'Connell came, with one Irish member to support him. A large number of members (I think Buxton said twenty-seven), whom we called the West-India interest, the Bristol party, the slave party, went to him, saying, 'O'Connell, at last you are in the House, with one helper. If you will never go down to Freemasons' Hall with Buxton and Brougham, here are twenty-seven votes for you on every Irish question. If you work with those Abolitionists, count us always against you.'"

It was a terrible temptation. How many a so-called statesman would have yielded! O'Connell said, "Gentlemen, God knows I speak for the saddest people the sun sees; but may my right hand forget its cunning, and my tongue cleave to the roof of my mouth, if, to save Ireland,—even Ireland,—I forget the negro one single hour!"—"From that day," said Buxton, "Lushington and I never went into the lobby that O'Connell did not follow us."

Learn of him, friends, the hardest lesson we ever have set us, that of toleration. The foremost Catholic of his age, the most stalwart champion of the Church, he was also broadly and sincerely tolerant of every faith. His toleration had no limit, and no qualification.

I scorn and scout the word "toleration." It is an insolent term. No man, properly speaking, *tolerates* another. I do not tolerate a Catholic, neither does he tolerate me. We are equal, and acknowledge each other's right: that is the correct statement.

That every man should be allowed freely to worship God according to his conscience, that no man's civil rights should be affected by his religious creed, were both cardinal principles of O'Connell. He had no fear that any doctrine of his faith could be endangered by the freest possible discussion. Learn of him, also, sympathy with every race, and every form of oppression. No matter who was the sufferer, or what the form of the injustice,—starving Yorkshire peasant, imprisoned Chartist, persecuted Protestant, or negro slave; no matter of what right, personal or civil, the victim had been robbed; no matter what religious pretext or political juggle alleged "necessity" as an excuse for his oppression; no matter with what solemnities he had been devoted on the altar of slavery,—the moment O'Connell saw him, the altar and the God sank together in the dust, the victim was acknowledged a man and a brother, equal in all rights, and entitled to all the aid the great Irishman could give him.

I have no time to speak of his marvellous success at the bar; of that profound skill in the law which enabled him to conduct such an agitation, always on the verge of illegality and violence, without once subjecting himself or his followers to legal penalty, —an agitation under a code of which Brougham said, "No Catholic could lift his hand under it without breaking the law." I have no time to speak of his still more remarkable success in the House of Commons. Of Flood's failure there, Grattan had said, "He was an oak of the forest, too old and too great to be transplanted at fifty." Grattan's own success there was but moderate. The power O'Connell wielded against varied, bitter, and unscrupulous opposition was marvellous. I have no time to speak of his personal independence, his deliberate courage, moral and physical, his unspotted private character, his unfailing hope, the versatility of his talent, his power of tireless work, his ingenuity and boundless resource, his matchless self-possession in every emergency, his ready and inexhaustible wit. But any reference to O'Connell that omitted his eloquence would be painting Wellington in the House of Lords without mention of Torres Vedras or Waterloo.

Broadly considered, his eloquence has never been equalled in modern times, certainly not in English speech. Do you think I am partial? I will vouch John Randolph of Roanoke, the Virginia slaveholder, who hated an Irishman almost as much as he hated a Yankee, himself an orator of no mean level. Hearing O'Connell, he exclaimed, "This is the man, these are the lips, the most eloquent that speak English in my day." I think he was right. I remember the solemnity of Webster, the grace of Everett, the rhetoric of Choate; I know the eloquence that lay hid in the iron logic of Calhoun; I have melted beneath the magnetism of Sergeant S. Prentiss of Mississippi, who wielded a power few men ever had. It has been my fortune to sit at the feet of the great speakers of the English tongue on the other side of the ocean. But I think all of them together never surpassed, and no one of them ever equalled, O'Connell. Nature intended him for our Demosthenes. Never since the great Greek has she sent forth any one so lavishly gifted for his work as a tribune of the people. In the first place, he had a magnificent presence, impressive in bearing, massive like that of Jupiter. Webster himself hardly outdid him in the majesty of his proportions. To be sure, he had not Webster's craggy face and precipice of brow, nor his eyes glowing like anthracite coal; nor had he the lion roar of Mirabeau. But his presence filled the eye. A small O'Connell would hardly have been an O'Connell at all. These physical advantages are half the battle. I remember Russell Lowell telling us that Mr. Webster came home from Washington at the time the Whig party thought of dissolution a year or two before his death, and went down to Faneuil Hall to protest; drawing himself up to his loftiest proportion, his brow clothed with thunder, before the listening thousands, he said, "Well, gentlemen, I am a Whig, a Massachusetts Whig, a Faneuil Hall Whig, a revolutionary Whig, a constitutional Whig. If you break the Whig party, sir, where am I to go?" And says Lowell, "We held our breath, thinking where he *could* go. If he had been five feet three, we should have said, 'Who cares where you go?'" So it was with O'Connell. There was something majestic in his presence before he spoke; and he added to it what Webster had not, what Clay might have lent,—grace. Lithe as a boy at seventy, every attitude a picture, every gesture a grace, he was still all nature: nothing but nature seemed to speak all over him. Then he had a voice that covered the gamut. The majesty of his indignation, fitly uttered in tones of superhuman power, made him able to "indict" a nation, in spite of Burke's protest.

I heard him once say, "I send my voice across the Atlantic, careering like the thunder-storm against the breeze, to tell the slaveholder of the Carolinas that God's thunderbolts are hot, and to remind the bondman that the dawn of his redemption is already breaking." You seemed to hear the tones come echoing back to London from the Rocky Mountains. Then, with the slightest possible Irish brogue, he would tell a story, while all Exeter Hall shook with laughter. The next moment, tears in his voice like a Scotch song, five thousand men wept. And all the while no effort. He seemed only breathing,

> "As effortless as woodland nooks
> Send violets up, and paint them blue."

We used to say of Webster, "This is a great effort;" of Everett, "It is a beautiful effort;" but you never used the word "effort" in speaking of O'Connell. It provoked you that he would not make an effort. And this wonderful power, it was not a thunderstorm: he flanked you with his wit, he surprised you out of yourself; you were conquered before you knew it. His marvellous voice, its almost incredible power and sweetness, Bulwer has well described:

> "Once to my sight that giant form was given,
> Walled by wide air, and roofed by boundless heaven.
> Beneath his feet the human ocean lay,
> And wave on wave rolled into space away.
> Methought no clarion could have sent its sound
> Even to the centre of the hosts around;
> And, as I thought, rose the sonorous swell,
> As from some church-tower swings the silvery bell.
> Aloft and clear, from airy tide to tide
> It glided, easy as a bird may glide.
> Even to the verge of that vast audience sent,
> It played with each wild passion as it went:
> Now stirred the uproar, now the murmur stilled,
> And sobs or laughter answered as it willed."

Webster could awe a senate, Everett could charm a college, and Choate cheat a jury; Clay could magnetize the million, and Corwin lead them captive. O'Connell was Clay, Corwin, Choate, Everett, and Webster in one. Before the courts, logic; at the bar of the senate, unanswerable and dignified; on the platform, grace, wit, and pathos; before the masses, a whole man. Carlyle says, "He is God's own anointed king whose single word melts all wills into his." This describes O'Connell. Emerson says, "There is no true eloquence, unless there is a man behind the speech." Daniel O'Connell was listened to because all England and all Ireland knew that there was a man behind the speech,—one who could be neither bought, bullied, nor cheated. He held the masses free but willing subjects in his hand.

He owed this power to the courage that met every new question frankly, and concealed none of his convictions ; to an entireness of devotion that made the people feel he was all their own ; to a masterly brain that made them sure they were always safe in his hands. Behind them were ages of bloodshed : every rising had ended at the scaffold ; even Grattan brought them to 1798. O'Connell said, "Follow me : put your feet where mine have trod, and a sheriff shall never lay hand on your shoulder." And the great lawyer kept his pledge.

This unmatched, long-continued power almost passes belief. You can only appreciate it by comparison. Let me carry you back to the mob-year of 1835, in this country, when the Abolitionists were hunted, when the streets roared with riot, when from Boston to Baltimore, from St. Louis to Philadelphia, a mob took possession of every city ; when private houses were invaded and public halls were burned, press after press was thrown into the river, and Lovejoy baptized freedom with his blood. You remember it. Respectable journals warned the mob that they were playing into the hands of the Abolitionists. Webster and Clay and the staff of Whig statesmen, told the people that the truth floated farther on the shouts of the mob than the most eloquent lips could carry it. But law-abiding, Protestant, educated America could not be held back. Neither Whig chiefs nor respectable journals could keep these people quiet. Go to England. When the Reform Bill of 1831 was thrown out from the House of Lords, the people were tumultuous ; and Melbourne and Grey, Russell and Brougham, Lansdowne, Holland, and Macaulay, the Whig chiefs, cried out, "Don't violate the law : you help the Tories ! Riots put back the bill." But quiet, sober John Bull, law-abiding, could not do without it. Birmingham was three days in the hands of a mob. Castles were burned. Wellington ordered the Scotch Greys to rough-grind their swords as at Waterloo. This was the Whig aristocracy of England. O'Connell had neither office nor title. Behind him were four million people, steeped in utter wretchedness, sore with the oppression of centuries, ignored by statute.

For thirty restless and turbulent years he stood in front of them, and said, "Remember, he that commits a crime helps the enemy." And during that long and fearful struggle, I do not remember one of his followers ever being convicted of a political offence ; and during this period crimes of violence were very rare. There is no such record in our history. Neither in classic nor in modern times can the man be produced who held a million of people in his right hand so passive. It was due to the consistency and unity of a character that had hardly a flaw. I do not forget your soldiers, orators, or poets,—any of your leaders. But when I consider O'Connell's personal disinterestedness,—his rare, brave fidelity to every cause his principles covered, no matter how unpopular, or how embarrassing to his main purpose,—that clear, far-reaching vision, and true heart, which, on most moral and political questions, set him so much ahead of his times ; his eloquence, almost equally effective in the courts, in the senate, and before the masses ; that sagacity which set at naught the malignant vigilance of the whole imperial bar, watching thirty years for a misstep ; when I remember that he invented his tools, and then measure his limited means with his vast success, bearing in mind its nature ; when I see the sobriety and moderation with which he used his measureless power, and the lofty, generous purpose of his whole life,—I am ready to affirm that he was, all things considered, the greatest man the Irish race ever produced.

THE SCHOLAR IN A REPUBLIC.[1]

MR. PRESIDENT AND BROTHERS OF THE P. B. K:

A HUNDRED years ago our society was planted—a slip from the older root in Virginia. The parent seed, tradition says, was French,—part of that conspiracy for free speech whose leaders prated democracy in the *salons*, while they carefully held on to the flesh-pots of society by crouching low to kings and their mistresses, and whose final object of assault was Christianity itself. Voltaire gave the watchword,—

> " Crush the wretch."
> "*Écrasez l'infame.*"

No matter how much or how little truth there may be in the tradition: no matter what was the origin or what was the object of our society, if it had any special one, both are long since forgotten. We stand now simply a representative of free, brave, American scholarship. I emphasize *American* scholarship.

In one of those glowing, and as yet unequalled pictures which Everett drew for us, here and elsewhere, of Revolutionary scenes, I remember his saying, that the independence we then won, if taken in its literal and narrow sense, was of no interest and little value; but, construed in the fulness of its real meaning, it bound us to a distinctive American character and purpose, to a keen sense of large responsibility, and to a generous self-devotion. It is under the shadow of such unquestioned authority that I use the term " American scholarship."

Our society was, no doubt, to some extent, a protest against the sombre theology of New England, where, a hundred years

---

[1] Address at the Centennial Anniversary of the Phi Beta Kappa of Harvard College, June 30th, 1881.

ago, the atmosphere was black with sermons, and where religious speculation beat uselessly against the narrowest limits.

The first generation of Puritans—though Lowell does let Cromwell call them "a small colony of pinched fanatics"—included some men, indeed not a few, worthy to walk close to Roger Williams and Sir Harry Vane, the two men deepest in thought and bravest in speech of all who spoke English in their day, and equal to any in practical statesmanship. Sir Harry Vane was in my judgment the noblest human being who ever walked the streets of yonder city—I do not forget Franklin or Sam Adams, Washington or Fayette, Garrison or John Brown. But Vane dwells an arrow's flight above them all, and his touch consecrated the continent to measureless toleration of opinion and entire equality of rights. We are told we can find in Plato " all the intellectual life of Europe for two thousand years :" so you can find in Vane the pure gold of two hundred and fifty years of American civilization, with no particle of its dross. Plato would have welcomed him to the Academy, and Fénelon kneeled with him at the altar. He made Somers and John Marshall possible ; like Carnot, he organized victory ; and Milton pales before him in the stainlessness of his record. He stands among English statesmen pre-eminently the representative, in practice and in theory, of serene faith in the safety of trusting truth wholly to her own defence. For other men we walk backward, and throw over their memories the mantle of charity and excuse, saying reverently, "Remember the temptation and the age." But Vane's ermine has no stain ; no act of his needs explanation or apology ; and in thought he stands abreast of our age,—like pure intellect, belongs to all time.

Carlyle said, in years when his words were worth heeding, "Young men, close your Byron, and open your Goethe." If my counsel had weight in these halls, I should say, "Young men, close your John Winthrop and Washington, your Jefferson and Webster, and open Sir Harry Vane." The generation that knew Vane gave to our Alma Mater for a seal the simple pledge, —*Veritas*.

But the narrowness and poverty of colonial life soon starved out this element. Harvard was rededicated *Christo et Ecclesiæ ;* and, up to the middle of the last century, free thought in religion meant Charles Chauncy and the Brattle Street Church protest, while free thought hardly existed anywhere else. But a single generation changed all this. A hundred years ago there were pulpits that led the popular movement; while outside of religion and of what called itself literature, industry and a jealous sense of personal freedom obeyed, in their rapid growth, the law of their natures. English common sense and those municipal institutions born of the common law, and which had saved and sheltered it, grew inevitably too large for the eggshell of English dependence, and allowed it to drop off as naturally as the chick does when she is ready. There was no change of law, —nothing that could properly be called revolution,—only noiseless growth, the seed bursting into flower, infancy becoming manhood. It was life, in its omnipotence, rending whatever dead matter confined it. So have I seen the tiny weeds of a luxuriant Italian spring upheave the colossal foundations of the Cæsars' palace, and leave it a mass of ruins.

But when the veil was withdrawn, what stood revealed astonished the world. It showed the undreamt power, the serene strength, of simple manhood, free from the burden and restraint of absurd institutions in Church and State. The grandeur of this new Western constellation gave courage to Europe, resulting in the French Revolution, the greatest, the most unmixed, the most unstained and wholly perfect blessing Europe has had in modern times, unless we may possibly except the Reformation, and the invention of printing.

What precise effect that giant wave had when it struck our shore we can only guess. History is, for the most part, an idle amusement, the day-dream of pedants and triflers. The details of events, the actors' motives, and their relation to each other, are buried with them. How impossible to learn the exact truth of what took place yesterday under your next neighbor's roof! Yet we complacently argue and speculate about matters a thousand miles off, and a thousand years ago, as if we knew them. When I was a student here, my favorite study was history. The world and affairs have shown me that one half of history is loose conjecture, and much of the rest is the writer's opinion. But most men see facts, not with their eyes, but with their prejudices. Any one familiar with courts will testify how rare it is for an honest man to give a perfectly correct account of a transaction. We are tempted to see facts as we think they ought to be. or wish they were. And yet journals are the favorite original sources of history. Tremble, my good friend, if your sixpenny neighbor keeps a journal. " It adds a new terror to death." You shall go down to your children not in your fair lineaments and proportions, but with the smirks, elbows, and angles he sees you with. Journals are excellent to record the depth of the last snow and the date when the Mayflower opens ; but when you come to men's motives and characters, journals are the magnets that get near the chronometer of history and make all its records worthless. You can count on the fingers of your two hands all the robust minds that ever kept journals. Only milksops and fribbles indulge in that amusement, except now and then a respectable mediocrity. One such journal nightmares New England annals, emptied into history by respectable middle-aged gentlemen, who fancy that narrowness and spleen, like poor wine, mellow into truth when they get to be a century old. But you might as well cite the *Daily Advertiser* of 1850 as authority on one of Garrison's actions.

And, after all, of what value are these minutiæ ? Whether Luther's zeal was partly kindled by lack of gain from the sale of indulgences, whether Boston rebels were half smugglers and half patriots, what matters it now ? Enough that he meant to wrench the gag from Europe's lips, and that they were content to suffer keenly, that we might have an untrammelled career. We can only hope to discover the great currents and massive forces which have shaped our lives : all else is trying to solve a problem of whose elements we know nothing. As the poet historian of the last generation says so plaintively, " History comes like a beggarly gleaner in the field, after Death, the great lord of the domain, has gathered the harvest, and lodged it in his garner, which no man may open."

But we may safely infer that French debate and experience broadened and encouraged our fathers. To that we undoubtedly owe, in some degree, the theoretical perfection, ingrafted on English practical sense and old forms, which marks the foundation of our republic. English civil life, up to that time, grew largely out of custom, rested almost wholly on precedent. For our model there was no authority in the record, no precedent on the file ; unless you find it, perhaps, partially, in that Long Parliament bill with which Sir Harry Vane would have outgeneralled Cromwell, if the shameless soldier had not crushed it with his muskets.

Standing on Saxon foundations, and inspired, perhaps, in some degree, by Latin example, we have done what no race, no nation, no age, had before dared even to try. We have founded a republic on the unlimited suffrage of the millions. We have actually worked out the problem that man, as God created him, may be trusted with self-government. We have shown the world that a church without a bishop, and a state without a king, is an actual, real, every-day possibility. Look back over the history of the race : where will you find a chapter that precedes us in that achievement? Greece had her republics, but they were the republics of a few freemen and subjects and many slaves ; and " the battle of Marathon was fought by slaves, unchained from the doorposts of their masters' houses." Italy had her republics : they were the republics of wealth and skill and family, limited and aristocratic. The Swiss republics were groups of cousins. Holland had her republic,—a republic of guilds and landholders, trusting the helm of state to property and education. And all these, which, at their best, held but a million or two within their narrow limits, have gone down in the ocean of time.

A hundred years ago our fathers announced this sublime, and, as it seemed then, foolhardy declaration, that God intended all men to be free and equal,—all men, without restriction, without qualification, without limit. A hundred years have rolled away since that venturous declaration ; and to-day, with a territory that joins ocean to ocean, with fifty millions of people, with two wars behind her, with the grand achievement of having grappled with the fearful disease that threatened her central life, and broken four millions of fetters, the great republic, stronger than ever, launches into the second century of her existence. The history of the world has no such chapter in its breadth, its depth, its significance, or its bearing on future history.

What Wycliffe did for religion, Jefferson and Sam Adams did for the State,—they trusted it to the people. He gave the masses the Bible, the right to think. Jefferson and Sam Adams gave them the ballot, the right to rule. His intrepid advance contemplated theirs as its natural, inevitable result. Their serene faith completed the gift which the Anglo-Saxon race makes to humanity. We have not only established a new measure of the possibilities of the race : we have laid on strength, wisdom, and skill a new responsibility. Grant that each man's relations to God and his neighbor are exclusively his own concern, and that he is entitled to all the aid that will make him the best judge of these relations ; that the people are the source of all power, and their measureless capacity the lever of all progress ; their sense of right the court of final appeal in civil affairs ; the institutions they create the only ones any power has a right to impose ; that the attempt of one class to prescribe the law, the religion, the morals, or the trade of another is both unjust and harmful,—and the Wycliffe and Jefferson of history mean this if they mean anything,—then, when, in 1867, Parliament doubled the English franchise, Robert Lowe was right in affirming, amid the cheers of the House, " Now the first interest and duty of every Englishman is to educate the masses—our masters." Then, whoever sees farther than his neighbor is that neighbor's servant to lift him to such higher level. Then, power, ability, influence, character, virtue, are only trusts with which to serve our time.

We all agree in the duty of scholars to help those less favored in life, and that this duty of scholars to educate the mass is still more imperative in a republic, since a republic trusts the State wholly to the intelligence and moral sense of the people. The experience of the last forty years shows every man that law has no atom of strength, either in Boston or New Orleans, unless, and only so far as, public opinion indorses it, and that your life, goods, and good name rest on the moral sense, self-respect, and law-abiding mood of the men that walk the streets, and hardly a whit on the provisions of the statute-book. Come, any one of you, outside of the ranks of popular men, and you will not fail to find it so. Easy men dream that we live under a government of law. Absurd mistake ! we live under a government of men and newspapers. Your first attempt to stem dominant and keenly-cherished opinions will reveal this to you.

But what is education ? Of course it is not book-learning. Book-learning does not make five per cent of that mass of common sense that " runs" the world, transacts its business, secures its progress, trebles its power over nature, works out in the long run a rough average justice, wears away the world's restraints, and lifts off its burdens. The ideal Yankee, who " has more

brains in his hand than others have in their skulls," is not a
scholar ; and two thirds of the inventions that enable France to
double the world's sunshine, and make Old and New England
the workshops of the world, did not come from colleges or from
minds trained in the schools of science, but struggled up, forc-
ing their way against giant obstacles, from the irrepressible
instinct of untrained natural power. Her workshops, not her
colleges, made England, for a while, the mistress of the world ;
and the hardest job her workman had was to make Oxford willing he should work his wonders.

So of moral gains. As shrewd an observer as Governor
Marcy of New York often said he cared nothing for the whole
press of the seaboard, representing wealth and education (he
meant book-learning), if it set itself against the instincts of the
people. Lord Brougham, in a remarkable comment on the life
of Romilly, enlarges on the fact that the great reformer of the
penal law found all the legislative and all the judicial power of
England, its colleges and its bar, marshalled against him, and
owed his success, *as all such reforms do*, says his lordship,
to public meetings and popular instinct. It would be no ex-
aggeration to say that government itself began in usurpation, in the feudalism of the soldier and the bigotry of the
priest ; that liberty and civilization are only fragments of rights
wrung from the strong hands of wealth and book-learning.
Almost all the great truths relating to society were not the result of scholarly meditation, " hiving up wisdom with each curious year," but have been first heard in the solemn protests of
martyred patriotism and the loud cries of crushed and starving
labor. When common sense and the common people have
stereotyped a principle into a statute, then bookmen come to explain how it was discovered and on what ground it rests. The
world makes history, and scholars write it, one half truly, and
the other half as their prejudices blur and distort it.

New England learned more of the principles of toleration
from a lyceum committee doubting the dicta of editors and
bishops when they forbade it to put Theodore Parker on its
platform ; more from a debate whether the Anti-Slavery cause
should be so far countenanced as to invite one of its advocates
to lecture ; from Sumner and Emerson, George William Curtis, and Edwin Whipple, refusing to speak unless a negro could

buy his way into their halls as freely as any other,—New England has learned more from these lessons than she has or could have done from all the treatises on free printing from Milton and Roger Williams, through Locke, down to Stuart Mill.

Selden, the profoundest scholar of his day, affirmed, "No man is wiser for his learning;" and that was only an echo of the Saxon proverb, "No fool is a perfect fool until he learns Latin." Bancroft says of our fathers, that "the wildest theories of the human reason were reduced to practice by a community so humble that no statesman condescended to notice it, and a legislation without precedent was produced off-hand by the instincts of the people." And Wordsworth testifies that, while German schools might well blush for their subserviency,—

> "A few strong instincts and a few plain rules,
>   Among the herdsmen of the Alps, have wrought
> More for mankind at this unhappy day
>   Than all the pride of intellect and thought."

Wycliffe was, no doubt, a learned man. But the learning of his day would have burned him, had it dared, as it did burn his dead body afterward. Luther and Melanchthon were scholars, but were repudiated by the scholarship of their time, which followed Erasmus, trying "all his life to tread on eggs without breaking them;" he who proclaimed that "peaceful error was better than tempestuous truth." What would college-graduate Seward weigh, in any scale, against Lincoln bred in affairs?

Hence I do not think the greatest things have been done for the world by its bookmen. Education is not the chips of arithmetic and grammar,—nouns, verbs, and the multiplication table; neither is it that last year's almanac of dates, or series of lies agreed upon, which we so often mistake for history. Education is not Greek and Latin and the air-pump. Still, I rate at its full value the training we get in these walls. Though what we actually carry away is little enough, we do get some training of our powers, as the gymnast or the fencer does of his muscles: we go hence also with such general knowledge of what mankind has agreed to consider proved and settled, that we know where to reach for the weapon when we need it.

I have often thought the motto prefixed to his college library catalogue by the father of the late Professor Peirce,—Professor

Peirce, the largest natural genius, the man of the deepest reach and firmest grasp and widest sympathy, that God has given to Harvard in our day,—whose presence made you the loftiest peak and farthest outpost of more than mere scientific thought, —the magnet who, with his twin Agassiz, made Harvard for forty years the intellectual Mecca of forty States,—his father's catalogue bore for a motto, "*Scire ubi aliquid invenias magna pars eruditionis est;*" and that always seemed to me to gauge very nearly all we acquired at college, except facility in the use of our powers. Our influence in the community does not really spring from superior attainments, but from this thorough training of faculties, and more even, perhaps, from the deference men accord to us.

Gibbon says we have two educations, one from teachers, and the other we give ourselves. This last is the real and only education of the masses,—one gotten from life, from affairs, from earning one's bread ; necessity, the mother of invention ; responsibility, that teaches prudence, and inspires respect for right. Mark the critic out of office : how reckless in assertion, how careless of consequences ; and then the caution, forethought, and fair play of the same man charged with administration. See that young, thoughtless wife suddenly widowed ; how wary and skilful ! what ingenuity in guarding her child and saving his rights ! Any one who studied Europe forty or fifty years ago could not but have marked the level of talk there, far below that of our masses. It was of crops and rents, markets and marriages, scandal and fun. Watch men here, and how often you listen to the keenest discussions of right and wrong, this leader's honesty, that party's justice, the fairness of this law, the impolicy of that measure ;—lofty, broad topics, training morals, widening views. Niebuhr said of Italy, sixty years ago, "No one feels himself a citizen. Not only are the people destitute of hope, but they have not even wishes touching the world's affairs ; and hence all the springs of great and noble thoughts are choked up."

In this sense the Fremont campaign of 1856 taught Americans more than a hundred colleges ; and John Brown's pulpit at Harper's Ferry was equal to any ten thousand ordinary chairs. God lifted a million of hearts to his gibbet, as the Roman cross lifted a world to itself in that divine sacrifice of two thousand years ago. As much as statesmanship had taught in our previous eighty years, that one week of intellectual watching and weighing and dividing truth taught twenty millions of people. Yet how little, brothers, can we claim for bookmen in that uprising and growth of 1856! And while the first of American scholars could hardly find, in the rich vocabulary of Saxon scorn, words enough to express, amid the plaudits of his class, his loathing and contempt for John Brown, Europe thrilled to him as proof that our institutions had not lost all their native and distinctive life. She had grown tired of our parrot note and cold moonlight reflection of older civilizations. Lansdowne and Brougham could confess to Sumner that they had never read a page of their contemporary, Daniel Webster; and you spoke to vacant eyes when you named Prescott, fifty years ago, to average Europeans; while Vienna asked, with careless indifference, "Seward, who is he?" But long before our ranks marched up State Street to the John Brown song, the banks of the Seine and of the Danube hailed the new life which had given us another and nobler Washington. Lowell foresaw him when forty years ago he sang of,—

> "Truth forever on the scaffold,
>   Wrong forever on the throne;
> Yet that scaffold sways the future:
>   And behind the dim unknown
> Standeth God, within the shadow,
>   Keeping watch above His own."

And yet the bookmen, as a class, have not yet acknowledged him.

It is here that letters betray their lack of distinctive American character. Fifty million of men God gives us to mould; burning questions, keen debate, great interests trying to vindicate their right to be, sad wrongs brought to the bar of public judgment,—these are the people's schools. Timid scholarship either shrinks from sharing in these agitations, or denounces them as vulgar and dangerous interference by incompetent hands with matters above them. A chronic distrust of the people pervades the book-educated class of the North; they shrink from that free speech which is God's normal school for educating men, throwing upon them the grave responsibility of deciding great questions, and so lifting them to a higher level of intellectual and moral life. Trust the people—the wise and the ignorant, the good and the bad—with the gravest questions, and in the end you educate the race. At the same time you secure, not perfect institutions, not necessarily good ones, but the best institutions possible while human nature is the basis and the only material to build with. Men are educated and the State uplifted by allowing all—every one—to broach all their mistakes and advocate all their errors. The community that will not protect its most ignorant and unpopular member in the free utterance of his opinions, no matter how false or hateful, is only a gang of slaves !

Anacharsis went into the Archon's court at Athens, heard a case argued by the great men of that city, and saw the vote by five hundred men. Walking in the streets, some one asked him, "What do you think of Athenian liberty?" "I think," said he, "wise men argue cases, and fools decide them." Just what that timid scholar, two thousand years ago, said in the streets of Athens, that which calls itself scholarship here says to-day of popular agitation,--that it lets wise men argue questions and fools decide them. But that Athens where fools decided the gravest questions of policy and of right and wrong, where property you had gathered wearily to-day might be wrung from you by the caprice of the mob to-morrow,—that very Athens probably secured, for its era, the greatest amount of human happiness and nobleness ; invented art, and sounded for us the depths of philosophy. God lent to it the largest intellects, and it flashes to-day the torch that gilds yet the mountain peaks of the Old World : while Egypt, the hunker conservative of antiquity, where nobody dared to differ from the priest or to be wiser than his grandfather ; where men pretended to be alive, though swaddled in the grave-clothes of creed and custom as close as their mummies were in linen,—that Egypt is hid in the tomb it inhabited, and the intellect Athens has trained for us digs to-day those ashes to find out how buried and forgotten hunkerism lived and acted.

I knew a signal instance of this disease of scholar's distrust, and the cure was as remarkable. In boyhood and early life I was honored with the friendship of Lothrop Motley. He grew up in the thin air of Boston provincialism, and pined on such weak diet. I remember sitting with him once in the State House when he was a member of our Legislature. With biting words and a keen crayon he sketched the ludicrous points in the minds and persons of his fellow-members, and, tearing up the pictures, said scornfully, "What can become of a country with such fellows as these making its laws? No safe investments; your good name lied away any hour, and little worth keeping if it were not." In vain I combated the folly. He went to Europe, —spent four or five years. I met him the day he landed, on his return. As if our laughing talk in the State House had that moment ended, he took my hand with the sudden exclamation, "You were all right: I was all wrong! It *is* a country worth dying for; better still, worth living and working for, to make it all it can be!" Europe made him one of the most American of all Americans. Some five years later, when he sounded that bugle-note in his letter to the London *Times*, some critics who knew his early mood, but not its change, suspected there might be a taint of ambition in what they thought so sudden a conversion. I could testify that the mood was five years old: years before the slightest shadow of political expectation had dusked the clear mirror of his scholar life.

This distrust shows itself in the growing dislike of universal suffrage, and the efforts to destroy it made of late by all our easy classes The white South hates universal suffrage; the so-called cultivated North distrusts it. Journal and college, social-science convention and the pulpit, discuss the propriety of restraining it. Timid scholars tell their dread of it. Carlyle, that bundle of sour prejudices, flouts universal suffrage with a blasphemy that almost equals its ignorance. See his words: "Democracy will prevail when men believe the vote of Judas as good as that of Jesus Christ." No democracy ever claimed that the vote of ignorance and crime was as good in any sense as that of wisdom and virtue. It only asserts that crime and ignorance have the same right to vote that virtue has. Only by allowing that right, and so appealing to their sense of justice, and throwing upon them the burden of their full responsibility, can we hope ever to raise crime and ignorance to the level of self-respect. The right to choose your governor rests on precisely the same foundation as the right to choose your religion; and no more arrogant or ignorant arraignment of all that is noble in the civil and religious Europe of the last five hundred years ever came from the triple crown on the Seven Hills than this sneer of the bigot Scotsman. Protestantism holds up its hands in holy horror, and tells us that the Pope scoops out the brains of his churchmen saying, "I'll think for you: you need only obey." But the danger is, you meet such popes far away from the Seven Hills; and it is sometimes difficult at first to recognize them, for they do not by any means always wear the triple crown.

Evarts and his committee, appointed to inquire why the New York City government is a failure, were not wise enough, or did not dare, to point out the real cause, the tyranny of that tool of the demagogue, the corner grog-shop; but they advised taking away the ballot from the poor citizen. But this provision would not reach the evil. Corruption does not so much rot the masses: it poisons Congress. Credit Mobilier and money rings are not housed under thatched roofs: they flaunt at the Capitol. As usual in chemistry, the scum floats uppermost. The railway king disdained canvassing for voters: "It is cheaper," he said, "to buy legislatures."

It is not the masses who have most disgraced our political annals. I have seen many mobs between the seaboard and the Mississippi. I never saw or heard of any but well-dressed mobs, assembled and countenanced, if not always led in person, by respectability and what called itself education. That unrivalled scholar, the first and greatest New England ever lent to Congress, signalled his advent by quoting the original Greek of the New Testament in support of slavery, and offering to shoulder his musket in its defence; and forty years later the last professor who went to quicken and lift the moral mood of those halls is found advising a plain, blunt, honest witness to forge and lie, that this scholarly reputation might be saved from wreck. Singular comment on Landor's sneer, that there is a spice of the scoundrel in most of our literary men. But no exacting level of property qualification for a vote would have saved those stains. In those cases Judas did not come from the unlearned class.

Grown gray over history, Macaulay prophesied twenty years ago that soon in these States the poor, worse than another inroad of Goths and Vandals, would begin a general plunder of the rich. It is enough to say that our national funds sell as well in

Europe as English consols; and the universal-suffrage Union can borrow money as cheaply as Great Britain, ruled, one half by Tories, and the other half by men not certain that they dare call themselves Whigs. Some men affected to scoff at democracy as no sound basis for national debt, doubting the payment of ours. Europe not only wonders at its rapid payment, but the only taint of fraud that touches even the hem of our garment is the fraud of the capitalist cunningly adding to its burdens, and increasing unfairly the value of his bonds; not the first hint from the people of repudiating an iota even of its unjust additions.

Yet the poor and the unlearned class is the one they propose to punish by disfranchisement.

No wonder the humbler class looks on the whole scene with alarm. They see their dearest right in peril. When the easy class conspires to steal, what wonder the humbler class draws together to defend itself? True, universal suffrage is a terrible power; and, with all the great cities brought into subjection to the dangerous classes by grog, and Congress sitting to register the decrees of capital, both sides may well dread the next move. Experience proves that popular governments are the best protectors of life and property. But suppose they were not, Bancroft allows that "the fears of one class are no measure of the rights of another."

Suppose that universal suffrage endangered peace and threatened property. There is something more valuable than wealth, there is something more sacred than peace. As Humboldt says, "The finest fruit earth holds up to its Maker is a man." To ripen, lift, and educate a man is the first duty. Trade, law, learning, science, and religion are only the scaffolding wherewith to build a man. Despotism looks down into the poor man's cradle, and knows it can crush resistance and curb ill-will. Democracy sees the ballot in that baby-hand; and selfishness bids her put integrity on one side of those baby footsteps and intelligence on the other, lest her own hearth be in peril. Thank God for His method of taking bonds of wealth and culture to share all their blessings with the humblest soul He gives to their keeping! The American should cherish as serene a faith as his fathers had. Instead of seeking a coward safety by battening down the hatches and putting men back into chains, he should recognize that God places him in this peril that he may work out a noble security by concentrating all moral forces to lift this weak, rotting, and dangerous mass into sunlight and health. The fathers touched their highest level when, with stout-hearted and serene faith, they trusted God that it was safe to leave men with all the rights He gave them. Let us be worthy of their blood, and save this sheet-anchor of the race,—universal suffrage,—God's church, God's school, God's method of gently binding men into commonwealths in order that they may at last melt into brothers.

I urge on college-bred men that, as a class, they fail in republican duty when they allow others to lead in the agitation of the great social questions which stir and educate the age. Agitation is an old word with a new meaning. Sir Robert Peel, the first English leader who felt himself its tool, defined it to be "marshalling the conscience of a nation to mould its laws." Its means are reason and argument,—no appeal to arms. Wait patiently for the growth of public opinion. That secured, then every step taken is taken forever. An abuse once removed never reappears in history. The freer a nation becomes, the more utterly democratic in its form, the more need of this outside agitation. Parties and sects laden with the burden of securing their own success cannot afford to risk new ideas. "Predominant opinions," said Disraeli, "are the opinions of a class that is vanishing." The agitator must stand outside of organizations, with no bread to earn, no candidate to elect, no party to save, no object but truth,—to tear a question open and riddle it with light.

In all modern constitutional governments, agitation is the only peaceful method of progress. Wilberforce and Clarkson, Rowland Hill and Romilly, Cobden and John Bright, Garrison and O'Connell, have been the master spirits in this new form of crusade. Rarely in this country have scholarly men joined, as a class, in these great popular schools, in these social movements which make the great interests of society "crash and jostle against each other like frigates in a storm."

It is not so much that the people need us, or will feel any lack from our absence. They can do without us. By sovereign and superabundant strength they can crush their way through all obstacles.

" They will march prospering,— not through our presence ;
Songs will inspirit them,— not from our lyre ;
Deeds will be done—while we boast our quiescence ;
Still bidding crouch whom the rest bid aspire."

The misfortune is, we lose a God-given opportunity of making the change an unmixed good, or with the slightest possible share of evil, and are recreant beside to a special duty. These " agitations" are the opportunities and the means God offers us to refine the taste, mould the character, lift the purpose, and educate the moral sense of the masses, on whose intelligence and self-respect rests the State. God furnishes these texts. He gathers for us this audience, and only asks of our coward lips to preach the sermons.

There have been four or five of these great opportunities. The crusade against slavery—that grand hypocrisy which poisoned the national life of two generations—was one,—a conflict between two civilizations which threatened to rend the Union. Almost every element among us was stirred to take a part in the battle. Every great issue, civil and moral, was involved,— toleration of opinion, limits of authority, relation of citizen to law, place of the Bible, priest and layman, sphere of woman, question of race, State rights and nationality ; and Channing testified that free speech and free printing owed their preservation to the struggle. But the pulpit flung the Bible at the reformer ; law visited him with its penalties ; society spewed him out of its mouth ; bishops expurgated the pictures of their Common Prayer-books ; and editors omitted pages in republishing English history ; even Pierpont emasculated his class-book ; Bancroft remodelled his chapters ; and Everett carried Washington through thirty States, remembering to forget the brave words the wise Virginian had left on record warning his countrymen of this evil. Amid this battle of the giants, scholarship sat dumb for thirty years until imminent deadly peril convulsed it into action, and colleges, in their despair, gave to the army that help they had refused to the market-place and the rostrum.

There was here and there an exception. That earthquake scholar at Concord, whose serene word, like a whisper among the avalanches, topples down superstitions and prejudices, was at his post, and, with half a score of others, made the exception that proved the rule. Pulpits, just so far as they could not boast of culture, and nestled closest down among the masses, were infinitely braver than the "spires and antique towers" of stately collegiate institutions.

Then came reform of penal legislation,—the effort to make law mean justice, and substitute for its barbarism Christianity and civilization. In Massachusetts Rantoul represents Beccaria and Livingston, Mackintosh and Romilly. I doubt if he ever had one word of encouragement from Massachusetts letters; and, with a single exception, I have never seen, till within a dozen years, one that could be called a scholar active in moving the Legislature to reform its code.

The London *Times* proclaimed, twenty years ago, that intemperance produced more idleness, crime, disease, want, and misery, than all other causes put together; and the *Westminster Review* calls it a "curse that far eclipses every other calamity under which we suffer." Gladstone, speaking as Prime Minister, admitted that "greater calamities are inflicted on mankind by intemperance than by the three great historical scourges,—war, pestilence, and famine." De Quincey says, "The most remarkable instance of a combined movement in society which history, perhaps, will be summoned to notice, is that which, in our day, has applied itself to the abatement of intemperance. Two vast movements are hurrying into action by velocities continually accelerated,—the great revolutionary movement from *political* causes concurring with the great *physical* movement in locomotion and social intercourse from the gigantic power of steam. At the opening of such a crisis, had no *third movement arisen of resistance to intemperate habits*, there would have been ground of despondency as to the melioration of the human race." These are English testimonies, where the State rests more than half on bayonets. Here we are trying to rest the ballot-box on a drunken people. "We can rule a great city," said Sir Robert Peel, "America cannot;" and he cited the mobs of New York as sufficient proof of his assertion.

Thoughtful men see that up to this hour the government of great cities has been with us a failure; that worse than the dry-rot of legislative corruption, than the rancor of party spirit, than Southern barbarism, than even the tyranny of incorporated wealth, is the giant burden of intemperance, making universal suffrage a failure and a curse in every great city. Scholars who play statesmen, and editors who masquerade as scholars, can waste much excellent anxiety that clerks shall get no office until they know the exact date of Cæsar's assassination, as well as the latitude of Pekin, and the Rule of Three. But while this crusade—the temperance movement—has been, for sixty years, gathering its facts and marshalling its arguments, rallying parties, besieging legislatures and putting great States on the witness-stand as evidence of the soundness of its methods, scholars have given it nothing but a sneer. But if universal suffrage ever fails here for a time,—permanently it cannot fail, —it will not be incapable civil service, nor an ambitious soldier, nor Southern vandals, nor venal legislatures, nor the greed of wealth, nor boy statesmen rotten before they are ripe, that will put universal suffrage into eclipse: it will be rum intrenched in great cities and commanding every vantage ground.

Social science affirms that woman's place in society marks the level of civilization. From its twilight in Greece, through the Italian worship of the Virgin, the dreams of chivalry, the justice of the civil law, and the equality of French society, we trace her gradual recognition; while our common law, as Lord Brougham confessed, was, with relation to women, the opprobrium of the age and of Christianity. For forty years, plain men and women, working noiselessly, have washed away that opprobrium; the statute books of thirty States have been remodelled, and woman stands to-day almost face to face with her last claim,—the ballot. It has been a weary and thankless, though successful, struggle. But if there be any refuge from that ghastly curse, the vice of great cities,—before which social science stands palsied and dumb,—it is in this more equal recognition of woman. If, in this critical battle for universal suffrage,—our fathers' noblest legacy to us, and the greatest trust God leaves in our hands,—there be any weapon, which, once taken from the armory, will make victory certain, it will be, as it has been in art, literature, and society, summoning woman into the political arena.

But, at any rate, up to this point, putting suffrage aside, there can be no difference of opinion: everything born of Christianity, or allied to Grecian culture or Saxon law, must rejoice in the gain. The literary class, until half a dozen years, has taken note of this great uprising only to fling every obstacle in its way. The first glimpse we get of Saxon blood in history is that line of Tacitus in his "Germany," which reads, "In all grave matters they consult their women." Years hence, when robust Saxon sense has flung away Jewish superstition and Eastern prejudice, and put under its foot fastidious scholarship and squeamish fashion, some second Tacitus, from the Valley of the Mississippi, will answer to him of the Seven Hills, "In all grave questions we consult our women."

I used to think that then we could say to letters as Henry of Navarre wrote to the Sir Philip Sidney of his realm, Crillon, "the bravest of the brave," "We have conquered at Arques, *et tu n'y étais pas, Crillon*,"—"You were not there, my Crillon." But a second thought reminds me that what claims to be literature has been always present in that battle-field, and always in the ranks of the foe.

Ireland is another touchstone which reveals to us how absurdly we masquerade in democratic trappings while we have gone to seed in tory distrust of the people; false to every duty, which, as eldest-born of democratic institutions, we owe to the oppressed, and careless of the lesson every such movement may be made in keeping public thought clear, keen, and fresh as to principles which are the essence of our civilization, the groundwork of all education in republics.

Sydney Smith said, "The moment Ireland is mentioned the English seem to bid adieu to common sense, and to act with the barbarity of tyrants and the fatuity of idiots." "As long as the patient will suffer, the cruel will kick. . . . If the Irish go on withholding and forbearing, and hesitating whether this is the time for discussion or that is the time, they will be laughed at another century as fools, and kicked for another century as slaves." Byron called England's union with Ireland "the union of the shark with his prey." Bentham's conclusion, from a survey of five hundred years of European history, was, "Only by making the ruling few uneasy can the oppressed many obtain a particle of relief." Edmund Burke—Burke, the noblest figure in the Parliamentary history of the last hundred years, greater than Cicero in the senate and almost Plato in the academy— Burke affirmed, a century ago, "Ireland has learned at last that justice is to be had from England, only when demanded at the sword's point." And a century later, only last year, Gladstone himself proclaimed in a public address in Scotland, " England never concedes anything to Ireland except when moved to do so by fear."

When we remember these admissions, we ought to clap our hands at every fresh Irish " outrage," as a parrot-press styles it ; aware that it is only a far-off echo of the musket-shots that rattled against the Old State House on March 5th, 1770, and of the warwhoop that made the tiny spire of the " Old South" tremble when Boston rioters emptied the three India tea-ships into the sea,—welcome evidence of living force and rare intelligence in the victim, and a sign that the day of deliverance draws each hour nearer. Cease ringing endless changes of eulogy on the men who made North's Boston port-bill a failure while every leading journal sends daily over the water wishes for the success of Gladstone's copy of the bill for Ireland. If all rightful government rests on consent,—if, as the French say, you " can do almost anything with a bayonet except sit on it,"—be at least consistent, and denounce the man who covers Ireland with regiments to hold up a despotism which, within twenty months, he has confessed rests wholly upon fear.

Then note the scorn and disgust with which we gather up our garments about us and disown the Sam Adams and William Prescott, the George Washington and John Brown, of St. Petersburg, the spiritual descendants, the living representatives, of those who make our history worth anything in the world's annals,—the Nihilists.

Nihilism is the righteous and honorable resistance of a people crushed under an iron rule. Nihilism is evidence of life. When " order reigns in Warsaw," it is spiritual death. Nihilism is the last weapon of victims choked and manacled beyond all other resistance. It is crushed humanity's only means of making the oppressor tremble. God means that unjust power shall be insecure ; and every move of the giant, prostrate in chains, whether it be to lift a single dagger or stir a city's revolt, is a lesson in justice. One might well tremble for the future of the race if such a despotism could exist without provoking the bloodiest resistance. I honor Nihilism ; since it redeems human nature from the suspicion of being utterly vile, made up only of heartless oppressors and contented slaves. Every line in our history, every interest of civilization, bids us rejoice when the tyrant grows pale and the slave rebellious. We cannot but pity the suffering of any human being, however richly deserved; but such pity must not confuse our moral sense. Humanity gains. Chatham rejoiced when our fathers rebelled. For every single reason they alleged, Russia counts a hundred, each one ten times bitterer than any Hancock or Adams could give Sam Johnson's standing toast in Oxford port was, "Success to the first insurrection of slaves in Jamaica," a sentiment Southey echoed. "Eschew cant," said that old moralist. But of all the cants that are canted in this canting world, though the cant of piety may be the worst, the cant of Americans bewailing Russian Nihilism is the most disgusting.

I know what reform needs, and all it needs, in a land where discussion is free, the press untrammelled, and where public halls protect debate. There, as Emerson says, "What the tender and poetic youth dreams to-day, and conjures up with inarticulate speech, is to-morrow the vociferated result of public opinion, and the day after is the charter of nations. Lieber said, in 1870, "Bismarck proclaims to-day in the Diet the very principles for which we were hunted and exiled fifty years ago." Submit to risk your daily bread, expect social ostracism, count on a mob now and then, "be in earnest, don't equivocate, don't excuse, don't retreat a single inch," and you will finally be heard. No matter how long and weary the waiting, at last,—

> "Ever the truth comes uppermost,
>   And ever is justice done.
> For Humanity sweeps onward:
>   Where to-day the martyr stands,
> On the morrow crouches Judas
>   With the silver in his hands;
>
> Far in front the cross stands ready,
>   And the crackling fagots burn,
> While the hooting mob of yesterday
>   In silent awe return
> To glean up the scattered ashes
>   Into History's golden urn."

In such a land he is doubly and trebly guilty who, except in some most extreme case, disturbs the sober rule of law and order.

But such is not Russia. In Russia there is no press, no debate, no explanation of what Government does, no remonstrance allowed, no agitation of public issues. Dead silence, like that which reigns at the summit of Mont Blanc, freezes the whole empire, long ago described as " a despotism tempered by assassination." Meanwhile, such despotism has unsettled the brains of the ruling family, as unbridled power doubtless made some of the twelve Cæsars insane : a madman, sporting with the lives and comfort of a hundred million of men. The young girl whispers in her mother's ear, under a ceiled roof, her pity for a brother knouted and dragged half dead into exile for his opinions. The next week she is stripped naked, and flogged to death in the public square. No inquiry, no explanation, no trial, no protest, one dead uniform silence, the law of the tyrant. Where is there ground for any hope of peaceful change ? Where the fulcrum upon which you can plant any possible lever ?

Macchiavelli's sorry picture of poor human nature would be fulsome flattery if men could keep still under such oppression. No, no ! in such a land dynamite and the dagger are the necessary and proper substitutes for Faneuil Hall and the *Daily Advertiser*. Anything that will make the madman quake in his bedchamber, and rouse his victims into reckless and desperate resistance. This is the only view an American, the child of 1620 and 1776, can take of Nihilism. Any other unsettles and perplexes the ethics of our civilization.

Born within sight of Bunker Hill, in a commonwealth which adopts the motto of Algernon Sidney, *sub libertate quietem* ("accept no peace without liberty"),—son of Harvard, whose first pledge was " Truth," citizen of a republic based on the claim that no government is rightful unless resting on the consent of the people, and which assumes to lead in asserting the rights of humanity,—I at least can say nothing else and nothing less—no, not if every tile on Cambridge roofs were a devil hooting my words !

I shall bow to any rebuke from those who hold Christianity to command entire non-resistance. But criticism from any other quarter is only that nauseous hypocrisy, which, stung by threepenny tea-tax, piles Bunker Hill with granite and statues, prating all the time of patriotism and broadswords, while, like another Pecksniff, it recommends a century of dumb submission and entire non-resistance to the Russians, who, for a hundred years, have seen their sons by thousands dragged to death or exile, no one knows which, in this worse than Venetian mystery of police, and their maidens flogged to death in the market-place, and who share the same fate if they presume to ask the reason why.

"It is unfortunate," says Jefferson, "that the efforts of mankind to secure the freedom of which they have been deprived should be accompanied with violence and even with crime. But while we weep over the means, we must pray for the end." Pray fearlessly for such ends: there is no risk! "Men are all tories by nature," says Arnold, "when tolerably well off: only monstrous injustice and atrocious cruelty can rouse them." Some talk of the rashness of the uneducated classes. Alas! ignorance is far oftener obstinate than rash. Against one French Revolution—that scarecrow of the ages—weigh Asia, "carved in stone," and a thousand years of Europe, with her half-dozen nations meted out and trodden down to be the dull and contented footstools of priests and kings. The customs of a thousand years ago are the sheet-anchor of the passing generation, so deeply buried, so fixed, that the most violent efforts of the maddest fanatic can drag it but a hand's-breadth.

Before the war Americans were like the crowd in that terrible hall of Eblis which Beckford painted for us,—each man with his hand pressed on the incurable sore in his bosom, and pledged not to speak of it: compared with other lands, we were intellectually and morally a nation of cowards.

When I first entered the Roman States, a custom-house official seized all my French books. In vain I held up to him a treatise by Fénelon, and explained that it was by a Catholic archbishop of Cambray. Gruffly he answered, "It makes no difference: *it is French.*" As I surrendered the volume to his remorseless grasp, I could not but honor the nation which had made its revolutionary purpose so definite that despotism feared its very language. I only wished that injustice and despotism everywhere might one day have as good cause to hate and to fear everything American.

At last that disgraceful seal of slave complicity is broken,

Let us inaugurate a new departure, recognize that we are afloat on the current of Niagara,—eternal vigilance the condition of our safety,—that we are irrevocably pledged to the world not to go back to bolts and bars,—could not if we would, and would not if we could. Never again be ours the fastidious scholarship that shrinks from rude contact with the masses. Very pleasant it is to sit high up in the world's theatre and criticise the ungraceful struggles of the gladiators, shrug one's shoulders at the actors' harsh cries, and let every one know that but for "this villainous saltpetre you would yourself have been a soldier." But Bacon says, "In the theatre of man's life, God and His angels only should be lookers-on." "Sin is not taken out of man as Eve was out of Adam, by putting him to sleep." "Very beautiful," says Richter, "is the eagle when he floats with outstretched wings aloft in the clear blue; but sublime when he plunges down through the tempest to his eyry on the cliff, where his unfledged young ones dwell and are starving." Accept proudly the analysis of Fisher Ames: "A monarchy is a man-of-war, stanch, iron-ribbed, and resistless when under full sail; yet a single hidden rock sends her to the bottom. Our republic is a raft, hard to steer, and your feet always wet; but nothing can sink her." If the Alps, piled in cold and silence, be the emblem of despotism, we joyfully take the ever-restless ocean for ours,—only pure because never still.

Journalism must have more self-respect. Now it praises good and bad men so indiscriminately that a good word from nine-tenths of our journals is worthless. In burying our Aaron Burrs, both political parties—in order to get the credit of magnanimity—exhaust the vocabulary of eulogy so thoroughly that there is nothing left with which to distinguish our John Jays. The love of a good name in life and a fair reputation to survive us—that strong bond to well-doing—is lost where every career, however stained, is covered with the same fulsome flattery, and where what men say in the streets is the exact opposite of what they say to each other. *De mortuis nil nisi bonum* most men translate, "Speak only good of the dead." I prefer to construe it, "Of the dead say nothing unless you can tell something good." And if the sin and the recreancy have been marked and far-reaching in their evil, even the charity of silence is not permissible.

To be as good as our fathers we must be better. They silenced their fears and subdued their prejudices, inaugurating free speech and equality with no precedent on the file. Europe shouted "Madmen!" and gave us forty years for the shipwreck. With serene faith they persevered. Let us rise to their level. Crush appetite and prohibit temptation if it rots great cities. Intrench labor in sufficient bulwarks against that wealth, which, without the tenfold strength of modern incorporation, wrecked the Grecian and Roman States ; and, with a sterner effort still, summon women into civil life as re-enforcement to our laboring ranks in the effort to make our civilization a success.

Sit not, like the figure on our silver coin, looking ever backward.

> "New occasions teach new duties ;
> Time makes ancient good uncouth ;
> They must upward still, and onward,
> Who would keep abreast of Truth.
> Lo ! before us gleam her camp-fires !
> We ourselves must Pilgrims be,
> Launch our Mayflower, and steer **boldly**
> Through the desperate winter sea,
> Nor attempt the Future's portal
> With the Past's blood-rusted **key.**"

INDEX.

A.

Adam, William, 131.
Adams, Charles Francis, 232, 284.
Adams, John Quincy, 153, 206, 213.
Adams, Rev. Dr. Nehemiah, 120.
Alcott, Bronson, 122.
Alford, 78.
Althorp, Robert E., 274.
American Anti-Slavery Society, 51, 71, 254, 262, 330, 342, 373.
Anderson, Major, of Fort Sumter, 338.
Andrew, John A., 213, 297, 299.
Anti-Slavery Bazaar in Boston, 248.
Appleton, Thomas Gold, 29, 34, 49.
Appleton, William, 227.
Arabella, The, 15.
Austin, James Trecothic, 93.

B.

Banks, N. P., 281.
Bartol, Rev. Dr., 437, 452.
Beecher, Henry Ward, 67, 231, 331, 338.
Beecher, Rev. Dr. Lyman, 40, 66.
Booth, Wilkes, Lincoln's assassin, 340.
Boston Female Anti-Slavery Society, 59.
Boston Public Latin School, 34.

Bowditch, William L., 274, 419.
Breckenridge, John C., 302.
Bright, John, 330.
British and Foreign Anti-Slavery Society, 129.
Broadway Tabernacle in New York, 228.
Brooks, Preston S., 281.
Brougham, Lord, 128.
Brown, "Box," 221.
Brown, John, 330.
Buchanan, James, 284, 312.
Buckingham, Rev. Dr. Edgar, 42.
Buffum, Arnold, 68.
Burleigh, Charles C., 107.
Burns, Anthony, 269.
Burr, Aaron, 52.
Butler, Benjamin F., 54, 315, 386.
Butler, Mrs. Fanny Kemble, 52.
Butler, Pierce, 52.
Byron, Lady, 128.

C.

Cairnes, Professor, 330.
Calhoun, John C., 176, 204.
Channing, Rev. Dr. William Ellery, 67, 90, 122, 235.
Channing, Rev. W. H., 434.
Chapman, Maria Weston, 110.
Chapman, Mr. and Mrs. Henry G., 80, 107, 130.
Charles I. of England, 16.
Cheever, George B., 170.

Chesson, F. W., 330.
Child, David Lee, 108.
Child, Lydia Maria, 109, 308.
Choate, Rufus, 227, 276.
Clapp, Acting Mayor of Boston, 305.
Clarke, Rev. James Freeman, 406.
Clarkson, Thomas, 130.
Clay, Henry, 224, 227.
Cobden, Richard, 330.
Congdon, Charles T., 53.
Craft, William and Ellen, 221.
Crosby, Rev. Dr. Howard, 455.
Curriculum of the Boston Latin Public School, 35.
Curtis, Benjamin R., 273, 274.
Curtis, George William, 247.

D.

Dana, Richard H., Jr., 232, 269.
Davis, Jefferson, 312.
Dewey, Rev. Dr. Orville, 261.
Dickerson, Samuel, 339.
Dickinson, Anna E., 343.
Disunion Convention, 284.
Dom Pedro, 421.
Duchess of Sunderland, afterward of Argyle, 128.
Douglass, Frederick, 161, 202, 228, 232, 235, 315, 343, 369, 406.
Douglas, Stephen A., 302.

E.

Ellis, Charles, 274.
Emerson, 298.
English Abolitionists, 114.
Evarts, Jeremiah, 67.
Everett, Edward, 36, 73.

F.

Faneuil Hall, 91.
Faneuil, Peter, 91.
Fillmore, Millard, 232.
Fisk, Rev. Wilbur, 174.
Florida, 209.
Follen, Charles T. C., 108.
Folsom, Abigail, 263.
Fort Sumter, 314.
Foster, Stephen S., 263.
Fremont, John C., 283.
Free-Soil Party, The, 223.
"Friends, The," 122.
Froude, James Anthony, 403.

G.

Garrison, William Lloyd, 58, 62, 106, 123, 133, 338, 428.
Garnaut, Eliza, 217.
Garnaut, Phœbe, 217.
"Genius of Universal Emancipation," The, 63, 64.
Giddings, Joshua R., 284.
Goodell, William, 170.
Gould, A. B., 34, 36.
Gough, John B., 369.
Grant, U. S., 330, 336, 363, 399.
Greeley, Horace, 229, 399.
Green, Dr. Samuel A., 428.
Green, Miss Ann Terry, 79.
Grew, Miss Mary, 138.
Grimké, A. H., 55.
Grimké, Judge John F., 119.
Grimké, Sarah and Angelina, 119.

H.

Hall, Newman, 330.
Hallet, Benjamin F., 93, 273, 274.
Hallowell, Edward N., 331.
Hallowell, The Brothers, 305.

INDEX. 597

Harvard College, 38.
Harvard Law School, The, 49.
Harvard Washington Corps, The, 44.
Hauman, James W., 213.
Hedge, Rev. Dr., 435.
Higginson, T. W., 310.
Hildreth, Richard, 252.
Hillard, George E., Esq., 93.
Hoar, 'Squire, of Concord, 160, 212.
Holmes, Oliver Wendell, 29, 437.
Holt, Judge, 338.
Holyoake, George J., 407.
Hopkinson, Thomas, 54.
Howe, Julia Ward, 367.
Howe, Dr. S. G., 213.
Hughes. Bishop of New York, 158.
Hughes, Thomas, 330.

J.

Jackson, Francis, 107, 123, 274, 278.
Jackson, Rev. Dr. Sheldon, 479.
Jerrold, Douglas, 252.
Johnson, Andrew, 350, 361.
Johnson, Oliver, 101, 306. 320, 345.

K.

Kelley, Abby (Foster), 263.
Keyes, 'Squire, of Concord, 160.
Kirkland, Rev. Dr. John T., 38.
Kossuth, Louis, 248.

L.

Lafayette, 36.
Latimer, a mulatto, 164.
Lawrence, Abbot, 206.
Lee, Robert E., 293.
"Liberator," The, 66. 238.

Liberty Party, The, 169.
Lincoln, Abraham, 287, 302, 312, 335, 340.
Livermore, Mrs. Mary A., 116. 406, 475.
Lord, President of Dartmouth College, 175.
Loring, Ellis Gray, 108.
Loring, Edward G., 269, 276.
Louisiana, 205
Lovejoy, Rev. Elijah P., 88.
Lowell, James Russell, 351.
Lowell, Rev. Dr. Charles, 452.
Lundy, Benjamin, 63.
Lyman, Colonel Theodore, 370.
Lyman, Mayor of Boston, 59.

M.

Mann, Horace, 260.
Manning, Rev. Dr. J. M., 298.
Marcy, W. L., Governor of New York, 73.
Martineau, Harriet, 130, 475.
Massachusetts Anti-Slavery Society, 125, 168.
Mathew, Father, 134.
May, Rev. Samuel J., 106, 273, 274, 343.
McCarthy, Justin, 330.
McDuffie, Governor of South Carolina, 72.
Mercantile Library Association of Boston, 223.
Mill, Mrs. John Stuart, 236.
Mill, John Stuart, 330.
Milmore, Martin, 376.
Missouri Compromise, The, 205.
Morison, Rev. Dr., 46.
Motley, J. Lothrop, 28, 34, 39, 49, 399.
Mott, Lucretia, 130, 235.
Municipal Court of Boston, 22.

N.

National Philanthopist," The, 63.
Nasby, Petroleum V., 362.
Nebraska Bill, The, 267.
New England Anti-Slavery Society, 70, 112, 124, 168.
"Newburyport Free Press," The, 63.
Noel, Baptist, 330.

O.

O'Connell, Daniel, 128, 134, 155.
Otis, Harrison Gray, 22, 36, 219.
Otis, James, 91.

P.

Park, John C., 58.
Parker, Theodore, 122, 215, 228, 232, 247, 251, 273, 300.
Papists, 16.
Party, The Union, 302.
Phelps, Rev. Amos, 108.
Phillips, George William, 274.
Phillips, Hon. John, 21.
Phillips, Hon. Jonathan, 93, 122.
Phillips, John, founder of the Phillips Academy in Exeter, 19.
Phillips, John, the goldsmith, 20.
Phillips, Judge, 19.
Phillips, Mrs. John (née Sally Walley), 21, 30, 31, 37, 38.
Phillips, Rev. George, 15.
Phillips, Rev. Samuel, 18.
Phillips, Rev. Samuel (4th generation), 19.
Phillips, Samuel and John, founders of the Phillips Academy in Andover, 19.
Phillips, Samuel, merchant; 18.
Phillips, Wendell. 21.—Paternal home, 25.—Preaching to chairs, 27.—Childhood friends, 28.—Revolutionary traditions, 31.—First educational advantages, 34. — Becomes the friend of Charles Sumner, 34.—Loves athletic exercises, 35.—An attractive elocutionist at school, 36.—Matriculates in Harvard College, 37.—The friend of Quincy, 39.—Consecrates himself to God, 41.—His standing and classmates at college, 46.—Heard Daniel Webster for the first time, 48.—Graduated, 48.—Entered the Harvard Law School, 49.—Admitted to the bar, 52.—Meets Trelawny, 52.—A trip to Philadelphia, 52.—Acts as *cicerone* to Aaron Burr, 53.—First public honors, 53.—Opens a law office, 54.—Witnesses the Garrison mob, 58.—His attention drawn to the weakness of the law against popular prejudices, 60.—Forms the acquaintance of Miss Ann Green, 79.—Becomes personally acquainted with Garrison, 80.—His first Anti-Slavery speech, 82.—His marriage, 86.—First speech in Faneuil Hall, 95.—His career as lecturer, 114.—A member of "the Friends," 122. — General agent of the Massachussetts Anti-Slavery Society, 123.—Makes a trip to Europe, 125.—Agitating the emancipation of woman, 133.—Garrison honors him, naming his new-born son Wendell Phillips, 142.—Returns from

Europe, 148. — Addresses a large audience upon the occasion of O'Connell's appeal to the Irish in United States, 155. —Antagonizes the Constitution, 165 —His method as an agitator, 180. — Effecting the abolition of caste schools in Boston, 202.—Arguing against capital punishment, 214. — Stabbing the clergy with interrogation marks, 220.—Denouncing Kossuth's reticence on the question of slavery, 249. —Assisting in the formation of a moral reform society, 251.— Arrested for obstructing the process of the United States, 273.—Signed the call for a Disunion Convention, 284.—Occupies Theodore Parker's pulpit, 300.—Becomes a Union man, 315.—Organizes colored regiments, 331. — Refuses a nomination to Congress, 354.— Pleads for Female Suffrage, 361. —Advocates Labor Reform, 368.—Urges the cause of Temperance.—Nominated for Governor of Massachusetts by the Labor Reform and Temperance parties, 382.—In sympathy with the Irish cause, 403.—His views on finance, 412. — Religious views, 431-439.—Deals a blow to Harvard College, 463.—His last effort as an orator, 475.— The last words of public concern traced by his pen, 479.— Leaves this world, 481.—Burial and tributes to, *vide* Book IV., Chap. IV.—Estimate as an orator, Ib. Chap. V. — As a man, Ib. Chap. VI.—Phillipsiana, Ib. Chap. VII.

Phillips, William, 20.
Peace Congress, The, 306.
Pease, Miss Elizabeth, 129.
Pierce, Franklin, 254, 313.
Piers, Rev. John Tappen, 45.
Pierson, John H., 213.
Pillsbury, Parker, 263.
Powell, Mr. and Mrs. Aaron, 361.
Prelatists, 16.
Prescott, W. H., 227.
Puritans, 16.
Purvis, Robert, 343.

Q.

Quincy, Edmund, 39, 109, 201. 343.
Quincy, Josiah, 24, 38, 232.
Quotations from Pro-Slavery papers, 72.

R.

Redpath, James, 56.
Remond, Charles Lenox, 343.
Republican Party, Organization of the, 283.
Revels, Senator from Georgia, 374.
Rynders, Captain, 228, 246.

S.

Salem, 17.
Sargent, Rev. John T., 235, 251, 370, 416, 417, 421, 431.
Scott, Dred, 286.
Scott, General Winfield, 313.
Schurz, Carl, 413.
Sewall, Samuel E., 108, 228.
Seward, William H., 280, 287, 302, 351.

Shadrach, a fugitive slave, 243.
Sharp, Graneville, 173.
Shaw, Judge, of Boston, 164.
Shaw, Robert G., 331.
Sims, Thomas, a fugitive slave, 246.
Smith, Gerrit, 170, 246, 330.
Smith, Goldwin, 330.
"Sons of Liberty," The, 91.
Spencer, Herbert, 330.
Spooner, Lysander, 216.
Sprague, Peleg, 219.
"Standard," The, 152.
Stone, Mrs. Lucy, 406.
Story, Judge, 49.
Stowe, Harriet Beecher, 67, 252.
Stuart, Professor Moses, 175, 227.
Sumner, Charles, 34, 39, 49, 55, 78, 213, 232, 274, 281, 366, 399.
Sturge, Joseph, 130.

T.

Taney, Chief Justice, 286.
Tappan, Arthur, 65.
Taylor, General, 232.
Texas, The annexation of, 206.
Thatcher, Rev. Moses, 108.
Thayer, Dr. David, 308.
Thompson, George, 128, 145, 237, 253, 330, 338.
Ticknor, George, 201, 227.

Torrey, Rev. Charles T., 220.
Toussaint L'Ouverture, 321.
Trelawny, 52.
Tyndale, General, 340.

W.

Walker, Amasa, 284.
Ward, Rev. Samuel, 230.
Wayland, Rev. Dr., 175.
Webb, Richard D., 129.
Webster, Daniel, 214, 226.
Weiss, John, 435.
Weld, T. D., 74, 120.
Wells, Hon. David A., 427.
Wesley, John, 88.
Whittier, John G., 68, 107, 120, 421.
Wightman, Mayor, of Boston, 307.
Whig Party, The, 223.
Willard, Miss Frances E., 406.
Wilmot, of Pennsylvania, 209.
Wilson, Senator Henry, 284, 338, 339.
Wise, Henry A., Governor of Virginia, 342.
Women's Rights Convention, National, 247.
Woods, Rev. Dr. Leonard, 227.
World's Anti-Slavery Convention, 128, 129.